LONDON RECORD SOCIETY
PUBLICATIONS

VOLUME V
FOR THE YEAR 1969

LONDON RADICALISM
1830—1843

A Selection from the Papers of
FRANCIS PLACE

EDITED BY
D. J. ROWE

LONDON RECORD SOCIETY
1970

Introduction © D. J. Rowe, 1970

SBN 90095201 6

Printed in Great Britain by

W & J MACKAY & CO LTD, CHATHAM, KENT

The people here differ very widely from you at Manchester. You some of *you* at Manchester resolve that something shall be done and then *you* some of you set to work and see it done—give your money and your time and need none but mere servants to carry out the details. Our men of property and influence never act in this way—they themselves must be operated upon and that too with care and circumspection to induce them even to give us their *mites* and to permit us to put their names on the list of our General Committee. . . . London differs very widely from Manchester, and indeed, from every other place on the face of the earth. It has no local or particular interest as a town, not even as to politics. Its several boroughs in this respect are like so many very populous places at a distance from one another, and the inhabitants of any of them know nothing, or next to nothing, of the proceedings in any other, and not much indeed of those of their own. London in my time and that is half a century has never moved. A few of the people in different parts have moved, and those whenever they come together make a considerable number. . . . But isolated as men are here, living as they do at considerable distances, many seven miles apart and but seldom meeting together except in small groups. . . . With a very remarkable working population also, each trade divided from every other, and some of the most numerous even from themselves, and who, notwithstanding an occasional display of very small comparative numbers, are a quiescent, inactive race as far as public matters are concerned.

(Francis Place to Richard Cobden, 4 March 1840.)[1]

[1] See below, Document no. **114**.

I

The documents printed in this volume are concerned with political radicalism in London during the period 1830–43 and have been selected from the papers of Francis Place now in the British Museum. It is peculiarly necessary to begin by commenting on Francis Place, himself, because of his unique importance in, and impact on, radicalism, particularly in London, during these years. His importance for a study of radicalism lies in the fact that he not only belonged to most of the major radical movements in London during this period but was also a very active, even if 'behind the scenes', leader in them. His impact on London radicalism owed much to his experience and entrenched position and to his enormous range of political contacts. His radical past went back to the London Corresponding Society of the seventeen-nineties and he had established himself as the authority and chief organizer of radical local and national politics in Westminster by the end of the first decade of the nineteenth century. As such he had the ear of Sir Francis Burdett and Sir John Cam Hobhouse, the members of Parliament for Westminster throughout the twenties and early thirties, as well as other members such as Joseph Hume and J. A. Roebuck. In addition he had a wide range of contacts by correspondence with reformers, such as Joseph Parkes and Richard Cobden, throughout the country. These contacts gave him an aura of considerable importance among many radicals. Together with this he had a number of other advantages: much time and energy to devote to radical activity since he had retired from his tailor's business in 1817; an outstanding personal library, particularly of parliamentary papers and pamphlets and tracts published on radicalism; and exceptional ability as a thinker and organizer.

It will be seen, therefore, that a volume of documents drawn from the Place Papers will illustrate a period in the life of Place and will be influenced and constrained by him as much as it will illustrate radical activity in London. Some brief account of the man[1] is therefore necessary before considering the subject.

Francis Place was born 3 November 1771, son of Simon Place. He went to 'some sort of school from the age of four till he was nearly fourteen' at which latter age he was apprenticed to a leather breeches maker, having already shown an independence of spirit by refusing his father's suggestion that he should be apprenticed to a conveyancer. A brief connection with a set of dissolute drinking companions was soon thrown over for a life of care and frugality since at the age of nineteen, a year after becoming a journeyman at his trade, Place married Elizabeth Chadd. As Wallas noted 'This

[1] The general material on Place and his life is taken from G. Wallas, *The Life of Francis Place* (rev. edn. 1918) and Wallas' account of Place in *D.N.B.* In their turn these are based largely on Place's autobiographical material, British Museum, Add. Mss. 35142–54. For Place, see also W.E.S. Thomas, 'Francis Place and working class history', *Historical Journal*, v (1962), 61–70.

was the turning point in his career' and he determined to be sober, respectable and better their joint position in life. Place had early become a member of the Breeches-Makers' Benefit Society, which was as much a trade union as a benefit club. It organized a strike in 1793 for higher wages which led to Place finding himself unemployed and obtaining his first experience of industrial action. Although having no knowledge of the intention to hold a strike Place soon made himself one of its organizers, arranging methods by which the society's funds for strike relief could be raised but after three months the funds ran out, the strike was broken and Place was refused employment at his trade and remained unemployed for eight months. During this time he determined to study as many subjects as possible and put himself in the position to become a master. It was this period of his existence which, ever after in his dealing with working men, led him to tell them that however bad their circumstances they must never lose their self-respect.

At the end of 1793 one of his old masters relented and gave Place employment at his trade, thus enabling him to improve his living conditions. This employment lasted for only a few months at the end of which Place re-organized the Breeches-Makers' Society and obtained an advance of wages without a strike and also organized clubs for several other trades. In June 1794, a few weeks after the arrest of Thomas Hardy on a charge of high treason and at a time when the London Corresponding Society was losing members rapidly, Place took the brave but dangerous step of joining the Society which launched him on his career of political reform. He was soon elected as delegate for the local division of the society and became a member of its general committee. By the summer of 1795, at the age of twenty-three, having been recognized as a capable organizer, he was taking the chair at many of the meetings of the general committee. Here he adopted the attitude to which he was nearly always to remain true, that large meetings and agitation would not frighten government into granting reform and that the society should proceed slowly and quietly in educating the people to the need for good and cheap government. Place was proved correct by the Treason and Sedition Acts of 1795, and in 1797 he resigned from the society because of the violent attitudes of others on the committee. In 1798 the arrest of all the committee members in the Despard affair led to the collapse of the society.

During these years Place had slowly built up a private tailor's trade, having persuaded a number of drapers and clothiers to let him have cloth on credit. At first he made little money which meant great difficulties since by 1798 he and his wife had had four children (they were to have fifteen in all, of whom five died in infancy,[1] the last, twins, in 1817). He remained determined, however, and in 1799, with another poor journeyman, opened a tailor's shop, on credit, in Charing Cross. They prospered and were soon employing a number of workmen but his partner forced the liquidation of the business and bought the goodwill, leaving Place out of employment. This crisis brought out the best in Place. He found his creditors willing to advance money and within a couple of months, in April 1801, was able to open a larger shop also in Charing Cross on his own account. He organized the business well, doing little of the actual work himself, but obtaining

[1] Add. Ms. 35142, f. 20.

and waiting on customers while he employed journeymen. His business prospered and at its peak in 1816 brought in more than £3,000 in profit and in the following year he retired and handed the business over to his eldest son. During its first few years he devoted himself to the business, spending the remaining hours after work in reading and commenced the building up of the famous library behind his shop. With more time to spare, from about 1806, he began to take an interest in local politics, already showing his later suspicions of the Whigs and their pretensions as reformers, especially when they brought forward the ineffectual Lord Percy as candidate for Westminster after Fox's death. With a general election in 1807, Place and a few friends decided to bring forward Sir Francis Burdett, who had refused to stand again for Middlesex because of the expense. As Place said, they were 'as insignificant a set of persons as could well have been collected together' but Burdett was returned at the top of the poll, through no efforts of his own, but entirely as a result of Place and his friends who became acknowledged as the radical Westminster election committee.

These proceedings brought Place from his previous insignificance to the notice of a number of important contemporaries. In 1810 he made the acquaintance of William Godwin, whose scrounging of money from him soon broke the connection. Robert Owen asked him to read and correct the manuscript of his 'New View of Society', and James Mill, with whom he worked on the committee of the Lancastrian schools society, brought him into Jeremy Bentham's circle. At the age of forty Place was to be much affected by the ideas and theories of Mill and Bentham and was persuaded by the former to adopt the system of analysis and rational argument with which he later endeavoured to inculcate the London artisans. He took the attitude on education which was to remain with him 'that the generality of children are organised so nearly alike that they may by proper management be made pretty nearly equally wise and virtuous'. With both Mill and Bentham Place kept up regular correspondence and visits, and for both of them he read and commented on manuscript works. Of Bentham he wrote, 'I never read anything of his without being both wiser and, as I believe, better in consequence of that reading', and Bentham had a considerable influence on Place's thought and writing. Despite an intellectual capability which enabled him to play a part with these distinguished men, Place had not the literary style to put his ideas into print at a time when factual material alone was insufficient for success in publication. After one or two dismal failures in writing articles (which turned out to be dry, complicated and little read) in the eighteen-twenties, Place turned to a career as 'back-room boy'. Neither a speaker or writer himself, he provided many others, including Hume and Hobhouse, with the factual material on which successful careers were founded and names made.

To return to the chronological precis of Place's life, his growing acquaintance with men of political importance together with his success in the Westminster election of 1807 led to an increase in his political power in Westminster and in 1819 and 1820 he led the committee which supported the candidature of John Cam Hobhouse to win back the second Westminster seat (Burdett having held the first for the radicals) from the Whigs who had won it in 1818. In 1819 Hobhouse was beaten by George Lamb, brother of Lord Melbourne, but in the election in 1820, following the accession of George IV, Place and his fellow workers obtained the election of both Burdett and Hobhouse and they retained their seats without contest until 1833 with Place and his co-adjutors too powerful a force to be challenged.[1] During this period there was little need for Place's organization in Westminster politics and in 1830 he turned successfully to the management of Joseph Hume's election for Middlesex.

During the twenties Place was involved in a variety of schemes. His interest in education was not forgotten when he ceased working for the Lancastrian schools society. With Bentham he had collaborated on the latter's Chrestomathic high school plan and in 1823 and 1824 he worked with Thomas Hodgskin, George Birkbeck and others to interest working men in and collect money to found the London Mechanics Institute, later to become Birkbeck College. Place also became involved in the population dispute which was later to cause him such difficulty in his dealings with working men; they could not understand how he could support a Malthusian doctrine and still be aiming at their betterment. In 1822 he published the *Illustrations and Proofs of the Principle of Population* which of all Place's writing was the only book to reach the printing press. In it he took a neo-Malthusian attitude which, while accepting the principle put forward by Malthus, did not accept much of the detail such as the criticism of early marriage (which Place himself favoured as his own life showed) nor the view that the poor had no right to relief and that the Poor Law should therefore be abolished. Place throughout argued that Malthus' principle was correct and that the important thing was to do away with the debasement of the working man to which the existing relief in support of wages led. This view was upheld by the report of the 1834 commission on the poor laws which Place attempted to justify to the London artisans.[2] He firmly believed that the New Poor Law would improve the condition of working men and despite their hatred of it he refused to tone down his views in order to seek their approbation.

As with population so in most other fields of economic doctrine Place was at one with the classical economists, influenced as he was by his contacts with such men as James Mill and his son, John Stuart, and the French economist, J. B. Say. In 1826, long before Nassau Senior's famous report on the condition of the handloom weavers, Place had commented on the 'absurd proposals' for minimum wage legislation and abolition of power machinery which had been put forward to improve the position of the weavers.[3] His views on capital and the role of labour in production are clearly seen in his correspondence with his friend, the pre-Marxist economist, Thomas Hodgskin in the twenties and in his attempts to draw the

[1] Although Place remained largely in the background of the political affairs of Westminster he was still much noticed and the members of Parliament he supported had to accept many jibes as being the nominees of the 'radical tailor'. There were also laudatory notices of Place's work and power such as that in the *European Magazine*, new series, ii. no. 7 (March 1826), 227–33, where the saying of Archimedes 'Give me *place* for my fulcrum and I'll move the world' was first applied in this context.
[2] See **94**. Place obtained an agreement from the London Working Men's Association not to criticize the New Poor Law if he drew up the 'Charter', Add. Ms. 27835, f. 160.
[3] Wallas, *Life*, 181.

London artisans away from the labour theory of value.[1] He was an ardent and active free trader and finally, his addiction to classical economics, in the form of the free labour market, can be seen in his work to abolish the laws against combination of working men for trade purposes.[2] Place believed that trade unions were formed because of the oppression of working men by the anti-combination laws and that the abolition of the laws would lead to a reduction of combination, improved wages for workmen, since they would not be forced to accept work offered at any wage, less industrial strife and therefore an improved economic climate. In this respect his economic orthodoxy proved stronger than his concern for working men: he realized that in a free labour market the employee would be at a disadvantage but, in his view, still in a better position than under the existing system.

Place became involved in attempts to repeal the anti-combination laws after the prosecution of the compositors employed by *The Times* in 1810 and in the following year he prevented the London master tailors from obtaining an act of Parliament to put down the tailors' union. Thereafter he worked for repeal of the laws with no success beyond increasing public opinion against them, until in 1823 he persuaded Joseph Hume to bring the matter forward in Parliament, and in the following year a select committee was appointed to consider the embargo on the emigration of artisans and the exportation of machinery, as well as the laws against the combination of workmen. Circulars were distributed throughout the country inviting witnesses to come forward; these witnesses were carefully schooled by Place in his Charing Cross library and briefs were sent to Hume of the questions to be asked and the answers which the various witnesses would supply. The result of the committee's inquiry was, therefore, almost a foregone conclusion, although it could not be said that the committee was unfairly biased. Place and Hume did nothing to prevent hostile witnesses being heard and publicized the existence of the committee widely. Place was certain that the results of the committee would not be accepted by the House of Commons and he and Hume concocted a series of resolutions instead of a report, thinking that less exception could be taken to them, and altered to their own liking the bills based on the committee's work to be presented to Parliament. They then persuaded a number of members of both Houses not to speak to the bills and their passage through Parliament was almost unnoticed. In a rising period of trade in the mid-eighteen-twenties, however, Place's expectations of the result of passing the bills were unfulfilled and there were a series of strikes which led to a demand in 1825 for the re-enactment of the anti-combination laws. A further select committee was set up to consider the situation but Place and Hume by further strenuous efforts prevented the complete abolition of the right of working men to combine and left them free to combine for the improvement of wages and hours of work.

[1] 92.
[2] The importance of the anti-combination laws of 1799–1800 has been grossly exaggerated. They were little used and although their psychological effect was perhaps considerable, there were many strikes during the period 1800–24 when they remained unused—on Tyneside for instance there were strikes of the keelmen in 1809, 1819 and 1822 and of the seamen in 1815.

In the later twenties Place was involved in a number of minor schemes[1] but his work was interrupted in October 1827 by the death of his wife, a blow which left him unable to concern himself with the detail of politics and for some time he went on with 'matters of laborious research'. In February 1830 he remarried and was soon immersed in the political agitation, with which this volume of documents begins, leading to the Reform Act of 1832. From then until the early eighteen-forties Place's life was involved with the story which the following documents reveal. He became a major (probably the major) force in the London reform agitation, emerging from his usual situation as *éminence grise* to take the leading role in drawing up the memorial for the midnight deputation to Lord Grey in October 1831, and in the formation of the National Political Union.

In 1833 as a result of a loss of income[2] he was forced to move from Charing Cross to Brompton Square, his wife's house, but although out of the immediate area of Westminster politics and no longer within easy reach from the Houses of Parliament, he maintained most of his contacts. In the following years he was involved with the agitation for the repeal of the newspaper stamp duty, with the commission on municipal corporations and with an abortive attempt to reform the Corporation of London.[3] Thereafter he was on the fringe of the reform agitation raised by Chartism and was invited by the London Working Men's Association to become one of the London delegates to the Chartist National Convention, but refused because he thought it was a job for younger men (he was sixty-seven at the time). During the winter of 1839–40, with many Chartist leaders imprisoned, he worked to raise subscriptions for the benefit of their families and although he became infuriated with a group of London Chartists who broke up anti-corn law meetings he maintained his contacts with many individual Chartists. In 1836 and again from 1840 when it was revived, he was involved in the organization of the Metropolitan Anti-Corn Law Association which was relatively unsuccessful, failing in London to stir up anything like the interest in free trade which the Anti-Corn Law League did in Lancashire and the surrounding areas. Place's final active participation in reform came in organizing the Metropolitan Parliamentary Reform Association, the short-lived London equivalent of the Complete Suffrage Movement. It came at a time when there was little chance of obtaining the immediate reconciliation of middle and working classes for which some of its members hoped. Most of them were not prepared to become involved in the tedium of a long campaign to educate the people to play their rightful political part which was what Place wanted.

There can be little doubt that in the late thirties and the forties Place was slipping out of the active political scene. He had much more time for correspondence than ever before, writing enormously long letters to his fellow reformers. He had the time to get on with some of the historical writing which had always been one of his major aims, although, from his own point of view, one of the tragedies of his life was that he had always been too busy and too involved to do the writing he wished to do.[4] Had his situation been different there would have been no need to have 'written

[1] Wallas, *Life*, 186.   [2] *Ibid.*, 329–30.   [3] *Ibid.*, 330–50.
[4] This was even true as late as 1840 as a letter to S. B. Harrison shows, **120**.

against the clock' and his style might have been more interesting. Not that Place's manuscripts are always as wooden and repetitive as some comments passed by Wallas and Thomas would have us think—the proposed address of the Parliamentary Candidate Society[1] shows that Place could be vitriolic with his pen. Although they were growing old, Place and some of his fellow reformers remained true to the advanced radical ideas put forward in the Charter. They refused in 1842 to accept its name, because of the disrepute which that name might bring to any new movement as a result of the earlier activities of the 'physical-force' Chartists. Among middle-class radicals, although not so extreme as men like Feargus O'Connor, Place was probably too advanced in his ideas for the support of those on whom he really depended—the middle classes. As he wrote 'By the word "people", when, as in this letter I use the word in a political sense, I mean those among them who take part in public affairs, by whom the rest *must* be governed'.[2] Although much has been written of Place's interest in and work for the working classes in the fields of trade unionism, education, freedom of the press and political reform, this improvement Place expected to come largely through the agency of middle-class pressure and it was with the middle classes that he aligned himself. When he writes in the Reform Bill period of the power of the people to control the government,[3] he is thinking of the power of the middle classes and not of the working classes who were merely a numerical addition. The middle-class reformers were, however, too conservative for the ideas put forward by Place, as may be seen from the following documents. The provisional addresses drafted by Place to inaugurate the Parliamentary Candidate Society, for the Westminster reformers after Lord John Russell's 'finality' speech in November 1837, and to inaugurate the Metropolitan Parliamentary Reform Association, were all drastically altered by provisional committees of the proposed societies because Place's ideas were too advanced. It is possible that if, as in the late autumn of 1831, Place had come out into open political agitation, many middle-class reformers would have followed him in his advanced radical ideas. As it was he preferred to run the ubiquitous business committees of the various societies and do the behind the scenes organization. When at the age of seventy-one, he finally had his own way with an organization, the Metropolitan Parliamentary Reform Association, he was too old and the circumstances were unpropitious for any good to come of his leadership.

In 1844 Place suffered a stroke and a kind of brain tumour which left him unable to read or write for a year, but by 1846 for a short period he was again involved in public matters. Still unable to do much reading or writing he continued his devotion to his work by spending part of his remaining years in cutting notices, from the various newspapers he had collected, about working men and reform movements and pasting them in to the 'guard books' which form the Place Collection of newspaper cuttings. He died on 1 January 1854.

II

It is necessary to say a little in the way of introduction to London radicalism. In most countries the capital city is now and has been historically

[1] **8**.   [2] Quoted in Wallas, *Life*, 192.   [3] **50**.

an important centre for the raising and discussion of new ideas and theories and for the attempt to put into practice those which were considered acceptable to a body of reformers. In this London should have been no exception, since its possession of all the country's major authorities and especially the legislature made it an important focus for interest in change and it was also the only large centre of population in the country. In the eighteenth century this had been to a large extent true and London had been in the van of political reform movements. From the time of William Beckford there had been considerable interest within the Corporation of London in political reform,[1] which culminated in the Wilkesite activity, when the middle-class radicals obtained the backing of the London 'mob'. The mob had earlier been easily manipulated by the authorities but was now to become first the tool and later the willing accessory of radical leaders. In 1776 Major Cartwright, in his pamphlet *Take your choice* first formulated the advanced programme of political reform which was to remain the aim of reformers down to the Chartists and beyond. In 1780 a sub-committee of the electors of Westminster put forward a draft programme of reform (drawn up by Charles James Fox and Thomas Brand Hollis) which contained the six points subsequently adopted in the Charter. Westminster was one of the few parliamentary constituencies where enfranchisement resulted from paying 'scot and lot' and the electorate was therefore large and consisted of socially diverse groups—with many artisan voters. It was therefore prone to advanced ideas and as we have seen was to return two radicals in the eighteen-twenties. Marylebone was also an area of advanced political ideas and largely accounted for the advanced nature of Middlesex county politics, a seat represented at various periods by Wilkes, Burdett and Hume. The only other area of the country which vied with London for leadership in reform activity was Yorkshire and its county association led by the Reverend Christopher Wyvill.

Following the French Revolution and the publication of Tom Paine's *Rights of Man* there was an enormous upsurge of reform activity in many areas throughout the country but it was the London Corresponding Society with its correspondence with reformers all over the country which was considered to be the major influence (although the Sheffield society had probably as large a membership). From 1794, with obvious signs of repression of reform societies by the government, most of the provincial societies were disbanded or went underground; the London Corresponding Society was left as the only major reform organization endeavouring to encourage reformers in the provinces to nail their colours to the mast and ignore the danger of being labelled 'Jacobin', although provincial societies revived in the early months of 1795. As a result it was on the London society that most of the government prosecutions fell, marking a point after which London was no longer among the leading centres of radicalism.[2] Unlike the previous radicalism in London, which had been led and organized by the middle classes with working men to swell the numbers, the London

---

[1] L. S. Sutherland, *The City of London and the Opposition to Government, 1768–74*, Creighton Lecture, 1958 (1959).
[2] For a wide-ranging coverage of radicalism at this time see E. P. Thompson's stimulating account in *The Making of the English Working Class* (1963), 102–85.

Corresponding Society was basically composed of artisans and most of its committee were (like Place himself) artisans or tradesmen,[1] with a few professional men, surgeons and journalists. In this respect the London Corresponding Society represented an important step forward in radicalism, with working men gaining greater knowledge of their position in society and being prepared to put forward cogent demands for the reforms they desired (a similar development was to be seen at the same time in such towns as Sheffield). Such activity added considerably to London's radical heritage, but it was not to be a precedent for continuous working-class agitation, which declined in the first decades of the new century, what activity there was originating largely among the middle classes. The effect of the 1795 Treason and Sedition Acts was to be a rapid decline in membership and importance of the London Corresponding Society. The process of decline to the point of collapse was brought about in 1798 by the arrest of the whole committee of the society and a new act putting down reform societies among which the London Corresponding Society was named. This meant that London was without any radical organization of importance and from this blow it took a long time to recover. As we have seen there were in the first two decades of the nineteenth century parliamentary contests for both Middlesex and Westminster of importance from a radical point of view, but these were temporary and very much local affairs. London was never again during the period covered here to come firmly behind a reform movement without much delay and long after the provinces.

It is generally true of the first decade and a half of the new century that reform movements of any size were submerged under the fear of revolutionary France and under the legislation of 1795. Yet when radicalism revived, with the discontents at the end of the Napoleonic wars (discontents which were primarily economic rather than political in origin) the revival was of importance in the provinces rather than in London. In the after- math of Peterloo it was in provincial towns such as Newcastle that there were large meetings to support reform and considerable fears on the part of the authorities that rioting would follow, whilst in London relatively little occurred.

Similarly, the twenties was a period of relative quiescence from the radical point of view; at the end of the decade it was again from the provinces that most of the initiative came. When a reform organization was set up in London in 1830, the Metropolitan Political Union, it is interesting to note that it needed Henry Hunt of Lancashire fame as one of its prime movers, and also that it only lasted for a very short time. Apart from this there was some radical activity. As the following documents show there was a group (albeit a very small one) of London artisans, who, during the twenties had been imbibing Owenite and Hodgskinite doctrines particularly with regard to the labour theory of value. These were to provide the nucleus for the National Union of the Working Classes and for ultra-radical activity in London. There was also in London, as in most towns throughout the country, a considerable amount of parochial agitation, in the form of opposition to select vestries and to the payment of church rates. This provided experience and often the initiative which led

[1] *Ibid.*, 155–6.

individuals into general political reform movements.[1] But these movements were insufficient to lead to any general reform agitation in London until *after* the first Reform Bill was made public in March 1831; then there was a series of public meetings to congratulate the Whigs on their measure and to express the hope that it would be successfully passed into law. In other words people in London could be stimulated by events but were insufficiently interested to provoke events. Although this was generally true of people everywhere, there had been much greater reform agitation, before the Bill was published, in the provinces. Even following its publication, in London there were only a few small parochial reform associations established. Although there was a limited amount of agitation following the defeat of the Bill in committee in the House of Commons, it was not until the second Bill was defeated in the House of Lords in October 1831 that the National Political Union was formed as a general reform organization in London. Again it was events rather than theoretical desire which had provoked activity and the problem was to be seen again between November 1831 and April 1832 when there was little of interest in the parliamentary proceedings over the third Bill and the National Political Union had difficulty in keeping up its membership. One may go on to look at the lack of interest in reform of the Corporation of London in 1835–6 at the time when the Royal Commission on municipal government in the provinces was reporting on the necessity for change and the lack of interest shown by London men in Chartism.

Many reasons could be advanced for the relative quiescence of reform activity in London. It is obvious from the quotation printed at the beginning of this volume that Place was well aware of some of these reasons. The very size of London, which at first glance would lead one to expect considerable activity, actually proved to be an inhibitory factor. London was an impersonal place where it was difficult to obtain the contact necessary to organize agitation; active leaders might have lived several miles from each other; suitable meeting places were probably less common than in villages and small towns; there were few large workshops or places where a large number of people met together at work as there were in textile, shipbuilding, or mining areas and, as Place noted, the trades were often distinct from each other. No doubt the list of features like these explaining why London's experience was different from that of provincial towns could be continued. For instance, in the context of Chartism, Place's note that London 'had no local or particular interest as a town not even as to politics' was important since the regional strength of Chartism depended very much on particular local grievances, and London was too diversified to have such a grievance.

Beyond the political background, however, the economic conditions within an area have a considerable effect in determining the attitude towards radical activity. Although there were many distressed labouring groups in London, such as the coal-whippers on the Thames, they were relatively small in number and sufficiently diversified to prevent London being affected by the 'bread and butter' radicalism which became so important in the northern manufacturing districts. These apart, working

[1] For evidence on this subject for the borough of St. Marylebone see F. H. W. Sheppard, *Local Government in St. Marylebone, 1688–1835* (1958).

men in London were probably better off, in general, than their counterparts in provincial towns,[1] such, at least, was the reason to which several northern delegates to the Chartist Convention attributed Londoners' apathy to Chartism.[2] With regard to the apathy of the middle classes in London towards reform, it is impossible at the present time to give a satisfactory explanation. It may well be that an important factor lay in their poor relationship with the politically aware among the working classes. In the letter to Cobden, already quoted, Place went on to write,

> The leaders [of the working people], those among them who do pay attention to public matters, are one and all at enmity with every other class of society. . . . their opinions are pushed to extremes and are mischievous prejudices. They call the middle class—'shopocrats'—usurers, (all profit being usury)— money-mongers—tyrants and oppressors of the working people and they link the middle class with the aristocracy under the dignified appellation of 'Murderers of Society'—'Murderers of the People'.

One might hazard that the effect of the propaganda of the small group of ultra-radical working men was to make the middle classes fight shy of reform agitation for fear of stirring up more than they bargained for.[3]

III

The remains of the material collected by Place are in two separate groups of volumes in the British Museum, the Place Papers in the Department of Manuscripts and the Place Collection of Newspaper Cuttings, etc., in the Department of Printed Books. Neither is as strictly differentiated as their titles or places of abode might suggest. Although the Papers are mainly of manuscript material, including much correspondence,[4] they also contain many newspaper cuttings and printed documents illustrative of the particular topic on which Place was writing. Conversely the Collection, although consisting largely of cuttings from newspapers and printed documents, contains manuscript comment and some correspondence.

The range of Place's interests is illustrated by the wide variety of material which the two sources contain. There is, for example, material for a history of the theatre; copious notes on drunkenness, public manners and morals;[5]

---

[1] See for instance M. Hovell, *The Chartist Movement* (Manchester, 1918), 47–8.

[2] See Public Record Office, Home Office Papers 40/44, report of meeting in Portland Town, 25 March 1839.

[3] To some extent this is side-stepping the definitions of class. I have used the terms working and middle class as a shorthand form—meaning working men, from artisans to labourers—and white-collar workers, from clerks to employing manufacturers. These terms have been used for more than a century and are far from precise. According to temperament and other circumstances a man from the working class will often act in the way one expects from someone of the middle class. If, however, one attempts to define classes more accurately the difficulties with which one gets involved outweigh the benefits of the exercise for historical analysis. See for example R. S. Neale, 'Class and class-consciousness in early nineteenth-century England: three classes or five?', *Victorian Studies*, xii (1968–9), 4–32. It seems more sensible to use the shorthand but to realize its limitations.

[4] Place made, or had made for him, copies of much of his outward correspondence.

[5] For further information on this topic see B. Harrison, 'Two Roads to Social Reform: Francis Place and the Drunken Committee of 1834', *Historical Journal*, xi (1968), 272–300.

material on the corn laws and the efforts to obtain their repeal. Far out-weighing all the rest, however, is the material on political radicalism, stretching from the complete published materials and minutes of the London Corresponding Society, through a collection on Westminster elections in the first half of the nineteenth century, to the evidence on radical activity leading up to the passing of the first Reform Act, and then on to its aftermath of discontent and demand for further change in the following decade, including an unpublished narrative history, on which this volume of documents is based.

Among historians working on radical activity in the first half of the nineteenth century, the view has been expressed that the Place Papers have been overworked and too readily accepted without sufficient critical analysis of their accuracy and value. Since Graham Wallas,[1] Mark Hovell[2] and Julius West[3] first made general use of the Papers in the late nineteenth and early twentieth century they have rightly received much attention from historians of all kinds. This attention has, however, been patchy in its coverage. Following Hovell, much time has been devoted to the material on the Chartist period. It has not been overworked, however, something which is in reality impossible, since each generation has to rewrite history and has only limited tools with which to do so, and each successive historian of the Chartist Movement must reconsider those sources already used as well as attempt to find fresh evidence. The rest of the Place material on political radicalism has to a large extent been neglected. A detailed study of the London Corresponding Society has yet to be published; the material on Westminster politics, which provides a vast amount of information on the intrigues and procedures of local politics in a constituency with a wide social range of voters, has been little used; strangely the Place Papers have been relatively neglected for the first Reform Bill period with the exception of the material which implies that Place exerted pressure on members of Parliament to work for the passing of the Bill, under the threat of a social revolution if it were not passed; finally the various reform and radical societies, such as the National Political Union and the Metropolitan Parliamentary Reform Association have been largely ignored, along with the correspondence which shows how they were formed and run. Indeed one might say with considerable justification that radicalism in London, quite apart from the evidence the Place Papers provide for it, has been neglected,[4] a strange omission for a capital city and one which is only partially explained by the fact that radical activity gained little of a footing in London during this period (in itself something which needs explanation and deserves more study than it has received).[5] It is therefore justifiable to make more readily available these important documents, both those that are already well known and those which have been hitherto ignored.

On the question of bias in the documents—it would be unwise to claim

---

[1] Wallas, *Life* (1898).   [2] M. Hovell, *The Chartist Movement* (Manchester, 1918).
[3] J. West, *A History of the Chartist Movement* (1920).
[4] For instance the volume of essays, *Chartist Studies*, ed. Asa Briggs (1959), contains no section on London.
[5] See my article 'The Failure of London Chartism', *Historical Journal*, xi (1968), 472–87, and I. Prothero, 'Chartism in London', *Past and Present*, no. 44 (Aug. 1969), 76–105.

that material collected by any individual could be free from bias, although that is no reason for failing to publish the material but merely one for endeavouring to understand the nature of the bias. There has, perhaps, been a too great readiness to accept uncritically the evidence mustered by Place, in some writing which has made use of his material. This is, of course, poor historiography and is unfair to the man. The brief account, given earlier, of Place's life and connections will suggest the general direction of bias which might be expected to be found in his papers but more obvious details of bias appear in the documents following.

Like everyone else Place did not exhibit complete objectivity and took an abbreviated and unfair view of people and ideas of which he did not approve. Frequently in his accounts of meetings on reform he commented that Mr. —— made 'a long and rambling speech' when he did not feel like transcribing or paraphrasing it and/or when he disagreed with its sentiments. Occasionally this very brevity is more illuminating for the meeting or topic under consideration (as in the case of the lone Tory or reactionary view put at a Westminster reform meeting) than a long and tedious transcription would be. It must, however, be remembered that there were views on reform, other than those of Place and his colleagues, views which are still extant in manuscript and document form, but which are not included in this volume as they are not to be found amongst the Place Papers. Comparison with other material, such as the *Poor Man's Guardian* on the National Union of the Working Classes, proves illuminating in this respect.

A number of examples of the unfair attitude adopted by Place occur during the period covered by this volume. He criticizes the government for using spies, such as Popay, to infiltrate the radical movement but obviously fails to see that he was in no position to throw stones when he had been responsible for threatening government with revolution by that radical movement if the Reform Bill were not passed. Place also criticizes Sir Francis Burdett (with whom his relations had often been cool)[1] with regard to his hesitation in accepting the chairmanship of the National Political Union, but when Burdett accepts and maintains creditable control of the initial public meeting to form the union, he receives no credit from Place.[2] In other dealings Place could almost be described as two-faced. Before the formation of the National Political Union, Place argued against Burdett the necessity of giving the union some object beyond merely 'support for King and ministers in passing the Reform Bill'[3] and of continuing the union when the bill was passed. As a result the first object of the union was made 'To obtain a full, free, and effectual, Representation of the People in the Commons House of Parliament'.[4] Yet when the bill was passed Place showed little interest in continuing the union or for a number of years in doing anything to obtain the vote for the working classes. To some extent it may be said that Place adjusted his energies according to the circumstances and that in the mid-eighteen-thirties there was little demand for the extension of the franchise and therefore no point in wasting time and money in agitating for it. There remains, however, a suspicion that Place was not always genuine in the reasons he gave for his actions and that in 1831–2 he

[1] See *D.N.B.* [2] B.M. Add. Ms. 27791, ff. 116–17 and 29. [3] **25**.
[4] Handbill 3.

was anxious to attract the support of the working classes for the National Political Union for the sake of the effect this would have on Parliament rather than from any real desire to obtain their enfranchisement.

Place could also malign individuals from his estimates of their past attitudes and never revise his opinion in the light of new evidence. He criticized John Savage for wishing to prevent the formation of the National Political Union,[1] but failed to note subsequently in his narrative that Savage became a council member of the union and worked amicably within it to obtain the passing of the Reform Bill. Place was also guilty of criticizing in others a failing which he did not perceive in himself. For instance he criticized the list of pledges drawn up by the Liverymen of London, to be demanded of candidates for seats in the reformed House of Commons.[2] Yet his own pamphlet on pledges[3] was remarkably long and diffuse and in the section devoted to Law Reform expected candidates to pledge themselves to ensure 'the detection of crimes, and the certainty of speedy punishment', surely a visionary hope, and in general a much less reasonable proposition than that of the Liverymen which sparked it off.

The documents in the Place Papers can also be inaccurate because of Place's tendency to exaggeration. To belittle the importance of the National Union of the Working Classes at the time of the Reform Bill, he says it consisted of 'not so many as 500 members'[4] which was possibly true, but its membership figure was much less important than the fact that more than 1,000 people regularly attended its meetings. Yet when he wished to prevent the holding of a general meeting of the National Political Union on Hampstead Heath, Place claimed that 'more than half a million persons'[5] would attend and the dangers of riot were too great to risk the meeting. One should not, therefore, put unguarded reliance on the numbers which Place quotes. Similarly Place had the, not unusual, tendency to exaggerate the importance of affairs in which he was involved and his own part in them. He wrote that 'The formation of the National Political Union at this moment was of all but inappreciable importance'[6] in ensuring that the Whigs remained determined to pass the Reform Bill after its defeat in the House of Lords in October 1831 and the ensuing prorogation of Parliament. No doubt the National Political Union acted as an important 'ginger group' in London, but it was by no means the only reform association there, and to arrogate to it 'all but inappreciable importance' is to forget the agitation in the provinces and the pre-existence of organizations such as the Birmingham Political Union and the whole structure of contemporary society and politics. Similarly the documents covering May 1832 would suggest that Place and his pamphlet *Go for Gold* were the major reasons why the Duke of Wellington was prevented from forming a Tory administration.[7] As one of the few people with organizational ability within radicalism, and one who fed the more public radicals with ideas, there was some justification for his estimate of his importance but there is truth in the pun that 'He saw everything in Place yet failed to see everything in place'.

Place could also make mistakes and come to incorrect conclusions. In a letter to Hobhouse in November 1830 he wrote that 'the time is not yet

[1] 29. [2] 53. [3] 54. [4] 22. [5] 45. [6] 30. [7] 46 and 47.

come when a radical change can be made either so effectually as to prevent other similar changes, or so beneficially as to answer the purposes of any class of reformers'.[1] In the long run the assessment was probably correct but in the short term Place was as surprised and delighted as most reformers when Lord John Russell announced the Whig Reform Bill. He then changed his general attitude to one of accepting and working for the bill as being an effective reform. This view seems generally to have been held by all but the most advanced radicals, even a majority of the National Union of the Working Classes deciding to accept the Bill as an instalment. Only Hetherington's *Penny Paper*, with its 'the Mountain in Labour has been delivered—of a mouse'[2] article, and other similar comments, really saw how ineffectual the Bill would be in making immediate changes in the representation. Place was, however, able to change his opinions rapidly as fresh evidence altered the circumstances, and on 20 May 1832, with the Reform Bill only just passed through the House of Lords, he wrote 'the reformed house of commons at no great distance of time shall, as it must, prove how inadequate will be the reform bill to satisfy the expectations of the people'.[3]

With regard to the narrative history of reform it is important to note that Place is writing with the advantage of hindsight and not commenting on the events as they happen which is the impression given. The narrative on the Reform Bill period was written in the middle thirties and that on the London Working Men's Association and the Charter in the early forties (even so it is the earliest detailed account by a contemporary). To some extent this accounts for the farsightedness often seen in Place's remarks, but there is also genuine prescience in his writing. From the enhanced knowledge and experience of the people in the reform agitation he comments on the probability of aristocratic government disappearing and the people obtaining representative government 'exactly at the time when it can best be maintained, and that will be when the people have been prepared to carry it on with the least possible difficulty and the consequent certainty of reaping all its advantages'.[4] Similarly he realized that it was not the working classes who forced through the reform of 1832 (although their agitation was valuable) and that the Reform Act did not give parliamentary power to the middle class. He wrote 'the aristocracy lost no power over the House of Commons by the Reform bill, it was only changed'[5] and went on to show that repeal of the Corn Laws would be a greater blow to the aristocracy, a shrewd view which it has taken historians more than a century to resurrect. The material comprising the Place Papers is of as much importance, therefore, for Place's contemporary comment as for the factual information on radical activity, and the inevitable errors and areas of bias do not seriously detract from that importance.

IV

Selection of actual documents from the Place Papers and Place Collection proved difficult because of the vast range of material. The period

[1] 3. [2] *Penny Papers for the People*, 12 March 1831. [3] 50. [4] 50. [5] 120.

1830–43 was chosen because this is the period for which Place provides most material on radical activity in London. During the eighteen-twenties Place's material concentrates on education and trade unionism and after 1843, as a result of Place's severe illness in the following year, there is little material. Within the given fact that the greatest amount of material is on the agitation for the Reform Bill, the basic premises on which selection was made were to provide as far as possible a broad coverage for the whole period 1830–43 and to make considerable use of the less well-known material. Thus the detail of Place's comments and material on Middlesex and Westminster elections has been ignored, although documents illustrating radical activity have been freely drawn from Westminster meetings in particular, evidence of which is generally available because of Place's contacts there. It should not be considered that the level of activity in Westminster was typical of that of London in general, although it was probably similar to the action in Marylebone, another borough with a long history of radical activity. There were, of course, reform associations formed and meetings held throughout the metropolis but leadership belonged to Westminster and Marylebone.

Newspaper cuttings have been ignored, on the ground that this material is available elsewhere, except where part of a document depends for its meaning on an annexed newspaper cutting. Place, himself, relied heavily on newspaper cuttings, particularly of reform meetings, which he frequently transcribed into his narrative. As well as newspaper cuttings, Place's accounts of the numerous parochial and borough meetings held in London during the Reform Bill agitation have had to be ignored with the exception of a few examples. Similar treatment has been given to the accounts of and comments on meetings of the National Union of the Working Classes.[1]

There is unfortunately no material, beyond the initial account of its formation and its rules, on the Metropolitan Political Union formed in March 1830. It was of far greater importance than the citing of only one document in this volume may suggest, since it was the first reform organization in London leading in to the Reform Bill agitation. Its rules and organization provided a formula for later associations and, even though its existence was brief, it was particularly of importance for endeavouring to bring together the middle and working classes in agitation against the oligarchy which controlled the House of Commons. The Parliamentary Candidate Society has been treated at considerable length, partly because it has been neglected by historians and partly because of the intrinsic importance of the idea behind such an organization of inquiring, on a country-wide basis, into the opinions and conduct on public matters of past members of parliament and prospective candidates, to ensure that voters could elect members who were really anxious to reform the House of Commons. Quite naturally it was an organization which was unpopular with members of parliament and much contemporary opinion since the idea was advanced for its time. It is unfortunate that none of the reports on candidates have survived in the Place Papers.

The next major organizations, chronologically, are the National Union

[1] Add. Ms. 27791, vol. ii.

of the Working Classes and the National Political Union. Inevitably the detail on the latter is the greater because of Place's connection with it and comment on it is, of course, much more favourable than that given to the former, some of the members of which Place described as 'perfectly atrocious'.[1] As has been noted Place denigrated the importance of the National Union of the Working Classes on the ground of its small number of members and criticized them for their violent attitudes and refusal to compromise with the middle-class reformers. The union was, however, important not for its figures of actual membership but its effect on the large audiences, many of whom were not members, at its public and private meetings and for its psychological effect on those at a distance from London who believed, as even Place noted,[2] that most of the working men in London were united in that union. One has also to accept that there was an obvious necessity, both for Place and his followers in the National Political Union on the one hand and the ultra-radicals of the National Union of the Working Classes on the other, to exaggerate the evils of the other one in order to draw the uncommitted members of the working class to support them. Hence neither of them had a good word to say for the other, particularly since the National Political Union was most anxious to expand its membership among the working classes.

Little has been written on either the National Union of the Working Classes or the National Political Union, which between them epitomize the wings of the reform movement—the ultra-radicals wanting revolution (so at least their opponents including Place said)[3] and the middle-class philosophic radicals with their 'deferential' working-class followers. The National Union of the Working Classes well deserves some serious study as the training ground for working men in which the theoretical ideas of men like Owen and Hodgskin were discussed and made the creed of the rapidly developing consciousness of identity among some working men, which was one of the factors leading into Chartism. The National Political Union, of less intrinsic interest for the ideas it promoted, was nevertheless as important a manifestation of public opinion of the times as its better known Birmingham counterpart, although probably not of as much importance as Place implies. Surprisingly, the two unions had much in common in the way of membership and could not be differentiated on a simple middle- or working-class structure,[4] nor even in the way Place divided them, 'The great peculiarity causing a difference between the Political Unions and the Unions of the working classes was, that the first desired the reform bill to prevent a revolution, the last desired its destruction as the means of producing a revolution.'[5] The real difference between the two was much more complicated, perhaps depending on the temperaments of individuals rather than their social class, and has yet to be unravelled. Both unions were, however, transient, being dependent upon the excitement engendered by the introduction of the Reform Bill for their support and soon falling away. By the end of 1832, for instance, the attendance at

[1] 28.   [2] 22.   [3] 43.
[4] See my article 'Class and Political Radicalism in London, 1831–32', to be published in *Historical Journal*.
[5] 43.

council meetings of the National Political Union was dropping and the minutes were purely formal. There was some fresh enthusiasm with the election of a new council in February 1833 but decline to extinction recommenced in April of that year. It may thus be seen that the spirit of union was only a temporary one brought about by circumstances and did not herald a general reaction against the form of government.

The account in the documents and the remaining evidence in the Place Papers of the meeting of the National Union of the Working Classes in Cold Bath Fields in May 1833 which led to the death of policeman Robert Culley, and the events surrounding the inquest on his body, reflect the bias of both middle- and working-class radicals against the metropolitan police. This is a subject which is insufficiently well explained by Gavin Thurston[1] in his book on the affair (which in whitewashing the police provides as much bias in the opposite direction and is a useful antidote to Place's material) and which will bear further scrutiny by historians. There is little material on the unstamped press and the agitation for the repeal of the newspaper stamp duty in the mid-eighteen-thirties in the documents following. Despite the fact that Place was intimately involved with J. A. Roebuck and Dr. Black on the committee for promoting petitions against the stamp duty and in the *Pamphlets for the People*, little evidence of this agitation remains in his papers, apart from some correspondence.

The London Working Men's Association has been given limited space in the documents, partly because it is already well known and much of the material appears in Lovett's autobiography[2] and partly because the minute books of the association, although in the Manuscript Department of the British Museum, do not form part of the Place Papers. On the other hand the Metropolitan Parliamentary Reform Association is given considerable space since it is much less generally known and because of its ideological connections with the Complete Suffrage Movement of Joseph Sturge.

Beyond the fact that the documents give a more widespread and favourable impression of middle-class moderate radical activity than they do of working-class ultra radicalism, it may well be said that they express only the views of the literate and important radicals and not those of the mass of their followers and that there is a disadvantage in this. While it is undoubtedly true that the thousands who took part in the Bowyer/Powell procession[3] and the meeting to elect candidates to the Chartist General Convention,[4] had ideas on the subject of reform, to a large extent they took them from the leading reformers or had their own ideas moulded by them. Lack of knowledge of the opinions of the majority of people involved in the reform agitation is probably therefore not of great significance, particularly since, as I have argued elsewhere,[5] the mass of people in London were peculiarly disinterested in the subject and were only stirred up to follow the leading reformers at times of particular excitement in 1831–2 and 1839. There was probably greater continuous interest in reform during the forties with the various trades' chartist societies but this was at a time when the excitement and ability to draw crowds in London was largely over.

[1] G. Thurston, *The Clerkenwell Riot* (1967).
[2] *Life and struggles of William Lovett* (1876, reprinted 1967).
[3] **23**.   [4] **103**.   [5] 'Failure of London Chartism', *Historical Journal*, xi, 472–87.

A number of other points remain to be made about some of the contents of the documents. There has been a tendency among recent historians to denigrate the importance of the first Reform Act and it is certainly true that it did little to alter the type of representative in the House of Commons or to alter the methods of electing members to that House. It is, however, obvious from the documents that many ardent reformers were very surprised and delighted at the extent of the bill when it was first introduced and that they considered that it introduced considerable change. This is sometimes lost sight of in the light of the Reform Act's failure to live up to the change which was expected and because of the considerable reaction to that failure. Nevertheless the first Reform Act was a major step forward as compared with the very limited proposals for reform seen during the twenties. One should, however, be suspicious concerning Place's continual comments on the united spirit of the people with regard to the Reform Bill.

In a recent book Dr. Hobsbawm has continued the historical argument that in the years 1831–2, at the time of the agitation for the first Reform Act, England was near to revolution. He writes,[1] 'At no other period since the seventeenth century can we speak of large masses of them [the common people] as revolutionary, or discern at least one moment of political crisis when something like a revolutionary situation might actually have developed'. That this is an artificial and forced view of history is evidenced by the language used—'*something like* a revolutionary situation *might* actually *have* developed'. If his were a lone voice one would be less concerned about the impact of this view of the period on students of history, but it is in fact a much held view. E. P. Thompson in his stimulating study of the working class comes to a similar conclusion. 'Viewed from one aspect, England was without any doubt passing through a crisis in these twelve months [early in 1831 until the "days of May" in 1832] in which revolution was possible,' and 'In the autumn of 1831 and in the "days of May" Britain was within an ace of a revolution which, once commenced might well . . . have prefigured, in its rapid radicalisation, the revolutions of 1848, and the Paris Commune.'[2]

The importance of this question of nearness-to-revolution in 1831–2 for this volume of documents lies in the fact that Place is one of the authorities from whom evidence has been drawn to support such a thesis. Professor Rudé has recently written, 'Francis Place . . . had actually hoodwinked both Whig and Tory Members of Parliament into believing that if the Reform Bill were not conceded revolution would be unleashed in all the great cities of the Kingdom!'[3] Many quotations from the documents could be made to support this. The decision of the King, under the threat of violence, not to make a state visit to the Lord Mayor of London in November 1830 was 'the first step in the British Revolution'.[4] 'There seemed to be

[1] E. J. Hobsbawm, *Industry and Empire: an Economic History of Britain since 1750* (1968), 55.
[2] Thompson, *The Making of the English Working Class*, 808 and 817.
[3] G. Rudé, in a review of Thurston, *The Clerkenwell Riot*, in *Victorian Studies*, xii (1968), 117–19.
[4] 3.

but two things between which a choice could be made—the bill or a revolution.'[1] With the Reform Bill passed Place wrote, 'We were within a moment of general rebellion, and had it been possible for the Duke of Wellington to have formed an administration, the King and the people would have been at issue. . . .' and also 'But for these demonstrations [the mass meetings of the people, etc.] a revolution would have commenced, which would have been the act of the whole people to a greater extent than any which had ever before been accomplished'.[2]

This was not, however, always the attitude adopted by Place. His general view was of the necessity of preventing revolution[3] and of horror at the attitude of the ultra-radicals who wanted a complete upheaval. After talking to some of them in October 1831 he wrote, 'So thoroughly satisfied were these men that in a very few months "the people would rise and do themselves justice", that when *I expressed my doubts,* they became irritated . . .'.[4]

Most important of all, however, are the questions as to how far Place was genuine in his belief as to the nearness of revolution and how far he was trying to make a case, as Rudé has put it, in order to hoodwink the authorities to force the Reform Bill through. On 18 May Sir John Hobhouse wrote to Place informing him that 'there was to be a meeting in Downing Street at noon' and requesting a letter 'telling him all the facts I [Place] could and giving him my opinion of the state of feeling among the people as far as I could and my view of prospective results'.[5] Realizing that the Downing Street meeting would be an important one which would settle whether or not the Duke of Wellington should form an administration, and knowing his own standing with Hobhouse, Place quite naturally produced a strong-worded reply. 'If the Duke came into power now, we shall be unable, longer to "hold to the laws"—break them we must, be the consequences whatever they may, we know that all must join with us, to save their property, no matter what may be their private opinions. Towns will be barricaded . . . we shall have a commotion in the nature of a civil war . . . Here then is a picture not by any means over drawn . . . Think too upon the results. . . . think of the coming Republic.' etc.

It is difficult to believe that this was anything but gross exaggeration and it would seem reasonable to accept that Place was playing a double game with Hobhouse (whom he had before used because of his parliamentary position) and overstating a danger which his considerable knowledge of the people, especially in London, did not really justify. It is, however, possible that Place was led astray from the realities by the infectious excitement he encountered. There still remains, quite apart from this letter, a considerable number of comments by Place on the nearness of revolution as shown above, but it may be seen that these were part of the agitation leading up to the passing of the bill, when it was necessary to create a

[1] Add. Ms. 27792, f. 153 (April 1832).
[2] **50**. See also generally Add. Ms. 27795, ff. 141–8.
[3] It should, perhaps, be made quite clear that the revolution of which Place is writing is one to be initiated by the middle classes and backed by the numerical support of the working classes in order to destroy the power of the aristocracy, etc.
[4] **27**. The italics are mine.   [5] **48**.

climate to force the bill through, and in such circumstances one may expect a lot of hot air to be loosed. Finally, in his narrative comments (which he intended to publish) when the bill was passed, Place could hardly produce a *volte-face* and say that it had been a complete spoof after all.

There were, of course, people at the time who would have welcomed a revolution, even such a one as Place had in mind to secure the supremacy of the middle classes, but they were too few and insufficiently organized to have created one in the climate of the time. It is particularly worth noting that this was especially true of London, which as the capital city and the major population centre would surely have had some say in the course of a revolution. As a postscript on the question of revolution and organization, especially among the working classes, it is worth noting Place's comment in 1842, written one suspects with a feeling of sorrow, on the failure of Chartism,

> All these persosn thought as most of the politically associated working men still do, that—noise and clamour, threats, menaces and denunciations will operate upon the government, so as to produce fear in sufficient quantity to insure the adoption of the Charter—they have yet to learn that these notions and proceedings contain no one element of power—that the Government as mere matter of course will, as every Government must, hold people very cheap who mistake such matters, as have been mentioned, for power . . . they have not a glimpse of their own, much less of the actual condition or relation of the several portions of society, who must concur, before any great organic change can be even put in progress. . . .[1]

This comment is surely a more accurate conception of British politics and society in the period than is the one of nearness-to-revolution. It is a comment which may accurately be applied to 1831–2, for without the Whigs, who were the powerful element in reform, the Bill would have been doomed to failure. Despite the important role which Place arrogates to the political unions, the popular out-of-doors agitation provided only the chorus and filled none of the principal acting parts.

V

There remain a few minor points of detail with regard to the documents and their presentation. An approximate chronological order has been maintained throughout, except where one topic has been followed through to its conclusion, in the hope that this will make for greater ease of reading. In documents where Place has transcribed reports from newspapers there may well be errors involved in his transcriptions. No attempt has been made to check these against the originals; they have been included since they bring together diverse opinions and add to the chronological sequence of the documents. In the Place manuscripts there are frequent instances of inaccurate spelling and poor punctuation and they contain much incorrect grammar and faulty and confused construction. To some extent, no doubt, this resulted from the fact that they were hurried drafts of what was later intended to be a published history of reform movements in the period. In these respects the documents here printed have followed the original, except where punctuation has been added in order to clarify ambiguous or

[1] 120.

otherwise difficult sentences. *Sic* has been used sparingly to denote spelling mistakes and other casual errors in the manuscripts, although it has been omitted if the same mistake is repeated regularly. Beyond the comment provided in this introduction, the documents have been presented as in the original with no annotation beyond the dating and placing of otherwise unrecognizable material.

Finally I should like to express my thanks to the staff of the Photographic, Manuscript and Printed Books departments of the British Museum; to the staff research fund of the University of Newcastle upon Tyne for a grant which enabled me to have photocopies made of all the relevant documents, and therefore saved me the tedious task of transcription; to Dr. N. McCord, who has kindly read this introduction and corrected many of the errors which it contained in its original form (those that remain are, of course, my responsibility), and also made many useful suggestions which have been incorporated in it; and to Miss E. Clark for her painstaking efforts in producing the typescript.

D.J.R.

PLACE PAPERS

1. [Add. Ms. 27789, f. 145]

On the 8 March [1830] an immense meeting of the people principally the working people was held in the grounds at the Eagle Tavern in the City Road, for the purpose of forming a Metropolitan Union, Daniel O'Connell took the chair, and Henry Hunt took a conspicuous part in the proceedings. A council of thirty-six was appointed and Henry Hunt accepted the office of Treasurer. This appointment ruined the Union. Several who had been named on the council refused to act and nobody would subscribe money to be under the controul [*sic*] or the care of Mr. Hunt, and the Union was soon extinguished from want of money to pay its current expenses.

[Add. Ms. 27822, ff. 11–14. *Printed.*]

AUTHORISED COPY OF THE RESOLUTIONS ADOPTED AT THE GREAT PUBLIC MEETING, CONSISTING OF 30,000 PEOPLE, HELD *At the Eagle Tavern, City-Road, on Monday, 8th March*, 1830, FOR FORM-ING A METROPOLITAN POLITICAL UNION FOR THE RECOVERY AND PROTECTION OF PUBLIC RIGHTS. DANIEL O'CONNELL, Esq., M.P. IN THE CHAIR. METROPOLITAN MEETING.

At a public Meeting of the Merchants, Manufacturers, Tradesmen, Mechanics, Artisans, and other Inhabitants of the Metropolis, held at the EAGLE TAVERN, City Road, on Monday morning, the 8th March, 1830, the following Resolutions were entered into:—

DANIEL O'CONNELL, Esq., M.P., IN THE CHAIR

RESOLVED, 1st.—That the ruinous depression of the trade of the City of London and its Suburbs has been progressively increasing for many years past, and has now arrived at an extent never before equalled; and as all the great productive interests of the nation are suffering, we are convinced that the hopes of amelioration, which have been so long and so frequently held out, are altogether fallacious and delusive.

RESOLVED, 2nd.—That, in the opinion of this Meeting, the general distress which now afflicts the country, is entirely to be ascribed to the long, sanguinary, extravagant, and unnecessary wars, waged against the liberties of the people of AMERICA and of FRANCE; and this general distress has been greatly heightened by the gross mismanagement of public affairs; and that such mismanagement can only be effectually and permanently remedied by real Radical Reform in the Commons' House of Parliament; and this Meeting is also of opinion, that for the legal and constitutional accom-plishment of this great object, and for the further redress of public wrongs

1

and grievances, through the medium of reformed Parliaments, it is expedient to form a General Political Union between the middling and labouring Classes of the People in the Metropolis.

The plan of a Political Union, between the middling and labouring Classes of the People in the Metropolis, for the protection of public rights, with a Political Council attached to it, having been read to this Meeting, and the same having been duly considered—

RESOLVED, 3rd.—That it be approved, adopted, ratified, and confirmed, as the act of this Meeting, and of the Friends of real, that is, Radical Reform, resident in this Metropolis.

RESOLVED, 4th.—That the thirty-six Gentlemen hereby named, be appointed to the Political Council, for the year ending the 1st Monday in July, 1830, with power to add to their numbers, so that the whole do not exceed fifty; and on that day the Council shall be elected by the Members of the Union, agreeably to the Rules and Regulations.

COUNCIL

Henry Hunt	Charles Lane
Daniel O'Connell	William Lovett
Alexander Dawson	Robert Ellis
John Grady	Daniel French
Robert Mercer	F. A. Augero
John Wood	Daniel Barrett
Richard Phillips	C. J. Hand
Edward Waylen	George Ward
Emanuel Dias Santos	Thomas Barrett
Joseph Hume	John Henley
Otway Cave	James Watson
Charles Pearson	John Matland
H. Hetherington	P. Cavanagh
William E. Andrews	William Carpenter
Cornelius Griffin	John Cook
B. Warden	James Mee
John Cleave	C. E. Mawbey
James Walker	W. H. Jones

RESOLVED, 5th—That Henry Hunt, Esq., be appointed Treasurer.

RESOLVED, 6th.—That this Meeting pledges itself, collectively and individually, to support the objects of the Political Union by every just, legal, peaceful, and constitutional means.

RESOLVED, 7th.—That we recommend to all our fellow-citizens to subscribe to the Funds of the Political Union, so far as they can conveniently afford, and to obey all the just, legal, and constitutional advice of the Council, as far as they can be legally, constitutionally, and conveniently followed.

RESOLVED, 8th.—That the Petition now read to this Meeting be adopted as the Petition of the Inhabitants of the Metropolis, subject to such alterations as the Political Council may direct.

2

COPY. TO THE HONOURABLE THE COMMONS OF, &c. &c.

HUMBLY SHEWETH, That your Petitioners have long suffered under accumulated difficulties and intolerable distresses; their industry has become abortive, their skill and capital are without profit, their sufferings are daily increasing, their resources are wasting, and they are without prospect of change or relief.

That, having long reflected upon the primary and immediate causes of these misfortunes, your Petitioners ascribe them entirely to the want of a RADICAL REFORM of your honourable House; the members of which not being chosen by, or duly sympathising with, the people, have for a series of years compromised the nation's welfare, by erroneous and pernicious measures; and by a policy which prefers personal and particular interests to the general welfare of the whole of the community.

That to the want also of a RADICAL REFORM of the Representation, your Petitioners ascribe the ruinous war with the American Colonies, which ended in their separation from, and entire independence of, this country; that to the same fatal cause, your Petitioners ascribe the late bloody, long-continued, and unjust wars against the liberties of France, which your Petitioners believe were waged and carried on to prevent that reform at home, for which the people had so long and so earnestly petitioned.

That to the same cause, also, they ascribe the enormous debt of EIGHT HUNDRED AND FIFTY millions(!) and the oppressive and grinding taxes annually required to pay the interest of the same; to the same cause also your Petitioners ascribe the upholding of the unparalleled and prodigal establishments in time of peace, by taxes drawn from the people, who, at the same time, are suffering the severest, the most cruel and most degrading privations; privations abhorrent and inconsistent with the character of Englishmen, and disgraceful to the nation at large.

That to the same cause also, namely, the want of a RADICAL REFORM in the Commons House of Parliament, your Petitioners ascribe the utter neglect and shameful disregard of their distresses; the professed inability to relieve them, and the total indifference with which the petitions of the people have been hitherto received, and the accumulation of Fiscal Statutes, diminishing their personal independence; and restraining, by innovations of every kind, the privileges which have hitherto been the birth-right of all Englishmen.

That your Petitioners pray therefore that your honourable House will restore, in purity of form and efficiency of practice, the rights and civil privileges assured to them by their ancestors, in MAGNA CHARTA, in the Petition of RIGHT, and in the BILL OF RIGHTS; the fundamental principles of which, all the kings of England, from Edward the First down to George the Fourth, have, by their Coronation Oaths, been bound to maintain; and which guarantee civil liberty, by providing *that no man shall be taxed who is not represented in Parliament; and that none shall be imprisoned, fined, or destroyed, except by the verdict of his equals;* and which also guarantee individual property, by protecting, *even from debts 'to the Crown,* a man's tools and means of obtaining future subsistence!'

That your Petitioners further pray, that your honourable House will not

3

continue longer to oppose such measures as may be proposed for your own *radical* and *effectual Reform*; and your Petitioners make this prayer not only for their own benefit, the welfare of their families, and the salvation of their country, but for the preservation of your honourable House itself, which can only exist in power and honour through the voice, influence, affection, and confidence of the people.

And your Petitioners will ever pray.

RESOLVED, 9th.—That the thanks of this Meeting be given to the Chairman, for the able and impartial manner in which he has conducted the business of the day.

THE FOLLOWING ARE THE OBJECTS OF THE POLITICAL UNION

1st.—To obtain, by every just, legal, constitutional, and peaceful means, an Effectual and Radical Reform in the Commons' House of Parliament.

2nd.—To inquire, consult, consider, and determine, respecting the rights and liberties of the industrious classes, and respecting the legal means of securing those which remain, and recovering, through the modes sanctioned by the law, and by the principles of the free Constitution of this Realm, those which have been lost.

3rd.—To prepare Petitions, Addresses, and Remonstrances to the Crown, and both or either of the Houses of Parliament, respecting the *preservation* and *restoration* of Public Rights, and respecting the repeal of bad laws, and the enactment of a wise and all-comprehensive code of good laws.

4th.—To prevent and redress, by legal and constitutional means, all local PUBLIC WRONGS and OPPRESSIONS, and all local encroachments upon the rights, interests, and lawful privileges, of the Community.

5th.—To promote peace, union, and concord, among all classes of his Majesty's subjects, and to guide and direct the public mind into uniform, peaceful, and legitimate operations, within the strict limit of law and constitutional principles, instead of leaving it to waste its strength in loose, desultory, and unconnected exertions, or to deviate into any course which would deserve the condemnation of sober, rational, and just men.

6th.—To collect and organise the peaceful expression of the public opinion, so as to bring it to act upon the Houses of Parliament in a just, legal, constitutional, and effectual way.

7th.—To adopt such measures as may be legal and necessary for the purpose of obtaining relief for the NATIONAL DISTRESS, of rendering justice to the injured, and of bringing to trial, according to due course of law, any individuals, in whatever station, who may be found to have acted from criminal or corrupt motives.

8th.—To avoid all private or secret proceedings of any kind or nature, and all concealment of any of the views or objects of the Union.

9th.—To facilitate, for all persons clothed with any legal authority, full, free, and constant access to all the books, documents, regulations, and proceedings of the Union; it being the fixed basis of this Union, in all things to obey and conform to the Law, and in nothing to violate the spirit or even the letter of the Constitution.

4

THE FOLLOWING ARE THE RULES AND REGULATIONS OF THE POLITICAL UNION.

1st.—The Constitution of this Union is essentially popular. It admits, as equal members, all persons whatever, whose names shall be registered in the Books of the Union, so long as they shall conform to the Rules and Regulations of the Union.

2nd.—The general management of the affairs of the UNION is committed to a POLITICAL COUNCIL, chosen annually at the GENERAL MEETINGS of the MEMBERS OF THE UNION, and subject only to the control of such annual or other general meetings.

3rd.—All persons becoming members of the Union, are expected to contribute such donations, and annual or quarterly subscriptions, as they can conveniently afford, the subscriptions not being less than 1s. per quarter.

4th.—A general annual meeting of the members of the Union takes place on the first Monday in July. The members of the Union also meet whenever called together by order of the Political Council, or by a requisition signed by the Chairman or Deputy Chairman of the Political Council, and countersigned by the Secretary; or by a Requisition signed by any seven of the Political Council, or by not less than 200 Members of the Union. No General Meeting can be held unless the Requisition is advertised in three morning newspapers. The Secretary produces the books for inspection at all general meetings.

5th.—The General Meetings of the members of the Union choose annually, on the first Monday in July, the POLITICAL COUNCIL of not less than 36 individuals; into whose hands the disposition and expenditure of the funds of the Society, and the general management of its concerns for the ensuing year, are confided.

6th.—The Political Council cannot exist more than one year without being *re-chosen* by the general meetings. At the General Meetings each individual is put in nomination separately (or in such a way as the General Meetings may direct), and is declared a member of the council by the majority of members of the Union present. The Chairman decides on which side is the majority; unless a division is demanded by fifty members present, in which case a division takes place, and tellers are appointed on each side.

7th.—The General Meetings choose annually three Auditors for the ensuing year, who shall pass the accounts of the Council for such year; and in case two of such Auditors shall not agree in passing the accounts, the subject of difference shall be submitted to the General Meeting.

8th.—The General Meetings choose a Treasurer and Trustees, in whose hands the funds of the Society are deposited.

9th.—The Political Council meet weekly, or as often as they may deem necessary; at such meetings seven of them are competent to act; they keep a record of their proceedings, and they appoint General Meetings of the Society as often as may become expedient.

10th.—The Political Council appoint a Chairman, a Deputy Chairman, a Secretary, Collectors of Contributions, and such other officers, either with or without salaries, as may be found expedient.

11th.—The Council employ such solicitors and legal advisers as they may approve.

12th.—The Council employ the funds of the Society solely in effecting the objects of the Society, to the best of their judgment and discretion; and no money can be drawn from the treasurer or trustees, without *an order passed by the Council, and signed by seven of its members.*

13th.—No part of the funds of the Society can be expended in any object in which a member of the Council is personally interested, without the previous consent of two-thirds of the members of the Council present at a meeting specially called for the purpose of considering the subject.

14th.—The Council pay their own expenses. They hold no secret meetings. They have power to add to their number, and to dismiss from the General Meetings any persons disturbing the peace, or violating the rules and regulations of the Society.

15th.—No alteration of, or addition to, the rules and regulations of the Society can be adopted, without being previously submitted to the Council, and recommended by a majority to a General Meeting of the Society.

16th.—The subscriptions of all classes of his Majesty's subjects are invited in support of the Metropolitan Political Union, the objects of which being strictly conservatory, are calculated to restore the just rights and interests of the Industrious Classes; to confirm and preserve the constitutional privileges of every class of the community from all illegal violation whatever.

THE FOLLOWING ARE THE DUTIES OF THE MEMBERS OF THE POLITICAL UNION.

1st.—To be good, faithful, and loyal subjects to the King.

2nd.—To obey the laws of the land; and where they cease to protect the rights, liberties, and interests, of the community, to endeavour to get them changed by just, legal, constitutional, and peaceful means, only.

3rd.—To present themselves at all General Meetings of the POLITICAL UNION, as far as they conveniently can; to conduct themselves peaceably and legally at such meetings, and to depart to their respective homes as soon as the Chairman shall leave the chair.

4th.—To choose only just, upright, and able men, as members of the POLITICAL COUNCIL, and to dismiss them and elect others in their stead, whenever they shall cease to watch over and defend, THE RIGHTS, LIBERTIES, AND INTERESTS, OF THE MIDDLING AND LABOURING CLASSES OF THE PEOPLE.

5th.—To obey strictly all the just, legal, and constitutional advice of the POLITICAL COUNCIL, so soon as they shall be made public, and so far as they can legally and conveniently be followed.

6th.—To bear in mind that the strength of our Society consists in the PEACE, *order, unity,* and LEGALITY, of our proceedings; and to consider all persons as enemies who shall, in any way, invite or promote violence, discord, or division, or any illegal or doubtful measure, and to exclude all such persons from the Union.

7th.—Never to forget that, by the exercise of the above qualities, we shall

6

produce the peaceful display of an immense organised moral power, which cannot be despised or disregarded; but that, if we do not keep clear of the multitudinous and intricate chicanery which surrounds us, the corrupt Crown lawyer and hired soldier will probably break in upon us, and render all our exertions vain.

THE FOLLOWING ARE THE DUTIES OF THE MEMBERS OF THE POLITICAL COUNCIL.

1st.—To endeavour, to the utmost of their power, to carry into effect the OBJECTS of the POLITICAL UNION, by every just, legal, constitutional, and peaceful means.

2nd.—To use none other than just, legal, constitutional, and peaceful means.

3rd.—To seek no private objects of their own, and to use the funds of the Society solely in promoting the objects of the Union.

4th.—To watch closely the proceedings of the Legislature, and to present petitions and remonstrances to the Crown and both Houses of Parliament, whenever the rights, liberties, and interests, of the middling and labouring classes of the Community are invaded, or whenever they can be restored or secured.

5th.—To endeavour to devise the means of assisting to preserve the peace and order of this City and neighbourhood, during any political convulsions which may be brought upon the country, through the distress occasioned by the mismanagement of public affairs.

6th.—To consider and report upon the legality and practicability of holding CENTRAL MEETINGS of DELEGATES from the INDUSTRIOUS CLASSES, in the manner as similar kinds of meetings were lately held by the Delegates of the *Agriculturists* assembled at Henderson's Hotel.

7th.—To consider the means of organising a system of operation, whereby the public press may be influenced to act generally in support of the public interests.

8th.—In all their proceedings to look chiefly to the recovery and preservation of the RIGHTS and INTERESTS of the middling and labouring classes of the people.

9th.—To avoid any thing secret, private, or concealed, or in any way inconsistent with the spirit or letter of the Law or Constitution.

In conclusion, let it be ever held in mind, that the basis of this Union is obedience to the laws, and conformity to the principles of our Constitutional rights, so that any act or proceeding inconsistent with either the one or the other, is declared to be, and shall be held and deemed to be, utterly void as to all persons, save such as personally and individually take any part in such act or proceeding; and every such person is hereby declared to cease to be a member of this Union, and his expulsion is declared to be a matter of right.

All letters and communications to be addressed (post paid) to C.M. Riley, Secretary, at the office of the Metropolitan Political Union, 9, Red Lion Court, Fleet Street, or at the Globe Tavern, Shoe Lane, Fleet Street, London.

2. [Add. Ms. 27789, f. 189] *Copy*

Whitehall Nov. 7 1830

My Lord,

I am commanded by the King to inform your lordship, that his majesty's confidential servants have felt it to be their duty to advise the king to postpone the visit which their majesties intended to pay to the City of London on Tuesday next.

From information which has been recently received, there is reason to apprehend that, notwithstanding the devoted loyalty and affection born to his majesty by the citizens of London, advantage would be taken of an occasion which must necessarily assemble a vast number of persons by right to create tumult and confusion, and thereby to endanger the property and lives of his majesty's subjects.

It would be a source of deep and lasting concern to their majesties were any calamity to occur on the occasion of their visit to the City of London, and their majesties have therefore resolved, though not without the greatest reluctance and regret, to forgo for the present the gratification which that visit would have afforded to their majesties.

I have the honour to be my lord,
Your obedient servant,
Robert Peel.

The Right Honourable the Lord Mayor.

3. [Add. Ms. 35148, ff. 69–70]
To John Cam Hobhouse, Esq.,

Nov. 8 1830

My Dear Sir,

'Miracles never will cease'. Here am I, 'the furious republican' whose opinions have induced many to fear and more to hate him become a moderé, writing to you not to accelerate an instant, but to retard it, not a mere reform, but an actual change.

The folly of the King and his ministers have [*sic*] precipitated matters.

The paltry contemptible procession to Guildhall so sillily agreed to by the King could do nothing but mischief, and was sure to put an end to his popularity if it had done nothing else. The refusal to go even at the eleventh hour is the best course which could have been taken. I hope he has not been persuaded to it by ministers, but that he has peremptorily refused to go, and not withstanding his refusal will on any ground, mark his folly, it is much less foolish to stay away than to go.

Now comes the rub, opposition will observe no bounds. I do not desire that they should if they would take the proper course, and instead of endeavouring at once to turn out Ministers, they would rather try to keep them in office as long as they can, it would not be long. Their efforts should now be fully to expose the ministerial absurdities, especially that of the Kings intended visit to the Lord Mayor, thus encouraging the vile corporation to spend a considerable sum of the peoples money extorted from them under false pretences by these corrupt Corporators, the whole of the City Government being from the top to the bottom a burlesque on the human understanding more contemptible than the most paltry farce played in a booth at Bartholomew fair, and more mischievous than any man living is perhaps prepared to believe.

The King refuses to make a procession along the streets, and the Play Houses are from very fear to be shut up tomorrow. This is the first time, observe that apprehension of violence by the people against an administration as to induce them openly to change their plan of proceeding.

Put these matters in any way you please. Let them do all they can to reconcile themselves to the conduct of ministers, let them excuse it how they may, let them deprecate it as much as they please, let them practice self-deception to the greatest possible extent to persuade themselves that no material consequences can result from it, its nature cannot be changed, neither can they make it other than the first step in the British Revolution.

You know my opinion of the weakness of the present Government, you know my opinion that there never can be a *strong* government again in England until there has been a change even in its very form, and neither you nor any one else will argue the contrary against me. I then want no instant change of ministers. I am as certain as a man can be who is not desirous to cheat himself or to be deceived by others, that a present change of ministers would do more towards producing, or rather accelerating a revolution than all the other circumstances of the times taken together, and the time is not yet come when a radical change can be made either so effectually as to prevent other similar changes, or so beneficially as to answer the purposes of any class of reformers. Critically as ministers are circumstanced I doubt their courage to continue in office, if opposition within and without were to be ever so little countenanced by the King, and if they were to be ousted at once who are to come in. Not another Tory set. There are not tory materials of sufficient importance to build up an Administration which could continue in office to the end of the session. Not a whig administration, for spite of the wishes of their friends, here is hardly any thing but imbecility. Who would be minister, Earl Grey, look at him is he competent to the duty? No man will say he is. Are these the times when such a man however good his intention can advantageously be minister. The answer must be NO. The power would soon fall from his hands to light on some one,—who can say whom? The Marquess of Lansdown, why should the fact be concealed that he is in no way competent to the duties of the office. If he were minister he must be led by others, must be a hesitating, vacillating irregular and consequently mischievous minister. He would either be driven away or driven mad in six months. Lord Holland he has gone by, or rather circumstances have gone by and left him behind. He might have done in quiet times, he will not do now. If I am mistaken in these matters you will really do me a favour and some service by shewing me that I am mistaken, and you shall have my thanks.

If on the contrary I am not mistaken, do pray do all you can to prevent the unwise conduct of your friends in resisting ministers in such a way as to compel them to resign at once. Abuse their proceedings as much as you please, but beyond this do nothing to prevent them sinking gradually as low as possible, and there leave them to work themselves out of office, which will happen quite soon enough.

I do not fear any change however great it may be, I think the more complete the better, but I do both fear and abhor a premature change.

A letter was written on saturday last, by a fellow named Chubb, a vagabond pamphlet seller in Holy-well Street to Mr. Hume. This Chubb knows as well as any man can know how the vulgarity feel, he is acquainted with a multitude of vagabonds who are fit for any mischief. In his letter he says there is an intention among many to seize the Palace of St. James's as soon as the King's party have left it. The doing as he says is absurd and improbable, but you may depend upon it, some such project has been talked of to a considerable extent.

Information was given to the Police Commissioners that Henry Hunt was to lead 20,000 men from the Surrey side of the Thames over Black Friars Bridge to Ludgate Hill to pay their respects to the King, and to let him hear the sentiments of the people. That Hunt could collect and lead twice that number I have no doubt, but I do not believe that any such a procession would have taken place.

It has been said by some respectable persons that if the Duke went in the procession he would be shot, and I know well enough that if in the opinion of vast numbers of persons, shooting the Duke would lead to a fight with the Government there would be many willing enough to shoot at him.

I have seen a letter from the man, whom I consider the most influential man in England, Thomas Attwood of Birmingham, proposing an association to collect the names of persons in London who will pledge themselves to pay no more taxes, if ministerial interference should produce the probability of a war with Belgium, and I believe something of the kind will be done. There has long been growing a disposition to refuse paying taxes, but it [is] only now that rich men who have any influence have countenanced it. Now there are many such willing to take part in it.

Now mark the consequence. If any considerable portion of the housekeepers were to refuse paying taxes, and especially if this were to happen in London a revolution would be effected in a week spite of the Government and the Army. If taxes were refused it would instantly produce a panic. Bank of England notes would no longer circulate, and Government would be powerless. No one would bring a sack of flour, a bullock or a sheep to the London Markets. The moment taxes were really refused the shops would be all closed, decent people would remain at home, until the populace and the soldiers had fought and were reconciled; a provisional government would then be formed.

No man can tell what fortuitous circumstances may produce a revolution. A revolution when a very large body of the people shall desire one may easily be produced. If no other circumstance shall precipitate it here refusing to pay taxes whenever it may happen will certainly produce it. That it will happen before many years have passed away seems to me a reasonable expectation. You know my opinion, that when men ought to act, they should act promptly, and go through with the business be it whatever it may. You know that I have a great dislike to undertake any matter unless circumstances seem to warrant the conclusion, that it can be wholly and not partially accomplished. I have always held that when action becomes necessary, it is much better to risk doing wrong, than doing nothing, and if opposition had no choice I should say go on, don't hesitate a moment, oust the ministers as soon as possible, but they have a choice and may do mischief if they refuse, or neglect to take that choice.

Yours truly
Francis Place

4. [Add. Ms. 27789, ff. 187–90]

Nothing under the circumstances of the time could have been so ill advised as was that of ministers respecting the visit of the King to the Lord Mayor [9 November 1830]. If a protest had been wanted as an excuse to attack the people similar to the Manchester Massacre in 1819—it might have been found in such a proceeding, but this was not intended. Ministers were silly enough to suppose it would be a grand fete, and such they intended it should be, they saw nothing in it but the popularity of the King and their own glory; the feelings, and the power of the people when called upon to act for a specific purpose was wholly unknown to them. Of their disposition to resist whatever they might consider agression [sic] no matter by what means produced they had no knowledge, and saw in them nothing but mere mobs—and yet were [where] paltry assemblies had to a considerable extent benumbed them, they seem to have been in a curious state of contradiction each man with himself and with each other. Had the procession been persevered in there would have been a riot and much blood would have been shed, it is even probable that very serious consequences beyond this would have taken place. The 9 of November which always calls an immense number of silly people into the streets would have been a grand holiday for all sorts of people, all the working people would have gone forth, and with the notions they entertained, that they could fight, and the desire to prove themselves as valiant as the Parisians, and could beat the soldiers as they had done, might have led to a temporary defeat of them, and this by the extinction of trade—and the refusal to take Bank Paper might have produced a revolution. Even under any termination to a riot so general, as could not have failed to have taken place, the procession was a matter to be deprecated and if possible prevented. I did all I could, in every way I could, to convince every man I saw who had any influence of any kind, that it was his duty to use it to prevent the procession. I wrote to Ministers and laid my notions before them, without advising anything, but merely as suggestions for consideration. I still further explained to three different gentlemen who came to me from three different departments why the proceeding was absurd and dangerous, I advised and cautioned them and I believe convinced them of the absurdity of advising and the evil consequences which could not fail, to be the result of the procession, and I induced Mr. Thomas the inspector of police to represent the matter in its true light to every gentleman he might have an opportunity of speaking to whom he might think at all likely to influence others.

The weakness and foolishness of ministers became more and more conspicuous not only from day to day, but from hour to hour, and was condemned by every body. Their folly was indeed perfect, for at the very time they were making arrangements for the procession which they intended should increase the popularity of the King and strengthen their own government, at the very moment when they were getting up a grand cavalcade from the western end of Pall Mall to the eastern end of Cheapside, in which the King, the Queen, the Foreign Embassaders [sic]—themselves, and others were to form the principal part, they put into the Kings mouth, words which were sure to alarm and offend the people from one end of the Kingdom to the other, and they permitted the Duke of Wellington, to make his insulting declaration, without in the least anticipating the consequences of such conduct.

As their eyes were opened to the consequences of their conduct, they became alarmed, and at length succeeded in frightening themselves completely and in the blindness of their fear they proceeded to *fortify the Tower of London.* The Tower ditch had not been cleaned out for many years, and was choaked [sic] with mud, this was now to be cleaned away in a hurry. Fear is usually as ridiculous as it is blind, and so it proved in this instance, it hurried them on with such rapidity, that they let the water into the ditch without giving time to the labourers to remove their carts, barrows and planks and other implements, and all were therefore either swamped or floated about in the ditch.

One good resulted from their fears which would never have been accomplished by their wisdom, and that was giving up the intended visit to the Mansion House.

On Sunday the 7 November a letter signed by the Home Secretary Mr Peel was sent to the Lord Mayor postponing the intended visit. This letter was immediately published by the Lord Mayor under the sanction of the committee appointed to conduct the entertainment. It appeared in all the newspapers of the next day.

The Lord Mayor elect had written a letter to the Duke of Wellington, most probably a concerted letter, in which he advised the Duke, '*to come strongly and sufficiently guarded*'. Strange advice this from a Lord Mayor elect to the Premier—Guarded—like the King. The modest Duke could not take advantage of the honour suggested. Inflamatory hand bills had been distributed, probably at the expense of some ministerial tool to enable ministers to take advantage of them, as was proved to have been done on a famous occasion, but be this as it may, these things furnished an excuse for the letter to the Lord Mayor postponing the visit, a measure so proper in itself as not to have needed any such pitiful manouvres [sic].

Thus ended the monstrous absurdity and with it much of the recently acquired popularity of William the fourth.

5. [Add. Ms. 27789, ff. 265–6]

On the first of March [1831], the day on which Lord John Russell was to make his motion [on reform of the House of Commons], much anxiety was generally felt by the people in the metropolis, they were excited by the hope that a real reform would be proposed, but they were also disturbed by the fear that they might be disappointed. Persons who were usually neutral in respect to political matters had now become eager to obtain information and desirous that enough should be done at once to satisfy everybody.

I saw several members of parliament and a great many others respectable well informed well judging men, the feeling in all of them was alike and in all hope prevailed that a very considerable measure of reform would be produced.

I was alone in the evening anxiously expecting some one to come from the house to tell me what had occurred, at length a friend who had taken a report of about half of Lord John Russells speech for the Morning Chronicle came in and told me the particulars of the ministerial plan. It was so very much beyond any thing which I had expected; that had it been told to me by a person unused to proceedings in the house I should have supposed that he had made a mistake. Both I and my informant were delighted, and we at once took measures to cause it to be known in the coffee houses in the neighbourhood where it spread like wild fire, to great distances, and other persons being equally desirous as ourselves to spread the information left the house of commons to communicate the earliest news to their friends. One of these came to me as soon as Lord John Russell had concluded his speech, and in less than an hour from that time the intelligence was spread all over the metropolis. The next morning the joy of the reformers was excessive, the newspapers were bought in immense numbers and read with avidity, every body seemed well pleased and the exhiliration [sic] was very general. Nothing within my memory had ever before produced such general exultation and the conviction appeared to be as general that there needed only a determined unremitted vigilant course of conduct on the part of ministers to carry the measure through the house triumphantly.

6. [Add. Ms. 27789, ff. 276–8]

A great many people came to me, and urged me to call a public meeting of the electors of Westminster without waiting for the formality of applying to the High Bailiff to convene it, in the usual manner. . . .

The persons who met to prepare the resolutions were more than usually numerous about 40 attended—they agreed to do all that I proposed and I made out a business sheet, for the government of the proceedings in the public room when the time of the meeting was nearly arrived there being then, upwards of sixty persons in the room, an objection was made by some one to the resolutions respecting the duration of parliament and voting by ballot and some of the usual common place sayings about unanimity and embarrasment [sic] were used, but as Sir Francis Burdett took no notice of them, and very few of those present took part in the opposition the whole body went into the public room with the resolutions and petition as I had drawn them. The room was filled the proceedings went on with equal spirit and unanimity, and the resolutions respecting parliaments and the ballot were about to be put when Mr Hobhouse who had not only concurred in the resolutions and the petition but had voluntarily given five pounds towards the expenses of the meeting, after talking for some time with some gentlemanly looking men who had never before been seen at a Westminster meeting and have I believe never attended since, got upon the table at the call of the room, raised first by those near him, and told the company a tale of what had passed and of what was likely to pass at the house, insinuated first and then unequivocally asserted, that the resolutions and petition would have a bad effect in destroying unanimity—the word was echoed from many persons in the room, the mad man Pitt of the Adelphi, who had been averse from the beginning to the resolutions, had spoken against them but with no effect, vociferated unanimity and a clamour ensued which for a short time interrupted the proceedings—Sir Francis Burdett then repeated in part what Hobhouse had said amidst shouts of unanimity—and the resolutions and petition were withdrawn. Some one at the table who had been active in urging on and in supporting Hobhouse tore the petition into bits and threw it under the table. These were true whig tactics, they had been expected and no one of those with whom I had acted was at all surprised at the proceeding. The whigs as well as Hobhouse and his especial friends knew these were times, when in some respects, they might presume to go great lengths without inducing the reformers to come to any open quarrel, and the matter dropped. But Hobhouse did himself serious injury in the opinion of many of those who had worked hard to secure his return for Westminster, as was soon seen at the next election when scarcely any of them came forward in his behalf, as they had done on former occasions.

Resolutions

1. That this meeting calling to mind the long continued exertions of the Inhabitants of this City and Liberty, to procure a reform in the Commons House of Parliament, are highly gratified at finding, that the Kings Ministers with the consent and approbation of his Majesty have proposed considerable and greatly beneficial alterations in the mode of electing members to serve in that house.—In cutting off several sources of corruption, and in extending the right of suffrage to many places which have not hitherto enjoyed that right.
2. That the following address be adopted by this meeting, congratulating his Majesty on the good feelings he has evinced towards his people by his sanction of the plan of reform proposed by his ministers, and that it be presented to his Majesty by Sir Francis Burdett and John Cam Hobhouse Esq.
3. That to make the plan of reform proposed by his Majesty's Ministers effectual, and to prevent further changes, it is necessary, that the duration of Parliaments be limited to a period not exceeding three years.
4. That to secure to the electors of the United Kingdom the power to choose representatives freely—without being unduly influenced by the wealthy —and without being in dread of the powerful, it is necessary that their votes should be taken by Ballot.
5. That the following petition embodying these resolutions be adopted by the meeting signed by twenty one electors and be presented to the house of Commons by our representatives Sir Francis Burdett Bart and John Cam Hobhouse Esq.

The Petition

To the honourable the commons of the United Kingdom in Parliament assembled. The petition of the undersigned inhabitants of the City and

Liberty of Westminster on the behalf of themselves and their fellow citizens in public meeting assembled this 4th day of March 1831.

Sheweth.

That anticipating many of the evils which have fallen on the people from the want of their being duly represented in your honourable house, the inhabitants of Westminster have during the last fifty years repeatedly petitioned your honourable house to restore to their fellow subjects their share in the legislature, and have as repeatedly called on their fellow countrymen to aid them in this the most important of all proceedings for the honour the prosperity and the happiness of the nation.

That the people in many places have from time to time petitioned your honourable house for a reform in parliament, but your honourable house has all along disregarded the prayers of the people until their grievances have become all but insupportable, and have at last compelled them to demand, as with one voice, the reform they have so often prayed for, and which has as often been denied them, when they were less unanimous than they now are in their requests.

That your petitioners have heard with great pleasure that the Kings Ministers, with the consent and approbation of his Majesty, have at length resolved to attend to the request of the people, for a reform in your honourable house.

Your petitioners therefore conclude by praying that in any plan of Reform which may be submitted to your honourable house, you will please to provide for the shortening of the duration of parliaments to a period not exceeding three years—and for taking of the votes of the electors by ballot.

Francis Place, Charing Cross—Thomas De Veare, Lisle Street—John Dean, Regent Street—T. Erskine Perry, Piccadilly—Wm a Beckett, Golden Square—Geo. Harper, Piccadilly—D. L. Evans, 12 Regent Street—Thos. King, Hanover Street—Joseph Cowell, Brydges Street—Wm. Adams, Long Acre—James Pitt, Piccadilly—Henry Ledwick Stephenson—Thomas Wakley, Bedford Street—Wm. Pigou, Greek Street—Geo. Eliot, Maclesfield Street—John Paget—G. W. Lynden—Edward Evans, Jermyn Street—John Harding, 14 Beak Street—Thomas Evans, Beak Street—Robert Kemp, 6 Leicester Street.

7. [Add. Ms. 27789, ff. 121–2]

It is my intention to give an account of two societies. The first of which was called the Parliamentary Candidates Society. The second the National Political Union. The existence of these societies was brief but not unimportant and their proceedings inasmuch as they had any effect in helping to produce the great and highly important changes which were made in the years 1831 and 1832 are a portion of the history of the times, which if not now recorded in a somewhat detailed form may be lost, and future historians like their predecessors may have to describe events many of the causes of which were irretrievably lost. Events which from the deficiency of facts *appear* to have been produced by inadequate causes, conjecture and hypothesis to have been substituted, and applied to fill up the space left vacant by the want of those facts. It is, however, probable that so many of the causes as well those which tended immediately as those which tended more remotely to the recent changes have been noticed by persons who took part in producing these changes, as well officially and parliamentarily as otherwise, and will in time either be laid before the public or so disposed of, that access may be had to them and our late revolution be much more completely elucidated than any which has preceded it. To assist as much as I can in this matter is the principal reason why this account has been extended to its present length. It needs no apology and none is made for it.

It is not my intention to write a history of the proceedings during the progress of the Reform Bills day by day either in or out of Parliament, further than they are immediately connected with the National Political Union and the general feelings and conduct of the houses of parliament and the people at their public meetings. All beyond these matters will be a mere sketch. The proceedings in parliament day by day are in print, and they who wish for more particular information must consult the Mirror of Parliament—Hansard Debates and the voluminous papers printed by order of the two houses of parliament. I intend however to notice such occurrences in parliament as may seem necessary to make a connected account, and to give such information from newspapers and the minute books of the National Political Union as may make the circumstances be clearly understood.

8. [Add. Ms. 27789, ff. 320–6. Steps were taken during March 1831 to form the Parliamentary Candidate Society.]

Mr (T. Erskine) Perry wished me to meet some of his friends for the purpose of forming a society—to point out proper persons as candidates at the next election. I had not as yet determined to join any society, and I knew that his friends were like himself, young men of some fortune, many of whom were desirous to become members of parliament themselves. We talked the matter over [on 6 March], I told him of the applications which at the last election had been made to me to name proper persons as candidates, of similar applications to Mr Warburton, and of the much larger number which had been made to Mr Hume without our being able to name persons. I encouraged him to proceed, on two grounds, to enable electors to obtain proper candidates, and candidates to find electors. I pointed out to him the difficulties he would have to encounter, and the little satisfaction he would derive from his exertions, but I said he could not fail to do much real service to the people by any sensible display, as it would draw the attention of a vast number of them to the subject and tend to induce them to think more correctly on the matter in all its bearings; and that he ought in the first instance to be satisfied with effecting this much. That the next election could be at no great distance, as the present parliament would either be dissolved when the reform bill was passed, or in consequence of its refusing to pass it, and it was therefore very desirable that such a society as Mr Perry proposed should be commenced. That there were however several objections which he would do well to consider and fully to determine before he attempted its establishment

1. The persons whose names must appear before the public.

2. The presumption and dictation of which they would be accused.
3. The chance of its being countenanced by any considerable number of persons, likely to be useful.
4. The means—money—to carry it on, on a large scale.

Then as to its advantages.
1. Exposure of the acts of many of the enemies of reform in parliament.
2. The advantage to electors to whom it might serve as caution.
3. The certainty that some electoral bodies would be enabled to make a better selection than they could otherwise do.
4. Exciting generally a spirit of resistance to the usual domination of the tories.
5. The chance that it might be carried to a considerable extent and thus become extremely useful.

All these matters had been discussed by me and others long before I saw Mr Perry and I was therefore the more desirous to induce him to proceed with his project. . . .

On tuesday the 9th Mr Perry came again and said his friends had resolved to commence such a society as he had mentioned. I advised him to lose no time in establishing it—to have nothing ambiguous about it, to go the whole length even if it should frighten some of his friends away, that it was better to be defeated at once and to let the matter drop, than to go on tamely and after all be obliged to break up with discredit. A meeting for the purpose was he said to be held at his chambers in the Albany on the next day in the evening, and he urged me to draw up an address to the public for him to lay before the meeting. I had mentioned his scheme to every man I saw, and as all commended it, I undertook to draw up the address as he requested—for the meeting to be held the next evening. . . .

It was as follows. viz.

At the close of the last parliament several persons were requested to name gentlemen who entertained liberal opinions, were in other respects qualified and were willing to become candidates for seats in the house of commons. So great however was the difficulty that even Mr Hume the most likely of all men could not name gentlemen who were willing to become candidates for as many places as were indicated.

In several instances the committees who conducted the Westminster Elections since 1806 have been applied to, to designate properly qualified persons to become candidates but in no one instance were they able to comply with the wishes of the applicants.

Men well qualified for the office and worthy of public confidence have shrunk from the expence [sic], the corrupt practices and the self degradation which has all along attended popular elections, in almost every instance under the rotten borough and county nomination system. This system it is hoped and believed will by the praiseworthy measure of reform introduced by ministers be to a considerable extent destroyed, and the election of members to serve in parliament be much more at the command of the electors than it has hitherto been.

But this of itself will be of little real benefit to the people, and especially in places where for the first time they will have to exercise the right of suffrage; if unaided by previous information, they should be left exposed to the practice of adventurors [*sic*], who may be generally described as consisting of three classes.

1. Men whose vanity leads them to desire to become or to continue to be members of parliament.
2. Men whose families think they have a sort of prescriptive right to seats, because some members of their families have for a longer or a shorter time had seats in the house of commons.
3. Men of desperate fortunes to whom seats are necessary to enable them to live in a style very superior to that, which if they were not members they could maintain.

These are the three *great* classes of adventurers

The first consists, almost wholly of men who do not think any of the qualifications requisite for legislation are at all requisite, and they, of course, with some few exception possess none of the necessary qualifications.

The general conduct of these men may be described in a few words. They are seldom present in the house when any business of moment is before it. They never do any thing in the way of business themselves, unless it be some trifling matter which may enable them to make a display before particular persons, or procure for themselves some particular personal advantage. They are altogether absent during the greater part of the session, and when present serve only to aid the party to which they belong, or happen to be attached, to swell the majority, or to make the minority *respectable* in number.

If it were possible, in so grave a matter as legislation, in a country like this, that any man could be useless, this might be called the useless class, but no one can be useless, even the silliest and the meanest of all the members must be either useful or mischievous by his acts of commission or omission.

It may be safely affirmed of this class, that the vanity which prompts the man to seek the office will seldom prevent him being open to corruption in almost every shape, and experience proves that all such men with some very rare exceptions are corrupt.

Every man in the second class must necessarily be mischievous. Every such man goes to Parliament with his mind made up to serve himself and his family, at the expence of the people and should be most carefully shunned by the electors.

Of the third class little need be said. No man is so ignorant as to suppose that men of this class ever had or ever will have any object but their own personal interests. No man can believe they will ever be other than what they have been, enemies of the people, ready and willing to sacrifice their welfare and happiness in any and every way; no matter how atrocious the proceeding; at the suggestion or command of those who will pay them best, or place them in situations in which they may pay themselves from the plunder of the people.

These three classes mark the strong distinctions of caste, of the adventurers. Many however partake of the two first, preponderating towards the second, and in some instances towards the third class. The same may be said

18

respecting the second and third classes, preponderating in the same way but to a greater extent towards the third class. A correct analysis of any former house of commons would show many instances of famalies [*sic*] of the second class either placing their poorer members in the third class, or encouraging them to place themselves in it.

The whole of the persons composing these three classes, and they are a large number, may be considered as adventurers, in the broadest sense, and against every one of them the electors should most carefully guard themselves. This they cannot however do with any effect unless men properly qualified and in sufficient number be made known to them, by their connections, pursuits and opinions on public matters, being sufficiently and also as early as possible supplied to them.

One only means can be adopted for this important purpose. It consists of two parts viz.

1. Collecting the names etc. etc. of such men
2. Publishing them in such ways as may make them known to all.

No individual can accomplish this purpose, but a number of individuals associated can do all that is desirable with the greatest ease; whence it follows that a society for this purpose ought to be formed, and a number of gentlemen having considered the matter in all its bearings, have formed themselves into such a society, and to enable them to carry their purposes into execution have appointed the following committee.[1]

9. [Add. Ms. 27789, ff. 327–9]

On the morning of thursday the 10th I took the address to Mr Perry. The next morning I received a note from Mr Perry saying that 'the sub-committee met last night, that he had read the address to them, as mine, that it was exceedingly applauded and the ideas suggested in it appeared to take exceedingly'. He said 'it was agreed that the *names of some 30 or 40 as big wigs as possible should be obtained*, and then that a meeting should be called and a definite plan be settled.' I understood the meaning of this as well as any one who had been present did, each saw what sort of thing an honest plain address must be, and each saw too, that he was much too genteel a person, to like that his name should appear to such an address— each applauded it because he felt the force of the facts it contained, because he could not dispute the reasoning, and each therefore determined not to take a decided part in the matter. I saw at once that the proposal to obtain the names of some 30 or 40 eminent and conspicuous men was an adjournment *sine die* as not one of those who composed the 'sub-committee' would have made any effort to procure the consent of any one such person, and the resolution that it would be advisable to procure such names was virtually a dissolution of the sub-committee, as they called themselves. If they had spoken out truly they would have said, we see that we have commenced a proceeding which when examined appears to involve circumstances we did not contemplate, and requires, to make it efficient, proceedings which we do not like, and we must therefore proceed no further, if they had done thus

[1] See **10.**

they would have spoken the language of honest men, but this of all things is ever avoided by gentility; so they concluded that it was necessary to propose what was impracticable as an excuse for doing nothing. They were not at all aware, that most of them were to be acted upon by others and even by what is called their own feelings—and consequently to follow others, if others of equal consequence with themselves should undertake to manage such a society as they had timorously and genteely abandoned.

I therefore wrote to Mr Perry, objected to the resolution to obtain the names of from '30 to 40 big wigs'—said it was requisite to proceed with dispatch and that if his friends were slow in their motions others would take the matter up. To this Mr Perry replied as I anticipated he would, 'that he could not get the sub-committee to meet, that he could not use their names without their consent, and that the only way to get out of the difficulty will be for you to set on foot something of the same kind as *after all it is from numbers* and intelligence and *not from names* that any good will spring.'

I had seen so very many persons who said they would belong to such a society if I would undertake a share of the management that I was convinced a society might be established, which could not fail to be useful to some extent, however few were the members and however short its duration, and I therefore resolved to go on with it.

On friday the 11th I wrote a very long letter to Mr Hume, in which I told him seriatim what had been done, I inclosed to him a copy of the address I had written and I requested him to allow me to name him as chairman of the society. I gave him till sunday morning to decide. On the sunday morning Mr Gouger who had consented to become honorary secretary went to Mr Hume's, saw him, and brought back to me the copy of the address, and *his unqualified consent to become chairman* of the society. In the note which Mr Gouger brought from Mr Hume to me—he says—'I entirely approve of the plan of such an association, and shall take any part which may be thought proper, always having reference to my time of which I can spare but little. I doubt the propriety of going so largely into the objects as you do in the address. I think it may be sufficient without dwelling on the unfitness of many in the house, to state the qualities the new members should have and the measures you intend to take to propose proper candidates. You may therefore calculate on my feeble aid in the cause.'

10. [Add. Ms. 27789, f. 335. The meeting having been held, rules drawn up and a committee chosen, Place wrote the following comments.]

Thus was the *'Parliamentary Candidates Society'* instituted. As usual most of the persons who became members of it were timid, and unresolved. Before the meeting could be held I was pestered with the fears, and the objections these fears excited, in the shabby genteel persons, on whom it depended whether or not any such society should be formed, and this included the matter of the address. I was compelled to let Mr Perry and some of his friends emasculate the address, as it may by comparison be seen it was emasculated. I debated with myself the whole subject and had almost determined to have nothing to do with the proceedings, but at length resolved to enter into them, seeing that unless I took a very decided part no

20

meeting would be had and no society formed. I should have abandoned the matter altogether, had I not been satisfied that when a general committee was formed, and a sub-committee was by that general committee appointed, much might be done that would be found useful, and that even the comparatively little, which under the most adverse circumstances which could happen, would be of some and might perchance be of much consequence. I knew that even in such a collection of half whigs half reformers there would be all sorts of impediments, changes, abandonments and resignations, but that if only three could be found in the sub-committee who would hold together something, much perhaps, could be done and I therefore resolved to go on as long as a chance of producing even a slight effect remained.

[Add. Ms. 27789, f. 342. *Printed.*]

PARLIAMENTARY CANDIDATE SOCIETY, INSTITUTED TO PROMOTE RETURN OF *Fit and Proper Members to Parliament.*

COMMITTEE

Jeremy Bentham, Esq.	Colonel L. G. Jones.
Major A. Beauclerk.	Dr. Mackinnon.
Charles Beauclerk, Esq.	John Marshall, Esq. of Leeds.
Charles Buller. Esq, M.P.	Daniel O'Connell, Esq. M.P.
A. Buller, Esq.	Erskine Perry, Esq.
E. Lytton Bulwer, Esq.	John A. Roebuck, Esq.
W. B. Evans, Esq.	Mr. Alderman Scales.
Sir Francis Burdett, Bart. M.P.	Charles Brinsley Sheridan.
John Crawfurd, Esq.	Colonel T. Perronet Thompson.
Thomas Hobhouse, Esq.	Thomas De Vear, Esq.
Joseph Hume, Esq. M.P.	Daniel Wakefield, Jun. Esq.
Francis Place, Sen. Esq. *Treasurer*	Robert Gouger, Esq. *Hon. Secretary*

ADDRESS.[1]

The measures of REFORM brought forward by His Majesty's Ministers, which have been enthusiastically welcomed by the whole Kingdom, will require the exertions of the People themselves to obtain the grand object of a legislative body identified with the popular interest.

Hitherto, the men best fitted, by their intellectual and moral worth, to be representatives of the people, have usually shrunk from a popular election. The expence [*sic*], corruption, and degradation attending on that hitherto debasing proceeding, have deterred the honest-minded, and but too often left the field open to those who have had much wealth to squander, and few scruples to overcome.

It is hoped that this vicious system will no longer prevail; that places will be thrown open in which the honest candidate will have to stoop to no immoral acts, to practise no corruption, to truckle to no commands; and, that the people will be able to choose those who, by talent, industry, and probity, are fit to be popular representatives.

This power, however, will be of little avail, if it be not judiciously

---

[1] Place has added in manuscript, 'as it was altered in the Sub-Committee'.

21

exercised. Unless the electors be made acquainted with the character of the candidates who propose themselves—unless the men most worthy be brought to their notice—improper or inadequate selections will again be made; the same neglect of duty, the same corrupt practices, the same extravagant expenditure, which have hitherto been our degradation and our curse, will continue.

To prevent this evil, two things are required:—

I. To collect all necessary information respecting the character, talent, conduct, and connexions, of all persons who may be proposed as candidates for seats in the Legislature.

II. To lay this information, when obtained, before the public.

Experience has taught us, that, separately, individuals cannot perform this task. Applications for information have often been made by various bodies of electors, desirous of choosing honest and enlightened representatives. But no one being prepared to answer their inquiries, the praiseworthy wishes of the electors have been frustrated. The idle, vain, and profligate, have too often been chosen in the place of the industrious, upright, and enlightened. The unprincipled political adventurer, swayed only by personal interests, has usurped the post of the honest, single-minded patriot; and a people harassed, plundered, and oppressed, have but too well attested the vicious operation of a badly-selected legislature.

Similar applications will again be made; and unless care be taken, they will again prove fruitless.

What individuals cannot perform may be easily effected by an association; and for the purpose of obtaining the information required, and properly and adequately publishing it to the world, the present Association has been formed, under the name of the

PARLIAMENTARY CANDIDATE-SOCIETY;

and the persons above named have been appointed a Committee to carry the intentions of the Society into effect.

The beneficial purpose here in view would be greatly aided by numerous local societies. But such separate yet connected bodies cannot be formed, since the 57th Geo.III. c.19. s.25. forbids all communication between them. A Society has therefore been formed extending all over the country, of which any person may become a member on entering his name, address, and designation, in one of the Society's books, or by forwarding the same to the Secretary by letter; and on the payment of a subscription of not less than Five Shillings to the funds of the Society for the current year. Thus the *one* body may extend to the most distant parts of the country, and a correspondence carried on, to whatever extent may be desired, without any violation of the law.

The whole people may thus act as a *single body*, aiding one another with their money, their labour, and their information, for the great and common end of obtaining a good government.

Books have been opened at the Houses of Messrs. Ransom and Co. Pall Mall East; Messrs. Martin, Call, and Co. Old Bond Street; Messrs. Grote, Prescott, & Co. Threadneedle Street; Mr. Alderman Scales,

Aldgate; Mr. Agassiz, 223 Piccadilly; Mr. Charles Fox Smith, Blackman Street, Borough; Mr. De Vear, 44 Lisle Street, Leicester Square; and at the Office of the Westminster Review, Wellington Street, Strand.

The Secretary attends daily, from 11 to 4 o'clock, at the Crown & Anchor Tavern, Strand.

11. [Add. Ms. 27789, f. 352]

On the 23 March I received a note from Mr Hume as follows

My Dear Sir,

I entreat you to withdraw my name from the list of the committee as I find it will be to me and other members most injurious. We were attacked yesterday and the day before in the house, and *I find every opinion against my having anything to do with it publicly*. I will explain more when we meet.

The draft of the schedule I think requires much consideration before it is printed.

Yours in haste,
Joseph Hume.

12. [Add. Ms. 27789, ff. 370–3. *Printed.* Report of the progress of the Parliamentary Candidate Society.]

The Society did not, however, make the progress anticipated. The principal obstacles which impeded its immediate success, were occasioned by the dislike entertained, with very few exceptions, by the members of the House of Commons, to having their public conduct fairly presented to public view. From this wholesome exposure, which real representatives of the people who did their duty would court, which their constituents would expect and perhaps demand, honourable gentlemen shrunk as from contagion. The enemies of reform first took the alarm; their fears were soon spread amongst the friends of reform, too many of whom joined with eager haste in reprobating what their fears represented to them, as an unwarrantable interference with the conduct of public men; and, instead of supporting the Society as they ought to have done, and as but for the absurd deference they paid to the assertions of the enemy they would have done, they became its most active opponents. The people had so long been considered and used as mere tools, to make members of parliament, and members had so long possessed the power of acting as masters over the people, that what at some former period would have been admired and applauded, as proof of the honesty and independence of Englishmen, was now considered as little better than an arrogant revolt of slaves against the domination of their absolute governors.

The apprehensions entertained by members of the House of Commons, were even communicated to some members of the Committee of the Society; who therefore withdrew their names; but the Committee, perfectly satisfied that the duty they had undertaken was too important to be neglected, resolved to perform it to the utmost extent of all the means they possessed, or might possess; and this they have done. Although all the good has not been effected which the state of the public mind would have permitted, great and permanent advantages have been obtained. Opposition, and defection of friends, though they at first lessened, could not eventually prevent the beneficial influence of the Society's labours.

Electors generally have obtained the respect and admiration of the people at large. Time was, however, wanted to enable them, as well as the Society, to accomplish all, which otherwise might have been accomplished. The personal exertions so many electors have made—the sacrifices to which they have cheerfully submitted—the bribes openly offered, or disguised under so many names, they have spurned—the power to which in so many places they have been accustomed to bow, but which they have now defied —and the many corrupt influences they have contemned—are proofs sufficient of that honour and honesty which the true friends of the people have all along believed and asserted they possessed, but which their enemies, who wished to continue to be their masters, as constantly denied. These enemies are now compelled to yield them an unwilling but perfect respect, and have thus justified the admiration of their friends.

In many places in which the electors have really possessed the power, they have rejected the notorious enemies of reform, and have returned men on whom they can safely rely to promote that all-important measure.

In other places, the enemies of reform shrunk appalled at the firm countenance and determined conduct of the electors; they saw that the time of delusion and of arbitrary power was passing away, and they submitted to the growing influence of an intellectual people they could no longer hope to mislead.

This is a triumph at which the friends of mankind have reason to rejoice. The triumph has not been obtained without much labour, and with great difficulty. The Parliamentary Candidate Society has shared in both; and they hope it will be acknowledged they are entitled to some share of the honour.

The Society has carried on an extensive and useful correspondence with reformers in various parts of the country.

At the request of many bodies of electors, the Committee have furnished statements, and published accounts, of the speeches and votes of their former representatives since the general election in 1826, and in some instances for a much longer period; and they have reason to conclude, that both in preventing the enemies of reform from again soliciting the suffrages of electors, and in inducing electors to refuse them where they have ventured to solicit their suffrages, the Society has assisted in promoting the public good.

Time in this, as in most cases where the purpose has been a good one, has done much for the Society. Its objects are now better understood, its conduct is more duly appreciated, its utility more generally admitted, apprehension has subsided, and even calumny has at least for the present ceased. Much has been accomplished—much remains to be accomplished; and encouraged by their past success, the Committee have determined to continue their efforts. They confidently rely on the honest independent men who really and sincerely advocate Reform, for the assistance which will be necessary to enable them to render service to the public, to an extent which can only be correctly appreciated by those who have profoundly meditated on the modes by which an intelligent people may by honest efforts be influenced for their advantage.

The Society possesses but one means of influence, namely, collecting, and plainly and honestly stating facts, by which all may be enabled to judge of the fitness of candidates, and thus be warned against entrusting their property, their lives, and their liberty, to persons who are unworthy of such highly important powers. This influence will, by the measures adopted by the Society, be of much greater importance previously to the next general election, than it has hitherto been, or could possibly have been in any former period; and this they trust will not only be acknowledged, but acted upon, so as to enable them adequately to accomplish all the purposes they have contemplated.

In continuing their labours, they will carefully observe, and daily note, the conduct of all the members of the newly-elected parliament, during the great struggle about to take place for the present salvation and future permanent advantage of the people, who compose this noble commonwealth; and when the time shall arrive, that our good and gracious and patriotic King shall again, by a dissolution of the parliament, 'appeal to the sense of his people,' they will, without prejudice or partiality, publish an accurate account of the attendance, the absence, the speeches and votes of the members of the House of Commons; and when any discussion or decision of any national importance takes place, of the number of members present at such discussion and division.

The misconduct of a representative may be of *two* general descriptions. 1. He may speak or vote contrary to the public welfare; or, 2 He may abstain from either speaking or voting on the side of the people. The latter is the least ostensible, but the most insidious mischief. The absence of a member is as much a dereliction from his duty, as it would be were he to oppose himself directly and actively to measures intended for the public benefit.

The Society will therefore notice such conduct. The public will then know, not only when a member did mischief in a direct way, but when, by neglecting his duty, he did his utmost to permit others to do so.

The struggle is not yet over—the evil of misgovernment is not eradicated. Nothing short of the most strenuous exertions on the part of the people, can consummate the great work so gloriously commenced. In aiding the people to the best of its ability, and to the fullest extent of the means which may be furnished them, the Society will not be found wanting.

A permanent Office has been opened at the Crown and Anchor Tavern in the Strand, London; where all communications are to be addressed, and where contributions will be received.

The accounts of the Society have been made up, and with the documents may be inspected by the Subscribers during office hours, which are from 11 till 4 daily.

By order of the Committee
ROBERT GOUGER,
Secretary.

June 1, 1831

13. [Add. Ms. 27789, f. 374]

It was my opinion that the society should as it had promised cease to exist with the commencement of the new parliament, and employ the small sum which remained in paying the persons who had hitherto been employed in extracting from the parliamentary debates and other authentic sources the political acts of the members; to announce this and ask for donations to enable them to continue the work till near the eve of another election; then to revive the society by calling together, not the dandyish gentility, which was seeking to obtain seats in the house of commons; but such men as were unlikely to have any sinister views; men whose habits of business and intelligence would lead them to work without intermission or fear for the accomplishment of the real objects of the society. To publish in a volume as cheaply as possible the information collected—from which all might select whatever could be useful. It was only necessary to follow closely the plan in progress, to accomplish this proposal. In every case which had been published—the matter was carefully collated and verified—and in no instance that I ever heard of, was the society accused of making a false statement or even of having in any instance in any way exaggerated the facts. The opinion of the majority was that an effort should be made to continue the society, it wholly failed, no money was obtained, the small balance in hand was soon expended and the society died what is usually in such cases called a natural death.

14. [Add. Ms. 27789, ff. 294–5. A petition occasioned by the defeat of the Whigs during the committee stage on the reform bill on 19 April 1831.]

To the Kings most excellent Majesty
The humble petition of the undersigned inhabitants of Westminster
  Sheweth

That the unwillingness of your petitioners to delay the expression of their opinion at the present awful moment until a public meeting could be called, has induced your petitioners thus to address your most excellent majesty.

Your petitioners believe that the continuance of order and tranquillity throughout the empire depends entirely on passing the Reform Bill brought forward by your Majesty's ministers.

That the astonishing unanimity displayed by the great body of the people on the subject testifies how inseperably [*sic*] they think their dearest rights and liberties are connected with the success of that measure.

That your petitioners further believe that if the principles of the Reform Bill be nullified or invalidated that the most awful consequences will ensue, commencing either in the tumultuous proceedings of a resolute Scotch or a famished Irish multitude, or on the more gradual but not less complete convulsion which the refusal to pay taxes by large bodies of the [people] in England will inevitably bring about.

Your petitioners therefore pray your most excellent Majesty to insure the success of the Reform Bill, and thereby avert revolution bloodshed and anarchy by commanding the *instant dissolution* of the Commons House of Parliament.

And your petitioners as in duty bound will ever pray.

Copies of the petition were with a note of its having been delivered immediately sent to all the London newspapers and was printed in almost every one of them. Had the dissolution been delayed[1] but a very few days many hundreds of similar petitions would also have been presented.

15. [Add. Ms. 27789, ff. 251–2]

The proceedings of the people fully answered the purposes of ministers, as they served to fix them in office, to guarantee and support them; while they more than answered their purpose, respecting the measures to be taken to promote reform in the commons house of Parliament. That some among the ministers desired reform for its own sake may be safely admitted as truth. Others among them now desired it because they had committed themselves before they knew how far they would be obliged to proceed, and could not now back out, and all of them because such demonstrations had been made, and were still being made by the people as rendered it impossible for them to continue in office unless a very considerable measure of reform was proposed, and because they saw that any paltering with it would have the further consequence of producing commotions the end of which no one could forsee. So fully indeed, so far beyond their expectations had the proceedings of the people been carried that all retreat was cut off and however much some of them disliked the proposed bill they dared not openly dissent from it. The business—for such the people really made it was immense and was carried on as systematically as it could have been had there been an arrangement made for the whole of it, yet there was not even the smallest communication between places in the same neighbourhoods, each portion of the people appeared to understand what ought to be done and each did its part—as if it were an arranged part of one great whole. The systematic way in which the people proceeded, their steady perseverance, their activity and skill astounded the enemies of reform and produced an effect sometimes observed in considerable bodies of men, yet scarcely ever in a nation. The enemies of reform had so strong a feeling of the impossibility of any thing like a successful opposition that they remained in a state of comparative quiescence quite at variance with their proceedings on former occasions.

16. [B.M. Place Collection, set 63, vol. 2, f. 9. *Printed.*]

NATIONAL REFORM ASSOCIATION. DECLARATION AND RESOLUTIONS.

THE evils inseparable from mis-government, having at length pressed upon the people with a severity too great to be any longer quiescently endured, their first efforts have been directed to put an end to a system, the workings of which have entailed upon them such accumulated ills.

Thay have long been conscious, that a small but dominant faction has grown up in this country, which has usurped and wielded a controlling influence over the councils of the King, and the deliberations of the Senate;

[1] Parliament was dissolved on 22 April.

and that this faction has uniformly exercised its power for the promotion of its own exclusive and sinister interests.

The origin of this anomalous body, and the seat of its strength, are to be found in the defective state of the representative branch of the legislature, which, by enabling it to command a majority of votes in Parliament, has given it a direct dictatorial sway over the measures of government, and an unlimited and irresponsible power in the disposal of the nation's wealth. While such a faction is suffered to exist, no honest ministry can efficiently serve the King, nor can the People be in any degree assured of having their rights protected, or their welfare advanced.

Conscious of this truth, and of the injustice wrought by such usurpation, both King and People have resolved to put it down. Hitherto their efforts have been attended with success; but much yet remains to be done. The enemy is strong, and must be met with proportionate firmness. Experience has taught the people, that their power consists in numbers allied with intelligence. Let them then unite, and instruct one another. By these means alone, can they aid their Sovereign in his efforts to rescue them from out the hands of a faction, and to restore to them that salutary influence over public affairs, which justice entitles them to demand, and good policy dictates should be conceded to them.

Deeply impressed with the conviction, that the present crisis is eminently auspicious for such a course being adopted by the people, We, whose names are hereunto subscribed, have by this act resolved ourselves into a NATION-AL REFORM ASSOCIATION, with a view to use our utmost and united exertions to promote, on all occasions, such measures as shall be calculated to advance the real interests of the community, and give strength and stability to the empire at large—but more especially, at this particular juncture, to devote our best energies in assisting the King and his Ministers, to carry on the great measure of Reform now pending to a successful issue: and, forasmuch as it is probable, that on this measure being carried, another Parliament will be speedily summoned by the King, we deem it to be an indispensable duty on our part, to aid in securing the return of honest and talented men to represent the people in such Reformed Parliament—and also, to the end that these objects may be accomplished, and the Parliament so elected be made subservient to the general good, it shall be our endeavour, by discussion and through the medium of the Press, to diffuse among the people, *sound and practical knowledge* upon all political subjects, by which means we hope to create an enlightened public opinion, that shall be capable at all times of being brought to bear with an irresistible moral force, upon all important public questions, and be made productive of a permanent system of just policy and wise legislation.

For carrying into immediate effect these our intentions, we hereby agree to, and bind ourselves to the strict observance of, the following

RULES AND REGULATIONS.

I. That the name of the Society shall be, 'The National Reform Association'.
II. That any person desirous of becoming a member of this Association shall furnish the Secretary with his name and address, and subscribe his name to these regulations in the book prepared for that purpose; and there-

upon shall be admitted a member, and receive a ticket of admission to the general meetings of the Association.

III. That each member shall subscribe one penny a week to the funds of the Association, the payment thereof to be made at the general weekly meetings.

IV. That strangers may be admitted to the meetings of the Association upon being introduced by a member, or by application to the chairman of the evening.

V. That there shall be a Committee of management, for the purpose of arranging and conducting the general business of the Association.

VI. That a general meeting of the members of the Association shall be held on Saturday evening in every week, at the Crown Tavern, Museum-Street; the chair to be taken at half past eight o' clock.

VII. That there shall be a Secretary and also a Treasurer of the Association. The Treasurer to be accountable to the Committee for all receipts and disbursements, and he shall not be at liberty to make any disbursements without the authority of the Committee.

VIII. That the Committee shall at all times be open to the strictures of, and be responsible for their conduct to, the members; and that each member shall have free access to the books of account and proceedings of the Association.

IX. That one half of the Committee shall go out of office every three months, and an election thereupon take place to supply the vacancies; and that the old members shall be eligible for re-election.

Crown Tavern, Museum-Street, Bloomsbury, May 21, 1831

17. [Add. Ms. 27822, f. 37. *Printed.* Adopted 4 June 1831.]
RULES of the NATIONAL UNION OF THE WORKING CLASSES. One Penny.
DECLARATION OF THE RIGHTS OF MAN.
The members of the National Union, convinced that forgetfulness of and contempt for the Rights of Man, in a municipal state of society, are the only causes of the crimes and misfortunes of the world, have resolved to proclaim their sacred and unalienable rights, in order that they, by comparing the acts of the government with the ends of every social institution, may never suffer themselves to be oppressed and degraded by tyranny; that the people may always have before their eyes the basis of their liberty and happiness; the magistrates the rule of their conduct and duty; and legislators the object of their appointment. They therefore acknowledge, and proclaim to the world, the following declaration of the RIGHTS OF MAN.

I. The end of society is the PUBLIC GOOD, and the institution of government is to secure to EVERY INDIVIDUAL, the enjoyment of his rights.

II. The rights of Man in society, are liberty—equality before the laws—security of his person—and the full enjoyment of the produce of his labours.

III. Liberty is that power which belongs to a man of doing everything that does not infringe upon the right of another. Its principle is nature;—its rule justice;—its protection the law;—and its moral limits are defined by this maxim:—*Do unto others as you would that others should do unto you.*

IV. The law is the free and solemn expression of the public will:—it ought to be the same for all, whether it protects or punishes;—it cannot order but what is just and useful;—it cannot forbid but what is hurtful.

V. The right of expressing one's thoughts and opinions, either by the press or in any other manner;—the right of assembling peaceably;—and the free exercise of worship, cannot be forbidden.

VI. The necessity of announcing these rights, implies the existence of despotism on the part of the governors, or ignorance on the part of the people.

VII. Instruction is the want of all; society and government ought, therefore, to do all in their power, to favour the progress of reason and truth; and to place instruction within the reach of all.

VIII. A people have always the right of revising, amending, and changing their constitution:—one generation cannot subject to its laws future generations.

IX. Every adult member of society, has an equal right to nominate those who legislate for the community; thereby concurring through his representatives in the enactment of the laws.

X. Oppression is exercised against the social body, when ONE of its members is oppressed:—oppression is exercised against EACH MEMBER, when the social body is oppressed.

XI. When a government violates the rights of the people resistance becomes the most sacred, and the most indispensable of duties.

CONSTITUTION.

1. The constitution of this Union is essentially popular.

2. It admits as equal members all persons whatever, whose names shall be registered in the books of the Union, so long as they shall conform to its rules and regulations.

3. It holds all its members eligible to office by right, and selects from its own body its own officers and managers; recognizing only the following simple, rational, politic, and just principles in the determination of its choice;—namely, *virtue, intelligence, and capacity for the performance of duties.*

4. It confides the administration of its government, to a general committee, which committee derive their authority exclusively from the written or published laws of the Union; conformably to its letter and spirit.

5. It constitutes its general committee, upon the basis of representation, in the persons of all sub-committees, attached to branch or district divisions of the Union; of the delegates of all recognized trade, benefit, and cooperative societies; and of such other persons as shall be elected committee-men at the monthly meetings of the Union.

6. The committees of branch or district divisions shall be chosen as follows; —namely, Any member of the Union at a general meeting of the several

30

district divisions may nominate another as a committee-man; the said nomination to be put to the vote of the meeting, and the majority of votes to determine the election.

7. It declares a fund or capital essential to its strength and prosperity, it therefore imposes upon all its members, the obligation of contributing a sum not less than one penny per month, payable in advance; such fund, to be exclusively applied to the interests of the Union and the promotion of its objects. But should a greater sum be required to meet any pressing exigency, the committee may call a general meeting of the members to raise such subscription to a sum not exceeding one penny a week.

8. That the funds of the Union be invested in the hands of a treasurer appointed at a general meeting of the members.

9. The Union decides all propositions relative to its constitution, laws government, and objects; also the nomination and expulsion of officers and members, by the vote of a majority at a general meeting.

OBJECTS OF THE NATIONAL UNION.

1. The objects of the NATIONAL UNION are,—First, to avail itself of every opportunity, in the progress of society, for the securing, by degrees, those things specified in the preceding declaration of the Rights of Man.

2. To obtain for every working man, unrestricted by unjust and partial laws, the full value of his labour, and the free disposal of the produce of his labour.

3. To support, as circumstances may determine, by all just means, every fair and rational opposition made by societies of working men (such societies being part of the Union), against the combination and tyranny of masters and manufacturers; whenever the latter shall seek, unjustly, to reduce the wages of labour, or shall institute proceedings against the workmen; the character of which proceedings, in the estimation of the Union, shall be deemed vexatious and oppressive.

4. To obtain for the nation an effectual reform in the Commons House of the British parliament: the basis of which reform shall be annual parliaments, extension of the suffrage to every adult male, vote by ballot, and, especially, NO PROPERTY QUALIFICATION for members of parliament; this Union being convinced, that until intelligent men from the productive and useful classes of society possess the right of sitting in the Commons House of Parliament, to represent the interests of the working people, justice in legislation will never be rendered unto them.

5. To inquire, consult, consider, discuss and determine, respecting the rights and liberties of the working people, and respecting the just and most effectual means of securing all such rights.

6. To prepare petitions, addresses, and remonstrances [sic] to the crown, and both Houses or either House of Parliament, respecting the preservation of public rights, the repeal of bad laws, and the enactment of a wise and all-comprehensive code of good laws.

7. To promote peace, union, and concord among all classes of people and

to guide and direct the public mind, into uniform, peaceful, and legitimate operations; instead of leaving it to waste its strength, in loose, desultory, and unconnected exertions.

8. To collect and organize the peaceful expression of public opinion, so as to bring it to act upon the Houses of Parliament, in a just and effectual way.

9. To concentrate into one focus a knowledge of moral and political economy, that all classes of society may be enlightened by its radiation; the NATIONAL UNION feeling assured, that the submission of the people to misrule and oppression, arises from the absence of sound moral and political knowledge amongst the mass of the community.

10. To avoid all private or secret proceedings, all concealment of any of the views or objects of the Union, and to facilitate for all persons invested with legal authority a full, free and constant access to all books, documents, regulations and proceedings of the Union.

MEANS OF OBTAINING THESE OBJECTS.

The means proposed are,—

1. By the creation of a fund, constituted by an equal subscription of all the members of the Union, and by donations.

2. By the formation of branch or district divisions, having committees attached to them.

3. By convening frequent meetings of the Union, and of the branch or district divisions, for the purpose of agitating such measures as may relate to the principles specified in the Declaration of Rights; in the Constitution, and in the objects of the Union.

4. By the instrumentality of the public press.

5. By the publication and dissemination of pamphlets tracts, &c.

6. By the active talent, zeal, and industry of the representatives of the Union, in the members of the general committee of the Union; of the committees of branch or district associations; and of delegates from trade, benefit, and co-operative societies; and by such other means as may be deemed advisable.

GOVERNMENT.

1. The management of the affairs of the Union is entrusted to the general committee, as constituted by the 5th and 6th article of the Constitution.

2. The committees of branch or district associations shall appoint collectors, from among themselves, to receive the contributions of members; the delegates of trade, benefit, and co-operative societies, shall act as collectors to their respective societies; and the subscription shall be paid by the collectors and delegates to the persons appointed by the Union.

3. Every officer of the Union shall keep a true and proper account of all business transacted by him relative to the affairs of the Union, and a copy of such accounts shall be delivered to the secretary of the Union.

4. The general committee shall meet weekly, or as often as they may deem necessary:—at such meetings seven are competent to act;—they keep a record of their proceedings.

5. The members of the Union shall meet monthly, or whenever called upon by the general committee, or by a requisition signed by not less than 40 of the members.
6. The general committee shall submit a report every three months to a meeting of the members of the Union, which quarterly report shall state the amount of receipts and expenditure; the balance of cash in hand; the increase or decrease of members, the nature of their correspondence, and the general results of their labours.
7. The accounts of the Union shall be examined every quarter by three auditors, who are not on the committee, to be chosen by the members from amongst themselves at the monthly meeting, preceding the quarterly night; the said auditors to possess the power of demanding all receipts, vouchers, and necessary explanations from the committee and servants of the Union.
8. All books, documents &c. in the possession of officers of the Union shall be produced when demanded by the general committee.
9. The accounts of the Union shall be open to the inspection of the members at all reasonable times, whenever such inspection does not interfere with the progress of business.
10. That each member of the Union pay a halfpenny for his card.
11. That all bills for payment be examined by the committee, and no money whatever shall be paid until the committee have so determined.
12. No person shall be allowed to address the meeting in a state of intoxication; and if he attempt to interrupt the business, he shall be desired to leave the room.

By order of the Committee of the Union.

18. [Add. Ms. 27791, ff. 280–2]

The article numbered 2 under the head of '*Objects of the National Union*' is the base on which the association was founded, the *sole* inducement to its formation. Its projectors in the first instance wished to form a trades union for the purpose of raising wages and reducing the hours of working—with a view to the ultimate object the division of property among the working people but the persons they called to their assistance under the circumstances of the times, and the general agitation caused by the Reform Bills, at once converted it into a Political Union, leaving the proceedings of working mens trade unions as a secondary object, the main purpose being political, the trade portion as incidental, and the title of the society was changed from the 'Metropolitan Trades Union' to the 'National Union of the Working Classes and others.' The word others caused dissentions and motions were twice made to permit, 'None but *Wealth Producers*' to be members of the committee or to hold any office in the union. In discussing the proposition it was shewn that several of their leaders were not wealth producers in the meaning of the words, in the restricted sense the words were used, and the motions were not adopted.

The 3rd article under the same head was well adapted to the general feeling of the working people, and the two articles would have induced the working people in almost countless numbers to have become members of the Union had the leaders conducted them more rationally than they did.

Several of the leaders and principle speech makers were ill-informed men entertaining very narrow notions, some among them were utterly dishonest men whose purpose was confusion that they might plunder, and these notions scarcely disguised at all even in public and carefully inculcated privately, were inimical to the better part of working people and by the alarm they occasioned prevented vast numbers joining the union. Many however attended the meetings which were held publicly and weekly—at the spacious Rotunda in the Surrey Road at the Philadelphia Chapel Finsbury and occasionally at other places. Had the meetings been conducted in the quiet orderly manner, and the committee adhered steadily to either the one or the other of the two objects before noticed, or even to both of them, without abusing in open and gross terms every one who did not concur with them, and had they refrained from continually preaching up what was clearly understood to mean insurrection accompanied by its concomitant plunder, the extent to which the union would have spread, the vast numbers of persons who would have become members and the general effect it would have produced all over the country, would have induced the government to put it down, it being altogether an illegal association, conducting itself in direct opposition to the well understood enactments of two acts of parliament, as it was, it was of little present importance to the government, the members of which could not give themselves the trouble to think of the notions it was propagating among the working people throughout the Nation.

The Constitution as a scheme of government for a large body of working men is well conceived and well executed, and is creditable to the talents of the men who formed the committee which prepared it. It is judiciously arranged and the style is unexceptionable. It was found sufficient for all the purposes intended and never I believe underwent any alteration.

19. [Add. Ms. 27790, ff. 8, 9 and 11. Following the rejection of the second reform bill on 8 October 1831, Place wrote:]

Meetings were held on the saturday in many of the Metropolitan Parishes and many more were called for the monday. The Parish of Mary-le-bone had taken the lead respecting parliamentary interference for the regulation of vestries, and had succeeded in inducing a considerable number of parishes to appoint deputies to confer together in their mutual interests, the persons who in that parish had assembled frequently appointed a committee to watch over their interests and this committee now considered themselves a political committee in respect to the reform bill. They assembled and being joined by a considerable number of the inhabitants they issued the following notice.

The Lords have rejected the bill. England expects every man will do his duty. The parishioners of Mary-le-Bone will assemble at the Horse Bazaar at twelve o' clock on Monday next, to address the King, support his ministers and consult on the present state of affairs. Pursuant to a resolution passed at two preparatory meetings, the inhabitants are desired to devote Monday next solemnly to these objects, to suspend all business and shut up their shops.

Long before the time appointed the capacious square of the Horse Bazaar was not only filled but an immense number of persons—said to amount to 30,000 could not gain admittance. A call became general to adjourn to Hyde Park and it was announced that Mr Hume who had agreed to take the chair would meet them there. An orderly procession of the people immediately took place and an immense number, estimated at 50,000 congregated in the open space north of the Serpentine River. They had come nearly a mile to this spot and had waited some time when two gentlemen on horseback rode among them and told them that Mr Hume thought the meeting would be illegal if held out of the Parish and as Mr Maberly had granted the use of a piece of ground in Regents Park they requested the meeting would assemble there as speedily as possible. 'If any thing,' observes the *Chronicle* (very justly)

could have cooled the ardour of the people, who however proved themselves as ardent as patriotic, it was this demand upon their patience after waiting above an hour at the Bazaar, and dragging through the Park for an hour more; but nothing daunted they proceeded in good humour, to the Regents Park and arrived there between one and two o'clock. Several waggons were placed at the lower part of the grounds and the assembled multitude which before the chair was taken must have amounted to 80,000 persons formed themselves on the rising ground into a sort of semi-circle and the wind being in their faces, the majority could hear the proceedings.

Mr Hume took the Chair[1]
Large Placards were exhibited, one was
Englishmen
Remember it was the Bishops—and the Bishops only
whose votes decided the fate of the
Reform Bill

The other was—

England
expects that every man will
do
His Duty

Mr Hume—said it was no ordinary occasion which had called them together, and in the great and important measures they were about to discuss, every man from the King to the Peasant had a deep interest. He knew they would act peacably and orderly, and would not despair, as long as they had a Patriot King, a liberal ministry, and a majority in favour of the measure. They would tell the petty pitiful majority of the house of Lords that they had rights as Englishmen as sacred as their own and that an oligarchy which had usurped their rights should be compelled to relinquish their tyrannical power which they had so long exercised against the people. He respected the words of Lord Grey that he would stand by the people and the King so long as the King gave him his confidence, said he reposed confidence in his sincerity, and though ministers had not been so active in promoting the bill as they ought to have been, he hoped they would profit by experience and not coquet with the Tories,

[1] See Handbill 1.

MARY-LE-BONE REFORM MEETING.

At an extremely numerous MEETING of the PARISHIONERS of MARY-LE-BONE, held in the grounds of Mr. MABERLY, in the Regent's-park, that gentleman having accommodated his fellow parishioners with a place of meeting.

JOSEPH HUME, Esq., M.P. in the Chair;

The following resolutions were carried unanimously:—

That this Meeting have learned with deep regret and indignation that a majority of the House of Peers have presumed to reject the Bill proposed by a liberal Ministry—sanctioned by our patriotic King—and received by the people with gratitude and satisfaction. That this meeting cannot any longer tamely submit to this arrogant usurpation of the people's rights by any two hundred individuals ; but particularly so when many of that number have nominees in the House of Commons, usurping the people's rights, are also pensioners on the taxes of the country—in some cases to an extravagant and shameful amount ; and who are thus personally interested in upholding the present defective and corrupt system of representation and Government.—Moved by Mr. MABERLY, M. P., and seconded by Mr. EDWARDS, of Crawford-St.

Resolved,—That it is essential for the peace of the country, that, the Reform Bill having been rejected by the House of Lords, another Bill should be introduced into Parliament and speedily become Law, and that his Most Gracious Majesty be intreated to exercise all those powers granted to him by the Constitution, to effect that most desirable measure, and that an Address be forthwith presented to his Majesty, expressing our continued loyalty and devotion to his person and Government, and praying that he would exercise those powers. Moved by Mr. JOHN SAVAGE, seconded by Mr. OGILVEY.

Resolved,—That this meeting do [unanimously] express their cordial and heartfelt thanks to Earl GREY and His Majesty's Ministers for the efforts they have made to pass the Reform Bill in the House of Lords, and beg to assure them of the unabated confidence which this meeting places in their continued exertion to promote the Reform demanded by the nation ; and that this Meeting here declare their determination to support his Majesty's Ministers in every means they may consider necessary to ensure speedy success to that measure.—Moved by Mr. WM. SMITH, Esq. late Member for Norwich, seconded by Mr. R. NELMS, Oxford Street

Resolved—That this Meeting entertain the strongest feelings of gratitude to the King for the paternal regard he has manifested to the welfare and happiness of his people, and to assure him of our unabated and unalterable attachment to his Royal Person at the present crisis. That we beg earnestly to suggest the propriety of his Majesty's immediately dismissing those Peers, and other persons, who may be employed in the office of trust, honor, or emolument, including Placemen in the Royal Household, Lords-Lieutenants of Counties, and, in short, all persons holding at the pleasure of the Crown, and to retain those only who have advocated the rights of the People.—Moved by Mr. BAXTER, seconded by Mr. MITCALF.

That this Meeting unanimously pledge themselves to wait with patience, and cheerfully to pay the public taxes, until his Majesty's Ministers shall have had time to adopt the necessary measures, to secure the speedy passing of the Reform Bill into a law ; but at the same time [unanimously] to declare their fixed and unalterable resolution, if unfortunately an anti-Reform and Tory Administration should take the places of Earl Grey and his Colleagues, that this Meeting will immediately withhold, and persuade others to withhold by every legal means in their power, the payment of all tithes and taxes.—Moved by Mr: WARDEN, seconded by Mr. WEBB.

That this Meeting offer their cordial thanks to the great majority of the public press, who have so ably, and so perseveringly advocated the rights of the people.

That an Address founded upon the foregoing Resolutions be adopted, and presented to his Majesty at the next Levee.—Moved by Mr. POTTER, seconded by Mr. FLOOD.

ADDRESS.

THAT We, your Majesty's dutiful and loyal subjects, the Inhabitants of the Parish of St. Marylebone, in public meeting assembled, deeply sympathising with your Majesty upon the present eventful crisis, caused by the intemperate, and rash conduct of the House of Peers, in rejecting the Bill for amending the representation of the people in the Commons House of Parliament, feel it our duty to offer to your Majesty the assurance of our unabated and unalterable attachment to your Royal Person, and to declare our confidence in your royal wisdom and firmness, and to express our earnest hope that your Majesty will continue in office your Majesty's present Ministers ; and we further implore your Majesty to adopt the following measures, which we conceive to be indispensably necessary, to accomplish your Majesty's wish, in the amendment of the representation of the people:—

1st. To dismiss from all situations of trust, honour, or emolument, those Peers and others who have voted against the people's Bill, including Lord Lieutenants of Counties, Placemen in the Royal Household, and, in short, all persons holding any situation at the pleasure of the Crown, who may have so voted, as utterly unworthy to retain the same.

2dly. To prorogue the Parliament forthwith, and to assemble it again as soon as the law will permit ; to recommend your Majesty's present faithful advisers again to introduce to the House of Commons, without delay, a Bill for amending the representation of the people in the Commons House of Parliament, which shall be in unison with the feelings of your Majesty, and the wishes of the nation at large. And we hereby again give to your Majesty an assurance that we are prepared and resolved with our lives and fortunes to defend your Royal Person and the just prerogative of the Crown together with our own liberties against our domestic enemies, with as resolute a courage as we would against our foreign foes.

Resolved,—That the Committees and Delegates of the various Parishes and Wards, of the Metropolis and its vicinity be requested to assemble at the Crown and Anchor Tavern, in the Strand, on Wednesday evening, Oct. 12, at 6 o'clock to consult on the best means of giving effectual support to the King and his Government, and on the measures necessary to secure the peace and safety of the metropolis.

Thanks were then voted to Mr. MABERLY and Mr. HUME.

MULLIN. Printer. 3. Circus Street, New Road, Mary-le-bone

HANDBILL 1 Add. Ms. 27790, f. 10.

since it was vain to expect the tories could be induced to approve of measures favourable to the people. He said there must be either reform or revolution (immense cheering and cries of we will have it). It was because in case of a revolution the working and useful classes would be the greatest sufferers that he wished to effect a reform by constitutional means and hoped to avoid such a revolution as the Duke of Wellington wished should take place. He knew the people would not be drawn in to commit acts of violence (no—no) they would protect the property of the country (we will).

20. [Add. Ms. 27790, f. 13]

Some little explanation may here be necessary—the meeting was a meeting of the inhabitants of Mary le bone according to the notice which called it together, but considerably more than half the persons present were of the working classes from all parts of the town. Mr Savage and several others who composed the so called Mary le Bone committee were understood to be the promoters of the meeting and of these three or four were like himself leaders in the National Union of the Working Classes. Mr Savage was convinced that any attempt to procure more than the bill which had been rejected would fail and he wished therefore to see the bill carried as a first step to the more perfect reform he and others contemplated, but he was unwilling to lose his power among those who were more obstinate and less informed than himself by directly opposing their notions. He wished the whole of the working people to withold for the present their usual propositions and to make common cause in favour of the Bill, and this he effected to a very considerable extent. There had been a meeting of the non conformist working people at which resolutions demanding universal suffrage etc. had been voted, and he knowing he could not lead these men, wished to lead all who were not associated with them, and this his speech was better calculated to effect than any thing and every thing which had hitherto been done. The proofs however of the efforts made to demonstrate the consent of the working people to forego their claims and to support the bill were incessant and the result was plainly shewn by the procession two days after this meeting when the King held his levee at St James's.

21. [Add. Ms. 27790, f. 11]

The National Union of the Working Classes had on the Wednesday evening preceeding the rejection of the bill by the Lords at their regular weekly meeting, adopted a declaration etc.—and had placarded it until the time the St Mary le Bone meeting was held.

[Here follows a newspaper cutting reporting the meeting]

Last Wednesday evening, a numerous meeting of the members of the National Union of the working classes, took place at the Rotunda, Blackfriars-bridge.—Mr. WATSON was called to the chair.

The adoption of the declaration issued by the Committee was moved by *Mr. Lovett*, seconded by *Mr. Cleave*, in animated speeches, and carried unanimously.

'Declaration in behalf of the working classes by the committee of the National Union.—We declare individual property of every description, acquired by honest industry, or under the sanction of laws (however unjustly enacted), to be sacred; and that we will, by every means in our power strive to bring those to punishment, who seek individual wealth or gratification, by an invasion of the rights of others, instead of promoting the public good.

'Although we are, in many respects, the victims of property and the slaves of monopoly and individual wealth, yet we seek not redress in the chaos of confusion, or an indiscriminate struggle for pre-eminence we are only anxious that property should be turned into those channels which an enlightened legislature, chosen *by all*, should determine to be promotive of the happiness *of all*.

'We, therefore, assure all classes, not interested in existing corruptions, but who are desirous of promoting the happiness of mankind, that we will cordially co-operate with them in resisting and opposing tyranny of every description! and in seeking to procure for this country such institutions as shall, in the opinion of the majority, be deemed the most efficient to promote the greatest happiness of the greatest number.

'We further declare it to be our opinion, that the most safe, just, and honest mode of obtaining this object, is, by choosing a legislature on the principle of every man above the age of twenty-one having a vote—that he be protected by the ballot—that patriotism and intelligence be the only qualification for both electors and representatives, and that parliaments last but for one year.

'We, therefore, rely on the honest intentions of a Patriot King, and on his Ministers, who, we trust, have the happiness and welfare of this kingdom at heart; and not their own exclusive privileges and distinctions; and we hereby call upon them to unite their solicitations with those of a loyal people, so urging upon his Majesty forthwith, to take such measures as will lead with the least delay to the attainment of this just system of representation.'

The following resolution was moved by Mr. *Gast*, seconded by Mr. *Benbow*, and carried unanimously:—

'That this meeting, duly impressed with the importance of the present crisis, do hereby declare to the King's ministers and the country, that they will not be satisfied with any future measure for improving the Representation, which does not recognize the just right of every man to the elective franchise, the protection of the ballot, and no property qualification whatever, and in the expression of these sentiments we only echo the feelings of our fellow-labourers in all parts of the country.'

22. [Add. Ms. 27790, ff. 22–5]

In many places, the working people had withdrawn the claims they had made for annual parliaments and universal suffrage, with voting by ballot and had agreed to support the bill. But as has been noticed, the National Union of the Working Classes in London, had published a declaration against conceding any thing, had placarded the town with their address, and had called upon their fellow workmen all over the country to join with them.

The National Union was composed of a very small body; not so many as five hundred out of the many thousands which London contained were actually members of it; though the payment was but a halfpenny a week for a card, which admitted any person to a meeting and constituted him a member for one week. In the agitated state in which the people had been and still were the weekly meetings of this Union at the Rotunda on the Surry [*sic*] side of Blackfriars bridge were numerously attended and it sometimes happened that many who could not obtain admission made a crowd about the entrance, all who attended were inconsiderately classed as members and the society was supposed to be very numerous. The leaders were not more than twenty persons and they never at any time had more money at command than would pay their current expenses. So little indeed were the real circumstances of this union known that it was very generally supposed a vast majority of the working people in London were members and that they were under the control of its managers.

The bill having been rejected it was much feared that the working classes all over the country would take advantage of the circumstances and say we have hitherto refrained from insisting on our claims to Annual Parliaments, Universal Suffrage and voting by Ballott [sic], to accomodate [sic] ourselves to the times and that we might be no impediment to the passing of the Reform Bill. That Bill is lost and we are no longer disposed to concede anything, we will now insist upon our 'rights'—they can be as easily procured as can a limited suffrage which excludes us.

This apprehension had great effect on many people, who feared that a division of interests would give great advantage to the tories and with the other obstacles before them either set aside all chance of reform, and produce convulsion, or break down the ministerial project to something not worthy of acceptance. These were not unreasonable apprehensions.

Many well informed men among the working classes were indignant at being classed with the 'Rotunda people' and were with a vast many others desirous to shew their dissent from the proceedings of that body, and their concurrence in the reform bill. I saw many of them who from time to time complained of the conduct of the union, and I always advised them to get up meetings, trade meetings and meetings of working men indiscriminately; declare their opinions that they were competent to act as citizens and exercise the rights which Annual Parliaments, Universal Suffrage and voting by Ballot would secure to them, but that under the present circumstances of the country and the government, they were willing to suspend any demand for those rights, and were ready to support the Government in any way which could be necessary to promote the passing of the Reform Bill. Many were well disposed to assist in doing what I recommended, but none were willing to take the lead.

On sunday the ninth of October I had many people with me of which some notice will be taken presently. In the afternoon when I was alone there came to me, a very respectable looking man, Thomas Bowyer. I had heard of him and was desirous to see him; he was a journeyman bookseller, he introduced himself, and told me that he in conjunction with an attorneys clerk named Powell had a project to get up a great meeting of the working classes and others to form a procession and present to the King at his Levee to be held on the wednesday following an address from the working classes and others resident in as many parishes as time would allow them to consult and arrange with for that purpose. That the address should pledge the working people to stand by the King—his ministers the House of Commons and the Bill. He laid his scheme before me and I encouraged him all I could to proceed with it, gave him a circular note with the names of many persons to whom he might shew it, as well for pecuniary aid as for personal assistance and reference to others—and especially seperate [*sic*] notes to every person I knew who was at all influential in conducting the daily papers, requesting them to insert notices and laudatory paragraphs; and I recommended Bowyer to see and converse with them immediately. He and his friend Powell did so and obtained all the support they desired, and the project was immediately made public.

I gave him a note to Mr Young, Lord Melbournes private secretary, advised him to communicate freely with Young, but to tell him he did not come for either advice, approbation—or disapprobation—as he had resolved to go through with the business, and to let him know that the whole of it would be conducted in an orderly discreet way so that no one need fear any disagreeable results. This was done and when I saw Mr Young I repeated what I had said to Bowyer and advised him to keep the Police and the Soldiers out of sight. I told him there would be a great mob at the Palace whether there were or were not a procession, and that some mischief in the way of breaking windows would probably take place, as had always happened at times of great excitement, but that the men who went in procession would be much more disposed to prevent than to promote mischief.

I wrote to every member of Parliament I knew, informed him of what was going on and requested him to subscribe a trifle to pay the expenses which would be incurred.

Bowyer and Powell having devoted themselves to the business, proceeded with it in a very extraordinary manner as the narrative of Mr Powell will shew.

23. [Add. Ms. 27790, ff. 39–47. Place had written to Powell for an account of the procession to assist him in completing his narrative of political events. The following is as Place transcribed it from the original.]

Mr Powells account of the Procession 22 May 1834

To state briefly the multitude of events which were crowded into the small space of time to which you refer is matter of some difficulty, but, I will endeavour to make my personal narrative, which is I believe what you require, as sussinct [*sic*] as possible.

I must premise that for some time previous to the period in question I had in conjunction with Bowyer and some others got up a reform association in the parish of Bloomsbury, which though small was very active and useful especially in the way of propagandism, and which subsequently merged in the National Political Union.

On the morning of the 8 Oct. 1831 I was compelled to go down to Gravesend by the Steamer and thence to Chatham. Before I started I obtained in the City a copy of the Sun Newspaper published at half past 6 o clock, fringed with black, and announcing the loss of the peoples bill in the house of Lords by the frightful majority of 41. Never shall I forget the excitement which prevailed in the breast of every one at hearing the news. The morning papers were not out, the boat was crowded and the passengers were conversing in groups on the deck on rumours which had reached their ears. I was the only person on board who possessed anything like an authentic account, and, when the paper with a black border was seen in my hand, the passengers rushed towards me, I was instantly mounted on a chair and compelled to read the debate through from beginning to end. The excitement, the disapprobation, and approbation of the several speakers were as energetic as they could have been had they been the actual spectators of the scene which the report described. The denunciations against the Bishops were fearful, and when I came to Lord Greys noble declaration that he would not abandon the helm of affairs as long as he could be useful to his King and his country the very shores of old father Thames reechoed the reiterated shouts of applause. A kind of meeting followed in which most of the persons present declared their determination to return to town that evening, to stir in their respective parishes, and above all to pay no taxes unless measures were taken to carry an efficient Reform Bill. I hurried through my business, hastened to town the same evening, and found as I expected the rooms of the association crowded with members. A strong petition to the King was carried, calling on him to retain his Ministers—to dismiss the Bishops—to create new Peers, in short to do any thing to carry the bill. I told them that petitions would be useless, that the Tories had the upper hand and would keep it, and that the moral power of the people could be of no avail unless we gave the King and the Tories reason to expect it would be backed by a tolerable portion of physical power. I urged them to go up with their petition to the King themselves, and to use all their influence to prevail with the various parishes in London to do the same. My proposal met with a very cold reception. It was argued that the undertaking was too vast for persons having no influence, such as we were, to accomplish it and that the intervening space of time, from Saturday night to Wednesday morning was too short for any effectual demonstration to be made, and that a small shew in point of numbers would rather injure than promote our cause. This I may as well once for all observe was *the* difficulty, started afterwards wherever I went. It was the most serious difficulty I had to encounter. The character of the English is in this respect very different from that of the French, Englishmen are generally reluctant to make any attempt, unless they see an immediate prospect of success, but when they have once made up their minds to an attempt they are more energetic in following it up; but unless they see that the chances are greatly with them, the fear of encountering ridicule for making an abortive effort damps their energies and prevents their acting. The french are the reverse, and hence their progress is more rapid than ours.

I contended against the objection with all my might, I urged that nothing was impossible to the determined, and that it was not a question of our insignificance but of the state and feelings of the people, and that a spark which under some circumstances would be useless, would under others be alone sufficient to explode a powder magazine. I was warmly seconded by Bowyer, but the utmost we could accomplish was permission on our own responsibility to endeavour to bring it about.

We accordingly started on our pilgrimage, and from that moment 'till wednesday we scarcely had an hours rest.

I cannot detail our proceedings in the order they occurred, nor indeed the whole of them. Our first object was to visit leading reformers in the different parishes to suggest the matter to them, and also to start it through the press by means of paragraphs. Here again we had the same difficulties to encounter, and another arising from the variety of the leaders who did not like any interference. This we got over, by arguing that our views were disinterested and that we sought no notoriety, we urged them to put forward the project as their own. We did the same with the men in the parishes and piqued their pride by advising them not to be outdone by other parishes. We were successful and on sunday night became assured that the proposal would be supported by many at several parish meetings on Monday and Tuesday. We had also made some arrangements for a sort of committee. On the same evening we heard there was to be a meeting at Bethnal Green. A large and influential meeting of the working classes of that district. Whither we went and addressed them. We found that many of them were bitten with the Rotunda notions, and would do nothing unless we would forego the Reform Bill, and demand at once Annual Parliaments, Universal Suffrage and Voting by Ballot. I explained that we looked upon the Reform Bill as a stepping stone to these things, and we at length prevailed by creating a considerable diversion in my favour, numbers expressed their determination to attend, one or two of the leaders undertook to lay the matter before a parish meeting which was to be held, and on the day of the procession about 5000 of the inhabitants of Bethnal Green and its neighbourhood joined us in Portland Place.

In Clerkenwell, my own parish, though no housekeeper, we were more successful. We had previously in our character of propagandists converted a *Parochial* reform association held on Clerkenwell Green into a *Political* Reform association, and this was the lever by which we moved that Parish. We called a meeting for monday, at which meeting the room could not contain us, and we were obliged to adjourn to the Green. Here all the propositions we made were carried, with the greatest enthusiasm and arrangements were made, for meeting again on the Green on Wednesday morning. On tuesday the Parish meeting in favour of the Bill was held, but the Parish Officers being opposed to the parochial reformers tried to set aside the main proposition. They refused even the use of the Parish crier or bell-man. We therefore placarded the parish—got a dustmens bell went round the parish ourselves on tuesday evening, announcing the meeting and the procession and calling on other parishes to attend. By the time we cleared the parish the next morning we were 10,000 strong.

In St Lukes Old Street we met with no difficulty. We called on several of the leaders who embraced our proposition with eagerness. Their bell man was instantly sent round to summon a parish meeting. The Reverend Dr Rice the Rector took the chair. The Churchwardens supported the proposition and it was carried unanimously. The next day the Rev'd. Dr Rice followed the Parochial Authorities on Horseback and led the St Lukes procession which joined the Clerkenwell association in Claremont Square Pentonville and with them marched down Portland Place, the rendezvous for the Northern Parishes. Several other parishes in that neighbourhood which we had excited to attend, which sent detachments to us, but the meetings in parishes we were unable to attend. We had a large body from the parish of St Mary Islington.

In St James Westminster and the adjoining parishes, we were after some difficulty successful. In them we did not appear, but only consulted with the leaders, leaving them to make their own arrangements. They and also the Bloomsbury people joined us at the bottom of Regent Street.

The southern parishes, the last of which was St Mary Newington managed their own business in the same way. They also fell in at the bottom of Regent Street at the same time that the Mayor and Corporation of the City of London reached the spot.

The most formidable part of the procession came perhaps from the parishes which constitute the great borough of Mary le bone viz Mary le bone Paddington and Pancrass [sic]. With these Parishes we also had some difficulty on account as well of the reasons I have alluded to as of an internal jealousy among themselves. At last however we succeeded, by arguing with the leaders and by addressing the committees of these three parishes. Mr Thelwall, was one of these and he too was at first against us, but he afterwards yeilded [sic] to the reasons we urged, and to confidence conferred by deputies from various other parishes whom I induced to meet them. In this district Major Revell was of infinite service. The result was that the proposition being made to a great meeting of these parishes was received with immense applause. On the wednesday morning the procession from these parishes joined us in Portland Place in number of 20,000 to 25,000. There may perhaps have been other parishes in the procession but they must have been worked on by example and by the paragraphs in the newspaper.

The numbers of the procession were variously estimated by the newspapers at from 70,000 to 300,000—I think about 70,000 is near the truth, but taking into consideration the crowds which met and accompanied us on the line of march there might have been nearer 500,000. All the windows of the streets through which we passed were crowded with spectators the greater part of whom were elegantly dressed ladies, and Ribbons—Flowers —and Cockades were frequently showered upon us as we passed, accompanied with loud cheers waving of handkerchiefs and expressions of sympathy.

At many points of the road we were saluted with bands of music, some playing the dead march, others God save the King—and Rule Brittannia [sic]. Church bells tolled out as we passed. Flags and other items were hung out and with the exception of the mere City most of the Shop windows were closed, and business was suspended even in the private streets.

The march of so many citizens of the Metropolis to present petitions in person, and to wait until they had an answer; for that was our expressed determination; was not however viewed at the palace without alarm. Mr Hume and Mr Byng were requested by a high personage to meet us, which they did, and prevailed on the deputies to forego their original intention of claiming personal admission to the King, and to entrust them with their addresses, they promising to return an answer, it being arranged that the procession should wait in the Park in St James's Square, and the neighbouring streets. That a certain number of deputies from each of the Parishes should be admitted into the square in front of the Palace to communicate with the county members.

The favourable reception the King gave to the addresses and the enthusiasm of the people when made acquainted with it by the communication thereof through Mr Hume and Mr Byng, I need not describe to you who have had so much experience of their feelings on the Reform question.

The greatest order prevailed throughout, which shews I think that for young soldiers we were not bad generals, we had arranged that the files should be six, eight, or ten abreast and that each flank man should be known and responsible for the order of his file, and the consequence as was universally admitted was, that spite of the excitement which prevailed not a single disorder was committed by the persons composing the procession, unless indeed it can be called disorder to groan or cheer as the files passed by the houses of the friends or enemies to the Bill. Among the former the Duke of Cleveland was particularly well received.

Much too of the prudent conduct observed was owing to the equally prudent conduct of the Government. We had previously received a message from the police intimating that they knew we were the promoters of the scheme, and requesting to know our opinions on the propriety of employing the police force. We told them there was no danger if they would only keep the Police out of sight, and let all who did appear be in coloured cloaths. This advice was adopted and the result shewed its prudence.

The only disorders of the day were the attacks on the Marquess of Londonderry in the afternoon, this was by a mob with which we had no connection, and which he much provoked by his ridiculous display of pistols. And on the houses of the Duke of Wellington and the Marquess of Bristol. Both were by mobs and not by the procession. The procession did not go near the Duke of Wellingtons, and the men belonging to the procession actually seized those who threw stones at Lord Bristols windows and delivered them over to the Police.

There was a slight attempt by the Police and Soldiery who formed a line across the end of Pall Mall to prevent our progress but the attempt was as vain as were Mrs Partingtons endeavours to mop out the atlantic. They prudently gave way and the procession filed off part into the Park, part up St. James's Street and to different parts to await the answer to their addresses. When that answer was obtained they quietly left the ground and returned to their parishes by different routes.

For my own part exhausted almost to fainting by the excessive fatigue and excitement of both body and mind I had undergone for four days, but which till the task had been fully accomplished I had never felt, I threw myself into a coach and went home to recruit my strength by necessary rest.

This is the scant history of that memorable event without which I have heard it said by many well informed persons the present ministry would have been certainly thrown out and the Tories would have triumphed a second time.

It was a bold and a hazardous experiment, for our personal responsibility in case of a riot was very great. No such thing had occurred either before or since, for the class of persons comprising the procession were respectable house-keepers, shop-keepers and superior artizans, the bone and muscle of a nation.

There was at this time no general union; each parish acted seperately,

44

and even the leaders did not come into communication with one another. Unless therefore we had acted judiciously in keeping ourselves in the background and acting only as the medium of communication between them, we never could have prevailed on them to recognise the possibility of such an undertaking.

It has taught me a lesson. It has taught me that in speculating on human nature despight [*sic*] of forms and customs we can never err. It has taught me that no man is too insignificant to serve his country, or to promote the march of great events. Above all it has taught me the truth of a creed I was before disposed to entertain, that to the energetic determined and persevering nothing is impossible.

Few knew the secret springs of that great metropolitan movement. It is perhaps a curious chapter in the history of life, and one which strikingly illustrates the excited and combustible state of society at that period, for I repeat that few things more repugnant to the general habits, customs and prejudices of the middle classes of London than walking through the streets in a procession can scarcely be conceived, and yet we the promoters were young and unknown men. I have sometimes jestingly said, that if the ministry had any consideration for their old supporters the least they could do would be to offer me the first good place that became vacant.

John H. Powell.

24. [Add. Ms. 27790, ff. 54–9]

The meeting [on 12 October 1831] was held in pursuance of the resolution passed at the great Mary le bone meeting on the 10th by which 'the committees and delegates of the various parishes and wards be requested to assemble at the Crown and Anchor Tavern in the Strand on wednesday evening Oct. 12 at 6 o clock to consult on the best means of giving effectual support to the King and Government, and on the measures necessary to secure the peace and safety of the metropolis.' . . .

In the evening at 5 o clock I attended at the Crown and Anchor Tavern to meet Mr Perry Major Beauclerk and two others for the purpose of concocting a scheme for a Metropolitan Political Union on a large scale, to amalgamate as much as possible all classes without distinction. It was proposed to construct it as much as possible on the plan of the Birmingham Union omitting only such matters as related to the particular views of Mr Attwood respecting the currency. Soon after 6 o clock we were requested to go up stairs to a meeting of delegates from certain parishes who were assembled in consequence of the Mary le bone resolution.

The room in which the meeting was held was a very long room with tables down the middle at each side of which about twenty or twenty-five persons were seated, behind these close to the walls were other chairs, also filled with people; at the top on each side of the fire place and behind the chairman as well as at the bottom of the room were chairs—two or three deep and all occupied, on each side of the chair were a number of persons standing, upon the whole the number must have exceeded one hundred. On our entrance chairs were given to Major Beauclerk, Mr Perry and myself

45

about the middle on one side of the table. Mr Potter of Mary le bone was in the chair, and Mr Drake of Paddington was acting as secretary. The coversation was desultory. No one appeared to have thought of what was proper to be done, none seemed to entertain any notion respecting any precise mode of proceeding, all who spoke talked vaguely of being firm,—that is, as a working man at one of the public meetings said, 'staring at the Government,—staring at the Government firmly.' After much talking some one proposed, 'that it be recommended to Counties Cities Boroughs and Towns to appoint persons to meet forthwith in London to consider of the best means of giving support to the King and his ministers for the passing of Lord John Russells Bill, for reforming the house of commons! This absurd proposal led to a long discussion in which Mr Merle took a conspicuous part, his purpose was to prevent any thing being done, confidence he said was to be placed in Ministers who would of themselves do every thing which ought to be done. In this opinion several concurred, and some most ridiculous nonsense was uttered, one had been to St James's, another had seen an eminent commoner who had said something, another had seen a noble lord who had also said something, and *therefore* full reliance was to be placed in ministers—and the King was firm, and *therefore* again they had nothing to do but to use means to preserve the peace of the Metropolis; all were abroad and some seemed bewildered, suggestion upon suggestion was made, all to no purpose. Some of the really good and clever men who were present were vexed and ashamed to see men who were usually shrewd and energetic so completely deluded and stultified.

Several of these gentlemen were so offended by the proceedings that they were indisposed to take part in them. It appeared, to them, that nothing could be done at this meeting, that as soon as the intention to prorogue the parliament should be generally believed, the whole matter would be abandoned, and it was with some difficulty I persuaded them to remain, and compelled me in order to keep them in their seats to address the meeting. I said I should concur in the resolution of confidence proposed by some of the gentlemen who had called the meeting, if I like them were satisfied that ministers would act in the manner they concluded they would, but that I felt no assurance that they would do any one of the things they so confidently anticipated. That I could not help believing that if things were left in their present state, to their guidance with the apparent consent of the people we should never again see Lord John Russells bill in the House of Commons.—That no new Peers would be made,—That parliament would be prorogued 'till after Christmas, and they might easily estimate themselves the chances there were of the whole of their expectations becoming disappointed. That I would state several circumstances which would probably convince them that the view I had taken of the matter was a correct one, that at any rate I would state such facts, and lay before them such reasons as would prove I did not speak inadvisedly. I did so at some length, and this set the matter right. I pointed out to them the passage in the Chancellors speech which seemed to imply backsliding and had produced a suspicion that there were disagreements in the cabinet. I commented on the passage and on another in a speech of Lord Althorpe's made only two days previously in which he said, 'I do not mean to say that after the discussions and consideration the measure has gone through, some *modification* may not be made in it which without diminishing its efficacy may render it more perfect.' That I had had two communications with one of Lord Althorpes confidential friends, and more than one with a gentleman in office, and from what I had gathered from these two gentlemen I was compelled to conclude that the statement I had made was correct. I reasoned on all the parts as correctly and put the points forward as forcibly as I could, I was cheered as I went on, the whole appearance of the meeting was changed, and the business went at once into the right channel.

Mr Merle again interposed and while he was speaking I was dictating to Mr Perry the substance of two or three resolutions. When Mr Merle had concluded his exhortation, Mr Rogers, of St Giles, rose at the bottom of the table and without either preface or ceremony said, I move that Mr Place do now draw up a memorial to Lord Grey. The proposition was received with shouts of applause. It would have been about as useless as absurd for me to have either refused or hesitated, so I immediately wrote as follows.

'To the Right Honourable Earl Grey etc. etc.
The memorial of the undersigned

Sheweth

That your memorialists are resident in various parishes of the Metropolis, and have considerable knowledge and some influence in their respective localities.

That they have heard with astonishment that it is intended to prorogue the Parliament, and not to reassemble it again 'till after Christmas.

That they should neither do their duty to themselves, to their country, nor to the Government itself, if they did not assure your lordship, that it is their firm conviction that unless the parliament be prorogued for the shortest possible period of time,[1] (not exceeding seven days) and that the bill for reforming the parliament which has passed the house of commons, and been rejected by the house of lords, be then again introduced and the necessary means be adopted to secure its becoming the law of the land, this country will inevitably be plunged into all the horrors of a violent revolution, the result of which no one can predict.

Your memorialists therefore most urgently implore your lordships immediate attention to this memorial.'

The memorial was immediately carried by shouts—and while a fair copy was being made, the following resolutions were agreed to—

1. That this meeting has heard with feelings of dismay that it is intended to prorogue the parliament until after Christmas.
2. That this meeting composed principally of deputies from various parishes in the Metropolis is confident that the state of feeling in their respective parishes is of such a nature as to render a prorogation for so long a period of imminent and instant danger to the lives and properties of his Majestys subjects.
3. That this meeting urge upon his majestys government the necessity of immediately proroguing and reassembling the parliament, within

[1] Parliament was recalled on 6 December.

seven days, so as to enable them to reintroduce Lord John Russells bill without delay.

4. That a memorial be written to Lord Grey founded on the above resolutions.
5. That the memorial now read be adopted and signed by the gentlemen present.
6. That the memorial be conveyed to Earl Grey tonight by a deputation to consist of one gentleman from each parish.
7. That the thanks of this meeting be given to Mr Thomas Potter for his conduct in the chair.

Adjourned 'till friday at 7 p.m. in the same place.

Joseph Drake Hon. Sec.

As soon as a fair copy of the memorial was made it was handed round for the signatures of the persons present, and they who were to go as a deputation were named. It was then asked at what time the memorial should be presented when Mr Carpue said instantly, this was assented to by acclamation, and the 5th resolution was accordingly passed.

The moment the resolution was passed two gentlemen who had been seated against the wall behind the chairman, in the darkest part of the room and before whom others had been standing rose and with Mr Merle left the room. I had no doubt then, I have had none since, that the two gentlemen were there from the Treasury, and that they with Mr Merle went to Earl Grey and informed him of all the particulars.

25. [Add. Ms. 27791, ff. 33–5. Preparations for the National Political Union.]

Major Beauclerk and Mr Perry went to his [Sir Francis Burdett's] house and had an interview with him, when he at once with much cordiality agreed to be the Chairman, with the declaration that one of the objects of the union was to support the King and his minister against a small corrupt faction in accomplishing their great measure of Parliamentary Reform.

After the interview with Sir Francis Mr Perry came to me and we had a conversation on the objects of the Union, and I recommended a much more general object than merely 'supporting the King and his Ministers', which seemed to be all that Sir Francis desired to have done. It was necessary that we should make our declaration such an one as would induce the better sort of the working people to join us. There were two very substantial reasons for this. 1 to induce them by joining the union to prevent them being mislead [*sic*] by some, a very few persons, of their own class who were brawlers for what they called the rights of the working man, whose object was to keep them detached from every other class and to hold them in readiness to commit any mischief, should an opportunity offer. 2 we were very desirous that those among the working people who were discreet orderly well informed men should be associated as closely with us, and such as us, as a step towards leading the two classes to a better understanding and diminishing the animosity which prevailed among the working people against those who were not compelled to work with their hands for wages and 3 to hold up the example for imitation to other persons not only in London but in every town where a union might be established. After having finally settled what ought to be done, I consented to go to Sir Francis and talk the matter over with him.

On the 26 [October] I saw Sir Francis and explained our views to him minutely, he concurred in them. I then went to Mr Perry and we put the matter in writing, this Major Beauclerk and Mr Perry took to Sir Francis, he agreed to it, and that it should form part of the proceedings at the meeting to be held to form the union, and he suggested that it should be held on the monday following. This was agreed to.

26. [Add. Ms. 27791, ff. 307–9]

On the 24 [October] the usual weekly meeting of the Rotunda was held. The leaders had now acquired as they thought a great addition of power and to some extent the belief was correct, but they knew neither how to use it, or to cherish it so as to increase it. The proceedings at this meeting afforded proofs of the opinion they entertained that the time was come when the people might proceed from words to actions. It will be seen that there was considerable dexterity shewn on this as there had been on other occasions to avoid an open declaration of the intention of those who meditated mischief, as well as of those whose persuasion it was that a general insurrection of the working people could be obtained, and that it would be the means of establishing an equality of property, the only state of society as these men imagined in which there could be peace and happiness. Each of these parties were equally reprehensible for their conduct, since could they have succeeded the result in either case would be the same, the same horrible mischief be perpetrated, the same miserable results be produced.

The proceedings are thus reported in the Poor Mans Guardian [Here follows a newspaper cutting.]

Last Monday night, an adjourned meeting of the National Union of the Working Classes took place at the Great Theatre of the Rotunda, Blackfriars Road. The meeting was numerously attended; and there were many new members who paid their admission.

Mr. BENBOW was called to the Chair . . . .

Mr. Watson said, that in proposing the first resolution he felt a little embarrassed, in consequence of being so often obliged to throw himself on their indulgences. (Hear, hear.) He then read the following resolution:—
'That this meeting is of opinion, that unless the Working Classes be alive to their best interest, and enroll themselves in Political Unions throughout the country, and seriously resolve to put forth their opinions in a manner not to be mistaken, that they will be again duped and deceived, as they have often been, and remain the oppressed and degraded victims of the present corrupt system.'
Mr. Watson proceeded to observe, that unless they were organized they would be again duped. He considered it a disgrace upon civilized man to be any longer oppressed by Lords and Bishops, and that that class of persons dreaded nothing so much as a union of the people; because they were

aware, that if the people were but once united, their fate was sealed for ever; and he would ask, How could a manifestation of their union be known, but by an exhibition of their strength? (Cheers.) It was idle to expect justice could be obtained from Lords and Bishops, although events have proved, and that recently, that it may be extorted by their fears. They no doubt, at the present juncture of affairs, may attempt to intimidate the people; but he would maintain that it was legal for the people at present to meet in the open air. He however would not recommend force of any kind, for that was a nullity—at the same time he could not banish from his views or his man-hood the idea of an armed force assuming a dictatorial language to a united people. (Cheers.) The Whigs rang the alarm bell, and brought in a Reform Bill, which was scouted by the Lords: but for a moment suppose the people were united, and prepared a Bill themselves, for universal freedom to all, and went in a body with it to Parliament, 'who,' he would ask, dare refuse it? He begged to be distinctly understood to mean that he did not use such language in the shape of intimidation; on the contrary, he was merely going to suggest, and to prove the necessity of a field meeting, as in his mind that would be the best test of principle, as well as the only criterion to judge of their public virtue and courage. The country was anxiously looking for an example from the capital, and in that respect he would refer them to the organized parties in France, who turned out and raised the siege of Paris. (Cheers.). . . He concluded by giving it as his opinion, that in less than one month there would be in the city at least 100,000 members attached to the Union. (Great cheering.) . . .

Mr. Cleave, after an appropriate explanation, read the following Address:—

'To the National Union.

'We, your Committee, hereby inform you that, in order that this Society may be a real Union, and not a mere chaos, we propose,

'1st. That you should appoint class leaders for the different districts of the metropolis and its vicinity.

'2nd. That there should be on an average 25 members to each class, so that there may be 40 class leaders to 1000 members.

'3rd. That every member should call, or leave his name at the residence of his class leader, once a-week, or the class leader on the members, if more convenient.

'4th. That the list of class leaders be read over in the first general meeting of the Union, every month, and that each class leader be then either con-tinued or changed, according to the will of the meeting.

'5th. That each class leader shall keep a list of the names and residences of the different individuals who leave their names with him, and that he shall receive their monthly subscription and send it to the secretary.

'6th. That the services of the class leaders be perfectly gratuitous.

'7th. That the class leaders constitute a committee, which shall meet once every week at such time and place as shall be deemed most convenient.

'8th. That all the branches of the Union, who adopt the resolutions sub-mitted to them by this committee, be requested to send class leaders to this meeting, at the rate of one person to 25 members, on Friday evening, November 4, at eight o' clock. . . .

50

Mr. Osborne said that in consequence of the declaration[1] then read, and which met with such approbation, he would propose the following resolution, which he read.

'That a Public Meeting of the useful classes of London be held on the open space in front of White Conduct [sic] House, on Monday, November 7th, at One o' clock precisely, for the purpose of expressing their political opinions at this important crisis, of making known to the government and the country their wants and greivances [sic], and for solemnly ratifying a declaration of their principles.'

He was quite satisfied the North of England would instantly join us and than an irresistable force would be formed, and if the plan of organization was to be so acted on, there would be no necessity for friendly and benefit societies, for all would merge into a national society. He highly approved of the plan of placing twenty-five members under one class leader, and hoped that on the day of the grand meeting such a moral force would be displayed, as would convice their task masters that they could not any longer withhold from them their just rights. (Great cheering.)

The resolution being seconded was carried unanimously. . . .

Mr. Cleave then observed that in moving the adoption of the next resolution he did not look for or expect any other kind of victory except a legislative one, and read the resolution as follows:—

'That as our object is just, we wish our proceedings to be peaceably conducted; and, therefore, earnestly impress on every working man to conduct himself with order and propriety, and to consider himself a special constable for that day, for the purpose of enforcing peace from others, if necessary.'. . .

27. [Add. Ms. 27791, ff. 333–5]

The influence of the [National] union [of the Working Classes] had become extensive, and was increasing, it was felt, acknowledged and acted upon in many places, especially in the large manufacturing towns, in Bristol and in the southern and south western parts of England.

The resolutions passed at the weekly meetings of the Union in London, and the speeches made at these meetings being regularly published in the Poor Mans Guardian induced large numbers of the working people in the country to attribute an importance to the union it did not possess.

They were misled by the advertisements in the Guardian of meetings to be held in some part of London on several days in each week, these announcements made people at a distance conclude that the whole body of workmen were confederated together, and this was a powerful inducement to them to form unions in various places.

The leaders of all these unions, with but a few exceptions had suceeded [sic] in persuading themselves that the time was coming when the whole of the working men would be ready to rise en masse and take the management of their own affairs, i.e. the management of the affairs of the nation into their own hands, and efforts were made in various places and in various ways to ascertain their present strength, among these efforts may be reckoned the

[1] See Handbill 2.

51

DECLARATION

OF THE

National Union of the Working Classes.

" Labour is the source of Wealth."
" That Commonwealth is best ordered where the Citizens are neither
too Rich nor too Poor."   THALIS.

AT this moment of great Political Excitement, it is alike the interest, as well as the duty, of every Working Man, to declare publicly his Political Sentiments, in order that the Country and Government may be generally acquainted with the Wants and Grievances of this particular Class—in accordance with which we, *the Working Classes of London*, declare :—

First.—All Property, honestly acquired, to be sacred and inviolable.

Secondly.—THAT ALL MEN ARE BORN EQUALLY FREE ! ! ! and have certain natural, inherent, and unalienable Rights.

Thirdly.—That all governments ought to be founded on those Rights; and all Laws instituted for the *common* benefit, protection, and security of *all the People ;* and not for the particular emolument or advantage of any single man, family, or set of men.

Fourthly.—That all Hereditary Distinctions of Birth are unnatural, and opposed to the EQUAL RIGHTS OF MAN, and therefore ought to be abolished.

Fifthly.—That every man of the age of Twenty-one Years, of sound mind, and not tainted by crime, has a Right, either by himself, or his representative, to a Free Voice in determining the necessity of Public Contributions, the Appropriation of them, their Amount, Mode of Assessment, and Duration.

Sixthly.—That in order to secure the unbiassed choice of proper Persons for Representatives, the mode of voting should be by *Ballot*—that Intellectual Fitness and Moral Worth, and *not Property*, should be the qualification for Representatives, and that the duration of Parliaments should be but for *one year.*

Seventhly.—We declare these principles to be essential to our protection as *Working Men*—and the only sure Guarantees for securing to us the proceeds of our labour—and that we will never be satisfied with the enactment of any LAW or LAWS that do not recognize the Rights we have enumerated in this Declaration.

In order to ascertain the opinion of the Working Classes throughout the
United Kingdom, as well as all those who think with them, we hereby call

A PUBLIC MEETING

of the Useful Classes of London, to be held on the Space in Front of White
Conduit House, on MONDAY, November the 7th.
THOMAS WAKLEY, Esq. Editor of " The Ballot," will take the
Chair, at One o'clock precisely. For the purpose of Ratifying this Decla-
ration, and of passing Resolutions connected with the present state of affairs.
We, therefore, particularly press upon our Fellow-Labourers, in all parts
of the Kingdom, to re-echo these Principles on the same Day, in Public
Meetings throughout the Country.   Signed, J. WATSON, Chairman.
J. OSBORNE, Secretary.

Letters addressed (post paid) to the Committee at the Commercial Coffeehouse, Temple Bar, punctually attended to.

HANDBILL 2 Add. Ms. 27791, f. 50.

intended meeting in White Conduit fields, as well as the 'holiday' to which reference had been frequently made by Benbow at the meetings of the Union in London . . .

Much art was employed by those among the leaders in London who had purposes of their own to accomplish. They were compelled in words to pretend that persons and property were to be secure, while the whole tenor of what they said and what they did shewed that the true meaning of their words and actions was that the working people should seize and divide among them the whole wealth in the Kingdom.

That this was clearly understood by the members of all the unions of the working classes is sufficiently shewn by their proceedings. The same doctrine was admitted as sound by all, and sufficiently declared by the two lines.

> That we who work to make the goods,
> Should justly have them all.

Another persuasion was as generally prevalent, namely that they would probably have to fight the way to *their* possessions, of the result of which no doubt was entertained, by the leaders, and especially by the leaders in the country, by a great majority of the most active men of the union in London, by the members of the union generally and by the large number who were occasional attendants at their public meetings, yet no one had as yet shewn how they were to proceed.

There were, at this time, several delegates from Manchester, and some from other places in London. Most of these came to me and I conversed with them. So thoroughly satisfied were these men that in a very few months 'the people would rise and do themselves justice', that when I expressed my doubts, they became irritated, and on being pushed to extremities, they threw aside all disguise and declared their conviction that within a few months there would be a simultaneous rising of the whole working population, and then the proud tyrants who oppressed them and kept them out of their just rights would be taught a lesson, such a lesson as none before had ever been taught. They admitted it was probable that large numbers of their fellows would be slain in the contest which might, and probably would take place. A great many they said might perhaps be '*murdered*', but numbers would prevail and then ample revenge would be taken. They talked of the men they would lose as a matter of very small importance, a trifling sacrifice to obtain a great good, they said it would be of no importance to the great body, they would not be missed, and might as well be killed in so righteous a cause, as linger on in a life of privation and misery. I should be convinced by the circumstances which would take place that what they said was true. I need only wait until a commencement was made the result of which was certain.

28. [Add. Ms. 27791, ff. 47–57. Meeting to form the National Political Union.]

31 October

The whole of the proceedings of this day were remarkable and singularly perplexing. The meeting which preceded the public meeting was very extraordinary. The room in which the persons who were conducting the business was on the ground floor of the Crown and Anchor Tavern, it was about twenty five feet long and about twelve broad, before eleven o clock it was crowded almost to suffocation, the door which is at the bottom of the room and opens into the hall, was blocked up with a crowd of persons vainly endeavouring to gain admittance.

There was a strong muster of the men who led the meetings at the Rotunda, some of these men were remarkably ignorant, but fluent speakers, filled with bitter notions of animosity against everybody who did not concur in the absurd notions they entertained, that every thing which was produced belonged to those who by their labour produced it and ought to be shared among them, that there ought to be no accumulation of capital in the hands of any one to enable him to employ others as labourers, and thus by becoming a *master* make slaves of others under the name of workmen; to take from them the produce of their labour, to maintain themselves in idleness and luxury, while their slaves were ground down to the earth or left to starve. They denounced every one who dissented from these notions as a *political economist*, under which appellation was included the notion of a bitter foe to the working classes, enemies who deserved no mercy at their hands. Among these men were some who were perfectly atrocious. Most of these men were loud and long talkers, vehement resolute reckless rascals whose purpose was riot as providing an opportunity for plundering. They had drawn round them a considerable number of others like themselves, who were eager to commit any outrage which circumstances would permit, while by their plausible vehement and continued appeals to large bodies of the working people they had succeeded in persuading a vast number that the absurdities they promulgated were truths. They were now of opinion that the time was come when by a desperate effort they might be able to cause a successful insurrection and so completely had they succeeded in deceiving themselves that they supposed the whole body of the working people were of the same opinion as they were or were so far advanced towards it as to be easily and speedily led to adopt it. They therefore publicly proposed as well by hand bills and small publications as by speeches that the whole body of the working people should on a day to be named cease to labour at any kind of employment for others, and refuse again to be employed for a month. To take whatever they might during that time need from those who had whatever they wanted.

Benbow who at this time kept a coffee shop in Fleet Street near Temple bar had an evening meeting in one of his rooms of the most unprincipled of the persons alluded to, and here they concocted a plan for a public meeting of the working people to be held on the 7 November in an open space in the front of White Conduit House. To this meeting it was openly proposed that every man should come armed to preserve the peace. The weapon they recommended was a stave about twenty inches long of a proportionate thickness the handle of which was made smaller than the other part and was turned in furrows that it might be firmly grasped, a strong string was tied to the end of it to go over the wrist to prevent it being taken away or dropped. It is a formidable weapon, one blow with it would break a mans arm or fracture his skull. I bought one as a curiosity—it cost fourpence.

To pay the expenses of calling the meeting and carrying on of a correspondence with the country, they collected weekly, small subscriptions. For several successive days, and as the bill stickers were induced to side with them their bills were left uncovered while others were covered by the bill stickers according to their rule of permitting a bill to remain only a certain number of hours. Hand bills in vast numbers were distributed and placed in the windows of as many small shop keepers as would thus exhibit them. They had some peculiar facilities to effect this purpose in the men who attended their meetings at the Rotunda in the Surrey Road, living in all parts of the town and passing through it daily in all directions, a great number of whom would distribute the bills, see other working men in work-shops and other places and urge them to attend the meeting. Delegates were sent to every place where there was a meeting of working men for the purpose of inducing them to attend the meeting. One of the most vehement ill-judging of men, Mr Thomas Wakley, proprietor of the Lancet Medical Journal and the Ballot Newspaper was advertised as the chairman.

Wakley was in the room as the leader of the Rotunda men. He is a remarkably good speaker, a tall stout man, with fair hair and a rather florid complexion, he has a round full voice a somewhat low-lived swagger-ing air, a suspicious cast of countenance and would be a formidable fellow were he not as all such men are in most particulars, a coward, one of those who will fight hard and long when screened from danger, but will not fight at all where danger is present. He is physically and morally a coward.

These men came attended by many others to bully the proposers of the meeting and to possess themselves of the power of controlling the proceed-ings. I am a pretty resolute chairman, and know I think how to manage a tumultuous assembly, but it was with extreme difficulty I was able to manage this. A tumult was expected and it had therefore been determined to put me in the chair. I knew however that there were clever resolute men to support the chair, and I therefore resolved to go through the business patiently but resolutely to the end. One purpose of the mischief makers was to compel the chairman to quit the chair, to put Wakley into it, vote their own resolutions and then propose them at the public meeting. They knew well enough however that I was not to be driven away and so far their hopes were defeated.

Their proposition to call a public meeting in the open space opposite to White Conduit House was brought before the meeting by them and argued as the proper course in opposition to the proposed union, which they said was to be governed by aristocrats and shopocracy people for the purpose of keeping the working people in slavery. This was vehemently insisted on and the promoters of the union were stigmatised and condemned in no measured terms. Some check was however placed on several of them by the know-ledge they had of my good wishes for the welfare of the working people and of the exertions I made to serve them. After much time spent in angry debating and vilification I appealed to all the working men who were present, and to all who wished them well to support me not only as the chairman of the meeting, but as their well known friend, to submit and compel others to submit to the order of business in the way I was deter-mined to conduct it and they did so, after much noise and some confusion, I succeeded in compelling the refractory to observe the order of proceeding

I laid down, and something approximating to a regular discussion attended with many interruptions was had. When this had gone on for some time, I took the large posting bill calling the meeting at White Conduit House, and read it slowly to the company. I then said with their permission I would make some remarks upon the most material passages, and with the aid of the company would confine the discussion to these points. This was assented to by shouts and I proceeded to explain the meaning of the words used and the intentions of the parties to the meeting. I told them how the scheme had been concocted and by whom, and what must be the inevitable result if it were held, the rogues were obliged to hear me out, since it was evident, that interruption would cause their forcible expulsion from the room. The consequence of the exposition and anticipation of the consequences of the meeting if it were held induced Mr Wakley to declare that he had been named for the chair and had consented to take it without being aware that it would be so obnoxious to objections as he saw it was and he declared he would not take the chair at the proposed meeting but he would take care that his reasons for withdrawing from it should be well known.

The resolutions for the public meeting about to be held were now discussed. The disappointment occasioned by Mr Wakleys refusal to take the chair was displayed in the most vehement and offensive manner, and in the grossest words, this conduct and these words were equally unavailing and were not much regarded. Finding they could not produce the alteration of any one of the resolutions, nor procure the adoption of their own, they declared that as they were prevented doing one thing it was still in their power to do another thing—namely make a riot—this they were determined to do, and disperse the meeting.

This was said at the last moment when information was brought that Sir Francis Burdett had arrived and had gone up stairs to the committee room. This room was a very large one, it was taken for the use of those who were to manage the business at the public meeting nearly all of whom however had been detained below stairs.

On going to the committee room we found it crammed as the room below had been and Colonel Jones standing on a chair advising the people to retire that arrangements might be made for conducting the business of the meeting. This was just what the disturbers wanted, it afforded them another chance to produce a riot, and ardent and continued were their efforts to produce one. The scene in this room, where no regular chairman had been appointed, was one of intense confusion. Sir Francis Burdett was ill-disposed and intractible, his perverse conduct gave countenance and support to the rioters, the great room was crowded with persons eager to have the business commenced, when one of the rioters who had been in the committee room ascended the orchestre [*sic*] in the great room and told the company that the committee had declared against universal suffrage and the working people that they intended to exclude them from all their rights and aid the middle class to keep them down. That the working people had therefore no interest whatever in the meeting. This caused a prodigious sensation, and a great uproar followed, the noise of which induced many persons to leave the committee room to ascertain the cause, among them was Thomas Murphy who had been advocating the insertion of a resolution

56

that the union would never disperse until it had succeeded in obtaining annual parliaments and universal suffrage, but was not willing to go the length of his associates deliberately to produce a riot. To calm the turmoil he went upon the platform at the top of the room and being well known was attended to. He told the audience that he had just that moment left the committee room and he entreated them to have patience and hear the whole of the proposed resolutions before they came to any decision. He assured them that if they were not such resolutions as were calculated to secure the cause of the people he would not support them.

The large room was filled with people, the committee room was also filled, the passages were being blocked up by people coming in and it was plainly seen the meeting was by far too large to be held in the Tavern, Mr Wakley was therefore requested to go into the large room, state the circumstance and advise the company to proceed to the top of Serle Street in Lincolns Inn Fields—persons were dispatched to procure three waggons, the people proceeded to the spot pointed out, and as soon as it was possible to detach the necessary persons from the wrangle going on in the committee room the persons who were in that room moved off to Lincolns Inn Fields.

A Gentleman, an attorney in Portugal Street, the back of whose house and offices were in Lincolns Inn Fields, was prevailed upon to let us have the use of one of his offices and of the leads above the office, here were placed an arm chair, and a table and here Sir Francis Burdett commenced the business. Here too all the rioters were mingled with the promoters of the meeting and the spectators arranged themselves in front of the office on the ground.

These circumstances gave the rioters great scope for mischief, though they were by then cut off from all chance of making a riot. It was however expected they would propose amendments at variance with the intended resolutions, and that as not more perhaps than half of the people assembled could understand what was addressed to them it was probable that any amendments or new resolutions they proposed would be carried. But Murphy who did not at the moment agree with his co-adjutors, and Wakley who had partly cut them and greatly offended them, were now much feared by them, they apprehended that if they proceeded to extremities they would be opposed by their own two best orators, and could have no hopes of success against them, they as well as some among the managers compromised the matter as well as they could.

29. [Add. Ms. 27791, ff. 66–79]

The conduct of Sir Francis Burdett during the stormy proceedings at the Crown and Anchor Tavern made it doubtful whether or no he would take the Chair, he seemed resolved to have the business confined to one single point, that of an union to assist in promoting the passing of the reform bill, by declaring unbounded confidence in the King and his ministers. This was absurd, it was clear enough from the tone of all the public meetings, and of at least four fifths of all the newspapers that doubts were entertained respecting the intentions of the King and his ministers, doubts were also entertained of their capacity to fill as they ought to do their respective positions amid the expected turbulence, and of their courage to go through the trying times which all now began to see were near at hand. To expect that the people of London should declare unbounded confidence in all respects, or indeed in any one respect in either the king or his ministers was the height of folly—yet Sir Francis could not be made to see this, and he arrogantly demanded that all should succumb to his opinions, ignorant as he was of the actual state of the people, and obstinate as he was in determining not to believe any thing he disliked. His conduct in the chair in Lincolns Inn Fields was still more absurd and particularly offensive to those who were endeavouring to form the Union. To such a length were disagreements pushed by him that it was every minute expected he would abruptly leave the Chair and break up the meeting. The scene on the top of the office where he sat was one of continued confusion, the rioters endeavouring by every means in their power to impede the business and increase the disputing with the chairman. The motion made by William Lovett [that the Union should commit itself to trying to obtain universal suffrage], and the speech with which he introduced it was well calculated in such a meeting to produce the effect intended and it seemed wonderful that it was not adopted. Lovett was a journeyman cabinet maker, a man of a melancholy temperament, soured with the perplexities of the world, he was however an honest hearted man, possessed of great courage and persevering in his conduct, in his usual demeanour he was mild and kind, and entertained kindly feelings towards every one whom he did not sincerely believe was the intentional enemy of the working people, but when either by circumstances or his own morbid associations he felt the sense he was apt to indulge of the evils and wrongs of mankind he was vehement in the extreme. He was half an owenite half an Hodgskinite a thorough beleiver [sic] that accumulation of property in the hands of individuals was *the* cause of *all* the evils which existed. He believed that in endeavouring to procure the adoption of his resolution he was promoting the good of his own class.

John Cleave had become a sailor and was now the keeper of a coffee shop. He was a sturdy little fellow totally devoid of fear and like Lovett ready to undergo any persecution to bear any punishment. He was not however so well informed nor so placid a man as Lovett, he on the contrary was passionate and revengeful, and not at all scrupulous as to the use of any means of accomplishing his purpose the end of which was improving the condition of the working people. His notions were all vague, any change however brought about was in his opinion sure to be useful and this was enough to induce him to labour continually to promote changes.

John Savage at this time a Linen Draper in Crawford Street Mary le bone was an exceedingly ill-disposed malignant ignorant man, in failing circumstances, as fully desirous of producing general confusion as any one of those who have before been mentioned. He was a remarkably shrewd cunning fellow and could talk nonsense in a plausible way by the hour. He saw as he thought the means of dispersing the union and this was the reason he conducted himself in the way described in the newspapers.

Wakley more furious in his manner than either of these persons, more openly impudent, and scarcely better informed, scarcely knew what he was at or why he acted at all—he however saw in the motion he made a chance of being restored to favour with the Rotunda men whom he knew he had greatly offended by refusing to take the chair at the proposed meeting at White Conduit House. His conduct was essentially mischievous. Instead of approximating, as an honest man would have done to a better understanding between the working and middle classes they took the utmost possible pains to increase and perpetuate the animosities existing between them. In these particulars the conduct of most of the self appointed leaders of the union of the working classes was atrocious. It alarmed and disgusted every one but themselves. The proposed meeting at White Conduit House was for the purpose of ascertaining how far they could rely upon the mob for mischief and this they took no pains to conceal. Their small publications recommending abstinence from all sorts of labour for a month for the purpose of ruining the classes above them, and the open determination they expressed to live during the time on plunder, had made even persons who were well disposed towards the working people averse from having any sort of intercourse with them, this Wakley knew and he like a rogue as he was did his best to keep up the ill will between these classes of people.

There was great exultation when the resolution to appoint working men in equal *or greater numbers* than others on the council. They believed that this determination would drive away all the '*shopocracy*', that the management would fall into their hands, and they were in an excess of delight in having as they said completely beaten the aristocrats who were getting up an union to keep them down. It appeared pretty certain at the moment that it would not be possible under these circumstances to form an extensive union. This appeared to be the opinion of all those with whom I had been acting, we feared that an end had been put to the amalgamation in the union of those who were not working men with those who were working men. It had this effect to a much lamentable extent. It was however saved from immediate ruin by the extraordinary energy of my associates and the business-like way in which we proceeded.

While the vote of thanks which was not at all merited by the Chairman was being proposed I left the meeting and went to the Crown and Anchor Tavern expecting to be immediately followed by some of the exulting rioters and some of my own associates. Here I remained alone until I concluded no one would come and then I went home. Scarcely had I left the house however when a number of my friends and some few of the rioters came to the tavern, and immediately proceeded to business.

It was moved by Mr Roebuck and seconded by Major Beauclerk that a general meeting of the *members*—of the National Union be called for Wednesday week. This was carried unanimously.

It was moved by Mr Roebuck and seconded by Mr Charles Fox Smith that a select committee be appointed to carry the preceeding resolution into effect, and to devise plans for the election of the council. This was also carried unanimously. The following persons were appointed

Place	Murphy	To these five more were
Perry	Fox Rev'd	afterwards added making in
Beauclerk	Roebuck	the whole thirteen.
Wakley	Lovett	

Some of those who were put upon the committee were particularly obnoxious, but it was impossible to proceed without them and it was therefore determined to put as many of them on the committee as chose to go on and to fight them out.

There had been a large enrolment of members at the Tavern in the course of the day, and altho' nearly all of those who took tickets, took them only for one quarter and paid a shilling each—the sum received amounted to £23 9/-.

November 1st

I and my friends were early at the Tavern and remained there all day and until late at night. Between three and four hundred more entered their names as members, whenever any respectable working man took a ticket he was asked questions for the purpose of ascertaining if he were a Rotundanist and upon finding that he was not he was invited into the committee room, questioned as to his political notions, and requested to give the name or names and references to the character of any man or men whom he knew in his trade who was a sober discreet clever man, and many such men were designated. Almost every man who was invited into the committee room appeared to understand the men who managed at the Rotunda, disliked them much, and were willing to aid us as well as they could to promote the election of such working men for the council as were honest sensible well intentioned men having the confidence of their fellow workmen. Many of our coadjutors came in and as no time was to be lost; and no one in our circumstances was to be either idle or to regard the consumption of his own time, each of them was dispatched to see the workmen who had been named to us, enquire their characters of their employers and their neighbours and then to invite them to join the union with a view to their being elected on the council. The bill 'this is not an union' etc. and copies of all our publicacations were given to these men; as they were to every one who became a member, and in a few days we had a sufficient number of such men for the council, and the certainty that their fellow workmen would vote for them.

They who were constant attendants at the Rotunda and other such meetings were much more desirous of having nonsense talked to them for a penny a week or for nothing than to work for the good of others and to pay a shilling to put them into a position to do so, kept away from the union, and we saw very clearly that the mischief makers had no chance to become members of the council in any considerable number. We saw plainly enough that Wakleys resolution had produced the anticipated consequences, as a comparative few who were not working men joined us, and some of those who were not working men left us, still we hoped that if we could succeed in procuring a really respectable council we should be able to induce a large number of such persons to join us, and we were not mistaken.

The sum received this day at the Tavern for tickets was £18 15 9.

November 2

Mr Perry and others were at the committee room all day energetically systematically and successfully carrying on the business. Numbers of useful co-adjutors attended part of the day and went about on various necessary occasions.

The committee which had been summoned met in the evening, there were present.

Mr Place in the Chair.

Messrs Perry	A. Beauclerk	
Roebuck	T. Murphy	
Rogers	Lovett	
Franks	Wakley	
Fox	Cleave	— 12
C. Fox Smith		

There were also present of our especial friends.

Messrs Bowyer	Thos. Place
Longford	Harrison S.
Hickson	Wakefield D.
Rosser	Wakefield W.
Rennie	Ellis Wm.
Detrosier	

The meeting as had been anticipated was exceedingly turbulent almost a riot. The abuse ill humour and bad language used roused Roebuck and he attacked the Rotunda gentlemen who were present and absent who were represent[ed] by Lovett Wakley and Cleave, Cleave had been the most indiscreet and abusive, and on him Roebuck fastened. He used no ceremony but unmasked the Rotunda men completely; called them and their proceedings by their right names challenged them to do their worst, told them the working people were much too wise to be led by them and much too honest to be used by them for villainous purposes, that none of them would be elected to the council, and that unless they conducted them with becoming decency they would be treated as they deserved. The room was crowded to excess no one being refused admittance. The violence and virulence of those of the rotunda men who being members of the committee were allowed to make speeches had disgusted the spectators while we had succeeded in convincing the better sort of people who were present that we, not they, were really their friends. The rioters were not men to be subdued but they were overpowered and left in a condition no longer to do us any further mischief.

The business was now again in our hands the rioters were disregarded, disgraced in the opinion of all but themselves and gave us very little trouble.

From this time for some consequtive [sic] days several of us attended at the committee room all day long, and many of our best friends gave us whatever time they could spare, every thing went on satisfactorily, we had many good men to assist us as well in the room as in going about the necessary business out of doors. Nothing, which appeared likely, however remotely to assist us, was neglected, every thing that could be done was done and well done.

Great numbers of our printed papers were distributed.[1] The town was placarded daily, shops were supplied with bills for their windows and they

[1] See Handbills 3 and 4.

NATIONAL POLITICAL UNION.

DECLARATION OF OBJECTS.

1.—To obtain a full, free, and effectual, Representation of the People in the Commons House of Parliament.

2.—To support the King and his Ministers against a corrupt Faction, in accomplishing their great measure of Parliamentary Reform.

3.—To watch over and promote the Interests, and to better the Condition of the INDUSTRIOUS and WORKING CLASSES.

4.—To obtain the Abolition of all Taxes on Knowledge, and to assist in the diffusion of sound moral and political information.

5.—To join every wellwisher to his Country, from the richest to the poorest, in the pursuit of these important objects.

6.—To preserve Peace and Order in the Country, and to guard against any convulsion, which the Enemies of the People may endeavour to bring about.

RULES AND REGULATIONS.

1.—ALL persons whatsoever are admitted as Members of this Association, who shall cause their names to be entered in books prepared for the purpose, and shall conform to the following Rules and Regulations.

2.—All persons becoming Members of this Union shall subscribe One Shilling, quarterly ; and are requested to make such further donation, or annual or quarterly subscription as they can conveniently afford.

3.—All Members shall strictly observe the just and legal directions of the officers of the Union, to whom the management of its affairs shall be committed.

4.—The general management of the Union is committed to a Council of Seventy-two individuals, to be chosen annually at a General Meeting; and subject only to the control of such Annual or other General Meeting.

5.—The General Meetings choose annually three Auditors for the year ensuing, to pass the accounts of the Council.

6.—The General Meetings choose a Treasurer and Trustees, in whose hands the funds of the Association are deposited.

7.—An Annual General Meeting of the Members of the Union, is held on the first Thursday in the month of February.

8.—General Meetings may at any time be called together, by an order signed by the Chairman or Deputy Chairman, countersigned by the Secretary ; or by an order signed by fifteen of the Members of Council ; or by a requisition signed by 200 Members of the Union. The order or requisition for such Meeting to be advertized in three London Newspapers.

9.—At the Annual General Meeting, the Council, Auditors, Treasurer and Trustees, are chosen. The name of each individual to be proposed for office, must be sent in to the Council, fourteen days before the Annual Meeting ; balloting lists will then be prepared, and delivered to the Members, on application, three days previous to the Annual Meeting. The Scrutineers will be appointed by the Meeting.

10.—At the General Meetings, the Secretary shall produce the books for inspection ; and in the whole conduct of the Union, every species of concealment or mystery is to be carefully avoided.

11.—The Council (of whom fifteen form a quorum) meets weekly, or as often as it may deem necessary, keeping a record of the proceedings at each Meeting.

12.—The Council appoints a Chairman, Deputy Chairman, Secretary, Collectors of Contributions, and such other Officers, either with or without salaries, as may be found expedient.

13.—The Council appoints a Solicitor, and Legal Adviser to the Union, if occasion require.

14.—The Council shall watch closely the proceedings of the Legislature, shall call General Meetings, when necessary, present Addresses and Petitions to the Crown, and the Legislature, when the interests of the People are at stake, and generally use every exertion in furthering the objects of the Union.

15.—The Council employs the funds of the Association solely in promoting its objects, according to their best judgment and discretion.

16.—The Treasurer shall pay money only to orders passed by the Council, and countersigned by the Secretary.

17.—Alterations in the Laws must receive the sanction of two successive General Meetings.

POPLETT, Printer, 23, Milton Street.

HANDBILL 3 Add. Ms. 27790, f. 32.

NATIONAL

*Bill written by Mr
Parry on the 31. October
printed on the 1. Nov.*

Political Union.

THIS is not a Union of the Working Classes, nor of the Middle Classes, nor of any other Class, but of all Reformers, of the masses and of the millions.

The *National Political Union*, is essentially a Union of the People, and is the first instance on record of the Nation breaking through the trammels of class, to associate for the Common interest in a Common cause.

The first blessing of Reform therefore is already produced; among those who struggle for it, a brotherhood is established, and recurrence made to a manlier and more generous intercourse between the Rich and the Poor.

If the People associate, the interests of the People must inevitably prosper: With the Reform Bill, which 199 Lords and Bishops have rejected, and with the preservation of peace and order, are the interests of the People bound up. If then the People associate, the Reform Bill, and all its happy consequences, cannot be denied them, nor can peace and order be infringed.

In Birmingham and London, Political Unions are possible as well as necessary, because intelligence has become diffused in spite of the old Tory Governments that laid every species of Tax upon knowledge—but in Nottingham and Bristol the effects of *"happy ignorance"* are exhibited, and those who sowed the storm have reaped the whirlwind.

Whoever then is for Reform! for Reform, without Bristol Riots! for Reform, with all its benefits peacefully and therefore *certainly* attained! for Reform, in a word, with the People's House of Commons! let him enroll his name at the *Crown and Anchor Tavern, Strand*, in the *National Political Union.*

Sir FRANCIS BURDETT, Bart. M. P.
CHAIRMAN.

R. HEWARD, Prov. Sec.

Barnes, Printer, 44, Bridge-house Place, Newington Causeway.

HANDBILL 4 Add. Ms. 27791, f. 46.

were stuck up in public houses. The business was laborious but it was perfectly regular. Deputations were sent to several places to promote and to open Unions, I knew the law relating to political societies, but I had no doubt we might for a long time disregard it, and it was violated by the persons who went from the union to other societies but I took especial care that there should be no violation of the law by any authorised correspondence. As the business of opening Unions increased it became necessary for us to be more cautious. I therefore expounded the law and shewed that as it related to communications between societies when formed it had no relation to those meetings which were intended as preliminary to the formation of societies. They who went as deputies to promote unions were therefore instructed to go on vigorously until the moment the union was about to be formed and then to withdraw, the business was adroitly managed and all the speaking excepting *agreeing* to the articles for governing the union was gone through before it was actually formed. The leaders of every such union were made acquainted with the law and instructed how to proceed.

30. [Add. Ms. 27791, f. 25]

The Union was fully formed and the unusual if not unparallelled [*sic*] energy and activity of its conductors, with the eagerness of the people to join it changed the whole aspect of affairs. The impulse was felt and responded to all over the Kingdom, projects of unions appeared in immense numbers.[1] The formation of the National Political Union at this moment was of all but inappreciable importance.

31. [Add. Ms. 27791, ff. 94–5]

At a meeting held at Benbows house in the evening of the 9th November (This was a meeting of the committee of the Union of the Working Classes), the Commercial Coffee House, Fleet Street. A Mr Petrie one of the active Rotunda leaders, proposed a plan to drill the people in some way of his own so as to make them equal if not superior to the best disciplined troops. This motion was discountenanced by the Chairman Wm Lovett and was dropped.

Benbow moved. 'That the *Whig Union* of which Sir F. Burdett was at the head, was a jesuistical attempt of the committee of the National Union to cajole the working classes to employ their moral and physical force in support of the whig reform bill, and that no union deserved or ought to receive the support of the working people which did [not?] declare its purpose to be the obtainment of Annual Parliaments and Universal Suffrage.'

The Morning Chronicle which contains an account of this meeting reports.

That the chairman joined with Mr Watkins Mr Cleave and others in deprecating the introduction of the resolution on the ground that the union at the Crown and Anchor had not yet assumed any character and that it could not be

[1] See Handbill 5.

At a **MEETING**, held at *Prockter's Hotel*, Bridge Road, Lambeth, on Wednesday, the 16th of November, 1831, of a few Friends favourable to Reform in the Commons House of Parliament, it was deemed adviseable to form a *Union*, to be called the

Lambeth Reform Union.

The following Resolutions, Rules and Regulations were unanimously agreed to:—

1.—That it is highly expedient, at the present important crisis, that the real Friends of Reform, resident in *Lambeth*, should form themselves into an Amicable Union, for the purpose of affording every loyal and constitutional support to our most Gracious and Patriotic KING and his present MINISTERS, in carrying into a Law the Measure of Reform, to which the latter stand pledged to the country, and which has been approved of by the former.

2.—That it be recommended, that the intended Union be confined to the support of his Majesty and his Ministers in carrying into complete effect the intended measure of Reform.

3.—That, for the purpose of carrying such Union into effect, a Meeting will be held at the *Horns Tavern*, *Kennington*, on *Wednesday*, the 23d day of November instant, at Six o'Clock in the Afternoon (exact time), at which the Inhabitants of this Parish, who are Friends to the measure, are earnestly invited to attend; and it was proposed and agreed, that it be recommended that such Union be founded upon the above and following principles, and be governed by Rules and Regulations to the following effect, viz.:—

Principles.

1.—To obtain a full, free, and effectual Representation of the People in the Commons House of Parliament.

2.—To support the King and his Ministers against a corrupt Faction, in accomplishing their great measure of Parliamentary Reform.

3.—To join every well-wisher to his country, from the richest to the poorest, in this Parish, in the pursuit of such important object.

4.—To preserve peace and order in the Parish, and to guard against any convulsion which the Enemies of the People may endeavour to bring about.

5.—To give opportunities, by frequent public discussion, for eliciting the best means by which the above objects may be carried into execution.

Rules and Regulations.

1. All Persons whatsoever are admitted Members of this Association who shall cause their Names to be entered in Books appointed for the purpose, and shall conform to the following Rules and Regulations:—

2.—All Persons becoming Members of this Union shall subscribe One Shilling Quarterly, and such further Donations as they can afford.

3.—All Members shall strictly observe the just and legal directions of the Officers of the Association, to whom the management of its affairs shall be committed; and the affairs of the Union shall be conducted by a Committee of Twenty-one Members, to be chosen at a General Meeting, and subject only to the control of a General Meeting.

4.—The General Meeting to choose a Treasurer, in whose hands the Funds of the Association are to be deposited.

5.—General Meetings may at any time be called together by an Order, signed by the Chairman, countersigned by the Secretary, or by an Order signed by Six of the Members of the Committee, or by a Requisition signed by Twenty-five Members of the Union, and all questions to be decided by a majority, in the usual way.

6.—At the General Meetings the Secretary shall produce the Books for inspection; and in the whole conduct of the Union every species of concealment or mystery is to be avoided.

7.—The Committee, of whom Five are to form a Quorum shall meet Weekly, or as often as it may be deemed necessary, keeping a record of the proceedings at each Meeting.

8.—The Committee to appoint a Chairman, Secretary, and such other Officers as may be found expedient.

9.—The Committee shall watch closely the proceedings of the Legislature; shall call General Meetings when necessary; present Addresses and Petitions to the Crown and the Legislature, and, generally, shall use every exertion in furthering the object of the Union.

10.—The Committee shall employ the Funds of the Association solely in promoting its objects, according to their best judgment and discretion.

11.—The Treasurer shall pay Money only to Orders passed by the Committee, and countersigned by the Secretary.

JOHN MOORE, Esq. Chairman.
H. SAUNDERS, Esq. Hon. Sec. pro tem.

J. KNIGHT, Printer, 17, Gibson Street, Waterloo Road.

HANDBILL 5 Place Collection, set 63, vol. ii, f. 68.

known what its principles were to be until its rules and regulations were drawn up and agreed to at a public meeting of the members. It could not be said that the gentlemen had determined what the character of the union should be as they had left it to a general meeting of the members to be held tomorrow evening, (Thursday) to appoint a committee which should within a month from that day propose to another public meeting rules and regulations for the government of the Union. It was also to be borne in mind that there were to be 36 working men upon the committee, and the members of the Union of the working classes ought to go to the meeting tomorrow night and support the appointment of such men as would make the principles of the National Union their principles and its objects their objects (hear hear).

Major Beauclerk and other gentlemen had already declared that they would not accept the Whig Bill as a final measure (hear) and it was on that account that Mr Barber Beaumont and others were attempting to get up unions pledged to ask nothing beyond the bill for the purpose of cutting up the National Union.

Benbow withdrew his motion with the intention of submitting it to the next meeting of delegates.

32. [Add. Ms. 27790, ff. 242–3]

. . . [There] was issued another proclamation against 'Political Unions composed of separate bodies with various divisions and subdivisions under leaders with a gradation of ranks and authority,' etc. it then alludes specifically to the plan of the Birmingham Union in assuming to constitute themselves a municipal corporation,—and declares all such illegal.

Advantage was taken of this proclamation by the Tory papers to alarm the members of the various unions, some of which but not in considerable numbers abstained from attending the meetings, others were intimidated and prevented becoming members, and two or three unions consisting of very few persons dessolved [*sic*] their association and dispersed, among these was a very paltry one which had assumed the title of the Westminster Union, and was to consist of none but *respectable* persons. The National Political Union had previously published an abstract of the laws relating to political associations,[1] it was printed as a hand bill sent to every union known to the National Union, and freely dispersed in every direction. In the evening of the 22nd, four members of the Council of the Union having met together caused the following advertisement to be inserted in most of the London daily papers.

National Political Union
Royal Proclamation

To the editor etc.

Sir in consequence of the mis-statements of some of the evening newspapers upon the subject of the Proclamation relating to Political Unions, and the strong excitement it has occasioned. We as members of the Council think it necessary to state that the Proclamation *does not* apply to the National Political Union nor to the great majority of the Unions now in existence. The Proclamation is in fact, little more than a copy of the 'Laws relating to Political

[1] See Handbill 6.

National Political Union.

Law relating to Political Associations.

The Tories, during their half century of misrule, have heaped statute upon statute to prevent associations of the people. The acts which apply to Political Unions are the 39th Geo. III. c. 79, and the 57th Geo. III. c. 19. It will be seen by the following statement, that Tory Malevolence and Tory Lawyer-craft have been unable to prevent the formation of political associations at the present crisis.

The act 39 Geo. III. prohibited all sorts of correspondence and intercourse between societies whose proceedings were secret; and it also prohibited the appointment of delegates or other officers in all such societies; and it further declared that every such society was an illegal combination and confederacy, and that every member of such society, and every person not a member who held intercourse with such society, was amenable to the punishments mentioned in the act.

It did the same in respect to every political society which had any divisions or branches.

It did not prohibit societies which had no secret proceedings, divisions or branches, from holding correspondence with other such societies.

It did not prohibit the appointment of delegates, nor meetings of such delegates.

It was therefore lawful for any society which had no secret proceedings to correspond in any way it pleased with other societies; and to appoint delegates to meet and transact business with the delegates of other societies.

But during the administration of Lord Castlereagh, the liberties of the people, which had been very much abridged during the administration of Mr. Pitt, were thought to be still too great, and it was concluded that the more the intelligence and consequent good conduct of the people increased, the greater was the necessity to destroy their ' rights and liberties,' and an act was therefore passed with this intention, subjecting all political societies to the penalties of the act 39 Geo. III.

No political society can therefore hold correspondence or intercourse with any other such society, nor appoint delegates to confer with one another on any matter relating to the society.

These acts, disgraceful as they are to the legislature and to the nation, do not however prohibit any Union from recommending the establishment of other Unions. They do not prohibit any Union from sending instructions to any body of persons for the formation of other Unions.

They do not prohibit any Union from appointing delegates to meet persons desirous of forming unions, and assisting to conduct their proceedings *to the moment the Union is formed*, but all such interference must cease before such Union is declared to be in existence.

They do not prohibit any one from being a member of as many Unions as he pleases.

They do not prohibit any one from being a member of the councils of as many Unions as he pleases.

They do not prohibit any one from saying in any Union, or in the council of any Union, anything he pleases, as a member of the council or Union he is addressing, provided he is not, and does not take upon himself the character of a delegate.

Thus every man may see, what he may and what he may not do under these new-fangled laws, which his father or grandfather would have declared, the people of Great Britain never would submit to.

Barnes, Printer, 44, Bridge-house Place, Newington Causeway.

HANDBILL 6 Add. Ms. 27791, f. 173.

Associations'—put forth some days ago by this Union and now in the hands of the members.

	signed	H.B. Churchill
		R.H. Franks
Crown & Anchor Tavern		Matt.Powell
Nov.22 1831		E.H. Redman

33. [Add. Ms. 27791, f. 184. Council as at general meeting on 1 December 1831. *Printed.*]

NATIONAL POLITICAL UNION

Allen, Thos, 1 Penton-pl. Pentonville
Beauclerk, Major, 12, Chester-street
Buckle, John, Paper-buildings, Temple
Bowyer, Thomas, 32, Myddleton-street
Barratt, George, Winchester-street
Bennett, John, 23, Museum-street
Carrick, Jas. 44, King-st. Long Acre
Collinson, John, New Cut, Lambeth
Cumming, William, London Wall
Churchill, H.B., Temple
Coode, George, Union-row, Newington
Cramphorne, R., 50 Brewer-st. Somers Town
Cheeseman, Richard, 49, Gt Dover-st.
Drake, Joseph, 100, Edgeware-road
Draycott, F., 27, Duke-st., Bloomsbury
Elphinstone, Howard, Eaton-place, Grosvenor-place
Franks, Robert, Red-cross-street
Fox, Rev. W.J., Upper Clapton
Galloway, Alex., West-st., Smithfield
Gowan, Capt., Upper Baker-street
Harrison, Samuel, 23, Gt. Ormond-st.
Harrison, S.B., Temple
Hall, Thos., 7, Royal-street, Lambeth
Holmes, Thos., 1, Cross-st., Carnaby Market
Howell, Henry, 4, Argyle-street
Hall, Charles, 3, Archer-st., St. James's
Hickson, W.E., 20, West Smithfield
Hankin, H.B., 2, Catherine-st., Vauxhall
Knapp, George, College-hill, Vintry
Lawrence, Wm. 20, Pitfield-st., Hoxton
Lillingstone, Daniel, 94, Cheapside
Longmate, James, 7, Theobald's-road
Lane, W., 5, Bateman's-buildings, Soho
Lockett, Ed., 29, Isabella-st. Lambeth
Lovett, Wm. 19, Greville-st., Hatton Garden
Manwaring, Wm. Lambeth Marsh Gate
Machin, George, 76, Leadenhall-street

Murphy, Thos. 1, Commercial-place, Hampstead-road
Menteath, C.G.S. 34, Keppel-street
Mordan, Sampson, 22, Castle-street, Finsbury
Mongredien, A., George-st. Euston-sq.
MacDiarmid, Wm. 17, New-street-sq.
Millard, Wm. 19, Greville-street
Place, Francis, 16, Charing Cross
Perry, Erskine, Clairville, Old Brompton
Powell, J.H., 26, Chapel-st. Pentonville
Palmer, Rt. 9, Fountain-court, Strand
Pain, Jas., 29, Union-row, New Kent-rd.
Rogers, G., 58, High-st., Bloomsbury
Rigge, Jn. Bartholomew-pl. St Luke's
Revell, Major, Burton-crescent
Rainford, Ed., 12, Red Lion-passage
Rutt, John T., Newington-green
Redman, D.W., 14, Little Charlotte-st.
Reynolds, W. 44, Cheapside
Smith, Charles Fox, Stone's End
Saull, W.D., 15, Aldersgate-street
Shirley, John, 22, Castle-st., Finsbury
Stevenson, George, 39, Old Change
Stiles, Joseph, 20, Marsham-street, Westminster
Taylor, John, 4, Christopher-street, Finsbury-square
Thompson, Col. J.P. [*sic*], 14, Hampstead-road.
Thomas, Cartwright, 49, Broad-street
Turner, John, 24, Brook-st., Holborn
Vesey, Wm. 2, Seymour-pl., Walworth
Wagg, Mathias, 8, Charles-street, New Kent-road
Wallis, George, Elizabeth-st., Hackney-road
Ward, George Green, 30, Union-st., Mary-le-bone
Wakefield, Daniel, Gray's Inn
Watson, James, 33, Windmill-street

34. [Add. Ms. 27791, f. 222. Printed balloting list for the council of the National Political Union, February 1832, with figures added in manuscript.]

1st of the working class

A	B	Votes	Names	Business	Address	Proposed by
*12		425	Atkinson, H. T.	Working painter	2, North Crescent, Bedford Square	George Rogers
*9		512	Allen, Thomas	Map engraver	1, Penton Place, Pentonville	C. F. Smith
†	41	249	Augero, F. A.	Teacher	26, Hercules' Buildings, Lambeth	William Carpenter
†*	47	160	Brackenborough, Edward	Cabinet maker	16, Brownlow Street, Holborn	E. Norminton
*18		478	Bennett, John	Artists' pencil maker	Museum Street	D. W. Redman
*27		372	Berkeley, George S.	Teacher	44, Fetter Lane	George Wilkinson
*4		531	Bowyer, Thomas	Bookseller	32, Middleton Street, Clerkenwell	H. B. Churchill
†*	48	147	Baber, George	Clerk	32, Essex Street, King's Cross	B. Heenan
*10		511	Cheeseman, Richard	Brazier and Tinman	49, Great Dover Street, Southwark	E. Perry
*3		538	Carrick, James	Bricklayer	44, King Street, Long Acre	Rowland Detrosier
*6		535	Cumming, William	Carpet maker	Carpenters' Hall, London Wall	W. D. Saull
†	39	260	Draycot, Frederick	Carver and gilder	27, Duke Street, Bloomsbury	D. W. Redman
*35		335	Douglass, William	Coach maker	21, Frederick Place, Hampstead Road	S. M. Douglass
†	45	196	Grady, John	Attorney's Clerk & Student at Law	6, Pratt Street, Lambeth	John Hunt
*29		367	Hewitt, Daniel	Musician	Camden Cottage, Camden Town	H. T. Atkinson
*11		511	Hankin, H. B.	Figure Colourer	Carpenter's Buildings, Westminster	Erskine Perry
†*	46	171	Heenan, Benjamin	Clerk	39, Prince's Road, Kennington	George Baber
15		487	Irvine, J. G.	Optician	32, Kirby Street, Hatton Garden	W. D. Saull
*36		326	King, J. B.		5, James's Place, Hackney Road	William Wallis
*25		400	Knight, George	Teacher	Globe Lane, Bethnal Green	William Wallis
*5		528	Longmate, James	Pocket-book maker	7, Theobald's Road	Thomas Murphy
†	38	266	Lovett, William	Carpenter	18, Greville Street, Hatton Garden	George Rogers
†20		435	Leonard, H. P.	Reporter for the press	32, Stanhope Road, Strand	Thomas Murphy
14		487	Moore, William	Bookseller	Little Russell Street, Bloomsbury	J. H. Powell
30		367	Millard, William	Trunk maker	19, Greville Street, Hatton Garden	Thomas Bowyer
*19		474	M'Diarmid, William	Printer	17, New Street Square	W. D. Saull
*23		422	Milner, Thomas	Painter and glazier	37, Marsham Street, Westminster	J. D. Styles
*7		513	Mongredien, A.	Merchant's clerk	44, George Street, Hampstead Road	D. Wakefield
†*	40	259	Marsh, Joseph	Baker	3, Holland Place, Kensington	W. Midwinter
†*	43	202	Norminton, Edward	Dyer	5, Drury Lane	E. Brackenborough

1st of the working class

A	B	Votes	Names	Business	Address	Proposed by
*31		367	Norman, John	Book-keeper	5, Claremont Terrace, Durham Street Hackney Road	William Wallis
*21		435	Owen, Robert	Silk weaver	James's Place, Hackney Road	William Wallis
*17		482	Palmer, Robert	Printer	9, Tottenham Court Road	E. Perry
*	37	307	Pain, James	Brush maker	29, Union Place, New Kent Road	E. Perry
* 2		536	Powell, J. H.	Clerk	26, Chapple Street, Pentonville	H. B. Churchill
* 8		513	Redman, D. W.	Lithographic printer	14, Little Charlotte Street, Middlesex Hospital	C. F. Smith
†*	42	227	Ralay, James	Silversmith	15, Plummer Street, City Road	J. Detheridge
† 1		581	Styles, J. D.	Carpenter	37, Marsham Street, Westminster	R. Detrosier
*33		351	Sellis, John	Tailor	Church Street, Hackney	William Wallis
*13		495	Shirley, John	Pencil maker	22, Castle Street, Finsbury	D. Wakefield
*26		385	Tuson, William	Modeller	13, Dean Street, Soho	C. Reynolds
*24		417	Thomas, William	Tinplate worker	273, High Street, Borough	R. Cheeseman
*12		504	Wallis, William	Silk weaver	Hackney Road	Francis Place
*16		484	Wright, Henry	Working Goldsmith	Green Street, Leicester Square	E. Perry
28		372	Ward, G. G.	Machinist	30, Union Street, Mary-le-bone	E. Rainford
†*32		363	Wright, Charles	Agent and collector of rents	102, High Street, Holborn	Thomas Murphy
†	44	198	Watkins, David	Jeweller	109, Drummond Street, Euston Square	Dias Santos
*34		351	Wellard, Samuel	Tinplate worker	273, High Street, Borough	R. Cheeseman

2nd not of the working class

A	B	Votes	Names	Business	Address	Proposed by
†*32		340	Arnot, Sandford	Professor	2, South Crescent, Bedford Square	George Rogers
*30		429	Buller, Charles	Barrister	Athenaeum	J. A. Roebuck
*22		492	Beauclerk, Aubrey	Major in the army	12, Chester Street, Belgrave Square	D. Wakefield, jun.
*31		410	Burnard, J. P.	Surveyor	Holloway	Henry Revell
* 9		568	Churchill, H. B.	Barrister	Temple	Henry Revell
†	45	169	Cleave, John	Coffee house keeper	27, King Street, Snow Hill	F. A. Augero
†*28		466	Carpenter, William	Editor of Political Magazine	16, Great Union Street, Borough	John Cleave
*35		307	Cooke, William	Hatter	45, St. Mary Axe	E. C. Thomas
*19		517	Drake, Joseph	Window glass merchant	100, Edgware Road	Thomas Murphy
†	43	220	Dias Santos, Emanuel	No profession	2, Oxford Arms Passage, Warwick Lane	William Carpenter
*33		336	Elphinstone, Howard	No profession	Eaton Place, Pimlico	C. S. Menteath
*24		491	Evans, Thomas	Surgeon	Beak Street, Regent Street	Erskine Perry

Mark	Tally	No.	Name	Profession	Address	
1		624	Fox, Rev. W. J.	Minister	Upper Clapton	E. Rainford
8		571	Franks, Robert	Hatter	Red Cross Street, Barbican	Rowland Detrosier
†	46	159	Fall, George	Accountant	Doris Street, Lambeth	John Grady
*16		532	Gowan, Captain William	Officer	Upper Baker Street	R. Detrosier
*14		539	Galloway, Alexander	Engineer	West Street, Smithfield	E. C. Thomas
*	40	269	Harrison, S. B.	Pleader	Temple	D. Wakefield, jun.
†	47	154	Hunt, John	Soap boiler	Broad Street, Lambeth	E. Dias Santos
*23		492	Howell, Henry	Master tailor	4, Argyle Street, Oxford Street	D. Wakefield, jun.
†*	41	180	Hoile, John	Plumber	44, King Street, Long Acre	James Carrick
*18		518	Harrison, Samuel	Accountant	23, Great Ormond Street	R. Detrosier
*17		529	Hickson, W. E.	Shoe warehouseman	20, West Smithfield	Erskine Perry
5		592	Lillie, Sir John Scott, K.C.B.		North End, Fulham	Erskine Perry
6	42	579	Murphy, Thomas	Coal merchant	Commercial Place, Hampstead Road	Henry Revell
*		235	Michie, W. A.	Baker	30, Milbank Street, Westminster	R. Kemp
*25		477	Menteath, C. S.	Barrister	154, Albany Street, Regent's Park	George Rogers
*	38	298	Mordan, Sampson	Pencil manufacturer	Finsbury	D. Wakefield
†*	41	250	Newberry, William	No profession	Chenies Street, Gower Street	H. T. Atkinson
*	39	476	Noel, Robert R.	B.A.	Notting Hill	E. Perry
*11		275	Nash, Eleazer	Jeweller	9, Tavistock Place	Joseph Marsh
*7		561	Place, Francis	No profession	16, Charing Cross	R. Detrosier
*34		572	Perry, Erskine	Student at law	Old Brompton	R. Detrosier
*13		329	Potter, Thomas	Chandler	73, Crawford Street	Thomas Murphy
*20		550	Rainford, Edward	Bookseller	Red Lion Passage, Red Lion Street	R. Detrosier
3		515	Roebuck, J. A.	Barrister	Gray's Inn	Francis Place
2		595	Rogers, George	Tobacconist	High Street, St. Giles	Thomas Murphy
*29		609	Revell, Henry	Gentleman	Burton Crescent	Thomas Murphy
†36		430	Rutt, J. T.	No profession	Newington Green	Rowland Detrosier
*12		303	Savage, John	Draper	Crawford Street	Thomas Potter
4	37	554	Smith, C. F.	Draper	Stones' End, Borough	H. Revell
*		594	Saull, W. D.	Wine merchant	Aldersgate Street	Henry Revell
*21		302	Templeman, John	Bookseller	18, Percy Street, Tottenham Court Road	J. Whitford
*15		508	Thomas, E. Cartwright	Surgeon	49, Old Broad Street	H. B. Churchill
*10		536	Taylor, John	Merchant	4, Christopher Street, Finsbury	R. Detrosier
†27		567	Wakefield, Daniel	Student at law	Gray's Inn	Henry Revel [sic]
		476	Wakley, Thomas	Surgeon	Greenford, Middlesex	George Rogers

N.B. Members must strike out the names of those they do not intend to vote for. No more than 36 names must be left on each of the above lists; it may contain any smaller number.

[In the Place Collection, set 17, vol. 2, there are two balloting lists, annotated in Place's writing, 'List made by one and agreed to by several in the hope of excluding the dishonest men who would destroy the Union—viz Augero, Grady, Lovett, Cleave, Dias Santos, Fall, Hunt.' and 'Rotunda list made by Dias Santos, Grady and Fall'. In the above list those whose names were struck off the list by the Rotunda men are marked *, and those whose names were struck off by Place and his friends were marked †. Those unmarked were, presumably, acceptable to both groups. Columns A and B, respectively, show the positions, according to votes received, of those elected and those not elected.]

35. [Add. Ms. 27791, f. 147]

Balloting for the Council in the way it was done was under the circumstances of the case the best mode of election that could be devised. It was however a very defective mode, every member was required to select seventy two other members, to whom he would be willing if not as he ought to have been desirous to chuse to manage for him, this was absurd, not one man in the whole union could pick out seventy two such men, no man in the union could have the knowledge of seventy two men each of whom was at all qualified for the office he was to fill. The consequences were that many voted simply on the direction of others, those others themselves chusing by far the greater part of the persons to be voted for at random. Many voted only for a small number, and some confined themselves to the very few with whom they were acquainted. A very large number did not vote at all, because there were not more than from one to perhaps two with whom they were sufficiently acquainted to be able to decide as to their fitness. To be complete each member should have had but one vote for one candidate only. As it was, it was a good lesson to a large number of persons, in as much as it shewed them with what ease, certainty and precision and in how short a time the secret suffrages of a very large number of persons could be taken.

36. [Add. Ms. 27791, ff. 147–8]

        Feb'y 8 The new Council assembled
        Mr Rogers in the chair and 42 councillors

Mr Detrosier was appointed secretary for the ensuing year. A business committee of nine members was also chosen. In consequence of efforts making by some of the members to promote a public dinner on the day appointed by proclamation for a general fast, Mr Howell moved

'That a public dinner of the members of this union on the day which is commanded by his majesty's proclamation to be observed as a fast would operate prejudicially to the objects proposed by this institution.'

An amendment was moved in the following words

'That this council will not countenance any proposition for a dinner of the members of the union as such on the day set apart for a general fast.'

The amendment was carried.

37. [Add. Ms. 27791, ff. 376–8. Place's printed copy of the comments of the *Poor Man's Guardian* on the proclamation for a general fast, 11 February 1832.]

Friends, Brethren and Fellow-Countrymen,

When we first heard of a GENERAL FAST, we thought that *Perceval* was a madman; but it seems we must have been mistaken in our opinion, or else the government are suffering under the same mental delusion as himself; as witness the following:

Monday, Feb. 6

By the KING

A PROCLAMATION FOR A GENERAL FAST
WILLIAM R.

We, taking into our most serious consideration the dangers with which this country is threatened by the progress of a grievous disease, heretofore unknown in these islands, have resolved, and do, by and with the advice of our Privy Council, hereby command that a public day of fasting and humiliation be observed throughout those parts of the united kingdom called England and Ireland, on Wednesday the 21st day of March next ensuing, that so both we and our people may humble ourselves before Almighty God, in order to obtain pardon of our sins, and, in the most devout and solemn manner, send up our prayers and supplications to the Divine Majesty for averting those heavy judgments which our manifold provocations have most justly deserved; and particularly beseeching God to remove from us that grievous disease with which several places in the kingdom are at this time visited: and we do strictly charge and command, that the said public fast be reverently and devoutly observed by all our loving subjects in England and Ireland, as they tender the favour of Almighty God, and would avoid his wrath and indignation and upon pain of such punishment as may be justly inflicted on all such as contemn and neglect the performance of so religious and necessary a duty: and for the better and more orderly solemnizing the same, we have given directions to the Most Reverend the Archbishop and the Right Reverend the Bishops of England and Ireland, to compose a form of prayer suitable to this occasion, to be used in all churches, chapels, and places of public worship, and to take care that the same be timely dispersed throughout their respective dioceses.

Given at our Court at St. James's, this 6th day of February, 1832, and in the second year of our reign.

God save the King.

On the 6 feb'y at the meeting of the [National] Union [of the Working Classes] a resolution was adopted[1]

That this meeting hope that on the day appointed for a general fast (or sooner, if the people think fit), all sinecurists, placemen, and extortioners, whether in Church or State, who are now living in luxury and extravagance, upon the taxes drained from starving industry, may be made to disgorge and give up their ill-gotten plunder, as a humiliation to themselves, and a peace-offering to this patient and long-suffering nation.

[1] This sentence is in manuscript.

73

Some of the members proposed a feast on the fast day.

On the 20 feb'y at a meeting of the Union 'Mr Watson announced, the intention of having a procession on the fast day to make a display, not only of their numbers, but of their destitution, peaceably but publicly. He deprecated all violence as the conduct of a mob and not of thoughtful and sensible men'. The information was received with cheers.

On the 17th March notice was given in the Poor Mans Guardian thus. General Fast, on Wednesday at 11 o'clock the members and their friends will assemble in Finsbury Square from whence the whole will start in procession. 'Be soberly, be orderly for your enemy the devil goeth about like a roaring lion seeking whom he may devour.'

James Osborne Sec.

38. [Add. Ms. 27791, ff. 381–2. Place's copy of the *Morning Chronicle*'s comments.]

Precautionary measures of government to prevent tumults this day 21 March 1831.

The determination of the meeting held on monday night to call together the Union of the Working Classes, to move in procession through the streets of the metropolis in defiance of the Proclamation to the contrary has caused a considerable sensation in the public mind, and great fears are entertained, that among the anticipated thousands who are expected to assemble at the rendezvous in Finsbury Square this morning many will be found with a predisposition to create tumult and disorder. We hope these fears will prove groundless and that the day will pass over in as peaceable a manner as the promoters of the intended procession anticipate it will. To secure the public peace and suppress any disposition to riot extensive arrangements have been made by the Commissioners of Police. Upwards of 4,000 men will be quartered in different parts of the Metropolis under the command of their respective superintendents and inspectors. In Finsbury—Spital Fields—and at all the chief station houses at the east end, detachments of 400 and 500 men are ordered to assemble. The Kings Mews, Palace Yard, and Waterloo place, with Hyde Park and other stations at the west end will contain large numbers of the Police, all of whom are to take up their respective quarters before ten o clock this morning. All the ward constables throughout the City of London have received instructions to be in attendance at stipulated places and another description of force we understand has received orders to hold themselves in readiness to preserve the peace of the metropolis should it be menaced. The police offices will be closed, but all the officers of the various establishments have been required to attend. Magistrates belonging to the various offices will also be in attendance, to act if necessary.

39. [Add. Ms. 27791, f. 390. Place's printed copy of the *Poor Man's Guardian*'s account of the procession, 24 March 1832.]

Our readers are already aware, that a few days since the Committee of the National Union of the Working Classes issued a placard, calling upon the latter to meet them at Finsbury Square, for the purpose of walking round the metropolis in procession, and enjoying the fresh air. Immediately on the publication of this placard, however, a counter one was issued by Government, cautioning the people to abstain from joining any of these tumultuous assemblages.

Notwithstanding this, the Union, it would appear, determined to meet, and various notices were issued, calling on the people to assemble in Finsbury Square. Soon after eight o'clock in the morning, in pursuance of these notices, a considerable number of persons began to assemble in Finsbury Square, and to increase in numbers up to eleven o'clock, when there could not have been less than 20,000 men of the Political Unions alone present. The streets leading in every direction towards the Square presented immense masses of people moving towards it; and it is no overstatement to say that there were at least 100,000 persons on foot in connection with the object of the procession. Between eleven and twelve o'clock, the Committee of the Union, which had assembled at the Philadelphian Universalist Chapel, in Windmill Street, Finsbury, headed the people, who formed themselves into a procession, three or four abreast. They then commenced moving, and in the memory of the oldest inhabitants in the metropolis, there has not been so great a mass of people seen marching in procession and order through this part of the town. The leaders, who had a perfect command over the great body, consisted of five or six individuals, amongst whom were Mr Hetherington, the Editor of The Poor Man's Guardian, Mr Lovett, and Mr Watson.

Up to the hour of moving, we did not in the immense mass observe a single drunken man, or any disorderly spirit. Quiet and order seemed to be the wish of every man, and a peaceable display of the power of the people was apparently the object of the meeting. Having commenced the movement, the procession directed its course towards the City Road along the south and east sides of Finsbury Square, thence through Sun Street into Bishopsgate Street, from whence they turned down Cornhill, and proceeded along Newgate and Skinner Streets, thence down Farringdon Street, and up Fleet Street, towards Temple Bar. Up to this time there appeared not to be the smallest indication of riot or disturbance. Not a single individual was in possession of even a stick. On reaching Temple Bar, a party of police was drawn across the street, on the west side, armed with their staves, and the cutlasses already alluded to, for the purpose of preventing the procession moving westward. The supposed object which the body had for wishing to pass through the Bar, was to reach Palace Yard by that route, in which place it was understood they had some notion of forming themselves into a condensed mass again, and thence to disperse to their homes. Seeing, however, that their progress was resisted, the procession retrograded, and turned its course up Chancery Lane, and into Holborn, where they were also met by another body of Police, who showed the same intention to prevent them from advancing westward; but here, as at Temple Bar, the concourse was again directed by its leaders, who directed its course from this point towards Gray's Inn Lane. From Gray's Inn Lane they proceeded up the King's Road, where they were again met by the police. Guildford Street was next attempted, and having passed through Lamb's Conduit

Street and Great Ormond Street, they arrived in Queen Square. They next proceeded down Gloucester Street, but being met there also by the police they returned to Queen Square, and again through Great Ormond Street into Brunswick Square. They reached, through Hunter Street, the New Road, and then proceeded unmolested to Tottenham Court Road, having scouts before them to give notice whenever the police were seen approaching through any of the cross streets. The procession in its progress towards this place acquired considerable strength, every street pouring forth its contribution; hundreds of women followed in its train, each attaching herself to her friend or husband.

All the persons composing the procession were in excellent spirits, and they frequently called on those who lagged in the rear to hasten forward. These cries were at times intermingled with cheers, and now and then an excitement was caused by the exclamation of the outscouts, 'Here come the police!' The leaders, on this, turned round, and frequently exhorted their followers to be peaceable, and on no account to commit a breach of the peace. The eyes of the whole metropolis, perhaps the whole country, were upon them, and they should not disgrace themselves. Cheers and exclamations of assent followed such addresses. Sometimes a member of the procession would express a fear that the police and the military would resort to harsh measures, and cut them down with their swords. The leaders, and some of the leading members, endeavoured to repress such fears, and said if they committed no breach of the law—and surely it was none to walk the streets quietly—the police would not interfere. In this way the procession which quietly acceded to the measures of the police in preventing their progress through certain streets, went on until it reached Tottenham Court Road.

Just before the procession reached Howland Street, the out scouts came running back in breathless haste, with the intelligence that a large party of the police were concealed in one of the bye-streets. On hearing this, the advanced part of the procession, which the leaders again exhorted to be careful lest they allowed their passions to lead them into a breach of the peace, pushed hastily on. A small portion passed Howland Street before the police, who were stationed in Howland Street, could throw themselves across the road, in order to prevent the further passage of the procession. In consequence of their not being prepared for the steady advance of the procession, they were only enabled to make their passage through the first part, and prevent the further advance of the rear of the procession. When the Members of the Union were thus divided, and whilst the police were certainly in an awkward position, of which no advantage was taken, a pause of a few moments took place, the rear of the police stopping, and driving back, as well as they could, any straggler who attempted to pass in the way which they were disposed to prevent them from going. At length the head of the phalanx took off their hats, and having cheered their companions in the rear, they answered to the call by a rush forward, by which they broke the line of the police, and the procession was again united.

In consequence of this movement, a conflict took place between the police who were still near the advanced part of the procession and the members of the Union. The staves of the policemen (who at this part of the town were not armed) were freely used, and stones and other missiles were thrown from various directions. Several of the police were wounded, and a number of individuals received serious injuries from the truncheons of the constables before the affray terminated and the parties dispersed. Seven persons, who were considered to be most active in urging the others to resist the police, were taken into custody, and conveyed, amidst the most deafening yells, to Albany Street station house. The confusion that at one time prevailed, with the shrieks of a number of women who had followed the procession, caused the utmost alarm to exist in the minds of the inhabitants, who crowded every window from which a view of the scene could be obtained.

By the advice of some of the parties in the procession, the whole body were drawn into North Crescent, where one of the leaders addressed them nearly in the following words :— 'Gentlemen—You have this day shown the country your united strength, and you have conducted yourselves like peaceable, well-disposed men. Having now effected your object, I would now advise you to disperse, and to retire immediately to your respective homes.'

He then, with his friends, withdrew, and the crowd quietly dispersed.

[Lovett, Watson and Benbow, as the leaders, were later arrested for creating a disturbance but were acquitted on trial.]

40. [Add. Ms. 27792, ff. 12–17]

On the 14 March . . . motion was made [at the National Political Union] That the business committee be directed to propose a petition in energetic terms, calling upon the house of lords to pass the reform bill in its present state.

The motion gave rise to a vehement and long discussion, one party contending that timely measures ought to be taken, in every possible way to *prevent* the lords rejecting the bill, and that petitions which shewed the disposition and determination of the people would have their effect. Another party contended that petitioning the house of Lords would be worse than useless, in as much as such petitions tended to mislead the people by inducing them to believe their petitions would be attended to when it was well known to the council that they would have no attention whatever paid to them, that they neither produced any results on the peers nor were at all regarded by the aristocracy, who utterly despised the people, and persuaded themselves that they had the power in their hands by means of the soldiers to compel submission to whatever they might wish, and were eager to use the means. Several members of the council were of opinion that the lords would wilfully drive the matter to a desperate issue and have it decided by brute force, that it was therefore necessary to have the matter well understood by the whole body of the people, who could whenever they pleased put down the aristocracy.

The agitation caused by the motion was extreme, and as several desired to deliver their opinions, who could not on that evening be heard, the question was adjourned to the next meeting of the council. . . .

At the council of the National Political Union on the 21, Mr Churchill (barrister) was in the Chair and there were present thirty six other members of the council and an auditory of about 300 members of the union, the seats would not hold the audience and the space occupied by the council of the union was encroached upon for the purpose of accomodating [*sic*] the members with standing room.

As the reform bill progressed towards its end in the house of commons, the agitation among the people increased, the feelings which the conduct of the lords in throwing out the former bill had excited, were again excited, and the abhorrence of their conduct in their corporate capacity, an abhorrence which had been gradually increasing ever since the proceedings against the Queen in 1820–1821 was again shewing itself in many places. The appeal to the people by the National Political Union, in their address headed 'Crisis'[1] had now greatly increased the apprehensions and excited the feelings of large numbers of people all over the country. This appeal was in the nature of a call, including advice and it was as spiritedly as generally responded to. The feeling was becoming intense and there was a much stronger and more general inclination among the reformers to coerce the lords than to petition them. It was in this temper and under these circumstances that the council of the Union again met to discuss the motion. The discussion was *generally* very able though with respect to some three or four of the members injudicious if not absurd.

The prevailing desire of the audience was evidently to provoke the aristocracy to commit violence against the people. A notion was prevalent among considerable bodies of the working people that if the lords were to oust the ministers on the reform bill and get into power, the Duke of Wellington would attempt to govern by the army, this course they not only expected but desired, they doubted not that such an administration of the government would produce a revolution in which they might gain but could not lose. It was this expectation and desire which to a considerable extent prevented them joining the Political Unions in London, Manchester Bristol and other places, and to use no efforts to promote the passing of the bill. These notions were sufficiently expressed during the debate in the Council of the National political union and were gratifying to the spectators. The rational side was taken principally by Messrs Roebuck, Place, Perry, Noel and the Chairman, the revolutionary by Messrs Wakley, Rogers, Fox Smith and Carpenter. It was a debate well worth preserving as an example of the opinions and expectations of a very large portion of the people, a fair and unequivocal display in London of the state of the whole kingdom. It was however no where reported but in the Morning Chronicle by a man whose understanding was not equal to a clear conception of what he heard, and the account given in the Chronicle is utterly absurd.

When in the course of the debate it became apparent to some of those who opposed petitioning that the motion would be carried they shifted their ground and argued that if the lords would receive a petition which contained plain truths, so plain indeed that they could be comprehended by all men and be denied by none, it might perhaps be expedient to petition, not indeed on account of any attention the lords would give to it, but in

[1] See Handbill 7.

CRISIS.

ADDRESS TO THE PEOPLE OF ENGLAND,
FROM THE COUNCIL
OF THE

NATIONAL POLITICAL UNION.

The Council of the National Political Union invite the attention of their countrymen to the present critical state of the Reform Bill.

A second time this Bill, which is to be the charter of the people's emancipation, has, in spite of the desperate opposition of an expiring oligarchy, been carried through the House of Commons. Its course, nevertheless, has even in this branch of the Legislature, been in the highest degree tardy and difficult. No sign has appeared in the discussions which have taken place on this second appearance of the measure, that there is any mitigation of the hostility formerly felt and expressed towards it.

They who were its opponents in the commons before have proved so also on the last trial; the party composing the enemies of the people were not in this second instance less numerous, less bitter than before.

Taking this party in the House of Commons as a fair resemblance of the same party in the House of Lords, we may safely conclude that the conduct which in the House of Commons has been pursued as respects the measure, is but a foretaste of that which will take place in the Lords; as in the Commons hostility has been not less, as the number of its opponents has not been diminished, so we may rightly conclude that in the Lords also will that hostility be as fierce as before, and the ranks of our opponents in no degree lessened.

But this body was before sufficiently powerful, headstrong, and ill-intentioned, to defy the people, and set at nought their desires. They then rejected the Bill; and since the same motives, the same feelings, exist, we are justified in concluding that such is the conduct they will again pursue.

The House of Lords remains unchanged—unchanged as to opinions—unchanged as to numbers. They have no more wisdom, no more patriotism than before, no new creation has infused freshness and purity into the old mass of corruption. To this body thus unaltered, the Ministers of the Crown are about again to present a Bill quite as obnoxious to the enemies of Reform as the former one—again, are they about to subject the people's measure to defeat.

It is to this state of affairs that the Council of the National Political Union earnestly solicit the attention of their countrymen. The public energy alone can bring a remedy to the evil—if that be not powerfully, *significantly* manifested, the cause of PEACEFUL Reform will be lost for ever.

The Council of the National Political Union do, then, in this eventful crisis, anxiously call upon their countrymen, as friends of peace and good Government, again to come forward, and forcibly to express their determination to make the cause of Reform triumphant.

They intreat the people distinctly to signify their desires, to speak in so plain a manner that their wishes cannot be misunderstood, and in so forcible a one that they cannot be denied.

By Order.
ROWLAND DETROSIER, Secretary.

March 14, 1832.

N. B. The Secretary of the National Political Union attends from 10 till 10 every day in the week, at SAVILLE HOUSE, LEICESTER SQUARE, to enrol members; and the Reading Room in which are the daily newspapers, is also open to members during the same hours. Subscriptions to the Union, including Reading Room, One Shilling per Quarter.

BARNES, PRINTER, 7, BRIDGE-HOUSE PLACE, SOUTHWARK

HANDBILL 7 Add. Ms. 27791, f. 153.

[*sic*] might be a useful paper to the people. This was met by the assertion that the Council could say whatever it wished in a petition to the lords, which could not be rejected by them and might be printed for general distribution, and coming from the council of a large and influential body of people could not fail to produce a good effect, that some members of the Council who had thought much upon the subject and would if permitted prepare such a petition, one which should go far enough to satisfy the expectations of the most ultra among them and yet meet with no objection in the house of peers. Objections were much more likely to be taken to manner than to matter provided the wording was what was called respectful, and there need be nothing left to cavil at by any noble lord in the manner. After some further debating the offer was accepted and Mr Place, Mr Roebuck and Mr Mongredien were appointed a committee to prepare a petition.

On the 28 March, at the Council of the Union, Mr Styles a journeyman carpenter in the chair, and thirty seven other members attending with a crowded audience, Mr Place was called upon to report from the committee appointed to draw up a petition to the lords. When after some introductory observations he read a draft, which he said contained a series of facts in a plain form each of which he was prepared to shew were correctly stated. That it was his opinion, that petitions to parliament with very few exceptions ought to consist wholly of allegations of facts, each capable of being sustained by evidence and reasoning, but that petitions should not be encumbered with reasons, which it was desirable should be used by those who presented them, the allegations being used as texts by the speaker. The petition he held in his hand consisted of three parts.

The first related to the defective state of the representation, the efforts made to amend it, and the evil consequences the want of a more adequate and equal representation had produced.

The second related to the former and present state of the house of peers, their power and influence, and the means they had used and were still using to govern the country.

The third related to the intelligence and power of the people and the probable use which would be made of them if the Reform bill were again rejected. Its prayer was consonant to the allegations of the petition. He then read the petition, pausing at each of the three divisions and commenting thereon, for the purpose of shewing that there were abundance of proofs to sustain the allegations. He concluding [*sic*] by challenging those who were averse to petitioning because as they said petitions were useless, to shew that it was possible this petition could fail of being highly useful, since being produced and widely circulated it would tend to increase the rising spirit of the people and produce good effects upon many influential men, who would see in it that the power of the people might be called into action peaceably if so the lords willed it should be, physically if so the lords opposed it in an improper manner when the consequences to themselves would be of their own seeking and not the fault of the people. That it was only by the demonstrations made by the people that the Lords would ever be induced to consent that the Reform bill should become the law of the land.

He challenged those who objected that the lords would receive no petition which told them truths in plain language to say that this petition did not tell important truths in plain language, yet so worded as to insure its reception. That there was nothing in it which consistently with the rules and usages of the house could cause its rejection, and if any Noble Lord should be silly enough to cavil at it, the public would have the advantage of the discussion which would ensue, and of its being thus recommended to their notice.

The petition was then read clause by clause and some merely verbal alteration having been made it was adopted unanimously, ordered to lie during three days to receive the names of the members of the council, and then taken to Lord King with a request that he would present it to the house of peers.

41. [Add. Ms. 27792, ff. 249–54. On 8 May, following the motion of Lord Lyndhurst in the House of Lords, to postpone consideration of Schedule A of the bill, the disfranchisement of small boroughs, a number of reform meetings were held in London.]

Prompt measures were necessary, a considerable number of the members of the Council of the National Political Union assembled in the morning at Saville House, and determined to call a public meeting of the inhabitants of Westminster at the Crown and Anchor Tavern on the same evening. There was no time to consult with any of the leading inhabitants, so the room was taken, notice sent to the evening papers and a few placards were carried about the streets on boards, this was all the notice given. At 8 o clock in the evening the time when the chair was to be taken, more than twice as many persons as the large room would hold attended, great numbers had gone away and numbers of others who came were also obliged to go away. The meeting would have been immense could a place have been found to contain the people.

Mr Thomas Murphy was called to the chair. He stated the reasons which had induced the council of the Union to take the liberty of calling a meeting of the inhabitants of Westminster. He explained the purpose of the meeting and the course recommended to be pursued in a speech of great energy, well calculated for the time and circumstances of the case for which he was himself also well calculated. He was a fearless man, possessed with one desire which was the total destruction of the present government, and the substitution in its place of one purely representative. He as well as a considerable portion of his audience thought the time was close at hand when a thorough revolution would be effected.

The time had certainly arrived when prosecution by the government of Earl Grey was at an end, when no legal process against any one either for writing or speaking could be commenced, when any public general movement against the government could be opposed by any power but the force of arms in the hands of the soldiers of the regular army. It was concluded by vast numbers of the people, that if a great shew of their power and determination was made, the King would be thereby induced to concede power to his ministers to carry the bill either by the creation of peers or a prorogation of parliament for a few days and then to introduce the bill anew, meanwhile to come to an understanding with a sufficient number of peers, that in the event of their pledging themselves to Earl Grey to vote for the bill by some, and to absent themselves at the divisions that peers would not be made. It was concluded that if the people shewed themselves with the activity the circumstances of the case required, the king would not make common cause with the duke of Wellington. It became clearly seen, that if the king did make common cause with the duke, the people would at once be compelled to resort to force in self defence. These matters were openly laid before the audience by the chairman, and their consequences anticipated in a total and permanent change in the very form of the government. These sentiments were received with enthusiastic shouts of applause.

Mr Daniel Wakefield maintained the same opinions and anticipated the same results. He reprobated in severe but just terms the conduct of those Westminster men who in the preceding october had pretended to establish an union of the—as they called them—the respectable electors, trifled with them and with the public, and formally destroyed their own union on the publication of the Kings proclamation against illegal assemblies which had no reference to them, he called upon them to wash out that stain by energetic conduct at the present crisis of affairs, which their pusillanimity had helped to produce, by its baneful operation [upon] but too many of their fellow citizens and by furnishing what was considered a want of any strong desire in the people for the bill, and used by the tories against them. It was he said but too plain that they who mismanaged the matter so badly, did one thing and meant another, as the tories were now doing. He hoped the men of Westminster would now do their duty to themselves and the country. It was, he said, probable, that at the very moment he was speaking to them, the ministry of Earl Grey was being dissolved, and the reform bill doomed to destruction. If Lord Grey and his friends went out of office and the King put the Duke of Wellington and his friends into office, an attempt would be instantly made to coerce the people, to put down the unions, and all other assemblies of the people, and establish a military government in support of the aristocracy. He was satisfied the people would not permit any such government to be established, but it was better by early and resolute exertions to prevent any such attempt being made. The people he was sure would no more put up with such a government under the Duke of Wellington than the Parisian people would with such a government under prince Polignac. Cries of no, no, and long continued cheering. Will they—said Mr Wakefield—submit to have their privileges their liberties destroyed when they have in their own hands the power to prevent it.—shouts of no, no, and cheers—The time for action was close upon them, the time for merely talking was all but passed away, the eyes of the people must be turned towards the true remedy, and they must achieve it with their own hands. He recommended the open refusal to pay taxes, the example being once set would be immediately followed all over the country, the immediate consequence would not be the mere privation of the amount but by such other consequences on the circulating medium as would palsy the hands of a tory government, and totally disable them from doing any thing of importance against the people, would indeed ruin such a government irretrievably in a very few days. If the lords endeavoured to withold from the people, their rights, the people should do their duty to themselves and prevent them, they should at once withold the means and thus bring the matter to issue. No administration could now carry on the government without consenting to a reform to the extent, at the least of the bill before the lords, and if the tories came into office and attempted to delay that reform; the opportunity to save themselves from the consequences of such conduct would be lost. If the people at once resolved to take proper steps they would secure reform, if they delayed to take such measures, they would have to work through a revolution; and in as much as reform was better than revolution he doubted not that the people would secure the one to prevent the other.—Great applause—

He then moved an address to the King.

Mr H. B. Churchill seconded the motion. He did not expect much good from the adoption of the address, but it was the duty of the people in the first instance to leave no peaceable means untried. He was not at all disappointed at the turn things had taken with respect to the bill, nor did he much regret it. It was now the duty of the people to watch the waverers in their pretended guise of friends and prevent them from assuming the domination they hoped to attain. The people must refuse to pay taxes, and turn the consequences of their refusal to account in every possible way. If power went into the hands of the absolutes they must prepare their powder, and cast their balls.—Great Cheering—

The address to the King was then read as follows.

'The address of the undersigned persons, assembled at the Crown and Anchor Tavern in the Strand London on the 8th day of May 1832.

May it please your Majesty.

We your Majesty's faithful subjects, beg leave to express our thanks for the kindness and goodness of your Majesty towards the people, by the countenance and support given to your ministers in bringing forward and carrying through the house of commons, the bill for Reforming the Representation of the People—particularly for the energy and determination of your Majesty displayed in the dissolution of one parliament adverse to the Bill, and the prorogation of another parliament; when the Bill had been rejected by the lords.

We beg also to express our anxious apprehensions lest the bill should again be rejected, or should be mutilated by the lords, and in expressing our apprehensions, we beg leave to add also our sincere convictions, that should such a rejection or mutilation occur, the country and government will become a prey to tumult anarchy and confusion, terminating in the utter extinction of all the present privileged orders of society.

We therefore most earnestly and urgently implore your Majesty to exert the prerogative vested in the Crown for the good of the nation, and save us from the impending evils,—by creating a sufficient number of Peers, not only to secure the passing of the Reform Bill, but to enable your ministers to conduct the government in such a manner as shall insure the prosperity and promote the peace and happiness of the people.'

Messrs Wakefield—Churchill and Detrosier were appointed a deputation to present the address to Lord Melbourne.

Mr George Rogers had intended to move two resolutions which he was happy to see embodied the opinions of the company.

1st That it is the opinion of this meeting that a creation of Peers should take place sufficient to secure the passing of the Reform Bill unmutilated, as a measure absolutely essential to prevent the country from falling into a state of anarchy.

2nd That it be recommended to every town, parish, and hamlet to hold meetings and of every inhabitant to attend such meetings for the purpose of praying to create peers to meet the present emergency. In the process of his remarks he said the Tax Gatherer had called at his house for taxes but he told him to defer another call until the reform bill had been passed. Great cheering.

The Chairman said he had done the same, and the consequence was that when the tax gatherer last called upon him he said he could not collect any money in the neighbourhood, the people had followed his example and said, 'I will not pay any more taxes until Mr Murphy pays his'. Cheers.

Mr Carpenter said he also had refused to pay taxes, the time was come when instead of meetings wasting their time in sending useless addresses they would come at once to the serious determination, of not paying taxes until the bill were passed.

The resolutions of Mr Rogers were not pressed to a division on the suggestion that they might be proposed at a more formal meeting of the inhabitants of Westminster called by the High Bailiff of which notice had already been given.

42. [Add. Ms. 27793, f. 23]

At the National Political Union the officers and several members of the council were occupied during the day [10 May], enrolling the names and addresses of new members. In the evening the throng was so great that many hundreds could not be entered on the books. Vast numbers came from distant parts of the metropolis, among whom were many whose apprehensions of violence had hitherto deterred them from joining this or any other unions, these persons now declared their conviction that the unions must proceed with vigour in support of the reform bill at whatever hazard to individuals. Every accessible part of the building—the rooms, the hall, the passages and the stairs were crowded, and an immense crowd congregated in the Square in front of the house.

The enthusiasm of the people was beyond all description.

43. [Add. Ms. 27793, ff. 74–6]

On the 10th, in the evening, there was a meeting of the National Union of the Working Classes at which it is said upwards of 2,000 members attended, this was an exaggeration, the whole number of members was less than three fourths of that number, and of these it is not probable two thirds attended the meeting. The place in which they met would not entertain more than a thousand. A considerable number of persons who were not members attended outside the building, but the whole number within and without was under the great excitement which prevailed among the small number, of members.

The proceedings at this meeting clearly coined the disposition of the leaders and the feelings of the members.

Mr Parkins was in the Chair.

Mr Cleave moved a resolution as follows:—'That this union being anxious for the *welfare of their fellow workmen* recommend in the present state of affairs, an active preparation for the worst, combined with a sober and watchful solicitude for the preservation and happiness of all.'

The resolution was received with great cheering, and seconded by Mr Mee. He thanked the Tories for what they had done as it was at least a means of shewing up the Bishops, those black locusts, who have been long fattening on the country. The object of these men all along and under all circumstances had been to feather their nests, by plundering the people. The responsibility was now however thrown upon the people, and it would be their own fault if they now failed to recover their rights. Notices were posted up in several houses in the City, expressing that, 'No more Taxes will be paid for this House, until a Reform in Parliament has taken place'. Enthusiastic cheering and cries of that's the plan. Several other members spoke in the same strain, and all expressed satisfaction that the tories had rejected the Reform bill.

Mr Benbow proposed an address, in what the 'Poor Mans Guardian' called 'a long and able speech'—but did not report it.

The address was as follows.
To the Working Men of England
'These are the times which try mens souls!—Paine

'Brethren—At this momentous period, we request your attention. An era has arrived that has aroused you. We having suffered with you the wrongs heaped on the millions, by the successive oligarchies that have swayed the destinies of this great people, desire to warn you of the danger there is in your being misled by the Factions now contending for the spoil. Anxious for our own emancipation, we would earnestly caution you against being made subservient to the few. Viewing every where around us the dreadful effects of *virtual representation*, and knowing the chicanery of the crafty few, our political creed henceforth is, equal rights and equal laws, how best can we secure to ourselves such blessings? All our interests—all our experience proclaim aloud, by, *being men*! Men prepared to suffer much for the common good. Knowing what craft and subtlety will be used to seduce you, we feel it our duty to call on you to bend the whole energies of your minds to this all important object.

'Be prepared for every sacrifice:— remember he who is not for us, is against us, and they who would disunite us are our worst enemies. If we have not union, how shall we resist the tax gatherer? or rate collector? or how accomplish the glorious work of our regeneration? We therefore call upon you, our brothers to enrol yourselves in unions to effect these great objects! to cast aside your jealousies and contentions, and to unite all who will unite against the *common enemy*. Let order be our rule—union our motto—equal justice our object, and the happiness of all our aim and end.'

Several members in their speeches recommended the non payment of taxes. A refusal to accept any reforms offered by the tories. The non payment of tithes and even of rents. The withdrawal of money by Savings Banks and Benefit Clubs, and every exertion likely to promote reform in parliament.

In this discussion care was taken that no reference was made to the National Political Union or any other association the purpose of which was to promote the passing of the bill. At this union every one who dissented from their doctrine was included under the appellation of whigs, whose desire was to keep down the people, and therefore to be considered as enemies. The bill did not give the right of voting to the working people and it was evident the time was not yet come, when any effort to introduce universal suffrage would be countenanced by but a small number of persons of the working people, and of this the working peoples unions were the best possible proofs, they would hear of no proposition which did not include universal suffrage, and they were just at this time more mischievous than useful. 'Standing at ease' which had been recommended by them, meant, observing whatever might occur and taking advantage of any circumstance likely to push forward their purpose. The mistake those among them who meant honestly made was, that they could control those who might prove dishonest, as well as the mass of purely mischievous persons who might under peculiar circumstances be let loose on society.

The great peculiarity causing a difference between the Political Unions and the Unions of the working classes was, that the first desired the reform bill to prevent a revolution, the last desired its destruction as the means of producing a revolution.

44. [Add. Ms. 27793, ff. 84–5. Place's copy of the *Morning Chronicle*'s report on the state of public opinion on Friday, 11 May.]

. . . The people have made up their minds to have the bill, *coute qui coute*—they have long forseen the probability of the present emergency, and their conduct has proved that, while on the one hand they were not unprepared for the occurrence of this disastrus [*sic*] event, neither on the other do they want sufficient spirit and energy to enforce their determination in a manner which cannot fail to ensure success. The whole country seems to be animated by one spirit. Individuals bodly avow their determination to pay NO TAXES in MONEY and every meeting concurs in calling upon the house of commons to Cut off the Supplies, or Place them in the Hands of Parliamentary Commissioners, Not to be Applied until the Reform Bill shall be Passed into a Law. The utmost confidence is placed in earl Grey and his administration, the most resolute determination to place no reliance upon any other. His noble conduct in vindicating the honour and dignity of the people, by refusing to suffer the integrity of the bill to be invaded, and the nation to be insulted by a postponement of its just demands, has called forth a feeling of gratitude, love and respect for him, the full extent of which it would be in vain to attempt to describe. Last night the National Political Union led the way, a splendid meeting of 5,000 members assembled together—declared their devoted attachment to Lord Grey and Reform—

denounced the treachery which had been practised, and announced not only their determination to petition the commons to take the supplies into their own hands but one and all declared their determination Not to pay Taxes in Money till the Reform Bill shall become law. The people are rallying round the unions. Yesterday 1,200 more members enrolled themselves at Saville House. Today up to the hour we are writing many hundreds more have been enrolled—a body of about 100 from one factory alone marched up today in procession from the east end of the town and entered their names. The meetings of this Union will continue nightly until the bill be carried. Tonight also the National Union of the working classes will assemble, as will also the Bloomsbury Householders Union. At each of these strong resolutions will be passed and declarations will be made by individuals Not to Pay Taxes. The south western—Clerkenwell—Lambeth —Greenwich—Deptford—Cripplegate—East London—Whitechapel and other Unions have all announced meetings for the same purpose. The City of London has set an excellent example to the Empire—the Court of Common Council which assembles today, have denounced those who advised his majesty to act as he has done, as enemies to the people, they have declared the country to be in danger and have determined to continue to meet *de die in diem*. They have petitioned the house of commons to cut off the supplies until the Reform Bill be a law.—That petition has been presented, and has received the support of all the four city members.

Tomorrow the Common Hall will assemble, similar resolutions of confidence in Lord Grey—cutting off the supplies etc. etc. are to be proposed— they will declare that they have no faith in any reform proposed from any other source. It is said that a proposition will be submitted to the meeting to call upon the house of commons to suspend all public business till the reform bill be carried. A permanent reform committee of citizens will be proposed accompanied with a recommendation to every city, town and parish throughout the kingdom to adopt the same course. Requisitions are being signed in every ward of the City of London to call Wardmotes—and in every parish to call parish meetings. Ten or twelve parishes meet tomorrow, and thrice as many more in the course of the next day. Westminster will meet tomorrow, and a requisition has been forwarded to the High Bailiff of Southwark to convene a public meeting which will probably be held on saturday. Mary le bone—Pancrass [*sic*]—Paddington, Clerkenwell, St Lukes, Cripplegate, St Brides, St Clement, Lambeth and many other parishes are moving.

45. [Add. Ms. 27793, ff. 123–4. 11 May 1832.]

National Political Union

Mr Francis Place in the chair

The members of the council, and of the members as spectators was very numerous.

The principal purpose of the meeting was to discuss the propriety of carrying into effect the resolution of the General Meeting held on the preceeding evening, relative to calling a meeting of the various reform unions at a distance from the metropolis.

Mr Savage moved, that the Council of the Union shall hold a Public Meeting, to which shall be invited, members of districts—unions and parishes.

Mr Leonard seconded the resolution, which produced a long discussion when Mr John Taylor moved, that the further consideration of the instructions from the general meeting, be deferred to monday evening next at 8 o clock. This motion was seconded by Mr Millard—and carried.

This was a most important subject and considering the highly excited state of the people was discreetly managed, the generality wanted a public meeting to demonstrate the feeling of the people—many wanted a public meeting to outdo in respect to numbers the Birmingham meetings while some wished for a meeting for the chance of plundering. The council hardly dared to set aside the resolution of the General Meeting, and they dared not carry it into effect, they feared too that if the matter were referred back to a general meeting that the resolution would be confirmed and a special committee appointed to carry it into effect. It was plain to the most discreet and best informed members of the council that such a meeting could not be held without great danger of a premature riot. Hampstead Heath was the place designated, and thither had the meeting been called more than half a million of persons would have attended. People would have come from considerable distances, trade in London and its environs would have been suspended, and as no arrangement could be made to engage the attention of all present to the same subject at the same time, ample scope would be given to the mischievously disposed to hold separate meetings on the ground and propose and carry their own resolutions; this was known to many of us as a matter determined upon by several leaders of working men who did not concur in the plan and proceedings of the National Political Union, and to these all the miscreants and vagabonds in the metropolis would have clung. This too was not a thing to be said if it could be avoided, but still it had been determined that it should be said not only in the council of the Union but at any general meeting of its members, and arguments be offered why the members of the council who took this view of the case could not consent to carry the order of the General Meeting of members into effect. Nothing at the moment could have been more favourable to the Tories nothing so injurious to the cause in which the people were engaged than the riotous proceedings of a mob, and a firm resolution of many members of the council was taken to use every possible means to prevent the holding of such a meeting.

46. [Add. Ms. 27793, ff. 146–8. 12 May 1832.]

In the afternoon, the deputies from Birmingham, other deputies and several persons who were not deputies came to my house. They had been in various parts of the metropolis had conversed with many people merchants, bankers, traders, and members of parliament, all whom they had seen as well as themselves were greatly excited at the no longer doubted intelligence that the King had ordered the duke of Wellington to form an administration, they observed that such was the dread of his probable conduct and so strong the desire to prevent him doing mischief that already, his protest on the second reading of the bill on the 7 May was reprinted, placarded and distributed with a caution to the people against permitting him to govern them. It was generally understood that the duke would endeavour and would probably succeed in forming an administration of desperate men and proceed at once to put down the people by force, cost whatever it might. No one present, however doubted that the people would put down the Duke, and each was ready to do his best for that purpose. It was quite certain that the bulk of the people would rise *en masse* at the call of the Unions, and the deputies now in London and other Cities. It was now considered necessary that as soon as it was ascertained that the Duke had formed an administration, all the deputies, excepting three, sent by the three principal places should return home and put the people in open opposition to the government of the Duke. While the leading reformers in London should themselves remain as quiet as circumstances would permit, and promote two material purposes. 1. Keeping the people from openly meeting the troops in battle, supposing the soldiers were willing to fight them. 2. to take care, to have such demonstrations made as would prevent the soldiers being sent from London, if it should turn out as seemed next to impossible that the mass of the people did not make these demonstrations themselves.

It was very clearly seen that if a much more open and general run for gold upon the banks, the bankers and the Bank of England could be produced, that the embarrassment of the Court and the Duke would be increased, and that if a general panic could be produced the Duke would be at once defeated. To this purpose the attention of us all was turned, and many propositions were made to increase the demand for gold. Several suggestions were made, several hints were adopted and agreed to be put in train, but some measure which would operate extensively and at once was still desired and this put us into a perplexity, respecting the means of accomplishing this purpose. Among the persons present were two Bankers, and although they were likely to be inconvenienced greatly and perhaps to be considerable losers they entered very heartily into the business. There was a general conviction that if the Duke succeeded in forming an administration, that circumstance alone would produce a general panic, and almost instantaneously close all the banks, put a stop to the circulation of Bank of England notes and compel that Bank to close its doors, and then at once produce a revolution. The question therefore, among us, was. Can we adopt means to cause such a run upon the Banks, as may either intimidate the Duke and induce him to give up the attempt to form an administration and coerce the people, or prevent him having the means of aggression if he persists in his attempt. It was thought we might succeed in one, and if in the first, prevent the second, and consequently the revolution which though much deplored was no longer feared. While the discussion was going on some one said, we ought to have a placard, announcing the consequences of permitting the Duke to form an administration and attempting to govern the country, to call upon the people to take care of themselves by collecting all the hard money they could and keeping it, by drawing it from Savings Banks, from Bankers, and from the Bank of England. This was caught at, and Mr Parkes set himself to work to draw up a Placard, among the words he wrote were these,—we must stop the Duke—These words struck me as containing nearly the whole that was necessary to be said, I therefore took a large sheet of paper and wrote thus.

TO STOP THE

DUKE

GO FOR

GOLD.

I held up the paper and all at once said, that will do—no more words are necessary. Money was put upon the table and in less than four hours, the bill stickers were at work posting the bills. The Printer understood to work all night, and to dispatch at four o clock on the next—sunday morning—six bill stickers each attended by a trust worthy man to help him and see that all the bills were stuck in every part of London. Other persons were engaged to distribute them in Public houses and in shops wherever the people would engage to put them up, to send them to the environs of London by the carriers carts, and thus cause as general as possible a display at once. Parcels were sent off by the evening coaches and by the morning coaches of the next day to a great many places in England and Scotland and with some of these parcels a note was also sent requesting people to reprint them as posting bills and as hand bills.

47. [Add. Ms. 27794, ff. 84–6. 15 May 1832.]

Between 2 and 3 o clock in the afternoon a report was spread that the King had sent for Lord Grey, and this report being confirmed it passed from mouth to mouth with amazing rapidity. Men ran about spreading the news in every direction, each putting his own surmises and wishes as facts and every one believing whatever he heard. The general conclusion which each drew for himself was that Earl Grey and his colleagues would be at once restored to office with full power to carry the Bills for England Scotland and Ireland. Every body concluded that if Lord Grey were restored to power it must be conditioned that he should have the power mentioned, full confidence was placed in his integrity in respect to the bills and few enquired by what means he was to accomplish his purpose, that was left to him, as no one doubted he would take all the security the case demanded and could be obtained to enable him to accomplish his purpose. The demand for Gold which had been rapidly increased stopped at once; no purpose was now to be accomplished by any such means, all danger of loss by holding of Bank Notes was at an end and balances were safe in Bankers hands. The gratulations and congratulations of the people were extravagant beyond description.

The restoration of Lord Grey was rationally considered a matter of immense moment, a change from impending—nay almost commenced civil commotion, to peace and prosperity, every mans life and property was safe, and every one feeling this to be the case the extravagance they enacted may well be excused, as might also be the general persuasion that Lord Grey being sent for was the same as being restored to power on his own terms.

In the evening I wrote to Mr Grote as follows

We may now sing 'Glory to God in the highest' the bill is won, won too without the help of the City Life and fortune men. It will now be the peoples bill and Lord Grey the peoples minister.

You and I can afford to differ, and may perhaps at times improve each other by differing. I expected to have seen in the Standard a simple denial from you, no more was necessary. It is taking the chance of too much personal abuse, and mischief to write any explanation to newspaper people.

Here is the conclusive answer to your note of yesterday, containing your, what?—Oh! arguments against Go For Gold—shewing that it was no go at all, just as an early copy of the Standard was brought to me containing your letter to the Editor, came a great man,[1] who seeing the placard Go For Gold on my table, pointed to it and said, in a tone of admiration, 'that's the settler, that has finished it,' this he said without any hesitation or reservation before a gentleman, whom he had never before seen. When the gentleman was gone, he told me that 'the placard and some other matters of less importance had worked out the reformation'. Earl Grey was with the King. That 'there had been fears of a hitch of a very extraordinary nature', that others might occur and if any did occur he would come and relate them to me; in the evening. It is now 11 p.m. and as he has not called I conclude that all is going on well. I shall I expect see him again tomorrow morning.

The great man came to me from other great men, greater than himself to ascertain my opinion of the chance there was that the excited people would become quiescent on Lord Grey and his colleagues being restored to office. I pledged my existence that they would be perfectly quiescent on the restoration of Earl Grey etc. provided that he in the Lords and Lord Althorpe in the commons made sufficiently clear and plain declarations that the bills unmutilated should, so far as depended upon ministers be carried.

I went to the National Political Union in the evening every one of the large rooms was crowded to excess all the people in high glee, all well disposed as could be wished, Now do pray recollect that Go For Gold was only an enlivener. I told you it would send the country to the Bank of England and send the Bank of England to the Palace of St James and thus stop the Duke, It has done its duty well.

Yours truly,
Francis Place

16 May 9 a.m. When I look at the City news in the Chronicle this morning—see what the Bank Directors did, and hear as I did yesterday the great man applaud the placard I am mightily pleased with the result. As for risks any thing everything was to be risked 'To Stop the Duke'.

'Go for Gold & Stop the Duke' is my motto.

48. [Add. Ms. 27794, ff. 278–80]

Several persons came to me before eight o clock in the morning, each filled with apprehension, each having his own version of what had happened, all however had come to the same conclusion,—resistance to the Duke at

[1] Sir John Cam Hobhouse. See Add. Ms. 27794, f. 87.

any cost and in every possible way. Others came in and at about half past eight, a gentleman came with a message from Sir John Hobhouse. He said there was to be a meeting in Downing Street at noon, and Sir John wished me to write a letter to him, telling him all the facts I could and giving him my opinion of the state of feeling among the people as far as I could and my view of prospective results. I therefore as soon as I could dismiss the persons who were with me, and shut others out, for a time, wrote as rapidly as I could the following letter. In quiet times, or in troubled times, when matters were not so far gone as they were now, the letter might have been thought treasonable, but on the day it was writen the memorable 18 May 1832 when all were ready and willing not only to write treasonably but to act treasonably, there was nothing very remarkable, much less extraordinary in my sending such a letter to his Majesty's Secretary at War.[1]

18 May 1832

Dear Sir John

I am again becoming anxious, you promised to come and tell me what was going on, in case of any peculiar difficulty, or any hitch—or any thing conclusive. I have not however seen you, and spite of my desire to believe that *all* may go right I cannot satisfy myself that *any thing* is going right.

Last night at the National Political Union I had much of difficulty in appeasing many members of the council. The persons who assembled in the Great Room and in the passages were gloomy and sulky. This mornings newspapers will make things worse. The moment it was known Earl Grey had been sent for, the *Demand for Gold* ceased. No more placards were posted, and all seemed to be going on well at once. Proof positive this of the cool courage and admirable discipline of the people. We cannot however go on thus *beyond to day*. If doubt remain until tomorrow, alarm will commence again and panic will follow. No effort to STOP The DUKE—by GOING For GOLD was made beyond a mere demonstration and you saw the consequence. What can be done in this way has now been clearly ascertained and if new efforts must be made they will not be made in vain. Lists containing the names addresses etc. of persons in every part of the country likely to be useful have been made. The name of every man who has at any public meeting shewed himself friendly to reform has been registered. Addresses and proclamations to the people have been sketched, and printed copies will, if need be, be sent to every such person all over the kingdom—means have been devised to placard towns and villages, to circulate hand bills and assemble the people. So many men of known character, civil and *military* have entered heartily into the scheme, that their names when published will produce great effect in every desirable way. If the Duke came into power now, we shall be unable, longer to 'hold to the laws'—break them we must, be the consequences whatever they may, we know that all must join with us, to save their property, no matter what may be their private opinions. Towns will be barricaded—new municipal arrangements will be formed by the inhabitants and the first town which is barricaded, shuts up all the banks. GO FOR GOLD it is said will produce dreadful evils,—

[1]A copy of the letter is to be found in Add. Ms. 35149, f. 150 r & v.

we know it will, but it will prevent other evils being added to them. It will STOP THE DUKE. Let the Duke take office as premier and we shall have a commotion in the nature of a civil war, with money at our command. If we obtain the money he cannot get it. If it be but once dispersed, he cannot collect it. If we have money we shall have the power to feed and lead the people, and in less than five days we shall have the soldiers with us. Here then is a picture not by any means over drawn—not too highly coloured, no, not even filled up. Look at it, it is worthy the serious contemplation of every man. Think too upon the results. Think of the consequences to the public creditor—to the Church—the King—the Aristocracy—think of the coming Republic.—Think of the certain destruction of those from whom opposition may be apprehended, and you will at once discover how all depends on Earl Grey being restored or not being restored to office. You will see the fearful necessity there is for prompt proceedings to *compel* the King to request his services, and to enable him to possess sufficient means to accomplish his purposes. Keep him up for Gods sake. Let us have one man worthy of a statue in every town and village, and let us have through him and his colleagues (we can have it in no other way) peace among ourselves, safety comfort and prosperity.

If I am to meet the people at the great meeting tomorrow night, in Leicester Square, with doubts, all but infinite mischief may follow.

If the meeting at the London Tavern on Monday is to take place whilst doubt remains—all may be ended. GO FOR GOLD may then settle the matter at once.

Yours truly
Francis Place

49. [Add. Ms. 27794, f. 336]

Livery of London Reform Committee
Guildhall, 18 May 1832

At a numerous meeting of the committee it was resolved unanimously. That the committee hails with heartfelt satisfaction the declarations which were last night made in both houses of parliament by his majesty's ministers, which they regard as the first determination not to enter into any compromise with their opponents, or with any unconstitutional advisers of the crown and that they will not retain office unless they are enabled to carry the great measure of reform without mutilation or curtailment.

That deeply impressed with the conviction that the stability of the throne and the peace of the country depend upon the speedy accomplishment of this important measure, this committee cannot but deprecate these perilous delays which are interspersed as the expiring efforts of a desperate faction, the effects of which on the present state of the country, must be to paralise [*sic*] the arm of industry destroy public confidence in the commercial world and put to fearful hazard the best interest of society.

Robert Franks,
Hon. Sec.

The committee meet daily at Guildhall at 10 o'clock precisely.

50. [Add. Ms. 27795, ff. 26–9]

Sunday May 20th 1832

Thus ended the week, and thus ended the eleven days of Englands apprehension and turmoil, the memorable eleven days, of probably as much importance to the country as any which ever occurred.

Left quietly alone on the sunday morning I wrote the following observation.

'The impending mischief has passed over us, thanks to the inlightened state to which large masses of the people have attained; thanks indeed to their foresight, the steady conduct of their leaders and the unlimited confidence the people felt in themselves, and that which they placed in the men who came forward in the common cause. But for these demonstrations a revolution would have commenced, which would have been the act of the whole people to a greater extent than any which had ever before been accomplished. Now, relieved from all present apprehension, the sunday was indeed a day of repose, of solid gratulation, and satisfaction to the people generally, in every rank and station. Of disappointment, bitter disappointment, however, to some who were opposed to any change whatever, persons by whom the inevitable consequences of increased intelligence of the people was not recognised, and who therefore supposed that the power still remained in the hands of the aristocracy to compel submission to their will, these people felt the disappointment deeply. They would have pushed matters to extremities in the full persuasion that success was certain. Disappointment to others who were unwillingly convinced, that with a house of commons which had twice passed the Reform Bill, with nearly all thinking people in the kingdom to support them, were not at all likely to deviate from the line of conduct they had so steadily followed, and that even were it possible for them to do so, had they been so disposed, it was made impossible by the conduct of the people who felt that they were pushed to the last extremity, and determined to go through with the business to which they had devoted themselves. These persons were too circumspect to attempt, to subdue the house of commons and the people by any power that the King and themselves possessed. They therefore submitted to inevitable necessity, after having made as courageous an opposition, as any set of men could make, and carried that opposition to the utmost possible extent. Of the disappointment of those to whom a state of confusion however short would have been advantages [sic] it is scarcely worth the trouble of alluding. Sunday was then a day of real repose.

'Here let us hope the turmoil will end. We were within a moment of general rebellion, and had it been possible for the Duke of Wellington to have formed an administration, the King and the people would have been at issue, it would have been soon decided, but the mischief to property, especially to the great Landowners and the Fundholders—and personally to immense numbers would have been terrible indeed. Yet upon the coolest calculation, it would have been by far less terrible, than that which must have resulted from, a submission to the Duke of Wellington and the Army. His acceptance of office, and his attempt to exercise the power conferred

94

upon him would at once have put a stop to business of every kind, and thrown hundreds of thousands of persons out of employment without the means of subsistence. Barricadoes of the principal towns—stopping the circulation of paper money—and consequently the supply of the markets; and the falling to pieces of the government. The mischief to the country would at the moment have been nearly as great as an actual civil war, though the continued mischief would have been much less. Happily the general demonstration of resistance compelled the Duke to withdraw and made it necessary for the king to recal [*sic*] Early Grey to office, with the assurance of means to carry the Reform Bills unimpaired and unmutilated in their principal clauses. The bold honest discreet men who took the lead during the eleven days from the 7th to the 18th of the month have saved the country.

'I always doubted the courage of the people, as well as their judgment to do, at the right time, the thing which might be most requisite to produce the greatest amount of good, on any great emergency. There had however been no means at any time of judging correctly on this subject, the people never in any case having acted for themselves, but always as the tools of some party for party purposes, even when national good was the result this was the use which was made of them. This was indeed the first time they ever combined of their own free will for a really national purpose and this it is which marks the era as of more importance than any former proceeding, which makes it prospective of still greater importance as the first of an inevitable series, which from time to time will increase the power of the people and lessen that of the government until it has either totally destroyed it by a violent ebullition, or quietly absorbed it.

'Thanks to the King and his stultified advisers. Thanks to the Duke of Wellington for his blind courage. Thanks to the tory Lords for their ignorance of the people, since it is to these things we owe the demonstrations and communication all over the country of the knowledge and power of the people, and the assurance it has given to all that these important particulars were about equally shared by them in every part of Great Britain.

'The thorough conviction they have now obtained of the moral power to control the government, and the confidence that conviction will give to them when the reformed house of commons at no great distance of time shall, as it must, prove how inadequate will be the reform bill to satisfy the expectations of the people. Even a year ago the people as a body may be said to have been essentially loyal, desirous to support the government of the King—the Bishops—the other Lords and the Commons, but the weakness and meanness of the King—the unholy arrogance of the Bishops— and the determination of the Peers to rule as of old, when the people were ignorant, besotted easily led and easily intimidated. Much of this absurd loyalty has now been destroyed and can never again exist. The demonstrations made by the King—and the Lords have shaken these absurd notions, and compelled the people to progress towards entertaining republican opinions to an extent which no one had anticipated.

'So great a change in so short a period, which from its very nature must be permanent never was so generally and so effectually manifested by any people. Kings and Lords will of themselves, if permitted, in time go quietly out of existence, and as it may be hoped, at least in this country, representative government will be established without tumults or any extensive convulsion. The only apprehension which can reasonably be entertained of any considerable disturbance is want of patience of the people. If they be not too much in a hurry representative government will be produced exactly at the time when it can best be maintained, and that will be when the people have been prepared to carry it on with the least possible difficulty and the consequent certainty of reaping all its advantages.'

51. [Add. Ms. 27795, ff. 164–5. 23 May 1832.]

The Council of the National Political Union

Mr Wm. Carpenter proposed, 'that the members of the National Union of the Working Classes, be admitted to the meetings of the Union on producing their tickets.'

Mr Carpenter was a member of both Unions and more disposed to promote the views of the Working mens, than those of the National Union. His purpose was so to amalgamate the two, that as the Bills for Reform were now sure to be passed and the members of the National Union would rapidly decrease, the leaders of the Working-mens Union should have the predominance in both Unions. It has been shewn that the leaders of the working mens union had endeavoured to prevent the formation of the National Union, but having failed in their endeavours, some of them had subsequently joined it for the purpose of embarrassing its proceedings and had suffered no opportunity to escape which promised the smallest chance of success, and these efforts had always received the countenance of Mr Carpenter. The leaders of the working mens Union, were of opinion that their own class could compel the parliament to consent to enact Universal Suffrage and they believed that, then, they by their numbers could and would elect men of their own class to parliament, to put in practice, their peculiar notions of political economy and an equalization of the possession of property. They thought they saw, the means of establishing a government which would compel all to work, and that all by working a few hours each day might produce in abundance every thing that mankind ought to desire to have, the whole produce and commodities being made common stock and served out equally to all. There would then they said no longer be the competition among men which had hitherto been their ruin;—no profit-mongers—no usurers—no shopocracy—no money-mongers—this doctrine inculcated by Mr Robert Owen was not only considered the true one, the only true one, but like the professors of every other, *only true doctrine*, they hated and would had they the power, have either compelled conformity or destroyed those whose opinions differed from theirs. The National Political Union was therefore held by them to be their enemy, and therefore to be opposed on every possible occasion.

Mr Carpenter who had previously to this time been a preacher was a shrewd cunning, voluble fellow, precise, plausable [*sic*] and persuasive. He made a long and very ingenious speech which was replied to by several of the members.

The Morning Chronicle contained the following short account of the proceedings [*Printed*].

NATIONAL POLITICAL UNION.—The Council of this Union held its weekly meeting last evening: but its discussions were occupied principally in considering the propriety of a Motion introduced by Mr. William Carpenter, to permit the Members of the Union of the Working Classes to become auditors at the Meetings of this Union. Mr. Carpenter produced many arguments in favour of his Motion, particularly the reciprocal benefit likely to result from Members of either Union being permitted to attend the Meetings of the other, so as to incorporate both in the bond of amity and similar prospects and objects, and to annihilate all feelings of hostility that might exist between both bodies. He was supported by Major Beauclerk, but was opposed by Messrs. Place, Churchill, Revell, Leonard, and Wallis, because the Motion would be unjust to the Members of this Union, who have at present not room to attend the Meetings—because the subscription to the Union is so small as to exclude none, even of straightened circumstances—and because it would be illegal, as it rendered the Union amenable to the Act against Corresponding Political Bodies. It was hence considered imprudent and unjust, as well as inexpedient and illegal, and was, therefore, negatived: but not from any feeling of hostility to the Members of any other Union, though, to give the preference to one Union would be an invidious distinction, little gratifying that body and odious to all the other Unions, which might be denied on demanding the same favour. No other discussion occurred, and the Council adjourned at a late hour.'

52. [Add. Ms. 27796, f. 313]

On the 25 June [1832] the quarterly General Meeting [of the National Union of the Working Classes] was held at Theobalds Road.

The Secretary made a statement of the affairs of the Union. He said that, though they [*sic*] were not many fashionable reformers among them, their numbers had doubled during the last four months. A short time ago they were compelled to meet in any place they could meet with, but the Union, had made a great step and secured a place to itself, and similar places would be taken in different parts of the Metropolis. (Cheers)

The balance of money in hand on the 12th April was   £10–8–7

The receipts since that time amounted to   £42–16–4

The Profit Mongers might smile at this as a small amount, but it was as much as they could spare out of what was left them.

The expenditure was £29–7–4, leaving a balance of £13–8/-

The income of the Union had increased £16 a month.

Mr Benbow moved the appointment of Auditors—he said, the fact that the number of members had been doubled since the last quarterly meeting, proved that it had its effect upon some of the working men.—He believed that there were at least 10,000 *efficient* members of the Union. (Cheers) By the word *efficient* he meant, not what their enemies would imply by it, mere pecuniary efficiency, but men who did their duty and observed the laws of the Union. Then he had to congratulate them on the possession of the place to meet in, and the prospect of having others. This he might well do when he recollected that a few months ago they were turned out of the Rotunda. He eulogised a free press, and recommended the extention [*sic*] of

Unions—Sir William Jones, who was good authority, had said—'It is my deliberate opinion that the people of England will never be happy, in the majestic sense of the word, unless 200,000 of the Civil state can be ready in twenty four hours notice to enter the field without rashness or disorder.' (Cheers)

By the laws of Edward 1 every man ought to have a Halbert, an axe and a large knife, and if that law had been still duly observed, Sir Robert Peel's Military Police could not have been established, there could be no necessity for it.

Auditors were appointed.

53. [Add. Ms. 27796, ff. 45–8]

Preparations in anticipation of the passing of the Reform bills had been making in many places for the purpose of selecting candidates for the forthcoming General Election. Many persons had announced themselves as Candidates, and almost all of them in their addresses had put forward pledges as to future conduct. Some of these were full, direct, and clear, some were few, and many were doubtfully or vaguely expressed.[1]

It was evident that in places where the people would for the first time be called upon to exercise the right of voting for representatives would be benefitted by a clear exposition of the nature of Pledges, and the printing out such as might reasonably be required of every candidate who professed himself a reformer. The bill was considered a means to an end and not at all as Lord Grey and some of his colleagues represented it a final measure. It therefore became necessary that some recommendation on the subject of Pledges which would apply to all persons and might be used in all places should originate somewhere and in no place could it originate so well as in the Council of the National Political Union and by no body could such a paper when composed be so fully and so usefully distributed. This was one of the principal reasons which induced me to write it, there was also another reason scarcely less important which will be noticed presently.

The subject of Pledges occupied the attention of all the more active reformers, meetings had been held resolutions had been passed and it was evident that many more meetings would be held and many more sets of resolutions would be passed. All that had been done in this way had been ill done, all differed, many very widely and no pledges could be generally adopted.

The propriety of exacting any pledge was questioned by some well disposed persons, others made no question of the matter, but insisted that no pledge whatever should be demanded or even expected. Others and these by far the most numerous body wished to exact pledges for even the most minute particular, on very many indeed, respecting which the widest difference of opinion existed.

By those who were the most rational and best qualified to judge, it was thought advisable that the opinions of candidates, on all the great leading questions should be accurately obtained, and pledges on these alone demanded.

[1] See Handbills 8 and 9.

TO THE INDEPENDENT

ELECTORS OF WESTMINSTER.

GENTLEMEN,

A Dissolution of Parliament being shortly expected, I venture to solicit the honor of becoming your Representative, and I do so with the greatest confidence of success, because I am prepared to promise and pledge myself to much more than any Man has hitherto done, in soliciting that honor at your hands. In fact, Gentlemen, what they have hitherto promised, viz. *the immediate Abolition of Slavery, the Repeal of the Assessed Taxes, the Reduction of the Army, the Reform of the Church, the Vote by Ballot, and the Shortening of Parliaments,* are mere trifles, unworthy of the genius and invention of a Promise-Maker or pledged Candidate. Knowing that it would not be at all difficult, they should have gone still further, and pledged themselves, as I will do, that from the moment I am placed in Parliament,—

1st.—The Government shall be carried on at no expense whatever, and this will be a great improvement, as we shall thus obtain the protection and benefits of the Social State, without paying a farthing for it.

2nd.—That no Army shall be kept up for the defence of the Country and the Colonies, or that, if kept up, it shall be at the sole cost of the Army, and it must provide for itself in the best manner it can.

3rd.—That if the Navy be retained (the propriety of which I very much doubt) it shall be determined, that every Ship of War shall henceforth become a little Republic, in which nothing shall be done but by the expressed wish of the majority of the Crew, and that not a Helm shall be altered, nor a Sail shifted, but by the Vote of that majority, and such vote to be taken by ballot.

4th.—That not only shall flogging in the Army and Navy be abolished, but that all punishments for offences against any of the Laws, whether civil or military, shall be immediately done away with, *and the Judges be directed, on conviction before them of any Offender, merely to admonish him, and civilly request him not to repeat the*

crime, and then discharge him, apologising for having detained him so long.

With respect to the Kingly Office, I have not yet fully determined; but as the institution is ancient, I propose to give it a fair trial, and shall leave it in its present state for one year longer.

All these things, Gentlemen, I promise to effect, and, of course, if I promise they will be done; and if any Elector should think of any thing which I might have promised but have not, I beg him to attribute it to inadvertence, and to consider me as virtually pledged to any thing he may think of, since I should regret exceedingly to lose a Vote through any such oversight.

A Candidate, in a neighbouring District, has put forward as one claim to the favor of the Electors, that he is without funded or landed property, and is consequently a completely independent man, but, Gentlemen, I have still higher claims to be considered, as independent of all the incumbrances of property, since I am at this moment in insolvent circumstances, as a large body of Creditors can prove to your entire satisfaction. I will only further state, that I shall at all times be accessible to my Constituents, and for this purpose shall every Morning, from 9 to 11 o'clock, stand at the corner of Covent Garden Market, to receive instructions from any Lady or Gentleman who may be passing, as to my plan of conduct during the remainder of that day.

All these Pledges, Gentlemen, I will have written on sheets of white paper, and a copy presented to each Elector, signed with my own hand; and, I trust, that as I have now completely outbid every other Candidate, you will consider me as the ONLY PLEDGED MAN, and you will, when we come to the Hustings, order the LOT to be immediately knocked down to

Your very humble Slave,
and most cringing Candidate,

PETER PROMISE.

Westminster, Nov. 23rd, 1832.

O. ODELL, PRINTER, 69, KING STREET, GOLDEN SQUARE.

HANDBILL 8 Add. Ms. 27844, f. 78.

EXTENSIVE FAILURE!!!

To be Sold by Auction,

ON THE PREMISES,

LISLE STREET, NEWPORT MARKET,

SEVERAL CURIOUS LOTS OF

Unredeemed Pledges,

AND OTHER PROPERTY;

AMONGST WHICH WILL BE FOUND SEVERAL

LARGE SPLENDID BANNERS,

Made of beautiful Silk, mounted on Staves of Blue and Gold, with suitable Inscriptions and Emblematical Devices, amongst which are the following strikingly displayed

IN LETTERS OF " PURE" GOLD,

" Westminster's Pride and England's Hope."
" Purity of Election."
" See the Conquering Hero comes," &c. &c.

LIKEWISE,

A LARGE SPLENDID CAR,

A LA ROMAN,

Chastely and magnificently Decorated, and Mounted on Four Wheels,

WITH THE

FOLLOWING INSCRIPTION, DELINEATED IN GOLD ON A SUPERB CRIMSON GROUND,

" Old Glory."

But the most remarkable Lots which will be submitted, and to which the attention of the Public, who may honour the Property with a View is invited, are several

UNREDEEMED PLEDGES,

Bearing date 1818-19-20, and subsequent Years, and which from their depreciated Value, owing to the certainty that they will never be Redeemed, must be Sold for any thing they will fetch.

The Property of THE RUMP, Lisle-street, Newport Market,

That Body having no further use for them.

CARDS TO VIEW, AND CATALOGUES MAY BE HAD OF

J. JACKSON,

AT HIS ROOMS, RATHBONE PLACE, OR AT COVENT GARDEN CHAMBERS.

N. B.—Wanted, for the purpose of being forwarded to Ireland, 500 Second-Hand CAT-O'-NINE-TAILS, in good Flogging Condition; a liberal Price will be given.— Apply as above, or at 42, Berkeley Square.

On hand, a few Copies of that much-admired Work, entitled, " MILITARY AND NAVAL FLOGGING DEFENDED, AND SHOWN TO BE THE MOST HUMANE AND CONSTITUTIONAL MODE OF KEEPING BRITISH TARS AND SOLDIERS IN SUBJECTION. By J. C. H.

J. BROOKS, PRINTER, 421, OXFORD STREET.

HANDBILL 9 Add. Ms. 27844, f. 138.

The first meeting on the subject which reported its proceedings was a meeting of the Liverymen of London who had formed what during the passing of the bill, from the resignation of Earl Greys administration, had sat continually at Guildhall. This committee assisted by a number of new electors for the City held a meeting at the Guildhall on the 19th of June—for the purpose of considering, if any—and what Pledges should be demanded from candidates for the City of London, when it was resolved that a sub-committee of 7 Livery-men and 7 of the new electors should be appointed to draw up such resolutions as might seem to them proper and to report to the General Committee as soon as possible.

On the 22. They made their report, and the General Committee adopted the resolutions reported to them, and ordered that they should be laid before a general meeting of Electors. A deputation was then appointed to wait upon the Lord Mayor to request he would allow the use of the Guildhall for the meeting.

The resolutions were

1. That for *one* man to represent *another* means that he is to act for *that other* and in a manner agreeably to *his* wishes and instructions.

2. That members chosen to be Representatives in Parliament, ought to do such things as their constituents wish and direct them to do.

3. That therefore it appears to this meeting that those to whom the law now commits the sacred trust, of the power of chusing members who are to represent their non-voting neighbours as well as themselves, ought to be scrupulously careful to chuse no man on whom firm reliance cannot be placed, that he will obey the wishes and directions of his constituents.

4. That in order to obtain the best possible ground for such reliance every candidate ought in the first place, to give the Pledges following—to wit—That I will omit nothing within my power, to cause, in the very first session,

A total abolition of Tithes.

A repeal of the assessed taxes.

The Taxes on malt.

The Taxes on Soap.

These having been repealed, I pledge myself to the immediate consideration of the—Revision of the Corn Laws

To do everything in my power to cause

The abolition of all sinecures—and all unmerited pensions

A repeal of the Act of daring usurpation called the Septennial Act.

I will at all times, and in all things, act conformably to the wishes of a majority of my constituents deliberately expressed, or I will resign to them the trust with which they have honoured me.

5. That we the electors of the City of London pledge ourselves to each other, and our country, that we will give our votes to no man who will not give the above pledges, and we earnestly recommend to our fellow electors in every part of the Kingdom to make and strictly to adhere to the same determination.

Neither the sense nor the stile [*sic*] of these resolutions were likely to recommend them to the adoption of any body of electors but their having laid them before the public somewhat increased the necessity for something better to be done.

54. [Add. Ms. 27796, ff. 144–7. *Printed.*]

NATIONAL POLITICAL UNION. ON PLEDGES TO BE GIVEN BY CANDIDATES (By Francis Place)[1]

To the Electors of the United Kingdom.

The Council of the National Political Union consider it their duty to state in the shortest and clearest way they can, the opinions they entertain, and the reasons on which they are founded, respecting the pledges which, under *present* circumstances, should be given by those who may become candidates for seats in the ensuing parliament.

It is well known, that, under the rotten borough system, the people had no real choice of representatives—a majority of the House of Commons was nominated and placed there by the Lords and a few rich Commoners, and indeed, with few exceptions, they who sought to be members were men whom the people, if left to themselves, would not have chosen. Men properly qualified for the office and worthy of public confidence very generally shrunk from election contests: the toil, the expense, the degradation necessary to obtain a seat for any but a pocket borough, was such as an honest man could seldom be found willing to encounter and submit to; and very few such men were therefore at any time to be found in the House of Commons.

The Reform Bill has, to a considerable extent, abridged the power of those who have hitherto had the composition of the House of Commons in their hands, and has given to the people in many places the right of choosing for themselves, and on that choice may depend the well being of the nation. The power to choose representatives will, however, be of little value, unless it be honestly exercised. To be useful, electors must not so much consider what may at the moment seem most likely to promote some particular interest—what may be most gratifying to some particular feeling, moral, religious, or political; but what, under the circumstances in which the country is placed, will be most likely to be beneficial to the whole of the people: they may safely believe that, in promoting the great interests of all, they cannot but promote in the best possible way, and to the greatest possible extent, the interests of individuals. Laying aside, then, such local and particular feelings as may interfere injuriously with the interests of all, they will seek for and accept, as candidates, none but men whose characters are good; whose particular interests are not at variance with those of the public, and on whose integrity they can satisfy themselves reliance may be placed. Much better is it that a man should refuse to vote at all, than that he should vote for any one of whose untrustworthiness he entertains doubt.

It will in many cases happen, that the person who is put forward, or who puts himself forward, as a candidate, will be unknown to the electors. In other cases, he will be known to many, but not to all. In other cases again, he will be known to all, either by his public conduct, or by public report of his conduct. In the last of these cases, a man's merits may, perchance, be known to an extent which may make it unnecessary to require pledges; but such a man will never hesitate to give them. Pledges may then be taken

---

[1] This has been written on the printed pamphlet, presumably by Place himself.

from all. Every elector should recollect that his representative is elected for the unreasonably long period of SEVEN YEARS, and that he may therefore set his constituents at defiance for that period.

It is then indispensably necessary, that the conduct, as well private as public, of every candidate should be scrutinized, and the result made known, and that pledges should be given by him to the electors in the most solemn manner.

The duties of electors may be summed up in very few words.

1. Relinquishment of all petty interests and feeling for the public good.
2. Strict inquiry into the characters, public and private, of candidates.
3. Demand of pledges, under the hands of candidates.

There is no intermediate course—there can be no compromising with these duties, without dishonestly betraying the sacred trust each elector ought to exercise for the public good.

The consequences of any compromising, or paltering, must be a betrayal of the public interests, and the return to parliament of political adventurers who speculate on a seat in the House of Commons to promote their own sinister interests, and those of their confederates, to enable them to plunder and debase the people.

The House of Commons has but too generally been composed of three descriptions of persons, viz:—[this section is almost identical to the wording of Place's suggested address for the Parliamentary Candidate Society in 8.]

The whole of the numerous body of persons who compose these three classes may be designated adventurers, no one of whom ought to find a seat in the new parliament. Against every such person electors should resolutely guard themselves, and this can only be done by careful inquiries as to their characters, public and private, and by taking such pledges as no one can violate without shewing himself to be a villain.

The pledges to be given by candidates should be as general as possible; the understanding as to their execution as particular as possible. No man should be expected to attempt any thing at such an unseasonable time as would subject him to the imputation of folly;—no one should bind himself in such a way as would compel him to perform such acts to save his pledges, as would make him a hypocrite: much must be left to the judgment of the representative, who, if he be, honest, will seize every opportunity to promote the good of his country, and convince his constituents that he has not given pledges without intending to perform them. He will, therefore, on all proper occasions originate motions, and will support every measure which can in any way tend to promote the great reforms of which the Reform Bill may be taken as the basis.

The pledges then that candidates should be required to give seem to be

I. PARLIAMENTARY REFORM

This includes

1. Shortening the duration of Parliaments.
2. Voting by Ballot.

If the whole nation were divided into electoral districts, and the votes were taken by ballot, parliaments could not be too short, nor the right of voting too extensive.

At *present*, the duration of parliament should be limited to three years.

The advantages of voting by ballot have been ably and conclusively shown in the 25th number of the Westminster Review. A careful abridgment of the article has been made, and may be had of the secretary, at the Union Rooms, Saville House, Leicester Square, at 7s. a hundred for distribution.

II. LAW REFORM

This includes a thorough revision of all laws—common, statute, civil, criminal, ecclesiastical, local, parliamentary, and municipal; the abolition of all arbitrary jurisdictions; the abridgment, as much as may be possible, of vexation, delay, and expense; the detection of crimes, and the certainty of speedy punishment; abolition of barbarous and cruel punishments, and the adoption of such punishments only as are commensurate with offences.

III. FINANCIAL REFORM

This includes reduction of taxes to the greatest possible extent; reduction of all over-paid salaries and pensions, as well as payment of every kind, from the highest office in the state to the lowest; the total abolition of all sinecures, all useless offices, and all unearned pensions.

It is advisable that indirect taxes, and especially those which press heaviest on trade, manufactures, commerce, and the comforts of the people should be repealed in preference to direct taxes. Had there been none but direct taxes, the public never would have submitted to be taxed to one half the amount they are at present taxed.

IV. TRADE REFORM

This includes the abolition of ALL monopolies, and more especially the Corn Law monopoly; the free admission of all sorts of produce for manufacturers, and indeed of free trade in every respect, that the greater number may no longer be compelled to purchase any thing at an advanced price that the profits of a very small comparative number may be unduly increased.

V. CHURCH REFORM

This includes—

1. Equalization to a great extent of the church establishment. Every dignitary of the church preaches poverty and wallows in wealth. Great wealth being condemned as incompatible with *the true* religion, none of its ministers should therefore be wealthy.

2. Ceasing to compel any one to pay for the maintenance of any particular doctrine he does not approve.

3. Abolition of tithes in the fairest way and in the shortest time possible.

VI. ABOLITION OF SLAVERY

This includes the freedom of every person, of every colour, and every shade of colour; holding of persons in slavery is UNJUST, atrocious, and cruel; abolition of slavery without compensation to slave holders is also

UNJUST, but it is inevitable, and therefore less *unjust* than retaining them as slaves. It becomes then the duty of the legislature to emancipate all slaves, with the least injustice, as well to slave holders as to slaves themselves, and in as little time as possible, compatible with the smallest amount of evil.

VII. TAXES ON KNOWLEDGE

These are the stamp duty on newspapers, the excise duty on paper, and the duty on advertisements.

The National Political Union have published the Debate on Mr Bulwer's motion on this subject, with notes.

These seven pledges, occupying as many lines, appear to the council to be sufficiently comprehensive and exact; such as no honest man can refuse to give, and every elector should demand.

ROWLAND DETROSIER
Secretary

JULY 11, 1832

55. [Add. Ms. 27796, ff. 316–18]

On the 23rd of July a meeting of the [National] Union [of the Working Classes] was held. Mr Benbow in the Chair. Mr Duffey proposed the following resolution.

That the members of this union in town and country, be requested to urge on all the necessity of demanding pledges from the candidates who offer themselves to their notice including all the great principles laid down in our, '*Objects and Laws*'.

56. [Add. Ms. 27796, ff. 321–2. Place's comments on the above proceedings of the National Union of the Working Classes.]

These proceedings shewed nothing but pure imbecility, circumstanced as the working classes were they had no power, no influence, they could neither intimidate their landlords with whom they lodged as had been proposed, nor even set about, much less persuade those who had votes; as had been recommended to vote as they wished, nor to obtain pledges from candidates, yet most of the leaders and perhaps nearly all their auditors entertained a vague notion that they could operate in all these ways. The leaders, like other fanatics imagined they had great power, and also like other fanatics, altho' they never had the most remote chance of carrying any one of their resolutions into effect, they proceeded as if they were continually effecting some of their purposes and progressing in all of them.

This was the character of the Union during the remainder of its existence and hence the history of them and other such bodies might be closed, but as that history which to some extent marks the temper of the active part of the working people, as it afterwards caused some uneasiness in London in consequence of an attempt at a public meeting, as well as of the assistance it gave to *Trades Unions* and to an immense meeting and procession of working people, which caused the government, to assemble a large body of troops in the Metropolis I have deemed it advisable to continue the narrative.

57. [Add. Ms. 27796, ff. 80–2]

While the English Reform Bill was before parliament it was not possible for me to persuade any member of Parliament with whom I was acquainted that in consequence of certain clauses in the bill, a very large portion of the electors in the Scot and Lot Boroughs would be disfranchised and that the number in each of the Boroughs would be a much smaller one than could be supposed by the returns made to parliament of the number of persons returned as eligible to vote. This being the case no one would interfere to prevent the mischief, now however when the bill had become law and the agitation, and enthusiasm to have the bill without taking the trouble to understand its operation, had subsided; I was able to explain to several of them what really was the condition in which the bill had placed the Borough voters. After much labour I induced Colonel Evans the member for Rye to move for certain returns which would officially prove that the representations I had made were correct. Colonel Evans therefore made his motion and two returns were obtained.

I also succeeded in convincing Mr Warburton, Mr Hume, Sir John Hobhouse and several other members that the defects in the Bill were of great importance and that the character of the new parliament might be decided against the reformers by the state into which the Boroughs had been put by the Bill. They conversed with other members and thus caused considerable uneasiness among many of them, and put ministers in an awkward situation.

58. [Add. Ms. 27796, f. 103]

Apprehension of the consequences, of the rate paying clause and the mode of registration directed by the bill, did not cease with the passing of the bill, nor the prorogation of the parliament. These apprehensions, and the necessity of doing whatever might be necessary relative to the forthcoming elections aroused the activity of the Political Unions, which would otherwise have subsided, and they continued in this state for some time.

There was also some disposition among the people in the Boroughs to agitate the matter, but after the long continued efforts the people had made and the energy with which they made it, the loss of time and expense of money it had occasioned, no very considerable effort on the present occasion was possible.

Some leading men in the Parish of St John finding that a small proportion of the householders in their parish were qualified to vote at the expected general election even by the payment of rates, without reference to taxes, drew up a case and sent it to Mr Chitty, who returned a long see-sawing opinion, from which nothing could be learned, beyond a leaning to a beleif [sic], that they who had not paid all rates and assessed taxes due on the 5 of April before the 31st of July would be disfranchised.

This induced them to call a meeting of the Parishioners, and an application to me to draw an Address to the King, explaining their case and praying for a remedy.

A very numerous meeting of the householders was held on the 23rd of August, when several parishioners made speeches very much to the purpose, in which it was clearly shewn that it was not possible for the electors to conform to the directions of the act.

1st. Because they could not clearly comprehend the meaning of some of the clauses.

2nd Because they could not know what rates and taxes ought to be paid under the act to enable them to be legally put upon the register.

59. [Add. Ms. 27796, ff. 164–5]

Table 1

Great care and much pains were taken to ascertain the state of the several parishes which compose the City and Liberty of Westminster and a Table made therefrom was printed in the Morning Chronicle on the 22 of August 1832. The table which follows is more accurate than it was possible to make one at the time of publication.

Names of the Parishes	Number of Rate Payers	Number polled in 1818	Number qualified to vote 31 July 1832
St George	5,144	2,211	22
St James	2,884	2,066	180
St Martin	2,218	1,748	1,500
St Clement etc.	2,205	1,289	320
St Ann	1,322	901	490
St Margaret	1,900	896	271
St John	1,796	659	153
St Paul etc.	631	447	10
	18,100	10,217	2,946

It will be observed that more than half the number of persons who had paid *the rate*, and were so far qualified, were in the Parish of St Martin. There was a dispute going on in this parish and a temporary rate of very small amount had been laid to raise money for present emergencies, and it was the collection of this rate which caused the number to be so high.

N.B. This table has no reference to the payment of Taxes.

Table II

Abstract of the Registration for Westminster as printed by the High Bailiff previous to the General Election in December 1832.

Names of the Parishes	£10 House-holders	Scot & Lot Holders	Totals	Rate Payers
St Ann	322	125	447	1,322
Clement	780	88	868	1,975
George	2,511	802	3,313	5,144
James	606	383	989	2,884
John	402	241	643	1,796
Margaret	547	422	969	1,900
Mary le Strand	89	12	101	230
Paul	271	48	319	549
Savoy	38	12	50	82
Martin	1,222	427	1,649	2,218
Totals	6,788	2,560	9,348	18,100

Number of Rate payers	18,100 ⎫	No. less than Rate Payers 8,752
Number registered as voters	9,348 ⎭	

Electors polled in	1807	10,542 ⎫	
	1818	10,277 ⎱	These were all the contested elections from
	1819	8,365 ⎰	1807 to 1832
	1820	9,280 ⎭	

Very few more than 4,000 voted in 1832, and consequently only about half as many as polled at any one of the above elections—and not half as many as at any one of the other three Elections.

What rule the overseers went by in making the distinction between £10 householders and Scot and Lot voters, could not be learned by me but I conclude those who appear as Scot and Lot voters were favoured persons who were in arrears for rates.

N.B. There are no rated houses paying a less rent than £10 per annum.

60. [Add. Ms. 27796, ff. 177–9]

Parliament was expected to be dissolved as soon as preparations could be made for carrying the enactments of the bill, and especially those which respected registration into practice.

The few and feeble efforts which had been made to procure such amendments in the English reform bill as have been mentioned,[1] had been met by a wilful misrepresentation and perversion of the law, and a scheme had been put in practice by which a considerable number of unqualified persons in the Boroughs might be fraudulently put upon the register instead of the small number who were legally qualified.

The attention of the people had taken a new direction, in consequence of the numerous addresses of candidates for seats in the house of commons, and the necessity there was in most places for the peoples endeavours to find men whom they thought qualified to represent them.

There was great scarcity of properly qualified candidates, and this caused many applications to every public man to be made to find if they could such persons as would suit the enquirers. It was difficult to procure any, and utterly impossible to find many men properly qualified and having the appropriate aptitude for the office of legislators. Very few such men would consent to become candidates.

The reasons were many. Some were engaged in pursuits or occupied with business which in justice to their families they could not abandon and to whom, under such circumstances a seat was not at all desirable. Others were not rich enough to pay the expenses of Election contests and the people had not virtue enough to put them into parliament free from expense; some very [few] instances alone excepted.

Others again who might have been willing to pay the election expences [sic], were satisfied that they could not do their duty to their country without incurring expenses, either wholly beyond their means, or to an extent which they were not justified in incurring.

Another class of persons, those who were by no means *so well qualified*

---

[1] See Handbill 10.

108

NATIONAL POLITICAL UNION.

To the Honorable the Commons of the United Kingdom of Great Britain and Ireland in Parliament assembled.

The Petition of the undersigned sheweth,

That being members of the Council of a society called the National Political Union, they think it their bounden duty to request your Honorable House not to permit the introduction of any clause into any Bill which may be brought before your Honorable House, " to amend the representation of the people," which clause may require the *payment* of *rent, tax*, or *rate*, to enable any person otherwise qualified to vote for a member of your Honorable House:

Your petitioners submit that it is scarcely within the province of the legislature so to interfere between landlord and tenant, tax and rate collector and tax and rate payer, as to deprive an elector of his right of suffrage on the ground that he has not paid the demand of his landlord, the tax gatherer, or the rate collector:

That if a man is to enjoy the right of suffrage in consequence of his occupying a house or premises of a certain value, all interference of the legislature should stop there, *payment* of *rent, taxes*, and *rates* being matters between individuals who can appeal to the laws, and should therefore have no reference whatever to the exercise of political rights:

That a clause requiring *payment* of rent, tax, or rate, must inevitably lead to disputes and ill will between parties, to endless litigation, vexation, and expence; to bribery, corruption, and perjury; and to a great increase of crimes of every kind:

That the important exercise of suffrage should be free and uncontrouled; but such a clause will be destructive of the freedom of multitudes of electors; will make the return of many members to your Honorable House a mere contention of the purse, and will cause the perpetration of many enormities in almost every city and borough in the kingdom:

That all the evils pointed out to your Honorable House are well known to have existed at, and been consequent on, elections for the city and liberty of Westminster:

That at elections for the said city and liberty, non-payment of poor's rate has been held to be a disqualification of an elector:

That many persons in the said city and liberty have been induced to withhold payment of poor's rate in the confident expectation that it would be paid for them by candidates for a seat in your Honorable House, and many other persons, who could but ill afford to pay the rates and who were in arrears, have entertained the same expectations:

That these expectations, whether they were the result of poverty or of a mean and corrupt disposition, were rarely disappointed; the practice being common to bribe voters by payment of poor's rates, to vote for the candidate on whose behalf the money was paid:

That in numerous instances electors were, by the payment of rates, induced to commit the foulest perjuries, and thus demoralized and degraded, became worse members of society than, but for these scandalous practices, they would have been:

That candidates for seats in your Honorable House participated in and promoted these atrocities; and the men who had thus become suborners of perjury, demoralizers of the people, and instigators of crime, have sat in the House of Commons as pure and upright senators, to make laws for the punishment of guilt, and to secure and increase the moral dignity of the people:

That these scandalous practices and lamentable consequences are common in other places, acting reciprocally on the wretches suborned and the villains who suborned them, both parties being nearly equally infamous:

That these atrocious practices subvert the freedom of elections, and drive the honest man from the hustings to make way for the rogue, who, if he be rich, too often succeeds in his nefarious purpose, by causing the baser and many of the poorer of the electors to depend on his purse; whilst in other cases, and between rogues, bribery in the shape of poor's rate has often led to a contest of who shall bribe highest:

That shortening the duration of polls will in some places tend to diminish these evils, but will not prevent them in any place:

That schemes will be devised and adopted by which these evils will be perpetuated; and should these evils, which are at present confined to particular places, be made applicable to all places, the greatest injury will be done to the community:

Your petitioners therefore pray, that your Honorable House will not permit the insertion of a clause in any Bill for "amending the representation of the People" which shall require payment of *rent, tax,* or *rate*, from any one otherwise qualified to vote for a person to represent him in your Honorable House.

HANDBILL 10 Add. Ms. 27822, f. 44.

for the office of representatives of the people were similarly circumstanced, and thus the difficulties of the people were greatly increased.

An instance occurred in my own case as it did in the case of several, probably many others. A deputation of respectable persons from one of the new Boroughs came to invite me to become a candidate on the assurance that the electors would themselves pay all the election expenses, and all expences I might incur in travelling, and they assured me that if I consented my election would be certain.

I was not at all ambitious of a seat in the house of Commons, but I should hardly have considered myself at liberty to refuse compliance with the request had not other circumstances made my acceptance altogether indiscreet, probably ruinous to me. From my connection with the working classes in various places and the intercourse I occasionally had with manufacturers, a very large portion of the parliamentary business of these classes and probably the whole in relation to the working people would have been put upon me. Others too would have reasonably expected my cooperation and assistance in consequence of the amendments I had proposed in the reform bill (England) and in every kind of reformation in Church and State.

It was therefore clear to me that if I attempted to do my duty as undoubtedly I should have done would have consumed every hour of my time, and occasioned an expense of money which I could not afford. I estimated this expense at £500 a year, and I knew that unless that sum was expended in the rent etc. of a place appropriated for business, in the salary etc. of a secretary and probably an assistant to him, in extra postage, stationary [sic] and various incidental expenses, that I should be an inefficient member which I was not willing to consent to become. These matters I stated, and fully explained to the deputation, and told them that whatever expenses as a member of parliament I was compelled to incur must either be paid by the persons who elected me or I could not consent to become a candidate for a seat in the house of commons. This necessarily put an end to the business.

61. [Add. Ms. 27796, ff. 195–6. *Printed.*]

NATIONAL POLITICAL UNION, SAVILLE HOUSE, LEICESTER SQUARE, October 26, 1832, EXTENSION OF THE OBJECTS OF THE UNION, 'KNOWLEDGE IS POWER'.

The Council of the National Political Union, anxious to redeem the pledge given by them, to 'assist in the diffusion of sound moral and political information,' have made arrangements to promote this object at the cheapest possible rate. The expense will be so moderate, as to place the contemplated advantages within the reach of almost every man in the community; and if the support given to the Council in their endeavours to extend the blessings of knowledge should enable them, they intend to reduce the sum now fixed to a still lower rate.

They call on the industrious classes to avail themselves of the advantages thus offered—advantages which, on such terms, cannot be secured but by means of UNION.

They call on the wealthier classes to co-operate with them in the noble cause of the 'diffusion of knowledge'. By their *subscriptions*, they may give greater efficiency to a plan which presents means of instruction to those whose circumstances have hitherto necessarily excluded them from most intellectual enjoyments; and by their *donations of books*, which will be extensively circulated amongst the members of the Union, they may enable hundreds to store their minds with really useful knowledge.

They call on all well-wishers to social improvement, of whatever station, sect, or class, to assist in bettering the intellectual and moral condition of the people. 'There has never been any object in the history of nations which more amply merited, or could be more efficiently served, by the co-operation of all good citizens and honest men.'

The means by which it is proposed to attain these important purposes, are,

1st.—By the delivery of Lectures on political and other useful subjects, including natural and experimental philosophy, literature, and the arts.

2d.—By Discussions amongst the members on questions of general interest.

3d.—By a Library of circulation, in addition to the present Reading Room.

It is further proposed to establish classes and elementary schools, for the study of languages, etc. as soon as the funds will permit.

The members only of the National Political Union will be admitted to the Lectures and Discussions, on the payment of one shilling per quarter, in addition to the present subscription, and one penny admission to each Lecture or Discussion.

The members only will be admitted to the use of the Circulating Library, on the payment of one shilling quarterly.

Donations in money, books, and apparatus, are earnestly requested.

62. [Add. Ms. 27796, ff. 200–2]

The plan proposed by the committee, adopted and ordered to be carried into effect by the Council, communicated to the members of the Union and intended to be made public in every way likely to be useful, did not suit the views of those whose selfish purposes extended no further than their own accomodation [*sic*] at the expense of others. These men therefore associated with themselves every ill-conditioned member whom they could persuade to concur with them, and every silly one whom they could delude, and of whom they made a bad use. They quarelleled [*sic*] with the servants of the Union, turned the quiet reading room into a debating room, in which full swing was given to the worst passions, the most disgraceful language and most reprehensible conduct. Efforts were at first made to appease, and to conciliate, and these failing, to suppress their proceedings, these also failed. They proceeded in their course ill used the servants, and then made formal complaints against them to the Council. They disgusted and drove away every respectable member who came to the reading room,—they injured the Union in every possible way. The consequence of their conduct in addition to the quiet state into which the people had sunk after their long continued and vehement excitement tended rapidly to the destruction of the Union. So small was the number who at once renewed their tickets, and paid their shillings, that it became evident, to the Council they could not maintain the ordinary expenses much less carry out the enlargements of the objects of the Union which they had persuaded themselves would be supported by the members and the public, and that any attempt to do so would speedily bring ruin on the Union and involve it [in] debts for which a portion of the Committee would be ultimately responsible.

The violence of these disorderly people increased daily, and no probable termination of their conduct could be anticipated; the Council were therefore called upon to consider all the circumstances in which they were placed and to take such measures as might enable them to avoid the impending danger.

Under these circumstances the usual weekly meeting of Council was held. On the 7 November, Mr Millard in the Chair and ten Councillors.

The conduct of the persons alluded to was exceedingly annoying. On this occasion they and a number of misled members occupied a considerable portion of the seats, and interrupted the Council, which after some time adjourned without having done any business.

A special meeting of the Council was held on 10th, Mr Rainford in the Chair and 19 Councillors.

Mr Harrison on the part of the Business committee communicated the reason why the Special meeting had been called. He said that the excitement which had caused so large a number of persons to become members of the Union had passed away and a large number had on that account refrained from renewing their tickets. That the conduct of some of the members had driven away a large number also, and the consequence was an almost cesession [*sic*] of members and subscriptions. It therefore became the duty of the Business Committee to invite the Council to the consideration of the present state and future prospects of the Union.

Mr Harrison then laid before the Council a statement of receipts and expenditure since the last account, and a statement of the future expenses to which the council as a body had made themselves liable.

The Council resolved itself into a committee and after some discussion it was resolved. That a cheap room be taken in a central situation, to enable the Council to make its expenditure correspond with its income.

A committee was appointed to carry the resolution into effect. It was then resolved that the committee be instructed

1. To give notice to the proprietor of Saville House that we shall quit the premises at the expiration of the ensuing week.

2. To give notice to the members that the money which has been paid by them for lectures and the circulating library will be returned to each of them upon demand.

3. That the newspapers be immediately discontinued.

4. That notice be given to the officers of the Union that their services will not be required at the end of one month from the present time.

5. That all members for the present quarter requiring the return of their subscriptions be repaid and their names erased from the books of the Union.

63. [Place Collection, set 63, vol. 1, f. 200]
Special Meeting of Council

Saville House Leicester Square
Thursday 22 Nov. 1832

Present Mr Thomas Murphy in the Chair

W. B. Hankin	A. Mongredien
E. Rainford	S. Harrison
W. Cooke	D. W. Redman
J. Longmate	C. Wright
J. Savage	W. D. Saull
J. D. Styles	G. S. Berkeley
G. G. Ward	C. Fox Smith
S. Arnot	R. Franks

The following report was presented from the Standing Committee.

The Committee report that in consequence of a past resolution of Council the reading room was closed on Saturday the 17th inst. & the publications discontinued—the secretary and assistants have received a months notice to leave—the different rooms occupied by the Union given up to the Landlord last Tuesday, the tables, forms etc. removed to a room for the present hired for the purpose & that the room occupied by the Secretary has been re-engaged at ten shillings per week where the business of the Union will continue to be transacted.

The Committee have specially summoned the Council in consequence of some propositions received from a deputation of Members who being desirous of perpetuating the Union have suggested that a room or rooms should be engaged to be used as a reading room or for conversation, discussions & lectures, the estimated expense including rent, attendance, candles, coals & newspapers would be about £50 per quarter this sum to be raised by the Members without touching the funds of the Union excepting that part subscribed this quarter and which was promised to be returned to those who required it—the members engage to raise the remainder—but before they do so they the deputation consider it necessary to ascertain whether the Council will sanction this plan & also if they will allow the management to remain in the hands of a committee one half Council & one half Subscribers, other minor suggestions were made which will be found in the annexed propositions.

Propositions presented to the Committee by a deputation of nine members of the Union viz Messrs Langley, Smith, Pearce, Mason, Baker, Gains, Davis, Nyse, Scarfe.

1st To recommend the taking of premises suitable for our accommodation for reading, discussions & lectures as far as our means will allow.

2d That the Committee to manage the same be composed of members of the Council & members of the Union in equal proportion.

3d The rules for the conduct of such rooms or room to be submitted to & sanctioned by a general meeting to be called by the Council.

4 That as Sect'n 2 Clause 3 says 'that every species of concealment or mystery is to be carefully avoided' will your committee allow extracts to be made from the address book on a requisition signed by six members.

113

5 That Mr Langley be requested to deliver the above.

The Committee have only to add that upon a conference with the deputation the Committee decided that they had no authority to accede to the propositions but agreed to refer them to a Council to be specially called for the purpose.

It was then after some discussion moved by Mr Savage, seconded by Mr Saull.

That the means of defraying the expences [*sic*] of rooms for reading, discussions & lectures not being sufficient and the probability of their being raised not being evident to this Council they regret that they cannot accede to the first recommendation.

Carried unanimously.

64. [Add. Ms. 27796, ff. 205–8. Place on the extinction of the National Political Union.]

1833

The Union was now virtually extinct. For some time past its use as a *Political* Union had ceased, was at an end.

Such Associations can never flourish but in times when the people are greatly and justly excited, by some particular movement of the Government, or when some great difficulty occurs and the government either from incapacity or wilfulness becomes apathetic, in either case the people will sometimes, not always, determine that a change of some sort shall be made. All other ebullitions are merely party contests in which the people are sure to be sacrificed whichever faction triumphs.

Circumstances such as these have hitherto been of rare occurrence in this country, they will be less and less rare in future, public opinion is only of recent growth but it will continue to grow with increasing rapidity, and will become more and more potent. It is only of late years that the masses of the people have ever shewn a deliberate disposition to act together for any purpose. This it is which makes an administration which is feeble in all other respects, strong against the people, who will, in ordinary times submit to almost any oppression so it be brought upon them slowly and quietly, and as it is in every way the practice of those who govern, as well as of the class of society, to govern for their own convenience and advantage solely, and not for the people generally, they act accordingly. It is only when they who compose the government have gone on in this way for a considerable time and met with little or no interruption that having become secure and consequently careless, they commit some gross error, which rouses the people to a shew of resistance. It was the supposed security of the government and the contempt it necessarily engendered for the people which induced the Duke of Wellington to make the uncalled for declaration which unseated the Tories and compelled the Whigs to propose a reform of parliament in the House of Commons. It was this flagrant act of folly into which the Duke was misled by his notion of security and his consequent misconception of his power that gave the advantage to his opponents at the moment the people were disposed to support them that led to the transactions which have been recorded. It was all these circumstances operating at the same time that roused the people to take the active part they did in their own affairs. Whenever this happens it puts the people so much out of their ordinary way—is so incompatible with their habits, so injurious to them in many ways, that having once interfered to any considerable extent, they fall back and sink to a considerable extent into a state of acquiescence from which much time and much ill usage can alone again rouse them. In a state of this kind they were placed at the commencement of the year 1833.

The Reform Bills were passed, the new parliament was about to meet and the people were quietly waiting for its opening in vague expectation that when assembled it would do something though they did not know what.

Any effort to keep up the Union, as a *Political* Union would have been absurd, and could not have succeeded. . . .

Many amongst the best members of the National Political were desirous to perpetuate the Union, not indeed as a Political Union but as a place of instruction. Many of those members who had headed the discontented, having first made them discontented, had left the Union and it was not at all doubted that many more would neglect to take out their tickets for the new quarter. Thus freed from men who would have kept up an evil spirit of contentious animosity it was intended to make an attempt to establish a reading room, a weekly lecture, a circulating library, and school in which Arithmetic—some Geometry—Geography—Grammar might be taught to the young members. They were individually willing to give some money and endeavour to induce others who were not members to contribute in the same way. I was consulted respecting this scheme, and from the experience I had of such projects was compelled to believe that it would not be found practicable.

65. [Add. Ms. 27796, ff. 336–8. Printed advertisement in the *Poor Man's Guardian*.]

That at the assembling of the first '*Reformed*' Parliament, we prepare and present a challenge, or invitation, from a specific number of the '*National Union of the Working Classes*' (to be appointed for that purpose) to meet a like number of Members of the said Parliament, for the purpose of discussing the justice of the claims of the non-electors to equal representation.

On the 17 [December 1832] the resolution proposed in the preceding advertisement was moved at the usual *general* meeting of the [National] Union [of the Working Classes].

The chairman proposed it as one of vital importance and took some pains to convince his audience that his assertion was correct.

Mr Duffey opposed the motion, he wondered how such nonsense had got into the Guardian, and could not tell how the committee could propose such buffoonery. The proposition was only calculated to make the Union look ridiculous and contemptible. He might not be applauded for saying this, but, he would never court their applause on any but just and proper grounds. What was it they had laid before them for their consideration?—

just nothing, or what was worse, that which was nonsensical or mischievous. It was just the thing to gratify their enemies. Challenge the Parliament indeed. There was no question it was a piece of buffoonery altogether. As to the competition of talent that was nonsense. There would be men of talent in the house who were their friends. Hume—O Connell—Cobbett—Fielden and others. (cheers) Let them then abandon this, quixotic—paltry—and disgraceful resolution, and let their friends act on right principles for them, while they, the Working-classes, gave them an influential direction. Before they could achieve any thing, they must conquer the prejudices of public opinion. If they boasted of talent, they should shew it by being judicious, their bravery should be directed by sense and discretion. If they shewed the feeling of what the *Times* called the *Destructives*, the country would turn away from them with horror, but if they acted wisely, they would convince both Whigs and Tories they were not the wretches they were said to be. What more could the enemy desire to have than the power to exhibit this resolution in the house of commons. He was ashamed to be one of a Union whence such a thing could emanate—rather let there be no Union than such a proposition as this. He had before censured the committee, and a more disgraceful act than this could not have been brought forward.

He continued for some time in the same strain, when the Chairman asked several times who seconded the motion, but no one doing so, it dropped.

This was followed by a furious altercation which continued for some time when the meeting broke up without any resolution having been passed.

66. [Add. Ms. 27796, f. 213. National Political Union. *Printed.*]

COUNCIL
Elected 4th February, 1833

Brookes, John, Oxford-street
Bohm, W.H., 17, Chad's-place
Bennett, John, 28, Hart-st, Bloomsbury
Berkeley, George S., 44, Fetter-lane
Barker, T.B., 4, Charles-place, Walworth
Blake, Robert, 8, Stephen's court, Tottenham-court-road
Blake, George, 8, Stephen's court, Tottenham-court-road
Bainbridge, Dr J.N., 88, St Martin's-lane
Burnard, J.P., Formosa Cott., Holloway
Barnes, W., Bridge-house-pl., Newington
Cheesman, R., 49, Great Dover-street, Southwark
Cumming, William, 68, London-wall
Cumming, R.D., 68, London-wall
Carpenter, W., 16, Gt Union-st, Boro'
Churchill, H.B., Temple
Curwood, John, Temple
Cooke, William, 45, St Mary Axe
Coode, Geo., Temple
Douglass, Wm, 21, Frederick-place, Hampstead-road
Draycott, Fred., Duke-st, Bloomsbury
Drewett, Joel, Harper-street, New Kent-road
Epps, Dr John, Berners-street
Evans, Thos, Beak-st, Regent-street
Fox, Rev. W.I. [*sic*], Upper Clapton
Franks, Robt, Redcross-st, Barbican
Goodwin, Sam., Manor-place, Walworth
Galloway, Alex., West-street, Smithfield
Hankin, H.B., 11, Granbourn's-buildings Vauxhall
Harrison, S., 23, Great Ormond-street

King, J.B., 5, James'-place, Hackney-road
Longmate, James, 7, Theobald's-road
Lee, J.G., 12, Newton-street, Holborn
McDiarmid, Wm, 17, New-st-square
Mongredien, A., 44, George-street Hampstead-road
Moore, Richd, 13, Compton-st, Soho
Milner, Thos, 37, Marsham-street Westminster
Millard, Wm, 19 Greville-st, Hatton Garden
Murphy, T., Commercial-rd, Hampstead
Mordan, Samp., Castle-street, Finsbury
Norman, J., Claremont-terrace, Hackney-road
Noel, Rt.R., Notting-hill
Owen, Robert Dale, 4, Crescent-place
Owen, R., James'-place, Hackney-road
Powell, J. H., 26, Chapple-street, Pentonville
Perry, E., 25, Chester-st, Belgrave-sq
Place, Francis, 16, Charing-cross
Redman, D. W., 14, Little Charlotte-st, Middle-sex Hospital
Roberts, John, 66, Basinghall-street
Revell, Henry, Burton-crescent
Rogers, Geo., High-street, St Giles
Rutt, J.F. [*sic*], Newington-green
Rosser, Chas, Skinner-street
Rainford, Edward, Red Lion-passage, Red Lion-street
Styles, J. D., 37, Marsham-street, Westminster
Sellis, John, Church-street, Hackney
Skinner, John, Lant-street, Borough
Saull, W.D., Aldersgate-street
Smith, C. Fox, Stones'-end, Borough

116

Simpson, H., New-street, Covent-garden
Sewell, John, Rockingham-pl., Kent-rd.
Tucker, Robt, Pepper-street, Borough
Templeman, John, 18, Percy-street, Tottenham-court-road
Thomas, Cartwright, 49, Old Broad-st
Taylor, J., 4, Christopher-st, Finsbury
Todd, John, Garnault-place, Clerkenwell

Upton, Geo., 64, Queen-street, Cheapside
Ward, G.G., 30, Union-st, Marylebone
Wood, W.R., 17, Cumberland-street
Wright, Chas, 102, High-st, Holborn
Wright, Henry, Clerkenwell
Wallis, William, 19, Elizabeth-street Hackney-road
Wakefield, D., jun., Gray's-inn

67. [Add. Ms. 27796, ff. 251–2]

Sometime previous to the election of the new Council on the 5th and 6th of February several of those members whom I most respected urgently requested me to permit my name to be put upon the list of candidates. They argued that unless we remained united and worked together as circumstances required, the government of the Union would fall into the hands of those who had caused the late dissentions, be by them conducted in an improper manner, be involved in a heavy debt and terminate in a very disreputable way. That it was possible and some of them thought it probable there might be a rallying of the members and a useful Institution for the working people established. I had no expectation that these hopes and expectations would be realised. I was satisfied that the working people would not subscribe in sufficient numbers nor consent to pay a sufficient subscription to keep up any such institution among themselves, and the time was gone by, at least for the present when others, not of their class would assist them to an extent at all likely to be useful. I however consented to have my name put upon the list, and promised to work with them for the accomplishment of their project until circumstances should prove, that their expectations could not be realised, that I should then cease to attend the meetings of the Council and would at any time resign my seat in the Council. I was elected, and attended the subsequent meeting on the 11 of february, when finding that the number of members who had renewed their tickets was so small that their subscriptions would be wholly inadequate to carry on the Union for any purpose whatever, I did not attend again, and I informed the business committee, that I was ready to resign my office or to attend on any emergency to prevent any injudicious proceedings.

Matters had now come to a crisis, several of the most useful and respectable of the members of the Council had resigned and their places were filled by others whose names stood next on the balloting list. Some of these were ill conditioned men, ignorant, self willed, and intent on their own convenience only.

The Union had degenerated in every respect and could not be sustained any longer. It was clearly shewn that if; as many wished; an attempt was made to keep the Union in an active state of existence a very considerable amount of debt would be incurred and for which a comparatively small number of members of the council would be responsible. I therefore agreed to attend with several others at the meeting this evening [5 June] and make an attempt to convince the council, that it was impossible to keep the Union in existence for any useful purpose and that the only rational course they could take was to bring it to a close as soon as possible.

Much pains were taken to accomplish these ends, but all our efforts were useless, and this determined me to resign.

117

68. [Add. Ms. 27796, ff. 290–1]

National Political Union
Abstract of Treasurers Cash Account 1831, 1832, 1833

	£	s	d		£	s	d
1831 Nov. 1 to July 31 1833 Subscriptions and donations received	1,217	15	2	Rent and occasional hire of rooms	358	13	6
Admission to meetings of the Council	28	18	–	Printing	285	16	9
Sale of pamphlets and tracts	31	6	9	Advertising and posting bills	109	13	8
Sale of medals	10	19	9				
	1,228	19	8	Newspapers etc. and reading room	53	8	2
Sale of books and furniture	34	11	4	Salaries clerks etc.	341	18	4
Subscribed by members of the Council	16	–	–	Sundries stationary [sic] coals, oil furniture etc.	190	–	7
	1,339	11	–		1,339	11	–

Quarterly Abstract of Cash Accounts

Receipts	1 Nov. 1831 to 31 Jan. 1832			30 Apr. 1832			31 July 1832			31 Oct. 1832			31 Jan. 1833			30 Apr. 1833			1 July 1833			Totals		
Subscriptions etc.	416	16	10	102	8	10	462	13	7	59	9	5	25	13	–	97	4	6	53	9	–	1,217	15	2
Council meetings	3	4	6	10	14	–	6	16	4	5	15	11	1	1	10		9	9		15	8	28	18	–
Sale of tracts	7	11	–	3	12	11	3	9	1	2	–	6	–	–		9	5	11	5	7	4	31	6	9
Sale of medals	–	–	–	–	–	–	10	19	9	–	–		–	–		–	–		–	–		10	19	9
£	427	12	4	116	15	9	483	18	9	67	5	10	26	14	10	107	–	2	59	12	–	1,288	19	8

Donations & sale of books 50 11 4

£1,339 11 –

Payments																								
Rent etc.	109	3	–	36	13	6	46	5	–	47	10	–	16	5	–	48	17	–	53	10	–	358	13	6
Printing	79	7	–	–	–	–	99	17	9	33	4	–	7	3	6	43	6	6	22	8	–	285	16	9
Advertising etc.	40	4	6	4	15	–	8	–	2	12	–	6	1	1	–	29	12	3	14	3	–	109	13	8
Reading room	2	8	9	8	3	9	17	9	5	20	9	–	4	17	3	–	–		–	–		53	8	2
Salaries etc.	64	7	9	64	3	–	69	8	6	65	19	3	25	6	–	19	2	–	33	11	10	341	18	4
Sundries	61	17	9	22	15	5	33	17	1	41	16	11	8	7	–	11	14	9	9	11	8	190	–	7
£	357	18	9	136	10	8	274	17	11	220	19	8	63	9	9	152	12	6	133	1	9	1,339	11	–

69. [Place Collection, set 63, vol. 1, f. 265. National Political Union.]

Final Balance Sheet of National Political Union
Jan. 28 1834

	£	s	d			£	s	d
Balance in hand at close of the union	£16	6	1½	By various disbursements since the close as per cash book		£47	8	6
Cash rec'd for books etc.	36	1	4½	Balance in hand see below		4	19	–
	52	7	6			52	7	6

Cr.	£	s	d			£	s	d
By Baxter Crown & Anchor	£23	2	–	Dr. Mr Rainford	£2 2			
1834 July 1 Settled by cheque for disc't	21 – – / 2	2	–	Rogers	16			
				Smith (Strand)	7			
				J. D. Styles	1 14			
	£23	2	–			4	19	–
				Balance required		18	3	–
						£23	2	–

The above Acc't included the sum of £21 voted by the Council to the Secretary as remuneration for his services a few weeks previous to closing the Union but does not include any thing for the attendance which he has been necessarily compelled to give to the business since that period.

The Cash book is of course open to the examination of any parties interested in the business and I shall be most happy to give to such any explanation they may require.

J. D. Styles

70. [Add. Ms. 27796, f. 292]

The Radical Club

On the night of the 5 June 1833 when I and several of my most esteemed friends, who were present at the Council of the [National Political] Union, resigned we walked up Holborn together, talking of the way in which the men into whose hands the management of the Union had fallen, would conduct it and the almost certain consequence, debt and disgrace they would bring upon it, unless they should find themselves incompetent to the charge they had taken upon themselves and abandon it, which some of us anticipated as all but certain, in which case it was suggested that we should be ready to take the matter up and bring it to an honourable close. This was asented [sic] to by all. When we were about to seperate one of us I believe Mr Rainford, said it was a pity that we and others who had acted so well together should become wholly disunited when Mr Samuel Harrison, one of the most considerate and honest hearted men I have ever known, proposed that some plan should be adopted to bring us together occasionally. This produced a conversation which ended in an agreement that as many of us as could make it convenient should meet on a day then named and consider of a plan. We met accordingly and agreed that the best mode would be to form a small club, to consist of as many of the members of the Council of the Union as we should hereafter select as original members, and that such as chose to join the club should be proposed by some members and be ballotted for.

71. [Add. Ms. 27796, f. 295. *Printed.*]

RULES of the RADICAL CLUB. Established 4th July, 1833.

I. That the Annual Subscription be Twenty-five Shillings.

II. That Persons of the Working Classes be admitted on payment of Ten Shillings yearly.

III. That when any Person, not a Native of Great Britain or Ireland, but a temporary resident in this country, shall be elected a Member of the Club, he shall not be called upon to pay any Subscription.

IV. That Annual Payments be made in advance on or before the first day of July in each year, or in proportion for new Members elected at any other period.

V. That the Society dine together four times in each year, on 30th January,— April, 4th July, 31st October, the expense of each dinner to be paid from the Subscription, and not to be less than Five Shillings or more than Seven Shillings for each Member.

VI. That every Person proposed to become a Member be nominated by two Members in writing, the nomination to be delivered to the Secretary at least fourteen days previous to any General Meeting; the Secretary must give notice to the Members of each such nomination, and the Persons proposed shall be ballotted for at the next Meeting of the Society.

VII. That on the nomination of any Candidate the Proposer or Seconder shall attend and answer as far as he is able any question which may be put to him respecting the qualifications of the Person proposed.

VIII. That when any Person proposed shall be elected a Member, his Proposer or Seconder shall pay the first Subscription on the night of the Election.

IX. That if on ballotting the number of black balls shall amount to one fourth of the whole number in the box, the Person proposed shall not become a member.

X. That if any Member should by his improper conduct become generally obnoxious to the Members, on requisition signed by four Members the subject shall be discussed at the next General Meeting after notice given in the summons to all the Members, and the question of his expulsion decided by ballot, a majority of votes of the Members present deciding.

XI. That a Committee of five shall be chosen from the Members annually in July, who shall have the superintendence and controul [sic] of the Affairs of the Society,—they shall call Meetings of the Members whenever in their opinion it may seem expedient—arrange and give the proper notices respecting the Quarterly Dinners, and keep regular Accounts and Minutes of all Proceedings.

SAMUEL HARRISON
23, Great Ormond Street   Secretary

71*a*. [Add. Ms. 27796, f. 296 *Printed*. Membership of the Radical Club at 29 January 1838]

William H. Ashurst, *New Bridge Street, Blackfriars*
Alfred Austin, *49 Doughty street*
Alexander Baylis, *8 New Basinghall street*
Samuel Baylis, *Whitecross street, Cripplegate*
J. Roberts Black
Thomas Brooksbank, *14 Gray's-inn square*
Samuel Courtauld, *Bocking, Essex*
George Charlwood, *Covent garden*
H. S. Chapman, *2 Tillotson place, Waterloo bridge*
H. B. Churchill, *2 Raymond buildings*
William Cooke, *43 St Mary Axe*
George Coode, *26 Euston place, New road*
John Crawfurd, *27 Wilton crescent*
William Cumming, *Carpenter's hall, London wall*
John Duce, *9 Wilmot street, Bethnal green*
Howard Elphinstone, *19 Eaton place, Belgrave square*
John Epps, *89 Great Russell street, Bloomsbury*
Thomas Falconer, *Gray's-inn square*
Edward Farn, *14 Gray's-inn square*
Edwin W. Field, *41 Bedford row*
William J. Fox, *366 Strand*
Charles J. Fox, *67 Paternoster row*
Robert Franks, *Redcross street, Barbican*
Alexander Galloway, *West street, Smithfield*
Thomas Gibson, *Hanger's lane, Tottenham*
George Glazier, *16 Titchfield street, Marylebone*
G. J. Graham, *21 Basinghall street*
W. P. Gaskell, *Cheltenham*
Samuel Harrison, *4 Cottage green, Camberwell*
C. J. Hector, M.P., *Reform Club, Pall Mall*
G. H. Heppel, *Mansion-house street*
William Hickson, jun., *13 Park Lane Piccadilly*
Joseph Hume, M.P., *Bryanstone square*
J. B. King, *2 Bartholomew lane*
William Lawrence, *Pitfield street, Hoxton*
James Longmate, *4 Princes street, Red-lion square*
J. T. Leader, M.P., *8 Stratton street*
James Murray, *8 Suffolk street, Hackney road*
John Melville, *16 Upper Harley street*
John Milner, *149 Albany street*

Sir William Molesworth, Bt. M.P., *Reform Club Pall Mall*
Augustus Mongredien, *21 Finsbury square*
Edward Mottram, *Little Britain*
M. Mazzini, *9 George street, New road*
Daniel O'Connell, M.P., *Reform Club, Pall Mall*
Robert Owen, *Mark Lane*
J. Osborne, *25 Bucklersbury*
Erskine Perry, *Chester street, Grosvenor place*
Joseph Phelps, *44 Paternoster row*
Francis Place, *21 Brompton square*
Michael Prendergast, *21 Castle street, Holborn*
William Pritchard, *Gordon court, Doctors' Commons*
Thomas Prout, *229 Strand*
Edward Rainford, *86 High Holborn*
Samuel Revans, *Austin Friars*
Henry Revell, *Burton crescent*
Elias Regnault, *Camberwell and Paris*
Nathaniel Saxton, *Bankside*
W. D. Saull, *Aldersgate street*
James Savage, *Bethnal-green road*
Charles FoxSmith, *64 Queen street, Cheapside*
J. D. Stiles,*27 Stamford street*
J. C. Symons, *Radnage, Stokenchurch, Bucks*
J. T. Selles, *15 St Mary Axe*
John Travers, *St Swithin's lane*
John Taylor, *17 Kent terrace, Regent's Park*
Richard Taylor, *Red-Lion court, Fleet street*
Peter A. Taylor, *5 Euston square*
T. Perronet Thompson, *13 Hanover terrace, Regent's Park*
J. B. Tomalin, *1 Riches court, Lime street*
Dr Usiglio, *9 George street, New road*
William Wallis, *19 Elizabeth street, Hackney road*
John Wade, *4 York terrace, Camberwell new road*
R. G. Welford, *Stockwell, Surrey*
William Williams, M.P., *Watling street*
Effingham Wilson, *Royal Exchange*
D. W. Wire, *St Swithin's lane*
William Weir, *Glasgow*

72. [Add. Ms. 27797, ff. 4–7]

On Monday the 22nd of April [1833] at a meeting [of the National Union of the Working Classes] held at the Rotunda in St Georges Fields. Mr Parkins, late editor of the Christian Corrector in the Chair.

Mr Cleave proposed the following resolution

'That we view with indescribable indignation the guilty speed with which the new secretary for Ireland has cooperated with Lord Anglesea in carrying into execution the infamous coercion bill, notwithstanding the repeated assurances to the contrary, both expressed and implied, made by the Whig Ministers in the house of commons, and by Sir John Hobhouse in particular at his second election; and therefore, we solemnly call on our Irish brethren to take the subject of a convention of the people into their most serious consideration.'

Mr Cleave spoke of the character of the bill and of some proceedings at Kilkenny. 'The resolution called upon them to take into their serious consideration the calling of a National Convention, and he was sure that until that was done and the Irish Nation put Daniel O Connell at the head of an Irish Republic the people of Ireland could procure no releif [*sic*].' (loud cheers)

Mr Mee seconded the motion. He observed that the lying press of the day told us the Reformed Parliament would do everything for us, and that we must therefore dissolve our Unions. They deceived us and we will not be deceived again. He was sorry the Irish members of parliament who were expected had not attended the meeting, as they would have seen the sympathy and fellow feeling of the working classes for their brethren in Ireland, and it might tend towards bringing about a closer connexion between them (cheers). They would likewise have become acquainted also with their determination to take their affairs into their own hands. They wanted to meet Irish delegates in London to form a *National Convention* (hear hear) and found a system of universal equity. It might be said, that he was a leveller—that he wanted to do away with the privileges of certain classes— they were right who said so. (cheers) It might be said you don't respect the laws, it was true they could never respect laws made without their concurrence calculated to injure them and benefit the privileged classes who enacted them (hear) men who had no feelings in common with the working people. Their interest was to make partial laws ours to make universal laws, and sure he was that the justice of the principle would ensure a certain victory. (cheers) He instanced the budget as proof that they had no desire to benefit the working man, and they would never do any thing to benefit him until they were compelled. (cheers) They were for keeping up the hereditary privileges which were brought into this country by that bastard of a Fish Fag—William of Normandy. He thought the people would be much to blame if after the lives of the present possessors, they retained their plunder any longer.

The resolution was agreed to unanimously.

Mr Yearly—then brought forward the resolution, which had been adjourned, as proposed by Mr Lee. Mr Plummer seconded it. [A resolution to call a national convention.]

Mr Cleave proposed an adjournment, the business was too important to be passed without further discussion. Adjourned.

The proceedings of this Union were strangely conducted, neither of these resolutions which seemed to the members to be matter of much importance had originated, or been even adverted to, in the General Committee of the

121

Union, nor is there in the minute book up to this time any notice respecting a National Convention. There is however the following entry under date, 17 April 1833. 'General Committee, Bowling Square Chapel. On the motion of Messrs Cleave and Mee a sub committee to consist of Messrs Preston—Coddington—Cleave—Mee—Petrie—Yearly—Fowler—Brown and Plummer, be appointed to prepare resolutions for the meeting to be held at the Rotunda on the 22nd instant.'

In all other societies of which I have had cognizance, the business to be brought forward at *general* meetings was prepared by the Committee or Council—or Managers—or Directors. But in this Union many motions were at once proposed and without notice not only to the members in general meetings, but to the members so assembled with a large body, generally as large sometimes much larger than the members, of persons who were not members, but strangers admitted by payment at the door as auditors for the evening.

In the present case the motion which was made by Mr Lee was probably adopted by the sub-committee and therefore again proposed by Mr Yearly —and that the resolution proposed by Mr Cleave was framed upon it, yet neither of those motions were stated to have been recommended by any committee, but were entertained simply as the motions of Mr Cleave and Mr Yearly.

73. [Add. Ms. 27797, ff. 11–16. Proceedings at a subsequent meeting of the National Union of the Working Classes, 8 May 1833.]

It was resolved that 500 double Crown Placards be printed announcing the meeting in the following form.

A PUBLIC MEETING
will be held on the Calthorpe Estate
COLD BATH FIELDS
On Monday next May 13 1833 at Two o Clock
To adopt preparatory Measures for holding a
NATIONAL
CONVENTION
The only means of Obtaining and Securing the
Rights of the People
By order of the Committee of the National Union of the Working Classes
John Russell Sec.

The following resolutions were finally adopted by the committee.
Resolutions for the Meeting in Cold Bath Fields on May 13 1833

1st. That this meeting disgusted at the barefaced hypocricy [*sic*] of the miscalled representatives of the people in the house of commons, take this opportunity of publicly declaring to their fellow countrymen, that until the working people of Great Britain and Ireland, obtain Universal Suffrage, they will be the dupes of designing factions.

2nd. That this meeting convinced of the ignorance of the many relative to the *Rights of Man,* (fostered by the designing few, who hold those rights in contempt) is the fatal cause of all the ills which afflict mankind, hereby proclaim the following declaration, to the end that the people may always have before their eyes the basis of their liberty and happiness, the Magistrates the rule of their conduct and duty, and Legislators the object of their appointment.

Declaration of Rights

All men are born equally free and have certain natural and unalienable rights, any infringement on which is a gross violation of the laws of nature and ought to be resisted;—consequently all hereditary distinctions should be abolished, as being unnatural and opposed to the equal Rights of Man.

The end of Society being the public good, and the institution of government being to secure to every individual the enjoyment of his rights, all government ought to be founded on those rights, and all laws instituted for the common benefit, protection and security of all the people, and not for the particular emolument or advantage of any man, family or set of men.

The Rights of Man in Society are Liberty, Equality, Security and the full enjoyment of the produce of his own labour. Liberty is that power which belongs to a man of doing every thing that does not infringe on the rights of another. Its principle is nature, its rule justice, and its moral limits are defined by this maxim—'Do unto others as you would that others should do unto you.'

The Law is the free expression of the public will, it ought to be the same for all whether it protects or punishes; it cannot order but what is just and useful, it cannot forbid but what is hurtful.

A people have always the right of revising, amending and changing their constitution, one generation cannot submit to its laws future generations.

Every adult member of society has a right to a free voice (either by himself or his representative) in making the laws which he is required to obey, and in regulating the amount and appropriation of public contributions.

Intellectual fitness and moral worth and not property should be the qualifications for representatives, and the duration of parliaments should be but for a year.

Statement of Grievances

The necessity for announcing these rights implies the existence of grievances, we therefore, the unrepresented classes of the Metropolis enumerate the most prominent of the evils under which we are now suffering.

1. Individual appropriation of the soil, which is the natural right of all; from whence arises that odious impost on the first necessary of life the tax upon corn.

2. The law of Primogeniture, by which the spurious portion of society are fastened like leeches upon the industy of the country.

3. The Funding System which has created a thousand millions of debt and deluged the world with human blood.

4. Hereditary and exclusive legislation passed by a corrupt and selfish

few which has produced and maintained among others the following National Curses.

I. An Hereditary Monarchy costing at the least 3 millions per annum

II. A Civil List of Male and Female Pensioners 1 million   do

III One hundred and thirteen privy councillors costing £600,000 per Annum

IV. A Law Church Establishment costing 9 millions per Annum

V. A Debt requiring for interest alone   35 millions   do

VI. A Standing Army costing   7 millions   do

To these may be added Inclosure Laws—Mortmain Laws—Game Laws —Stamp Laws—Trespass Laws—Subletting Laws and Excise Laws— Impressment for Sailors—Tithe Exactions—with expensive erections of Palaces—Prisons—Churches—Barracks—Workhouses. Monopolies in Commerce—Monopolies in trade—Taxes on Knowledge—Taxes on houses —Taxes on the light of heaven; with a thousand other fertile sources of oppression through the medium of indirect taxation on the labour and industry of the productive classes of the community.

3. That this meeting calls the attention of their fellow countrymen to the aforementioned glowing declaration of Rights and to devise the most effectual means of carrying them into effect.

In the preceeding resolutions which were agreed to by the General Committee of the Union it will be seen that the intention to call a National Convention was abandoned. No notice being taken thereof in any one of the resolutions.

In the meetings of the sub committee who prepared the resolutions as entered in the minute book of the Union, it does not appear that any member said a word respecting any proposition to be made at the meeting respecting a National Convention.

All the proceedings of the committee of the Union were probably, (the leading members say certainly) made known to the Government, they had they say nothing to conceal and an inspection of their minute books confirms so far as such a document can the truth of the assertion. Nothing seems to have been said at their committee which was not said at their public weekly meetings at which reporters attended and were accomodated [sic], yet their reports were scarcely ever inserted in the Daily papers and the reporters were consequently not paid for by their proprietors. That they did nothing they wished to conceal is not to be doubted.

Mischief was meditated by some of the members of whom Mr Petrie was now the leader. This man had been a soldier during several years and had seen much service. He had or thought he had grounds of complaint which were not attended to at the War Office, and this it was supposed induced him to become a member of the Union. He was one of the most violent of the members. He now suggested that, as the meeting would consist of an immerse multitude that they should move off the ground at the conclusion of the business in two columns one to attack the Bank the other the Tower of London. In these suggestions he shewed what some considered dishonesty, and this it has been said was the reason of his being objected to as Chairman of the meeting, when in the committee on the 8th he was named for that office, and Mr Mee was appointed.

At a meeting of the committee on the 10th a letter was read from him as follows

Bulls Head Court May 10 1833

Mr Russell
      Sir
            I request that you will present this note to the sub committee.
            'When faction rules and wicked men hold sway,
            The post of honour is a private station.'

The conduct of the majority of the committee, on wednesday evening (the 8th) which not only justifies me, but compels me to state that the respect I owe to myself prevents me from taking any part whatever in the business of the public meeting on Monday next.

George Petrie

Preparations were made for the meeting—two vans were hired. Movers and seconders of the motions were appointed. The placards were ordered to be posted. Four men with boards on which placards were to be pasted were ordered to be hired.

74. [Add. Ms. 27797, f. 15. Printed government notice banning the meeting.]

Whereas, printed papers have been posted up and distributed in various parts of the metropolis, advertising that a public meeting will be held in Coldbath Fields, on Monday May 13th, to adopt preparatory measures for holding a National Convention, as the only means of obtaining and securing the rights of the people;—And, whereas, a public meeting holden for such a purpose is dangerous to the public peace, and illegal:—All classes of his Majesty's subjects are hereby warned not to attend such meeting, nor to take any part in the proceedings thereof.

And notice is hereby given—That the Civil Authorities have strict orders to maintain and secure the public peace, and to apprehend any persons offending herein, that they may be dealt with according to law.

By order of the Secretary of State.

75. [Add. Ms. 27797, ff. 16–20]

The notion of their being a great Public Meeting was clearly given up, the ultimate organization being the vague resolution that the sub committee which consisted of Petrie—Lee—Mee—Bayley—Yearly—Preston and Plummer, in all seven—But Petrie and Bailey [*sic*] having resigned—the whole was left to five men no one of whom was at all know[n] out of the Union, neither were they of much weight in the Union.

It does not appear from any entry in the minute book that the presence of even, such men as, Cleave—or Hetherington—or Lovett were expected to attend and the whole matter was as wretched as any such thing could be. It is more than probable that this sub-committee of five would have given up the whole matter had they not lacked the resolution, to encounter the charges and sarcasm of those who would have availed themselves of the circumstances to annoy them.

In the first instance the projectors of the meeting had persuaded themselves that all the world had their eyes upon their proceedings, and they imagined that nothing more was necessary than a public meeting in which the people should be called upon to send deputies to London to form what they called a convention to induce them to comply with their request, as they proceeded however this absurd expectation left them, and the proclamation even such as it was convinced them that there was no likely hood of any assemblage worthy the name of a public meeting at all likely to be held.

It would, be impossible on the whole to conceive any thing more absurd and contemptible than were the proceedings of the Union respecting this meeting.

With the knowledge that they who called the meeting, lacked the means of accomplishing any purpose, whatever, either for evil or good, with the certain knowledge that any resolutions which the persons who took part in the meeting could propose would produce no effect whatever, Government could not fail to conclude that no meeting of the least importance could be held, and that there needed a very small portion of the police force and none of the Army to keep the peace. 50 police men could have kept the ground and all the approaches to it clear and that too without any incivility or much annoyance to any one. Whatever other force the Government might have thought it prudent to assemble should have been carefully concealed, instead of being thrust into notice unnecessarily.

Lord Melbourne knew well from experience that if the Government did not desire to commit outrages on the people, but were desirous as became men charged with the grave duty of governing such a nation as the British People composed, and were therefore more desirous of preventing than of punishing that they needed do no more than has been alluded to to insure that peace, and had their purpose been to preserve they would most certainly have so acted.

This was also well understood by at the least some of the Police Superintendents, one of whom, and one too of the most respectable and best informed of them, told me that with ten men he could have kept the ground clear of people and that too without producing ill temper and scarcely any annoyance whatever. This he proposed to do but was not attended to.

In fact the members of the Sub-committee in whose hands alone the whole matter rested wanted an excuse for withdrawing and this as Lord Melbourne will [well] knew could have been easily supplied; but he and his coadjutors who were vigorous only against the common people had made immense preparations for display, on the use of which they would have followed the example of Lord Castlereagh and his coadjutors, and grounded some bad laws on the result of their own mis-conduct. It would have been no great stretch of either disposition or power in Lord Melbourne who supported and justified and thanked the men who committed the Manchester Massacre to have played the bad game over again in London if the opportunity had offered. The administration was at this time courting the Tories, they had done much in endeavoring [sic] to please them, and a resolution to put down and keep down the people which the present occasion appeared to afford would have done much in the way of reconciliation between the two parties. They however did too much, and may be said to have failed in every particular, the consequence of which was, hatred towards them on the part of the common people, contempt on that of the Tories.

The following account of the proceedings is taken from the daily papers of the 14th.

The best and I have reason to believe that which is nearest to the truth is from the Times—as follows.

It commences by saying the meeting was called by placards and forbidden as illegal by Proclamation—and it goes on thus.

'Notwithstanding this mandate by 12 o clock about 300 persons had assembled on the ground, but none of the leaders of the intended meeting were among them.

'Shortly after 12 a strong detachment of the Metropolitan Police marched into the neighbourhood and took up their quarters in the Riding School (near the place of meeting). Colonel Rowan and Mr Mayne the two Commissioners of police as also *Lord Melbourne* had arrived. The two Commissioners were accomodated [*sic*] at a house in the neighbourhood attended by two clerks. Mr. Laing the Magistrate of Hatton Garden Office was stationed in the House of Correction as were other magistrates and a strong body of the Police force. Two officers of the 1st Regiment of Life Guards were on the spot in plain clothes, who kept up a constant communication with their regiment a detachment of which was under arms and ready at a moments warning.

'Matters remained in this state till near 2 o clock when the number of people had greatly increased, we should say there were between 3,000 and 4,000 present. Some doubts were expressed by some of the persons assembled as to the meeting taking place as no caravan or hustings was prepared.

'During this time the committee consisting of 6 persons were holding their council at the Union Public House, Bagnigge Wells, and some discussion arose among them as to which of them should ascend the hustings first, and after much time had been spent in arranging this point which they considered most important, a young man named James Lee undertook to open the proceedings by proposing a person to take the chair.

'Shortly before 3 o clock a caravan which had been hired for the purpose took its station and instantly young Lee jumped into it followed by a person named Mee and several others. Lee waved his hat several times which was answered by the shouts of the assembly. The owner of the van however did not like the appearance of things, and instantly drove off, the committee jumping out of the van. Lee was then carried on the shoulders of some of the mob to some railings and being there supported he proposed that Mr Mee should take the Chair which being seconded by some person Mr Mee stood up, and addressed the meeting. He called upon those present to beware of those hirelings of the government who were paid to induce them to commit a breach of the peace. Just at this moment a large body of members of the Union came up with colours and banners and took their position around the Chairman who continued to address the meeting.

127

'About 200 of the police force of the A division, followed by as many of the others marched up to the railings with their truncheons ready for action. The mob gave way a little but Mee the Chairman never moved until he saw the danger which awaited them, and then Mee jumped down and effected his escape amongst the Crowd.

'The scene that followed was dreadful. The Police furiously attacked the Multitude with their staves felling every person indiscriminately before them; even females did not escape blows from their batons, men and boys were lying in every direction weltering in their blood and calling for mercy. The inhabitants from their windows and balconies cried Shame! Shame!! Mercy! Mercy!! but the Police men continued their attack which they kept up for several minutes. A large space of ground within our view was st[r]ewed with the wounded, besides others who were less injured and were able to crawl to a surgeons. A policemen belonging to the C Division 95 named James [sic] Culley was stabbed to the heart by a man who was carrying a banner, and which he attempted to take from him. He walked a few paces and then fell dead. His brother John who belonged to the same division was also stabbed but not mortally. Serjeant Brooks of the C Division was also wounded through the thick part of his left arm.

'The following are the names of the persons arrested—then follows several names—and among them James Furzey [sic], and the writer observes—that it seemed to be believed, that Furzey was the man who murdered the Policeman, as a dagger with a sharp point, and a loaded pistol were found near the spot in a stable where he was standing after he had been arrested. The dagger corresponded with the wound in Culleys side and those of the other Police-men. The same man made a thrust at Mr Baker the Superintendant [sic] of the C Division and he must have fallen had not two policemen Merchant and Ossett, have struck his arm and taken him into custody.

'With the above exceptions we heard of no loss of life, but we should think upon a fair calculation from what the writer of this article saw there must have been 50 people more or less wounded.'

The Times condemned the Meeting and justified the dispersing of it—and in its leader in no way condemned the Police for making the Riot and ill using the people.

76. [Add. Ms. 27797, ff. 277–80]
Conversation with George Fursey respecting the stabbing of Brooks and Redwood two police constables.
Sunday 3 June 1838

Went to the house of George Fursey, Bricklayer in the Albany Road, Kent Road—(the same house he rented in 1833) and had a long conversation with him respecting the meeting held on the 13 May 1833.

I told him I had taken pains that he should be informed by some of his friends that I was collecting materials for an accurate account of the proceedings of the 'National Union of Working men and others', and especially just now of the meeting called by them on the 13 May 1833 in Cold

128

Bath Fields, for the Riot on which, and for the stabbing two police men at which, he was tried at the Old Bailey on the 5 July 1833.

That I had taken care he should be well informed who I was, as it was necessary for the elucidation of the matter that he should believe I was a friend to the working people and had no purpose in my enquiries beyond that of being enabled to do them justice.

I said I had been told by those who knew him well that he was an honest sedate man who would not deceive me, and that I trusted he would not. That unless it was quite agreeable to him to answer my enquiries fully and without the least concealment I was not desirous to question him at all, but that as I believed he had reason to conclude that I was the working mans friend, and as no fact if known could now do him any injury I hoped he would give me very fully the information I wished.

He said he had long known me by report and was not unacquainted with the good I had done the working people, and would willingly tell me truly and without any reserve whatever related to the whole facts of the case, so far as he knew them.

He was he said a member of the National Union etc.—and approved of the meeting—though he now confessed it was a very foolish proceeding. That he went to the meeting with a number of members of his own class accompanied by his friend Mr Simpson, each of them having a small flag in their hands, that they entered the ground by Calthorpe Street followed by their brother members and marched up to the place where Mee was standing upon a rail addressing the meeting. That they had scarcely reached the spot when a cry was raised of the police, he saw them coming, the people making an opening to let them up to the place where he was. Simpson said to him there will be mischief we had better go away, and instantly drew back with his flag which he threw down an area and got away being squezed [sic] out by the pressure of the people behind the Police. That he on the contrary held his flag staff in his *right hand* and called to the people to 'stand firm', He meant, don't run away; the police were at this moment beating the people, several of them (the police) rushed forward, some seized hold on him some struck at him with their staves and one seized his flag staff with both hands and a struggle ensued the staff was broken and he was knocked down, as soon as he was down he was struck by several police men his head was cut open and he was stunned, *No one of the policemen spoke one word to him*, he lost his flag was seized and taken away to a *Coach house* in which were several Policemen and here he was confined until he was marched away to the public office in Bow Street.

This he said was the whole transaction and all the words [?] in the world could make no more of it. The whole matter from the time the police was announced to his being knocked down, bruised in several places his head cut in two places and his being stunned could not have occupied *one minute*.

I then said but you stabbed Brooks and Redwood at the moment you were assaulted?

He. Oh, no, I stabbed neither of them I assure you, they & others pressed upon me, seized the flag and broke the staff knocked me down and stunned me when I was down. I do assure you most solemnly *I neither struck at nor stabbed any one of them.*

129

I. well that seems very odd. I concluded you were the man who had stabbed them both?

He. I again assure you that I did not. I had neither knife nor tool nor instrument of any sort with which I could stab any one about me on that day.

I. why it was given in evidence against you, that you were taken to a *Stable* where you sat yourself down in a stall on some straw with your back leaning against the wall, and that close by the place where you had been seated a poiniard [*sic*] was found?

He. Yes, I know it, but I assure you I *never was taken into a stable at all* and of course never sat down upon any straw in a stall. I was taken to a coach house, and no poniard, or knife or instrument was found upon me or in the place where I was confined. I had no such instrument with me, and I never struck at any one that day.

I. well that is very strange. How was it, this did not appear at your trial?

He. it was an ommission of Mr Phillips the Councillor. It was in his instructions, but he omitted it. When Mr Phillips said 'that is my case' and my trial was ended, I was uneasy on account of his never having questioned the witnesses respecting the place I was confined in and the more so as Popay the *Police Spy* who was in Court and with whom I was well acquainted was present, he [had?] come into the Coach House and said he was very sorry to see me in custody—I therefore mentioned the fact to one of the keepers of Newgate who was standing close to me, he had behaved with much civility to me in the prison and therefore I spoke to him. He said never mind, the jury does not believe one word the fellows have been swearing against you, Councillor Phillips knows what he is about so do you let him alone. I was afterwards told, that it was an inadvertence of Mr Phillips occasioned by his anxiety to procure me an acquittal.

I. do you know who it was that stabbed Brooks and Redwood or either of them.

He. I must solemnly assure you, I do not, I did not see any one stab them. I had no time to see any thing that passed. I was seized thrown down and stunned so suddenly, that I had no time to observe any thing. It is all as I have told you, it is every word sacredly true and it is all the truth. There is nothing else it is the whole.

My full belief is that it is the truth and the whole truth.

Fursey is as he was represented to me, a plain simple man, who would I have no doubt have told me he stabbed the man had he done so. He said they richly deserved to be stabbed, or knocked on the head for their wanton and ferocious cruelty, but he neither struck nor stabbed at any one, but he should not have been sorry if he had killed all who attacked him, for he thought a man had an undoubted right to kill any body who attempted to treat him as he was treated by the police men.

77. [Add. Ms. 27797, ff. 69–70. Place's comments on the verdict of justifiable homicide brought in against the unknown person who killed the police constable Robert Culley on Calthorpe Estate.]

Immediately after the verdict was given the morning newspapers attacked it, in almost every was [way] in which it was possible to attack it.

Some comments of the Editors and some of the communications sent to them shewed both the knowledge and the talent to make the most of it.

The laws relating to public meetings—the decisions of the Courts—the practice of such courts, and the opinions of many—legal—authorities were stated, as such, and then, in some, cases, unwarrantable inferences were drawn, and every case and circumstance which *made against the writers* were [*sic*] carefully suppressed by them.

The verdict was questionable if not actually incorrect in words, since it was the result of an inference only, and the jury were sworn to enquire into facts. It should however be observed that in a great many cases on which an inquest is held nothing but circumstantial evidence can be produced and yet from circumstances and appearances the jury are compelled to come to a decision which no one will question. So it is sometimes in other criminal cases no verdict can be given on any but circumstantial evidence, whether it be for acquittal or condemnation, and it is quite clear that the jury which sat on the body of Culley knew that they were going upon circumstantial evidence, and believed they were perfectly justified in finding that his death was a justifiable homicide. They believed, that Culley was stabbed by a man whom the police, he among the rest, assaulted, and put in bodily fear and danger, and for that reason the verdict which they gave was justifiable homicide. The evidence of this fact did not appear before the jury, and their verdict was consequently an inference from other facts.

They knew that no riot act had been read,—they knew that no proclamation to disperse had been made,—they knew that no attempt to preoccupy the ground by the authorities had been made,—they knew that the police force, (as it is called) were marched in order and blocked up nearly the whole of the persons who were assembled in the open space intended for the meeting.—They knew that even then, when every caution had been purposely omitted, for the purpose of misleading and entrapping of very absurd people that no attempt to take the leaders into custody was made in a decent orderly way,—and they must have believed; what, although they did not know it, turned out to be the actual fact, that no one altho' he attended the meeting yet if he conducted himself properly and did not commit a breach of the peace, nor in any way make a riot was not committing an indictable offence, as would have been the case had there been sufficient evidence to have borne out such a prosecution.

They knew it was in the power of Ministers—in that of the Magistrates, of the Commissioners of Police, either to have prevented the meeting or to have quietly dispersed it, and that they would have done one of these things probably the first if they had not intended to make an example of the people, and put them down by their own ill advised vigilance, a course of conduct no ministry well acquainted with the people of this country would ever have consented should have been used.

All these things the jury knew but they did not know specifically, how Culley came by his death. The verdict was therefore too precise and not fully warranted by the evidence.

The finding of the jury was therefore wrong, but not more so than many others much more important verdicts which have never been at all disturbed nor questioned in any court of law, or questioned by any authority

131

even when their errors have been proved, or made evident by the discovery of circumstances.

The quashing of this verdict as it afterwards was quashed, was an anomalous proceeding, and under all the circumstances of the case, done more for the purpose of establishing authority in the King and the judges than for any other reason. It will be seen by the proceedings that it was none at all in conformity to any act of parliament, or any usage since the keeper of the Kings conscience could in all such cases do just what he pleased, without being questioned by any one but his master, whose, in almost every case, tool he was.

78. [Add. Ms. 27797, ff. 238–44]

Meeting at the Crown and Anchor Tavern

On the 19th of June a public meeting was held at the Crown and Anchor Tavern in the Strand London. 'To take into consideration the circumstances connected with the after proceedings relating to the verdict of the Calthorpe Street Jury.'

The Great Room was densely crowded long before the time announced for the commencement of business. Colonel Evans the member for Westminster was to have taken the chair but he having sent a shuffling excuse, the chair was taken by Lord Dunboyne. Having opened the business.

Mr Carpenter addressed the meeting. He felt very strongly on the subject on which the company had assembled, and could not but comply with the wish of the managers to come forward and make the first resolution. It had been said that the meeting was hostile to the constitutional institutions of the country. This was absurd, when the very purpose of the meeting was to support one of [the] most important of these institutions. He thought the meeting might very safely leave the monarchy and the aristocracy to themselves to take care of such of these institutions as related to themselves or principally to themselves while the people looked to such of them as principally related the masses. He need not argue that it was the undoubted right of the people to meet and discuss political matters, that right was unquestioned. It was fully proved that the meeting in Cold Bath Fields was perfectly peaceable, and he believed the purpose of the meeting was both legal and constitutional; this was certain that notwithstanding the assertion of Mr Lamb in the house of commons, there was no disposition on the part of the people to break the peace. On the contrary they took every precaution in their power to prevent any such occurrence. They were quite orderly in their proceedings and did not evince any disposition to commit violence even after they had been ferociously attacked by the Police. He was present at the proceedings on that day, for the purpose of observing and noting the circumstances which might occur. He saw how the police before they commenced their attack upon the people stopped up all the avenues by which the people could have escaped. He had testified on his solemn oath that the Police commenced the attack while the people were perfectly peaceable. He saw the Police knock the people down. He saw them beat them with their staves when they were down and trample on them. He saw the Police beat two women most brutally—two innofensive [*sic*] women. (shame) But

132

as the meeting was well acquainted with the occurrences of the day he would dwell on them no longer.

He was confident the resolution would have the hearty concurrence of the meeting. The people had no reason for believing that the proclamation prohibiting the meeting proceeded from the Government, it might have proceeded from some individual to answer some sinister purpose as placards had proceeded on former occasions, yet purporting to proceed from the parties calling the meetings, of which there were some remarkable instances. (Loud cheers) Was it to be wondered at if the people, when thus treated should shew a disposition to resort to illegal means to obtain a redress of grievances. For the last 25 years the petitions of the common people, aye and their complaints in every form had been treated with perfect contempt by the Legislature and by the executive government. It was the sense of this which sometimes goaded them on to acts of which in their cooler moments they would disapprove.

Mr Carpenter moved. 'That it is the undoubted *right* of the British Subjects to assemble for the purpose of discussing their grievances, and petitioning the legislature for their redress or removal: and that the employment, under the sanction of a notice or proclamation issued by a secretary of state, of unnecessary violence, under the pretext of dispersing a meeting in Cold Bath Fields, (which had been permitted to assemble uninterruptedly) was highly censurable, and has a strong tendency to alienate his majesty's people from their dutiful and confident dependence on the constitutional laws, and their attachment to the government.' Mr Courtenay seconded the resolution.

[The following resolutions were also passed.]

That this meeting present their best thanks to the members of the Coroners Jury, convened at the Calthorpe Arms in Grays Inn Road on the 13 May last on the death of a police-man named Culley, slain in the attack on the people in Cold Bath Fields, for the sagacity and patience manifested in their performance of an arduous and painful duty, and in their unanimity of their verdict of 'justifiable homicide', by which they have ably assisted in maintaining the right of 'Trial by Jury'.

That the application made to the Court of Kings Bench by a law officer of the Crown to quash the honest and conscientious verdict of the Jury appears to be unprecented in the history of English Jurisprudence in as much that it was not contradicted that the jury had deliberated upon the evidence of all the witnesses permitted to be brought before them, was incorrupt, intelligible with the strict tenor of the oath they had taken; and that the quashing of such verdict of the court without evidence inquiry or investigation was novel, and has a tendency to subvert the trial by jury, and to diminish that sacred regard which has long been cherished as the great bulwark of british freedom.

That a petition be presented to the honourable the house of commons praying an inquiry into all the circumstances of the late proceedings in reference to the meeting in Cold Bath Fields; the Coroners performance or neglect of duty, the inquest, and the conduct of the police on that occasion, as well as the subsequent events connected therewith. That it be entrusted to Mr Hume for presentation and that Mr Roebuck, Col. Evans, Mr O

Connell and other honourable members who supported the petition of the jury, be requested to give this also their support.

79. [Add. Ms. 27797, ff. 251–2. Place's comments on the quarterly report of the National Union of the Working Classes for the period April–June 1833.]

This quarterly report shews very plainly the declining state of the National Union of the Working Men. All the Great Political Unions all those indeed which were not conducted by working men had either gone out of existence or were in a condition which disabled them from being efficient or capable of any thing beyond an occasional meeting and even this was not properly an act of the union but of some few of its leading members who used its name, but paid the expenses out of their own pockets, none of these unions having any money in the hands of its treasurer.

Those among the working people who had hitherto taken part in political matters were disappointed and chagrined, and by far the greater part of them were hopeless, they had no share in the suffrage, and were wholly abandoned by the middle classes. They had themselves however to blame for much of the neglect they now endured, and for the want of assistance they might have secured. They acted with great indiscretion and frequently with much injustice. Some of their leaders had on many occasions shewn a strong desire to lead them into mischievous courses. They had purposely offended all who were not of the working class, and had from time to time done much to alarm them, as well for what they call their liberty as for their property and consequently for their lives and property. This had a bad effect in two discetions [directions]. First in destroying all sympathy for them in every other class, and second in destroying confidence among themselves, sewing dissentions and animosities in their own class. This result was very clearly forseen and pointed out to them in the disputes they had with the National Political Union in October 1831. Caution was useless, they could not be advised, and the result of their perseverance in vilifying all who were not working people, drove away from them nearly every man who was in a condition and had a disposition to serve them. In their own class even there never were enough of them associated at any place to enable their managers to do what was requisite to make their proceedings to be made known, they never subscribed among themselves money enough to pay for the insertion of their proceedings in the newspapers, nor to publish occasional tracts or addresses for distribution.

It ought not however to be objected to the working men who took the lead among themselves that they demanded Universal Suffrage etc. No other suffrage would reach them and as they sincerely believed that nearly all the evils of which they complained were caused by bad government, and that the only remedy was in the members of the house of commons being fairly chosen by the whole of the male inhabitants of the country, they made a sacrifice whenever they consented to assist to procure for others, advantages in which they could not participate. This sacrifice was made by a very great number of working men but it never was made by any body of them, when they were formed into Unions. The members of the unions forming by far the smallest portion of the active body of working men. They would have done better and have had more influence had they gone on teaching their class; and inducing them to observe such conduct in their associations as could not reasonably have been objected to, but of this they were not capable. They had been misled and bewildered by the misty doctrine of Robert Owen and others who taught, to them, the agreeable doctrine that whatever was made by or was the consequence of any actions of any man belonged to that man, or that the *whole* produce of every community should be equally divided among such of the members of the community as were willing to perform equal shares of labour, and these notions made them look upon all who were not of their own class as their deliberate and determined enemies. They who entertained and still entertain these notions were and are an immense number of the working people, by far the greatest part of whom are fully persuaded that the working men in their unions and associations do not go as far as they ought to go, and this is the principal reason why but few comparatively join them, as it is the cause of great numbers leaving them after they have joined, and from these causes always keeping the whole number of working men politically associated too few to produce any important consequence. These were the causes which extinguished the National Union of Working Men and every other similar Union.

80. [Add. Ms. 27797, ff. 290–1]

The year [1833] ended leaving the [National] Union [of the Working Classes] in a state of much depression. The nonsensical doctrines preached by Robert Owen and others respecting communities and goods in common; abundance of every thing men ought to desire and all for four hours labour out of every 24. The right of every man to his share of the earth in common, and his right to whatever his hands had been employed upon. The power of masters under the present system to give just what wages *they* pleased, the right of the labourer to such wages as would maintain him, and his, in comfort for 8 or 10 hours labour; the right of every man who was unemployed to employment and to such an amount of wages as have been indicated, and other matters of a similar kind, which were continually inculcated by the working mens political unions, by many small knots of persons, printed in small pamphlets, and hand bills which were sold twelve for a penny, and distributed to a great extent, had pushed politics aside to a great extent among the working people. These pamphlets were written almost wholly by men of talent and of some standing in the world, professional men, gentlemen, manufacturers, tradesmen, and men called literary. The consequence was, that a very large proportion of the working people in England and Scotland became persuaded that they had only to combine as it was concluded they might easily do, to compel not only a considerable advance of wages all round, but employment for every one, man and woman who needed it, at short hours. This notion induced them to form themselves into Trades Union in a manner and to an extent never before known. These combinations, which were harmless, and useful, upon the whole, altho' they for a very short time caused some inconvenience

135

to many master tradesmen and manufactures [*sic*] and in many instances distress among the work people were necessary to convince the masses of the impossibility of their succeeding in the present state of society and induced a vast number of the best conditioned among them to conclude that the ends they aimed at could not be accomplished until the *whole* people were properly educated, and this persuasion with the signal failure of the Trades Unions will for many years to come prevent a repitition of the folly, and it is more than probable the increase of intelligence in the meantime will prevent such another effort from ever again being made, better means of arranging matters between masters and workmen will probably be adopted and the necessity for men striking to prevent the reduction of their wages, or to bring these up again when they have been reduced, and all the evil consequences which attend such strikes of the men, and of the masters also will be then avoided.

It was impossible under these circumstances that the National Union of the Working Classes, or any other such political unions could flourish or even exist at all, except as this in London did, as matter of form kept up pertinaciously by a few with scarcely any members to compose it.

81. [Add. Ms. 27791, ff. 241–2]   6 Oct. 1836

The following narrative was written by Mr William Lovett one of the most active and sensible among those whom he has named as conductors of the National Union of the Working Classes.

Mr Lovett is an honest sincere courageous man. He is a tall thin rather melancholy man about 32 years of age in ill health to which he has long been subject, at times he is somewhat hypocondriacal, his is a spirit misplaced. If instead of being a journeyman cabinet maker he had been so circumstanced as to have received only an ordinary share of education and the means of obtaining leisure, he would have read more extensively than [he] has been able in his state to do, he would have gone on improving himself, have associated with persons of greater acquirements than his lot has enabled him to associate with, he would have gone on from one improvement to another and would have become a remarkable and very useful man. His feelings for his fellow workmen are intense, and his close attention to small particulars in too many cases has prevented him obtaining knowledge of general principles, and caused him to be a *practical man.* It is not therefore at all surprising that Lovett should become a disciple of Robert Owen, an advocate of the absurd notions he entertained of appropriating the whole wealth of the nation to the use of all in common in his paralellograms [*sic*], nor that he like many others unable after a time to perceive that any progress towards the accomplishment of their wishes was made should abandon Robert Owen and his absurdities, to adopt other opinions and proceedings not less absurd respecting the production and distribution of every thing which results from the labour of mens hands, and maintain that the whole should belong to those by whose labour it was produced, and that he being as brave as honest should propagate his notions to the fullest extent of his means, and sometimes to make practical demonstrations, not apparently in accordance with the actions of a sensible

136

man, but it should be remembered that when a man, to any extent, becomes a fanatic, however well he may be informed, however correctly he may reason, and however rationally he may act on other matters, he acts to some extent absurdly in respect to the particular notions he entertains on the subject of his fanaticism, his monomania. This is the case of William Lovett. He however has to some extent relinquished his opinions and will probably as he becomes a better political economist become altogether a reasonable and valuable member of society.

It will be seen that the National Union of the Working Classes—never consisted of a very large body of actual members,* though it had considerable influence at particular moments. It would have been composed of more thousands than it reckoned hundreds, had it not been that some of its managers shewed themselves to be great rogues, who at their public meetings at the Rotunda a large place on the Surrey side of Black Friars Bridge, where weekly meetings were held, and at other places shewed but too plainly, that their object was by any and every means to possess themselves of the property of others, & to produce general confusion by which they hoped to gain. The Union had however great influence over a considerable portion of the working people, more especially in the great manufacturing counties. During the time the reform bills were before the parliament this was particularly the case, the attention of the whole people was then drawn to the subject, and the working people were quite as much excited as any class whatever. The ways in which their excitement was manifested, though unwisely in many respects directed, proved that there was an immense improvement among the working people as compared with other, not very remote periods.

The consequence of this excitement was a general persuasion that the whole produce of the labourers and workmens hands should remain with them, and this persuasion still remains, as an impediment to their progress in many important particulars.

* Mr Lovett says. From Mr Russell's (the secretary's) books of the Union it appears that, comencing [sic] with the 1 July 1832 the time when Mr Russell became secretary, the account stood thus.

1st quarter commencing	1 July—there were	86	classes—cash—	30	9	4½
2nd do do	1 Oct.	74		26	4	10½
3rd do	1 Jan. 1833	77		34	7	8
4th do	1 April	39		13	3	7½
Averaging per quarter		69		£104	5	7½

The above sum of £104 5 7½ gives 1,043 members paying two shillings each per year. Mr Russell estimates an equal number who paid only occasionally at times of great excitement and yet reckoned themselves members. 'A still greater number of persons attended our meetings who were admitted by paying a penny at the door.'

Now as each member paid a penny a week, or one shilling a quarter, the number will be just half the estimated number of 521 actual members, and the best enquiries I was able to make at the time satisfy me that about 500 was the actual number of the members. It is probable that there were 1,500 including those who 'paid occasionally yet were reckoned members'. The number who attended in the course of a year as auditors paying 1d or 2d for admission would amount to several thousands, there were several inducements to persons to go to these strange meetings once or occasionally. The Rotunda would probably contain 1,000 persons and I have seen hundreds outside the doors for whom there was no room within.

[Here follows Place's transcript of Lovett's account of the National Union of the Working Classes. The account printed here is from Lovett's manuscript, Add. Ms. 27822, ff. 15–27.]

July 26th   19 Greville Street Hatton Garden

Dear Sir

I feel ashamed in not having complied with a request you made me several months since, to furnish you with a narrative of the union of the working classes. Yet sir so many circumstances have transpired to prevent me from writing it (which I will not trouble you to enumerate) that now I have sent it you, I hope to claim your forgiveness. I informed you in my answer to your request, 'that I was no writer', and that consequently my narrative would be very imperfect as to all those essentials so necessary in any thing worthy of publicity. But as I presume that you only want the outline of facts and dates to fill up in your own style, I have not troubled you with many observations or opinions of my own unless were [sic] I thought they might serve to assist you. I have not filled up a considerable portion of it but have refered [sic] to what I think the best accounts, and information on the subject refered to, most of which I send you. I have shown what I have written to Hetherington and Watson and they have agreed on the authenticity of the facts contained in it. You will perceive that I have forborn to speak of the characters of those who took an active part in the union, the reason is, that they are as well known to you as to myself. And being one of them (though differing from many) I choose to be painted black or white as you may think we deserve; rather than attempt to dress up my companions, as if to show the good company I kept, or speak to others prejudice, claiming exceptions according to my fancy. If you want any further information within my power to supply, you may command my humble service.

I am no ways desirous than any save yourself should know of what I have written, it might beget bad feelings especialy [sic] amongst the prejudiced in my own class. I remain sir, an admirer of your present exertions in the cause of truth and justice.

                                                                    Wm Lovett.

The National Union of the 'Working Classes and others' sprung out of another association entitled the British Association for promoting Co-operative Knowledge. And in order to account for many of the peculiarities of the former, differing as it did from other unions of the same period, in its advocacy of first principles and abstract opinions of right and justice, as well as to asertain [sic] if possible the motives of those characters who took a conspicuous part in its proceedings; some little account of the latter might not be devoid of interest. The British Association was formed on the

11th of May 1829 [principally?] by a number of persons who belonged to a society just established in Red Lion Square, called the London Co-operative Trading Association. The object of which was to accumulate a capital for co-operative purposes, by dealing amongst themselves and acquaintances, and reserving the profits of the retail dealer. This Trading Association subsequently removed to jerusalaem [sic] passage Clerkenwell, and there it was that the British Association was projected. The persons most conspicuous in forming this association were James Watson, Wm Lovett, John Cleave, George Foskett, Robert Wigg, Philip and George Skene, Wm Millard, Thomas Powell and subsequently Henry Hetherington and Benjamin Warden. Those persons having read and admired the writings of Owen, Thompson, Morgan, Gray and others, resolved to be instrumental, to the extent of their abilities in disceminating [sic] their works throughout the country. They also sought, in the propagation of their principles, to avoid the course Robt Owen had steered, which they conceived had materialy [sic] impeded his progress; that of insisting on principles strongly opposed to the prejudices of the multitude; and condemning, though in his usual philanthropy, the Radical Reformers. By which proceedings they were led to consider him as a person inimical to their interests, and accordingly they attended his meetings and carried resolutions counter to his own. The persons above named therefore during Mr Owens visit to America, resolved to take up such parts of his system as they conceived would be appreciated by the majority of the working classes; and be the means of uniting reformers of every grade. Taking especial care to learn those subjects on which great differences of opinion existed, to time and uppertunity [sic]; or, when men having experienced the benefits resulting from a part of his system, they might be led to investigate the whole. They held their Committee meetings weekly, and meetings of their members and the public quarterly: they made arrangements by which those who had to address the public, had some time for preparing themselves, by which means those meetings were more interesting and effective. Their reports were published quarterly and distributed throughout the country, and as affording some proofs in favour of their policy, together with the novelty of their plans (as they forcibly impressed on the working classes the importance of Trading Associations) that in less than six months from their commencement they had been the means of forming upwards of two hundred of those associations, extending from one extremity of the kingdom to the other. They had their committees of correspondence giving advice and assistance and promulgating their co-operative views. Persons in remote parts of the kingdom hearing of their projects, and requiring information, were supplied with books on the subject; and in this manner more was done in the space of twelve months to disceminate Mr Owens peculiar views, than perhaps he had done himself during his long carrier [sic]. This society was also entrusted by benevolent individuals with considerable sums of money to apply to co-operative purposes, which they did in the employment of several Spitalfields weavers: eventually they opened a Bazaar at 19 Greville Street Hatton Garden for the purpose of disposing of the produce, and for facilitating exchanges between the societies in town and country. This part of their arrangements oweing [sic] to mismanagement was a failure. They had

139

not been more than twelve months in existance [*sic*] when Mr Owen returned from America, he commenced by condemning them as altogether opposed to his system and it was not till after a visit to Manchester at one of their delegate meetings, that he was induced to acknowledge their importance. Many of his most zealous disciples bowing to his first decrees had in the interim seceeded [*sic*] from their societies which had led to their breaking up, in addition, many of those who were strict religionists had been terrified from supporting the British Association on account of many of its members attending and supporting Mr Owens Sunday morning lectures. Eventually the funds ceased to come in, meetings could not be got up, printing could not be any longer paid for and dissentions respecting Mr Owens views led to the breaking up of an Association that did much good, and if it had continued, bid fair to do more than any association of working men about this period. It may be well to observe that many of those trading associations it had been instrumental in forming are still in existance, especialy in the north of England though the major part are broken up. It would seem that the great cause of their failure was the want of some law to secure their property—to sue and be sued in the name of their Treasurer, Secretary, or other officer; the want of which caused many individuals to make off with their funds—and by throwing great responsibility on others was the means of the most of them breaking up. To return however to the British Association *the central organ of all these societies*; some months previous to its dissolution, a few carpenters who were in the habit of meeting at the Argyle Arms Argyle Street, and being imbued with co-operative views were desirous of carrying out some modified plans of the British [Association], waited at the suggestion of Henry Hetherington on the committee for assistance. Henry Hetherington, Benj. Warden and George Foskett were accordingly appointed for that purpose and attended their first meeting at the above place on Wednesday the 2nd of March 1831. They first called themselves the 'Metropolitan Trades Union' and subsequently took the more extensive name of the 'National Union of the Working Classes and Others'. At this first meeting persons were appointed to draw up a circular to be sent to the Trade, Benefit, and Co-operative societies of London and its vicinity. Messrs Foskett and Warden addressed the meeting at great length; principly [*sic*] on the importance of the working classes as producers of wealth, and the consequent justice of their retaining a greater portion of it than they usualy [*sic*] did. About a fortnight from this period several hundreds of those circulars were issued, calling on the above societies to appoint one or more intelligent members of their respective bodies to meet at the Argyle Arms, for the purpose of arranging the details of a plan, and to draw up a constitution for the purpose of carrying the following objects into effect—

1st To obtain for all its members the right of electing those who make the laws which govern them unshackled and uninfluenced by any property qualification.

2 To afford support and protection individualy and collectively to every member of the Union; to enhance the value of labour by diminishing the hours of employment—and to adopt such measures as may be deemed necessary to increase the domestic comforts of working men.

The Union continued its meetings every Wednesday and the room was generaly crowded principly by delegates of societies—persons were actively engaged in attending Trade and other associations and inducing them to unite in this general union; Hetherington and Warden were especialy useful in this respect as they were in the habit of addressing working men and especialy prest [sic] those points on their attention which cannot fail to have their effect—such as the extremes of wealth and wretchedness, of ill paid industry and overpaid idleness and uselessness. The consequence was that the place of meeting was to [sic] small for their purpose; and they accordingly removed to the Assembly Rooms 36 Castle Street Oxford Market April the 20th 1831. At this place they were joined by G. Petrie, James Savage, John Russell, J. Osborn and others who publicly took part in their proceedings. Excepting their usual weekly meetings nothing of importance occured [sic] untill May the 25th when Hetherington, Foskett, Warden and two others brought forward the following 'Declaration and Rules for the Constitution and Government of the union', which after several nights discussion were adopted and printed for distribution. See Guardian May 27 1831.

After the adoption of the above declaration and rules considerable numbers of the working classes joined them. And as the affairs of the British Association were by this time brought to a close, the remainder of its Committee, consisting of John Cleave, James Watson, Wm Lovett, Julian Hibbert, and several others joined this *new* union. Those persons considering it a fit uppertunity for blending their own peculiar views of society, more especially of production and distribution of wealth, with those of the Radical Reformers. By which policy they soon innoculated [sic] many of those who previously stood alofe [sic] from the Co-operators, considering them as persons who retarded reform. Hence we find their resolutions and speeches partook more or less of a co-operative character, as well as of the extremes of radicalism; somewhat modified in violence of feeling from the radicals who preceeded [sic] them. Makeing [sic] exceptions however for two or three of the committee whose violence of temperment [sic] or prejudiced notions often betrayed them beyond those bounds of moderation prescribed by the majority. Wm Benbow about this time also joined them, and induced the Committee to hold their meetings at his Coffee House Temple Bar. They were held on Wednesday evenings and were open to all those members who choose [sic] to attend to *hear* their proceedings or even to *suggest* any thing they deemed important, but not to take further part in the business. At these meetings a general subject of discussion was selected which was discussed throughout the union at their different places of meeting; persons from the committee were also appointed to speak at their places, so to prevent delay or inconvenience, at the same time any other member was at liberty to speak but no strangers.

On the following June the prosecution of Henry Hetherington the printer and publisher of the Poor Mans Guardian, the father of unstamped publications; called for their additional energies and support, it being considered their leading organ. Not that reports of their proceedings were confined to it, as the Ballot newspaper, Carpenters Magazine and several others gave accounts of their meetings; but from the fact of it having been established for the purpose of deceminating cheap political information, and spreading ultra doctrines of reform on all subjects, it obtained the preference and first place in their estimation. As soon therefore as the prosecution commenced, they got up meetings on the subject, and passed several resolutions expressive of their determination to support, not only Hetherington by selling and purchasing his Guardian; but all others who might in any way become the victims of prosecution in endeavouring to deseminate cheap political knowledge amongst the people. They accordingly commenced subscribing towards a fund which they designated the 'Victim Fund', Wm Lovett was appointed the secretary and Wm D. Saull the Treasurer, a committee was also elected to govern and manage the fund. Though the sum subscribed was not considerable (about £360) they relieved nearly three hundred persons who were imprisoned for selling unstamped publications, either by rendering some small assistance to their families during their imprisonment, or supplying them with the means of purchasing other papers when they came out, and thus renewing the warfare against the government. By this means they kept [sic] up the exitement [sic] among the people against those odious laws, and by publishing the details of cruelty to which the prisoners were subjected, by petitions and remonstrances to the legislature, the exertions of this committee coupled with those of the Guardian who published in deffiance [sic] of the laws, were the most efficient means of generating that public opinion which now exists on the subject of abolishing all laws which impede the progress of knowledge. The ensueing [sic] month several delegates from the country being in London it was determined that the union should hold a public meeting on the subjects of just and equal representation and the prosecution of Mr Hetherington. A large meeting was therefore held at Portman Market Lisson Grove on Monday July the 11th Mr T. Wakley in the chair, several spirited resolutions were past [sic] on universal suffrage, vote by ballot and no property qualifications—as well as the following on the liberty of the press.

That this meeting views with alarm and indignation the repeated attempts of a Whig ministry to shackle the press by attempting to withhold from man the liberty of expressing his opinions and interfering with that great law of nature which when it gave him the power to speak, also gave him the right to speak as he thought.

In as much as the political events of this period arroused [sic] almost all classes to the consideration of some change; unless indeed those interested in corruptions and oppressions—and as no class had suffered more from the withering influence of corrupt men and measures than the working classes they fondly hoped that the national union, in conjunction with others, would enable them to rise in the scale of political power, and through the medium of just legislation better their social condition. Hence they looked fondly forward with hope, and joined in such numbers that it became necessary to divide their numbers into classes and to hold meetings in different parts of the Metropolis. Their prominent places of meeting were the following. The parent or central place of meeting at the Rotunda Blackfriars Road, Windmill Street Chapel Finsbury Square, Castle Street Assembly Rooms, at the Blind Beggar Bethnal Green, the Duke of York

Hammersmith, the Halifax Arms Mile End, at the Three Compasses Bermonsey [sic], the Yorkshire Grey Hampstead, at the Sydney Arms Commercial Road, the Lecture Room Theobalds Road and several other places occasionally. But perhaps the most usefull of their meetings were those of their classes. Whenever a person was selected by the Committee for his intelligence and fitness as a Classleader, he was written too [sic] by the Secretary, and the names of twenty five members the nearest to his residence were given him. He had also a printed form on which he entered the names of his class, and every week he received their subscriptions and entered them under their proper heading; the sum he received every night was added up before the members present, and he was bound to give it in to the secretary every fortnight, at the Classleaders meeting. The Classleader was also provided with quarterly cards for the members, for which sixpence was demanded from each; they could pay it at once if they choose, or if more convenient, one halfpenny per week, this card admitted them to all the meetings of the union. Their class meetings were generaly held at some members house, the classleader presided and some subject of discussion or conversation was selected; sometimes selections were made from books, the works of Pain [sic], Godwin, Owen, Ensor and other radical writers were generaly prefered [sic], as well as the unstamped political periodicals of the day; and in this manner hundreds of persons were made acquainted with books and principles of which they were previously ignorant. In addition to this the discussions and conversations generated and encouraged the tallent [sic] of public speaking among the members; so usefull in a country of corruptions and abuses, where its exercise becomes a duty.

Abundant subjects for excitement and discussion were from week to week aforded [sic] to the union. Hetheringtons second prosecution, and the almost daily imprisonment of some victim for selling the unstamped continued to perpetuate the political strife; exhibiting as it did the Tory trickery of the Stamp Commissioners on the one hand, and the cowardice and perfidy of the Whigs on the other, in permitting their rivals to triumph at the expence of their own *avowed principles*, and striving to conciliate hollow friendship; instead of seeking to promote the progress of truth and justice. Mr Hunts return for Preston, the massacres in Ireland, the prosecution of Lovett for refusing to serve in the Militia, were subjects for congratulation or bitter invective. This union also participating most cordialy in the feelings of the revolutions of France, Belgium, Poland and others, were the first to congratulate, and the last to celebrate their victories. The first Anniversary of the French Revolution was celebrated at Copenhagen House on the 8th of Aug. 1831. The following address to the French people was agreed to and a supper, speeches, dancing and amusements concluded the evening without drunkenness or confusion. (See P[oor] M[an's] Guardian for the Address Aug. 6th 1831 for Lafayette's answer Sep. 24th.)

Near this period, the time of the throwing out of the Reform Bill by the Lords, considerable anxiety was entertained by the shopkeepers of London, and wealthy individuals, respecting the feelings and views of the Working Classes; and more especially of those belonging to this union; as they were ultra liberals in politics, and always contended that their condition could not be permanently improved; while *property* was made the bassis [sic] of legislation. Those people therefore foolishly believed that the union meditated an attack on *their* property and that they sought by some scheme to dispossess them of it, and divide it amongst themselves. Now though the leading members of the union had taken considerable pains to explain their views, nay they even went to the extent of declaring that they would risk their lives to assist the ministers to carry the Reform Bill, as will be seen from the following address to his majesty agreed to at the Rotunda the 10th of Oct. 1831. (See P. M. Guardian Oct. 22 1831.)

This was not sufficient to satisfy the timidity of those, whose wealth is the bugbear of their fears, at most of their meetings, and in those papers devoted to their interests, something was said to distrust or condemn the Union of the Working Classes. In addition to this many of the union concerned that the committee did not go far enough at this crisis, in declaring their views *on all subjects*, connected with their political and social rights, but thought they had overlooked their own, in their anxiety to assist others. In order therefore to make known to all parties if possible clearly their views & intentions, as well as to promote in their opinion the progress of the measures then pending in parliament—they resolved to hold a large meeting in the open air, on Nov. 7th in the space in front of White Conduit House. Lovett and Watson drew up the following declaration of principles, together with the resolutions that were to have been proposed, they also consulted Mr T. Wakley who agreed to take the Chair on the occasion. (See Declaration P. M. G. Oct. 29 1831.)

This declaration was discussed in most of their class meetings, and read at many of their public meetings, previous to the grand meeting were [sic] it was to have been solemnly ratified. Previous however to its taking place several circumstances transpired to generate a very powerful feeling in the Metropolis against it being held. One of these circumstances were [sic] the riots in Bristol and the burning of the city, which took place after the Declaration was posted—another was some very improper language used by Benbow at a meeting in the Rotunda respecting his joy at the event; which language however was strongly deprecated by the Committee and members generaly—another was the fact of their intention to attend this public meeting each provided with a constables staff. The reason for this latter arrangement originated in several members of the union having been cruely illtreated by the Police when returning with the Marylebone procession from addressing the king on the Reform Bill, and they therefore resolved to protect themselves with similar weapons to those used by the police. The newspaper press therefore taking advantage of those circumstances soon generated such a powerfull sensation among the timid by the dread prophecies of burnings plundering and devestations [sic], that the government was induced to pour Regiment after Regiment into London, to swear in hundreds of special constables, to post cautionary bills, in fact to make as many preparations as if they feared the entry of some foreign foe; instead of a meeting of a few thousands of working men, to talk of their wrongs and to pray for a remedy. Takeing [sic] into account that their object in the first place was a *peacible* [sic], and by them understood to be a *legial* [sic] one—and feeling how powerfull the public opinion was against their intended meeting; and the power and means *they knew* government would

144

use to crush them—after their Committee had waited on Lord Melbourne to endeavour to convince him of their peacible intentions, they wisely resolved to put off the meeting. (See P. M. Guardian Nov. 12 1831.)

A large meeting of the union was held the following monday at the Rotunda and the Resolutions which were to have been submitted to the large meeting in front of White Conduit House were there unanimously agreed too.

The next great exitement of the members of this union was on account of the Bristol and Nottingham Special Commissions. Several public meetings were held and the following protest with 1,270 signatures obtained in a few hours was submitted by a deputation to the Secretary of State. (See Protest P. M. Guardian Jan. 28 1832.)

The 22 of March following the Ministry seeking to conciliate knaves and fanatics on the one hand as well as to feed the gullibility of the ignorant on the other put forth a proclamation for a general fast. No sooner did the members of this union hear of this farce, than they were actively engaged in asertaining [sic] how they could best show their contempt for this knavery or hypocrisy. They first thought of a public meeting on the occasion, but after consulting several eminent lawyers on the subject, they found that no exhibition of numbers could so effectually evade the laws, as by their walking peacibly through the streets of this Metropolis. They therefore resolved that a procession of the union should be held on this occasion after which they should adjourn to their classes or places of meeting and that the most able to afford it should help their poorer bretheren [sic] to *feast* and not *fast* on that day. (See P. M. Guardian March 24 1832.)

Soon after the procession Benbow, Lovett and Watson were arrested as the leaders of the procession and being bailed out, their trial took place at the sessions house Clerkenwell Green on Wednesday the 16th of May 1832. (See trial of Benbow Lovett & Watson—printed.)

Oweing [sic] to some disagreement with Benbow connected with this trial, Lovett and Watson sesceded [sic] from the Committee and though Mr Watson ocassionaly [sic] attended their public meetings the former took no part in their proceedings since that occasion. The Public meetings of the union about this period were attended frequently by Dr Wade, Mr Hunt, Mr Lawless and ocassionaly by D. O. Conelele [sic] and other members of parliament—Duffey, Mee, Lynch, Beck, Lee, Guthrie, Preston and others took part in their proceedings. The 29th Oct. following at the request of several of the Working Classes of Birmingham a Deputation of this union was sent to form a Union of the Working classes at that place. (See P. M. G. Nov. 3 1832.)

Various were the topics discussed throughout the union about this period but none so important especialy in its consequences as was the subject of a National Convention. About the begining [sic] of April 1833 Mr Lee a young man who had recently joined the union, and was elected on the Committee, proposed the following resolution, which was publicly discussed at a meeting at the Rotunda.

That the conduct of the pretended reformed House of Commons clearly demonstrates that to look for any amendment in the political condition of the Working classes untill they possess the power [of] electing their own

145

representatives would be little short of absolute insanity; and that this union conscious that such right will never be obtained so long as this country be cursed with a pampered Monarchy, an indolent aristocracy, and a bloated hierarchy, earnestly implore their brethren throughout the whole country to prepare themselves for a *Convention of the people* as the only mode by which they can devise means to extricate themselves from the grievous misrule under which they have too long and too patiently been suffering.

This resolution was discussed for three suceeding [*sic*] weeks, throughout the union, many were the arguments aduced [*sic*], but none so efficently as were urged by Messrs Lee, Mee and Petrie in calling upon them to send their own representatives to Parliament as Dan'l O Connele was sent by the men of Clare. Though the majority were evidently in favour of this project, yet a considerable number of the most intelligent were thoroughly opposed to it, nay, even in the committee it was carried by a small majority. Eventualy it was determined that a preparitary [*sic*] meeting should be held, which was advertized to take place on May the 13th at 2 o clock on the Calthorp [*sic*] Street Estate Cold Bath Fields. (See P. M. G. May 18 1833 & May 25. See also the Popay affair P. M. G. July 13 1833 & Aug. 24 1833.)

The union is now very weak in numbers & intelligence, great efforts have been made by their indefatigable secretary Mr Russell and a few others to rescussitate [*sic*] it but without effect, a few of the classes still hold together, and they have by the assistance of a few members of Parliament got up public meetings on great ocassions, yet only the shadow and name exists of a union, that scotched and terrified corruption, that exposed public plunderers & private peculators, and that planted the seeds of regeneration the fruits of which may be reaped by posterity.

82. [Add. Ms. 27819, ff. 5–12]

Circumstances which led to the formation of the [London] Working mens Association.

Aug. 1 1841

It is my intention to give a circumstantial account of the immediate causes and the progress of the political proceedings of the working people, from the commencement of the year 1836. Proceedings in themselves very remarkable and unexampled in this or any other country, and very unlikely to terminate until great changes have taken place not only in the relative condition of the working people but in the very form of the government itself. Many of the circumstances now operating upon all classes and many more which operate upon them all together with the increase of knowledge among the masses of the people, do and will tend towards a democratical form of government, and these from time to time will call forth the exertions of the working people in large bodies, who mistaking their want of more general knowledge than they will have, for the possession of full and complete knowledge will induce them to act most unwisely and to do a vast amount of mischief, for which however the government will probably be more to blame than the people from the course they will continue to take of

146

neglecting to adapt their conduct to circumstances and resisting innovations absurdly, until the time has gone by, matters which if adapted to the knowledge and condition of the people would be accepted with thanks, or received as boons, will be extorted by means which will be considered as forced submissions and tend to encourage demands, backed by powerful demonstrations before the nation at large will be prepared for them.

The amount of knowledge among the many is lamentably defective though its increase is certainly great. Some among the working people; a large number among themselves, but a very small number in comparison with their class; are much better informed, more rational and in all respects superior men, to any who could formerly have been found in their class.

But even these men, with few exceptions, have not yet arrived at that state when men rely upon themselves, they are still in but too many cases liable to be drawn aside from the true course and led into errors.

Many again who are neither so well informed as these men and generally not so honest are ready on every occasion when a display can be made to become leaders of large bodies and to influence still larger bodies—to make what they call demonstrations, most of them absurd and demonstrating nothing but their folly, the remainder leading to some extent to better modes of thinking in some particulars and it can hardly be doubted, that upon the whole, and notwithstanding the folly and mischief, progress is made in the inducement to a course which must lead, however slowly, to correct reasoning among multitudes who but for these demonstrations might not so soon have become reasoners, even to the small extent to which the mass of them may be led to reason.

The great body of the working people who take part in political proceedings are still open to the delusions of ill informed, and to dishonest agitators, the field of operation for whom has of late years been greatly enlarged. These ever active men, are enthusiasts as much misled, or nearly as much misled as those who follow them. The doctrines by which the people are misled are founded on what are called inherent indefeasible rights, which are made to include whatever particular object may be aimed at. By notions of equality in respect to property, and by the doctrine promulgated by Robert Owen now known under the name of Socialism. The most mischievous nonsense propagated is that which pretends, to assure the deluded people that poverty will by the adoption of the proposed measure be wholly removed, and that the time is all but at hand when these predictions will be accomplished. These to them mischievous notions called into actions as they had been for several years past, led them to the conclusion that they could associate nearly the whole of the working class in one great confederation which in a short time would gain possession of all the power and property of the nation, and compel the submission of all to their rule; never for an instant doubting that their rule would be the most wise and beneficent that could be imagined; be in fact, a millineum [sic], in which peace plenty and happiness would abound.

This infatuation which governed nearly the whole of the men who in any sense of the word could be designated politicians of the working class and many others who were not of their own class, but of almost every other class, tradesmen, manufactures [*sic*], gentlemen, clergymen and professional men were as it will be seen called into co-operation with the working men, and either lead [*sic*] or supported their schemes with zeal which though much abated in intensity will never be abandoned, but as repeated false steps and their consequent disappointments may teach them wisdom. As the best men in the working class proceed in their attainment of knowledge, they will cease to enforce their mistaken notions, and this will be called abandoning their caste by those who remain unenlightened, and these men, and such other men as have power over multitudes of other men and have sinister objects to accomplish will misinterpret to the many the actions and opinions of those who may have become more enlightened, and will represent them as enemies of the people whom they would be the best qualified and best disposed to serve, the people will continue to be misled, and will look upon their best friends as their worst enemies, and the more, these their friends may attempt to justify themselves and to defend themselves against absurd and false imputations the firmer will be the conviction of the misled ill judging multitude that they are enemies to be shunned. Progress in the capability of thinking more justly will however increase, various circumstances will occur tending to this result. Some of the leaders who have impugned their fellows will be convinced that they have decided absurdly and have acted accordingly and these will from time to time fall into the ranks of those who have been rejected by the people, will become a very considerable number and will slowly but certainly increase their influence. In the mean time many of the incorrigible leaders, and large numbers of those of their followers who are unteachable will be wearied out with continual and rapidly occurring disappointments and will draw off, to be replaced by better men, and notwithstand[ing] the times of inactivity and despair which will occasionally occur the progress of actual improvement in right thinking will go on with increased velocity.

Great allowance should be made for men who have never been taught to reason on causes and consequences. The principal cause of action in such men is the hope of being able to better their condition by increasing their real wages and securing constant employment. It is this hope which sustains vast numbers and prevents them from becoming altogether reckless, as some among them in whom this hope is extinguished are continually becoming. Others and these by far the largest number having toiled on for years will sink into that state when by *ordinary* means all chance of bettering their condition by increase of wages will continue their toil their energies being concentrated, so far as regards their employment in preventing the decrease of wages. To men circumstanced as these two descriptions are the hope of benefit from political associations is very alluring, and the only matter for surprise is that they do not proceed with more of outrage, and offence in various ways than those about to be noticed.

A great mass of our unskilled and but little skilled labourers among whom are the hand loom weavers, and a very considerable number of our skilled labourers are in poverty, if not in actual misery. A large portion of them have been in a state of poverty and great privation all their lives, they are neither ignorant of their condition nor reconciled to it, they live amongst others who are better off than themselves, with whom they compare themselves and they cannot understand why there should be so great a difference, why others who work no more, or fewer hours than themselves at employments not requiring more actual exertion and in many cases occupying fewer hours in the day should be better paid than they are, and they come to the conclusion that the difference is solely caused by oppression. Oppression of bad laws and aviricious [*sic*] employers. To escape from this state is with them of paramount importance, among a vast multitude of these people, not a day, scarcely an hour can be said to pass without some circumstance, some matter exciting reflection occurring to remind them of their condition which notwithstanding they have been poor and distressed from their infancy and however much they may *at times* be cheerful, they scarcely ever cease, and never for a long period cease to feel and to acknowledge to themselves with deep sensations of anguish their deplorable condition. To men thus circumstanced, any, the most absurd scheme which promises relief is eagerly seized and earnestly adhered to until long after it has failed, and is even then reluctantly given up, and is always accounted for by something having supposed to have happened which prevented the good the scheme held out from having been accomplished, and thus they remain as they were having learned nothing, ready to be again deluded by some other scheme, until they hopelessly abandon every effort either to serve themselves or others.

This state of delusion, of disappointment and despair will continue until even this poor class shall be rationally educated, not merely taught to read and write badly, but to use their intellectual faculties, made clearly to understand the meaning of the word Reasoning, and to Reason with something approaching to accuracy on the circumstances in which they are placed, their causes and consequences, the doctrine of Wages, Profit, Rent of Land, and Population, and the application of each to their own as well as to the condition of other persons. Difficult as it may seem to teach these things there is no real difficulty, each admits, of short and clear and conclusive definitions the grounds of which may be easily laid and as the children of the poor grow they may easily be taught to comprehend them thoroughly.

Every rational, well disposed man who for a short time only, will observe the mode and the extent of the reasoning such as it is, of ininstructed [*sic*], ill paid working people, will soon be satisfied, that in their state of toil and trouble and privation and all but hopelessness to which but too many of them are driven, that it is unjust to condemn them for easily giving credence to the delusions which from time to time are inculcated by men who are by them supposed to understand what they talk about, and especially as among them are the Attwoods—Muntz's [*sic*]—Fielden's Wakleys, and others, who frequently take advantage of circumstances to lead and mislead them most egregiously, who seriously point out remedies and at other times assure them that the nostrums they prescribe or administer to them will work their salvation, by causing plenty of work at all times, and double their wages.

Delusions the result of superficial and defective reasoning in men who ought to know better and whose position should make them careful neither to propose nor to support measures which may be injurious to the working

149

people whom they would willingly serve. Of fluent men who go about preaching & lecturing without understanding the subjects they talk about; of others well meaning men who are led by their feelings, and men who are more rogues than fools who are careless of consequences, willing to take the risk of being prosecuted, because it gives them importance, enables them to live upon their fellows and saves them from the much more disgraceable alternative of working for their living at employments they dislike, will one and all continue to produce considerable effect, and consequently continue to produce undesirable and mischievous results.

Proceedings analagous [*sic*] to those which have been noticed will continue sometimes with more, sometimes with less effect, will be more or less extensive, and never will wholly subside. The working people will never more desist from attempts to obtain the right of voting for members to represent the people in the commons house of parliament. No law can wholly prevent them, can wholly put them down, and it may be concluded as certain that laws made for this purpose would but increase the difficulty with the government which should proceed in this way. They would inevitable [*sic*] induce the people to proceed in much more reprehensible ways than they would otherwise adopt.

Proceed how they may some present evil will generally result from the movements of the people, and these will be more numerous and more extensive as wise measures of caution and of amelioration are neglected, or as more stringent laws may unwisely be made. It may therefore be rationally concluded, that the irritation the movements of the people will help to engender, coupled with the apprehension of loss of property, of power and patronage which the aristocracy in church and state cannot but entertain, and the offence they will give to the pride and importance which their long domination has consolidated, and to a considerable extent have blinded them will continue to prevent them seeing the consequences of their own actions, and be a bar to such conduct as might tend to put the evil day to a great distance. Many acts will therefore be done as well by the aristocracy as by the people to the great injury of both and impede the reconciliation of all classes with one another which must preceed any thing worthy the name of good government in this country.

The result is certain. The tendency towards democracy will increase continually. Its rate of increase will be constantly augmented even among those who are incapable as vast numbers are of perceiving the increase, visible as it even now is in the demeanour and language of all men who do not really compose the aristocracy, and with very few exceptions in nearly all if not indeed to some extent in every one of them. Such men as supported the long administration of Mr Pitt no longer exist, and cannot be replaced. However slow has been the change in some instances, still there is not one left who is now the man he would have been in the period from 1793 to 1803. If they were wise they would change still more rapidly than they are likely to do, would carefully observe the march of opinions and events and profit by them for the good of all themselves included, however much they might dislike to see their power and all which to them as a privileged body they most value slowly but continuously sliding from under them. This is not however to be expected from such a body and the people will therefore obtain their emancipation at much greater cost than they would otherwise have to submit to and the aristocracy as the result of their pride and obstinacy will probably be exterminated.

The hope remains but it is a faint one that this may not be the case, but that the whole body of the people exclusive of the aristocracy will as the time approaches when the government must become wholly representative be wise enough to keep their position without inflicting injury on any which can be by any means avoided, and thus set an example to the world of a great nation passing from an aristocratic domination to a wholly democratic government without civil war and bloodshed.

83. [Add. Ms. 35154, ff. 208–22. Dr J. R. Black's account of his attempts to form a society of working men in London, which led eventually to the London Working Men's Association. (Place used this account in writing part of his narrative history of working men's associations, Add. Ms. 27819, ff. 21–7.)]

About the middle of June 1834 Black sought Roland Detrosier and proposed to him a plan for the political organization of the working classes. He was slow in comprehending it. He admitted at once that nothing would be done for the working classes till they did something for themselves, but he could not at first see how the mere union of a few intelligent working men in political associations could effect a general organization of their class & lift them up in their own estimation & in that of the other classes of society. Eventually he understood the plan, seemed to enter warmly into it, and promised to set it going, first in London and as soon as one association could be well trained there, then in the other large towns. After waiting some weeks without any movement on the part of Detrosier, Black asked him to give him the names and addresses of some of the most intelligent & active working men in London that he might apply to them himself. Detrosier sent him to Lovett, saying that he was an excellent man & could introduce me to others. Black went to Lovett in Greville Street, Hatton Garden, but his manner was so cold and guarded that he did not open his business to him. He then sought J. D. Styles, as one of the most active & intelligent working men in London, but he failed for some time in finding him & when he did, Mr Styles was from peculiar circumstances at the time wholly unable to enter into the matter. He next went to John Gast, of whom he had heard through a working man in a conversation held between them in an archway in the Old Jewry where they had both stopt [sic] out of a hard shower of rain. Gast did not hope much from working men's associations, but he thought some good could be done with them & he was therefore willing to aid in forming one in London. He was to see some of his friends & speak to them upon the subject & if they thought well of it, Black was to meet them. Gast however failed in getting any one to see the thing as he did, and when Black saw him Gast was less than ever sanguine as to the success of the plan.

About this time or a little after in August Black made the acquaintance of Francis Place & they very soon became intimate friends, spending a great deal of time together & talking in the most unreserved & confidential

151

manner. To Mr Place he presented his plan of Political Associations of Working men, & he at once saw through the whole matter & in the most encouraging manner urged him to go on with it. From this time they worked together in carrying it out. Many of the most intelligent working men were in the habit of visiting Mr Place on Sundays for the purpose of asking his advice about private affairs or those of their Clubs & Trade Societies, Black regularly attended every Sunday & Mr Place & he let no opertunity [*sic*] slip of holding such conversations with them as would enable them to discover fit men as to ability, zeal, & leisure for their purpose. At last they determined to start an agitation for the Repeal of the Stamp Duty upon Newspapers, to give Black an opertunity of mixing himself actively with working men & others, and thus whilst promoting a general good enabling him to gather round him a sufficient number of proper men to start a London Association. This was done.

They got an office in Leicester Square in April 1835 where Black worked night & day at the Stamp Repealing Agitation & became acquainted with numbers of active working men. In the winter they removed the office to Tavistock Street & continued their exertions to obtain the repeal of the Stamp Duty. By this time many of the most intelligent & active of the working men in London were around Black, but finding their political views extremely crude, he formed classes ostensibly for teaching them Grammar, French, Mathematics etc. but while this was going on he selected & inoculated many of them with the principle of his plan. Here he & Mr Place got up the Committee for obtaining subscriptions for the relief of Hetherington & Cleave, on which committee were half working men, & half middle class men. During the operations of this committee, Black formed an association composed exclusively of working men for the Repeal of the Stamp Duty, which he and Mr Place thought a good preparation for their main design in that direction. This association issued an address, which was published in the Radical Newspaper & in all the unstamped newspapers, with the names & occupations of the members. After this Black broached the main plan in separate conversations to these & a few other working men, and when they had all thus agreed to it, he called them together, the plan was formally proposed, & they resolved to form themselves into a Working men's Association. The members met Black on Thursday night's [*sic*] & Sunday mornings to discuss & agree upon the rules. When every thing was nearly arranged, the 'Universal Suffrage Club' was started by some other persons, and a deputation from the committee of that Club was sent to the infant Working men's Association, inviting its members to join the Club & give up their plan. Great efforts were made thus to break up the Association, & much anger was felt & expressed by some of the more active promoters of the Club at their failure in doing so. In this affair, William Lovett, who was acting as secretary of the Association, Rob't Hartwell & Black, for their determined resistance to the Clubites, were, the especial objects of animadversion for some considerable time. For the want of means Black was obliged a short time after this to give up the political office in Tavistock Street, and the Association not being able to find a suitable place of meeting which they could afford to hire, William Lovett gave it free of all charge a room for its meetings in his own house in Greville Street.

84. [Add. Ms. 27827, f. 32. The following is the address mentioned in the previous document, as it was published in the newspapers. At the top of this published copy Place has written, 'Written by J. Roberts Black M.D. of Kentucky, May 1836'.]

ASSOCIATION OF WORKING MEN TO PROCURE A CHEAP AND HONEST PRESS

THE WORKING MEN of GREAT BRITAIN look around them, and discover that they live in the richest country on earth; yet a greater proportion of themselves barely exist, and trifling accidents in their affairs may doom them to irretrievable pauperism, or to the wards of a loathsome prison.

The working men of Great Britain are conscious that they live in the freest country on earth, with but one exception; yet they themselves are hardly above the condition of slaves. Unrepresented by the law-making power, their wants and their interests are wholly at the mercy of their rulers. Shut out of the courts of law as jurymen, and by the enormous expense of what is called justice, they are seldom seen in them, except when dragged there to be convicted for breaking statutes whose existence they were not permitted previously to know.

The working men of Great Britain live in a country remarkable for the extensive and rapid circulation of intelligence and information; yet they, themselves, are positively, and almost in express terms, denied any participation whatever in the benefits of the readiest, the commonest, the chief vehicle of knowledge—the newspaper.

Under such painful and oppressive circumstances, the working men of this country hailed with joy the first agitation for procuring a cheap and unshackled press; for, from it they hope for advancement in their knowledge, for improvement in their morals for increased sympathy of the other classes of society, for a share in the formation of public opinion, and through these, for all such ameliorations of their condition as would be consistent with the happiness of the community at large.

But now, after years of agitation, after sending into Parliament petitions upon petitions, after repeated promises held forth by ministers, and after the strongest assurances from the middle classes that they would make common cause with the working classes, till a perfectly free press should be obtained—after all this, what is the position of affairs on this subject? Simply this: the stamp duty is to be reduced to a point which will permit newspapers to circulate as freely among the middle classes, as if the press were actually free; while so much of the stamp-duty is to be retained, and such an inquisitorial law is to be enacted, in addition to all those now in force, as shall utterly prohibit the circulation of newspapers among the working classes. Or to express the same thing, by stating the proposition of the present ministry, a *minimum* stamp-duty of one penny is to be retained, by which, according to the acknowledgement of ministers themselves, no such newspapers as we now have can be legally sold for less than fourpence, a price working men cannot pay; while any peace officer or stamp officer is to be authorised to seize any person having an unstamped newspaper in their possession, and a single justice of the peace may commit him to prison for six calendar months, and not less than one month, unless a penalty of

153

£20 for each paper be paid. The conviction to be summary, and without appeal! And let it be remembered, as of a piece with this inquisitorial proposition, that the ministry lately procured an Act of Parliament, taking away all right of private citizens to lay informations for a violation of the stamp laws, and restricting this right solely to officers of the Government; so that the stamp laws now actually stand as so much arbitrary power for official dictation. Yes, incredible as it may seem when simply stated, these laws are wholly in official hands, to be dealt out according to their particular views; and, unfortunately for us, their particular views, are in direct hostility to the labouring classes, as is but too clearly shown by the fact, that of great variety of publications, equally in violation of the stamp laws, ministers have selected those, and those only, to base their prosecutions upon, which contain 'news and information' for working men.

Here, is a *minimum* stamp-duty of a penny, keeping up the price of legal newspapers to fourpence; with a multiplicity of obscure laws relating to newspaper stamps, all recognised in the new Consolidated Bill; with a proposed additional act of extensive and inquisitorial powers; with the right of resorting to these laws, taken from the community, and put solely into official hands; and with the demonstrated hostility of our rulers against our further improvement—the true position of working men is too painfully evident.

Now, as working men, we appeal to every honest heart amongst our fellow citizens, whose approbation we covet, if it is just to mark out our class for so cruel an exclusion from the countless benefits and peculiarly inestimable gratification of possessing newspapers? We appeal to every candid man in either the aristocratic or middle classes to say, if his particular class were thus, alone excluded, by inquisitorial and arbitrary laws, from reading newspapers at home, whether that class would tamely submit to such exclusion? And yet to no class does the reading of their own newspapers bring greater benefits, or higher enjoyment, than to the working classes—to no other class is the possession of newspapers so important—by no other class is this privilege so dearly prized. Let it not be expected then, that we will tamely submit to the uncalled for, and cruel oppression of being excluded from all participation in the press of our country; and above all at this moment too, when mainly by our co-operative exertions the press is to be thrown open to the middle classes;—many of whom seem but too much disposed to accept their bribe and to desert our cause, leaving us to the unscrupulous opposition of offended power. But we repeat, let it not be expected that working men will repose in silence and inaction under this bitterest oppression.

We know what is thought of us by the other classes of society, what is often said of us even by those who are really our friends,—that we have too little intelligence to perceive rightly our own interests—too little mutual confidence to become united—too few habits of temperance and providence to exercise moral courage—and too much subserviency to other classes to hold up our heads as men. We who now form this Association know otherwise, and we possess, it must be allowed by those who are acquainted with us, somewhat ample means of coming to correct conclusions with respect to our own class; but we hope to convince both our enemies and our friends

154

in the other classes of society, that the few last years have not past [*sic*] in vain, as regards the intelligence and morals of working men; and that the unstamped press, whatever the other classes of society may have thought of it, has not been more busy than profitable among that portion of the people who demanded and therefore purchased its 'millions of sheets a year'.

At all events, we, who this day form 'the Association of Working Men to procure a cheap and honest Press', have unanimously resolved:—

1. To appeal to our fellow-citizens of the other classes, from time to time, and in every way we can, till the press is, as it ought to be, perfectly free:

2. To stimulate our own class, in every possible way, to continual efforts in the holy cause of a free press:

3. To use every legal means in our power to organize a system of general intercommunication between leading working men throughout the kingdom for this beneficent purpose:

4. To resort to all legal and proper means of supporting and procuring CHEAP NEWSPAPERS:

5. To take steps for the dissemination of instructive tracts among our brethren throughout the whole country:

6. To do all we can to aid and succour our brethren when under any oppression legal or illegal, connected with the Press:

7. And never to cease our exertions till the Press is as free to the Working Man as to the Chancellor of the Exchequer himself.

Henry Ainsworth, 114, Bunhill-row
E. H. Baker, 22, Eagle-street, Red Lion-square
Charles Cole, 10, Fleur-de-lis-court, Norton Folgate
John Cray, 3, Seamore-place, Camden Town
Richard Cray, 16, High-street, Bow
John Duce, 9, Wilmot-street, Bethnal-green-road
John Farrell, 53, Heath-street, Commercial-road, East
J. Fox, 7, Scott-street
John Gast, 14, Lucas-street, Rotherhithe
G. Glashan, 6, George-street, Tower-hill
Jonathan Gray, 12, Wilmot-square, Bethnal-green-road
R. Hartwell, 35, Brooke-street, Lambeth
G. Hendley, 18, Putney-street, Whiteconduit Fields
William Kitran, 1, Princess-street, Spitalfields
William Lovett, 19, Greville-street, Hatton Garden
James Martin, 14, Tavistock-street, Covent Garden
D. M'Donnell, 25, College-street, West, Camden Town
T. Medway, Winchester-street, Bethnal-green
R. Moore, 20, Hyde-street, Bloomsbury
Anthony Morton, 73, Rahere-street, Goswell-road
R. Potts, 9, Crescent-street, Euston-square
Robert Raven, 3, Hanover-crescent, Milton-street
James Roberts, 23, Robert-street, Hampstead-road
J. Robinson, Tower-street, Tower Hamlets
John Rogers, 8, Newcastle-street, Strand
A. Sparks, 26, Noble-street, Willington-square

J. D. Styles, 7. Belvidere-road, Lambeth
J. Sturges, 8, Upper-street, St. Martin's-lane
J. Thomson, Blacksmith's Arms, Brook-street, Ratcliff

85. [Add. Ms. 35150, ff. 116–17]

To Mr Morton, Journeyman Carpenter

Dear Sir   Brompton 2 April 1836

My friend Dr Black has told me of your intention to form societies in various places to consist of working men for the purpose of mutual instruction and that you are coming to converse with me upon the subject.

Desirous as I have always been to facilitate every project likely to promote the well being of the working people I was much pleased on being informed of your intention, and therefore to save your time and prevent any misunderstanding I now send you some particulars and advice.

In the year 1795 I was one of 15 working men, all of us members of the London Corresponding Society, who met every sunday evening at an appointed hour, at one or other of our rooms, at these meetings each one of us in turn was chairman, and each of us in turn read a small portion of some useful book, and then each was requested to make his observations thereon. As many as pleased did so. Then another small portion was read and they who had not spoken were requested to make such observation as occurred to them. If any remained who had not spoken another portion was read and it was considered a point of honor that they who had hitherto been silent should speak. This course of discipline embarrassed most of us, but it compelled every one to think more correctly than we had been accustomed to do, and it either engendered or increased the desire and habit of investigation. It made us all eager to procure information on many subjects, it induced us to purchase books for our private use with such money as we could save, and which some of us had spent much less usefully, with me it laid the foundation of my library. It stimulated us all to learn many useful things, and to be much more precise in every way than we had been. Two, the most useful of all possible results were the consequence, we obtained correct notions on several important subjects and information on others which few of us had ever before contemplated. These inquiries increased our notions of our own individual respectability and helped to put every one of us in the way to become a master in his particular trade, and every one of us succeeded in permanently bettering his condition in life. See here an example, than which nothing ought to be more cheering to a working man, none which can to a really respectable working man be more consoling.

I strongly advise you and your friends to adopt a somewhat similar course, but to some extent improved course. Thus, to meet together either at one anothers rooms or in some common room where no expense beyond candles and perhaps fire will be incurred. If only half a dozen meet it will be sufficient as others will soon join you. Each man to pay 1/- on joining and 1/- a quarter to purchase books, and one penny at each meeting he attends, if necessary, for candles etc. You may go on adding to your number until it amounts to about 25, then make an offset of from 5 to 10 as may be most convenient, to those members who live at a distance but in the same direction, thus multiplying your associations continually, but having cognizance of each others meetings and occasionally holding a general meeting of all the members. By proceeding in this way you will collect together the best disposed and best informed men in the several trades in London and great indeed will be the benefit of your proceedings.

It is of much more importance that a small number of the best informed and most respectable men should meet in the first instance than a large number of men less qualified to promote the objects you have in view.

The best book I know of for the use of such meetings is 'Godwins enquiry concerning political justice and its influence on morals and happiness'. It will be advisable to purchase a copy of that work, and when your numbers will enable you to purchase another copy, to cut them up, and sew such chapters as may be selected in *very strong* brown paper covers. When you have two copies two members may read the same chapter at the same time, and by allowing two days to each to read those same chapters each will read it in the course of a fortnight and by reading one chapter under another, you can so arrange it that the chapter which shall have been read by each at his home could be read aloud again at the sunday evening meeting for discussion.

Several of the chapters which are most important are short and though they require some serious thinking do not present greater difficulties than ordinary men may overcome, if not completely at first, yet certainly by discussion and subsequent reading, and this is the great advantage of such institutions as we are now considering. The chapters I recommend to be first read are

1 The history of political society	in 8	pages
2 The Spirit of political institutions	10	do
3 The characters of men originate in their external circumstances 18		do
4 Human inventions susceptible of perpetual improvement	4	do
5 Of the equality of mankind	5	do
6 Of personal virtue and duty	10	do
7 Of rights	12	do
8 Of the right of private judgement	13	do

Here are 8 subjects every one of them of great importance and these with the probable adjournments of some of the discussions may serve for a quarter of a year, by which time many of the members will be competent to select as many other chapters as may be advisable for the purpose, and when these have been read and discussed as recommended, they may be again read and discussed with almost infinite advantage.

At the commencement of vol. 1 is a summary of principles, 5 pages, these may be advantageously read but not for discussion until all the selected chapters have been discussed, since without the knowledge which would be thus acquired it would be waste of time to discuss the summary.

There is an invaluable little work on the wages of labour which might be read and discussed in the same way on alternate sunday evenings or much more advantageously on the evening of some week day, as the general and particular subjects would be thus taught together. I will ascertain if any of the small treatises can be procured. Reading these works need not prevent the learning of any art or science since even a third evening in every week could not be spent in any way so advantageously. How great an amount of real learning, how much truly valuable information may be obtained by working men is known to scarcely any body, and no one can appreciate the benefits of knowledge of any kind until he has obtained it. The rules may be very simple. 1 Each man to pay 1/- per quarter in advance. 2 No eating drinking or smoaking [*sic*] to be allowed at any meeting. 3 Any member the least disguised by liquor to be at once expelled the meeting. 4 When there are 25 members, a certain number to form a new division. 5 One member in each division to be Treasurer and secretary. 6 Regular weekly communications with every division either in writing or by meeting of the secretaries. 7 The secretaries to report when necessary to their divisions

Yours truly
Francis Place

You may make any use you please of this letter.

86. [Add. Ms. 27819, ff. 32–5]

This was the first of a series of proceedings of a public kind taken by the working people in their own name, and emanating from a formal body which led to matters of very extensive and serious importance, and has in many cases proved disastrous mainly from want of patient perseverance. The false notions of their leaders, and the ready acquiescence of the too credulous people, faults from which it was not possible for the working people to be free from, any more than those are who are better off in the world, and better educated, and having much more leisure than men who are compelled to work twelve hours a day for a subsistence. These facets may indeed be said to pervade every class and are amongst the greatest impediments to improvement.

It will have been seen that there was great difficulty in getting up the Working Mens Association, that it required much time perseverance care and temper, and it may be fairly inferred that few men could have gone on with it as Dr Black did, and still fewer who could have established it as he did. The circumstances are curious in themselves and serve to shew how very difficult it is where there is no sinister interest in any of the parties to promote and consequently no disposition to pander to the mistaken notions of the people to induce them to become active in forming and conducting societies calculated to promote their own well being, the good to be done being remote. To shew this and to satisfy the readers that this was not a wild speculation got up to promote the personal advantage or to gratify the love of distinction of some silly person are amongst the reasons why this account, which is only a sketch has been written.

The plan of proceeding did not please many whose want of knowledge of the actual condition and notions of the disappointed disorganized working people, led them to anticipate proceedings by large bodies of them, some therefore who had taken part in the previous proceedings, abandoned the association, quarrelled with its members and in their eagerness to become notorious—popular—as they believed made an effort to form an association more conformable with their own notions.

158

At the head of these were Mr Feargus O Connor and Augustus Hardin [*sic*] Beaumont.

Feargus O Connor was the son of Roger O Connor the brother of Arthur O Connor who had been an exile in the United States of America ever since the Irish Rebellion in 1798. Feargus O Connor became a member of the House of Commons after the passing of the Reform Bills in 1832, and since he has ceased to be a member of Parliament he has taken whatever means he could to lead and mislead the working people. His associate Beaumont was a very extraordinary man, his excentricities [*sic*] sometimes bordered upon insanity, but he meant well to the working people at all times, even when his actions were most likely to be injurious to them. He would have served them had he known how but the abberrations [*sic*] of his intellect led him to adopt measures which while they injured him in his pecuniary concerns were producing consequences to them directly the reverse of his intentions.

The unfortunate state of Mr Beaumont and the ignorant self-willed perseverance of Mr O Connor were great impediments to the progress of the working people in the right way and the consequences of the exertions of these two men were the disunion and holding back of very considerable numbers of working people.

The first endeavour of O Connor and Beaumont was to prevent the publication of the Address of the working mens Association. Failing in this they next endeavoured by causing dissention among the members of the association to break it up, and failing to accomplish this, by direct means, they hoped to accomplish it by indirect means, they attempted to establish an 'Universal Suffrage Club', in the expectation that they should be able to induce them to become members of it.

Their proposition went to this, that the men who composed the club, instead of conducting their own affairs, should submit to have them ordered by O Connor and Beaumont, to this the working men would not consent, the society they had formed being an experiment for the purpose of ascertaining how far the men of their own class were able and willing to conduct their own affairs without leaders from any other rank in society.

Failing in this project, they set another on foot and on the 10 of June they published a paper headed thus.

'At a General Meeting of the Central Committee of the Metropolitan Radical Unions (there were no such unions in existence F.P.) held at the True Sun Office on Friday the 10 June 1836 for the purpose of forming a Working Mans Club, it was resolved,—unanimously that the following prospectus of the Club be published in the True Sun—Radical—and Unstamped Newspapers.'

This was followed by another address dated the 17 June.

These addresses were both signed   Feargus O'Connor Treasurer
                                       John Russell   Secretary

— — — — —

On the 24 June there was another pretended meeting of the Central Committee for forming a Working Mans Club, and an address was voted, this was followed by another to the Radical Reformers of Manchester from the pretended Universal Suffrage Club. The entrance to this Club was, it said, 20/- to be paid quarterly, and it was announced, 'That in consequence of representations being made by several bodies of working men of the high rate of entrance and subscription which would exclude them from becoming members of the Club. It was resolved to meet the wishes of the working men the entrance should be 2/6 and the annual subscription 10/- payable quarterly.'

Neither of these associations were established.

87. [Add. Ms. 27827, f. 33]

Published in June 1836 by the men who contend that all the produce of the earth and of manufactures and every thing else belongs to those by whose labour they are produced and to none else—They as they maintain being productive labourers all other being consumers merely.

[*Newspaper cutting.*] At a GENERAL MEETING of the CENTRAL COMMITTEE of the METROPOLITAN RADICAL UNIONS, held at the *True Sun* Office, on Friday, the 10th June, 1836, for the purpose of founding a WORKING-MAN'S CLUB. It was resolved unanimously, that the following prospectus of the Club be published in the *True Sun, Radical*, and unstamped newspapers:—PLAN FOR ESTABLISHING A WORKING-MAN'S CLUB. 1 Name. That the Club be called 'The UNIVERSAL SUFFRAGE CLUB'. 2 The objects. To elevate the moral, intellectual, and political character of the Working Classes; to afford them more opportunities for friendly intercourse with each other; and for forming a more substantial compact between them; and such men of learning, and political and moral integrity, as are desirous of making common cause with their less affluent brethren for placing happiness within the reach of all;—to soften, and eventually to subdue, the asperity of the aristocracy and middle classes towards the working portion of the people;—to prove to all their enemies the fitness of the working classes to manage their own affairs, both locally and nationally;—to maintain a powerful combination of talented and virtuous men, devoted to the public welfare, around whom the great bulk of the people may at all times rally in promoting all useful and important changes, instead of continuing to be but the instrument of one faction for the suppression of another, under pretence of reform, which has only been attended with additional injury and new insults to the people;—and finally, to establish perfect equality in the making and administration of the laws, as the only guarantee for securing to industry and real merit their just reward, and of ensuring peace and plenty, universal security and happiness. 3 The means. Are to raise a fund by donations from friends, and by the entrance-fees and subscriptions of members. 4 Application of funds. As soon as the funds will allow, a Club House shall be established, with suitable offices for conducting its various departments in a manner superior to any accommodation which the working man now has. 5 Advantages. The members to have free access at all hours—all kinds of information from newspapers, and the various periodical works of art and science—a library

160

to be opened for the members as soon as possible—the best accommodation for supplying members with all kinds of refreshments of the best quality at the cheapest rate. 6 Conditions. 1 It is expected that every man joining this Association shall be favourable to universal suffrage. 2 The entrance fee shall be five shillings, and the annual subscriptions shall be one pound, payable quarterly. 3 When 500 persons shall have paid the entrance money, the Club shall be considered founded; a meeting of members shall then be convened, for the purpose of electing, by ballot, officers and a committee to complete the arrangements upon the plan here laid down, and to draw up rules of management. 4 That after the formation of the Club, every candidate for admission shall be subject to the ballot—three black balls in ten to exclude. Resolved—That, till the formation of the Club, when the officers will be elected by ballot, the undernamed members of the Central Committee shall hold the offices set opposite their respective names provisionally:—Feargus O'Connor, Treasurer John Russell, Secretary. Resolved—That the Central Committee do continue to use all its energies in the formation of the Universal Suffrage Club, with power to add to their number. Resolved—That an Address to the Working Men of the Nation be prepared by the Central Committee at its next meeting. Every information will be given, and cards issued at the following places:— Mr HETHER-INGTON'S, Strand; Mr CLEAVE'S, Shoe-lane; Mr WATSON'S, City-road; Mr LOVETT'S Coffeehouse, Greville-street, Hatton-garden; Mr BEAU-MONT'S, Radical Office, Strand; Mr SAVAGE'S, Mechanic's Institution, Circus-street, New-road, Marylebone. Communications to be addressed, post paid, to the Secretary, 23, Princes-street, Portman-market.

88. [Add. Ms. 27819, f. 35]

The reduction of the Stamp duty on Newspapers was about to be enacted and the members of the working mens association had turned their attention to the formation of a political association, the matter was discussed, and was much impeded by Beaumont but they at length proceeded as the following extracts from their minute book will show. . . .

6 June 1836 'At a meeting of a few friends assembled at 14 Tavistock Street Covent Garden, William Lovett brought forward a rough sketch of a prospectus for the Working Mens Association. It was subsequently ordered to be printed for further discussion'.

At the next meeting 16 June Mr R. Moore in the Chair the prospectus was adopted; and a provisional committee of the following persons viz Hartwell, Hetherington, Lovett, Hoare, Morton, Baker, Glashan, Rogers and Sturges were appointed to draw up rules and regulations for the Association.

At the next subsequent meeting June 26 the following Rules were submitted and unanimously agreed to.

[Place did not include in his narrative the printed address which accompanied the rules, and the following is taken from a printed version in Add. Ms. 27835, ff. 247–50.]

ADDRESS AND RULES OF THE WORKING MEN'S ASSOCIATION, FOR BENEFITING POLITICALLY, SOCIALLY, AND MORALLY, THE USEFUL CLASSES.

ADDRESS[1]

FELLOW LABOURERS IN THE PURSUIT OF KNOWLEDGE AND LIBERTY.—We are anxious to express our grateful acknowledgements thus publicly, to those associations who have addressed us in the spirit of fraternity, and especially to those individuals who have so kindly assisted our missionaries in their exertions to form other associations.

It is a pleasing evidence of the progressive knowledge of those great principles of democracy, which we are contending for, to find kindred minds prepared to appreciate, and noble hearts seeking their practical development in the remotest parts of the kingdom.

But we would respectfully caution our brethren in other societies, strictly to adhere to a judicious selection of their members; on this, more than on any other of their exertions, harmony and success will depend. Let us, friends, seek to make the principles of democracy as respectable in practice as they are just in theory, by excluding the drunken and immoral from our ranks; and in uniting in close compact with the honest, sober, moral, and thinking portion of our brethren.

Doubtless, by such selections, our numbers, in many instances, will be few compared with the vicious many; but these few will be more efficient for the political and social emancipation of mankind than an indiscriminate union of thousands, where the veteran drunkard contaminates by his example, and the profligate railer at abuses saps, by his private conduct, the cause he has espoused.

In forming Working Men's Associations, we seek not a mere exhibition of numbers; unless, indeed, they possess the attributes and character of *men*; and little worthy of the name are those who have no aspirations beyond mere sensual enjoyments—who, forgetful of their duties as fathers, husbands, and brothers, muddle their understandings and drown their intellect amid the drunken revelry of the pot-house—whose profligacy makes them the ready tools and victims of corruption, or slaves of unprincipled governors, who connive at their folly, and smile while they forge for themselves the fetters of liberty by their love of drink.

We doubt not, that the excessive toil and misery to which the sons of labour are subject, in the absence of that knowledge and mental recreation which all just governments should seek to diffuse, are mainly instrumental in generating that intemperance, the debasing influence of which we perceive and deplore. But, friends, though we possess not the political power to begin our reformation at the source of the evil, we cannot doubt the efficacy of our exertions to check by precept and example this politically-debasing, soul-subduing vice.

Fellow-countrymen, *when we contend for an equality of political rights*, it is not in order to lop off an unjust tax or useless pension, or to get a transfer of wealth, power, or influence for a party; but to be *able to probe our social evils to their source, and to apply effective remedies to prevent, instead of unjust laws to punish.* We shall meet with obstacles, disappoint-

[1] See **88a** for Place's comments on this address.

162

ments, and it may be with persecutions, in our pursuit; but, with your united exertions and perseverance, we must and will succeed.

And if the teachers of temperance and preachers of morality would unite like us, and direct their attention to the source of the evil, instead of nibbling at the effects and seldom speaking of the cause; then, indeed, instead of splendid palaces of intemperance daily erected, as if in mockery of their exertions—built on the ruins of happy homes, despairing minds, and sickened hearts—we should soon have a sober, honest, and reflecting people.

In the pursuit, therefore, of our righteous object, it will be necessary to be prudent in our choice of members; we should also avoid by every possible means holding our meetings at public houses; habits and associations are too often formed at those places which mar the domestic happiness, and destroy the political usefulness of millions. Let us, then, in the absence of means to hire a better place of meeting, meet at each other's houses. Let us be punctual in our attendance, as best contributing to our union and improvement; and, as an essential requisite, seek to obtain a select library of books, choosing those at first which will best inform us of our political and social rights. Let us blend, as far as our means will enable us, study with recreation, and share in any rational amusement (unassociated with the means of intoxication) calculated to soothe our anxieties and alleviate our toils.

And, as our object is universal, so (consistent with justice) ought to be our means to compass it; and we know not of any means more efficient, than to enlist the sympathies and quicken the intellects of our wives and children to a knowledge of their rights and duties;—for, as, in the absence of knowledge, they are the most formidable obstacles to a man's patriotic exertions, so when imbued with it they will prove his greatest auxiliaries. Read, therefore; talk, and politically and morally instruct your wives and children; let them, as far as possible, share in your pleasures, as they must in your cares; and they will soon learn to appreciate your exertions, and be inspired with your own feelings against the enemies of their country. Thus instructed, your wives will spurn, instead of prompting you to accept, the base election bribe—your sons will scorn to wear the livery of tyrants—and your daughters be doubly fortified against the thousand ills to which the children of poverty are exposed.

Who can foretell the great political and social advantages that must accrue from the wide extension of societies of this description acting up to their principles? Imagine the honest, sober, and reflecting portion of every town and village in the kingdom linked together as a band of brothers,—honestly resolved to investigate all subjects connected with their interests, and to prepare their minds to combat with the errors and enemies of society—setting an example of propriety to their neighbours, and enjoying even in poverty a happy home. And, in proportion as home is made pleasant, by a cheerful and intelligent partner, by dutiful children, and by means of comfort their knowledge has enabled them to snatch from the ale-house, so are the bitters of life sweetened with happiness.

Think you a corrupt Government could perpetuate its exclusive and demoralizing influence amid a people thus united and instructed? Could a

163

vicious aristocracy find its servile slaves to render homage to idleness and idolatry to the wealth too often fraudently [*sic*] exacted from industry? Could the present gambling influences of money perpetuate the slavery of the millions, for the gains or dissipation of the few? Could corruption sit in the judgment seat—empty-headed importance in the senate-house—money-getting hypocrisy in the pulpit—and debauchery, fanaticism, poverty, and crime stalk triumphantly through the land,—if the millions were educated in a knowledge of their rights?

No, no, friends; and hence the efforts of the exclusive few to keep the people ignorant and divided. Be ours the task then to unite and instruct them; for, be assured, the good that is to be must be begun by ourselves. And is it not a task worthy of every generous mind, to endeavour to ameliorate the condition of humanity?

It has been said by some that our objects are exclusive, seeing we wish to confine our associations to working men. We reply, that judging from experience and appearances, the political and social regeneration of the working classes must be begun by themselves; and, therefore, they should not admit any preponderating influence of wealth or title to swerve them from their duty. By the laws of our Association all classes and conditions of men, whose character will stand the test of investigation, may be admitted to render us all the possible good they can desire—we only seek to prevent them from doing us evil. If they desire to impart to us their superior knowledge and advice, our laws permit them to do so on terms of perfect equality; but if they desire to rule and govern for their selfish interests, our rules oppose their domination. Let not however the men of wealth imagine that we have any ulterior designs inimical to their rights, or views opposed to the peace and harmony of society.—On the contrary, we seek to render property more secure; life more sacred; and to preserve inviolate every institution that can be made to contribute to the happiness of man. We only seek that share in the institutions and government of our country which our industry and usefulness justly merit. That the working millions may be induced to perceive their just interests and form themselves into Working Men's Associations,—and that those already enrolled may be urged by a sense of duty to their families and their country to persevere in their progress—is the ardent wish of the members of the London Working Men's Association.

Signed by the Committee, on behalf of the Association—
H. HETHERINGTON, Printer, Treasurer, 126 Strand
WILLIAM LOVETT, Cabinet-maker, Secretary, 6, Upper North-place, Gray's Inn-road

RULES. etc.

Among the causes that most contribute to the perpetuation of abuses and corruptions in every department of the state, and the indifference manifested toward the interests of the millions, none have been more pregnant with evil than the divisions and dissensions among the working classes themselves.

The great variety and clashing of opinions on all important subjects, political and social—the contradictory and deficient evidence relating to

164

the true condition of the labourer—the conflicting means suggested to remedy what each conceives to be the paramount evil—together with the bickerings and trifling of the most honest and influential amongst them—have long been subjects of regret and causes of vexatious disappointment.

Being convinced, then, that no reflecting and philanthropic mind can *witness* those scenes of misery that everywhere press upon his notice,—can *read* of the thousand wretched forms under which the demon of poverty tortures the millions, and at the same time *reflect* on the ample means wasted on folly and lavished on idleness—means sufficient to impart happiness to all, if wisely directed, without resolving to inquire into the causes of those evils, and to devise, if possible, some means of remedying or alleviating them.

And if the working classes themselves do not sympathise with each other, so many of whom have felt the bitterness of extreme poverty, how can they expect those, who, from their situations in life can scarcely form a conception of it, to feel or care respecting them? If they, whose interests are so identified, do not investigate the causes of the evils that oppress them, how can they expect others to do it for them?

A few persons, therefore, belonging to and associated with the working classes, having seen much of their state and condition, and knowing much more of their wants and necessities, sincerely lamenting their apathy to their *own affairs*, and their still more reprehensible dependence on wealth and power for their political and social rights, have resolved to use every exertion to form an Association, with the following objects in view:—

Objects

1 To draw into one bond of UNITY the *intelligent* and *influential* portion of the working classes in town and country;

2 To seek by every legal means to place all classes of society in possession of their equal, political, and social rights;

3 To devise every possible means, and to use every exertion, to remove those cruel laws that prevent the free circulation of thought through the medium of a *cheap and honest press*;

4 To promote, by all available means, the education of the rising generation, and the extirpation of those systems which tend to future slavery;

5 To collect every kind of information appertaining to the interests of the working classes in particular, and society in general, especially statistics regarding the wages of labour, the habits and condition of the labourer, and all those causes that mainly contribute to the present state of things;

6 To meet and communicate with each other for the purpose of digesting the information acquired, and to mature such plans as they believe will conduce in practice to the well-being of the working classes;

7 To publish their views and sentiments in such form and manner as shall best serve to create a moral, reflecting, yet energetic public opinion, so as eventually to lead to a gradual improvement in the condition of the working classes, without violence or commotion;

8 To form a library of reference and useful information; to maintain a place where they can associate for mental improvement, and where their brethren from the country can meet with kindred minds actuated by one

great motive—that of benefiting politically, socially, and morally, the useful classes. Though the persons forming this Association will be at all times disposed to co-operate with all those who seek to promote the happiness of the multitude, yet being convinced, from experience, that the division of interests in the various classes, in the present state of things, is too often destructive of that union of sentiment which is essential to the prosecution of any great object, that they have resolved to confine their members, as far as practicable, to the working classes. But as there are great differences of opinion as to where the line should be drawn which separates the working classes from the other portions of society, they leave to the members themselves to determine whether the candidate proposed is eligible to become a member.

QUALIFICATION FOR MEMBERSHIP—All persons of good moral character among the industrious classes are eligible to become Members of this Association.

MODE OF ELECTING MEMBERS—All candidates for admission must be proposed and seconded by Members; the proposer must give in the name, residence, and occupation of the person proposed, to the Secretary, on a general meeting night. The Secretary shall then submit the same to the Committee, for inquiry respecting the moral character and fitness of the candidate; they shall report the result of their inquiries to the next subsequent meeting. The Members present shall then determine on the election of the person proposed, and resolve, by a majority of three-fourths, whether he shall be admitted or not. The election to be decided by Ballot.

HONORARY MEMBERS OF THE WORKING CLASSES—Working men in different parts of the country may be elected Honorary Members without payment, who shall be entitled to all the privileges of the Association whenever they come to town.

HONORARY MEMBERS NOT OF THE WORKING CLASSES—Persons not of the working classes, but whom the Members believe are sufficiently identified with them, may be elected Honorary Members. They shall be allowed to take part in all debates or discussions, and to attend all meetings of the Association; but not to hold any office, or take any part in the management.

PAYMENTS—Each Member shall pay the sum of one shilling per month (in advance) towards supporting the establishment. He being in arrears three months, and not making a satisfactory excuse, shall have his name erased.

OFFICERS FOR MANAGEMENT—The business of the Association shall be conducted by a Committee of twelve, a Secretary, and Treasurer. It shall be incumbent on them to attend every *business night of meeting*, and keep minutes of the proceedings, and carefully perform those duties which the Association may from time to time require of them. The Treasurer shall make all purchases, and pay all bills, by a specific order of the Committee, and not otherwise; and make up a balance-sheet of receipts and expenditure every quarter, for the use of the Members. Should any of them be ill, and unable to attend, they shall send a written statement to that effect to the Association.

The twelve elected on the first Committee shall continue in office for three months; at the expiration of that period, the six lowest on the list shall vacate their seats, and six others shall be elected in their stead. At the end of every subsequent quarter, the six longest in office shall retire, whose places shall be filled up by a new election, agreeable to the following rule. The retiring Members may be re-elected.

ELECTION OF OFFICERS—A fortnight previous to the quarterly meeting, the Secretary shall make out a list of the candidates for office from a book kept for that purpose. The list having been printed, he shall forward a copy to each Member, and also inform him of the time of election. When they are assembled for that purpose, each Member shall silently deposit his balloting-list in a box on the table, he having previously struck out the names of all except those he wishes to be chosen. Two scrutineers shall then be appointed by a show of hands, who shall examine the lists and declare the names of the persons elected, who shall commence their duties the following week.

ON THE EXCLUSION OF MEMBERS—On the requisition of twenty Members who consider the conduct or character of any Member inimical to the objects of this Association, a general meeting of the Members shall be called, when all the circumstances connected with such conduct or character shall be investigated; after which, they shall determine, at once, (by ballot) whether such person shall be excluded from the Association or not.

VISITORS—Each Member may invite a friend (by ticket) to any meeting, except those devoted to the business of the Association. He may be allowed to address the meeting with the leave of the Chairman.

MEETINGS OF THE ASSOCIATION—They shall hold a *Quarterly Meeting* on the Wednesday nearest the general quarter-day for the election of officers.

They shall have a *General Meeting* every Tuesday, at half-past eight o'clock, for the election of Members, and for conducting the general business of the Association.

They shall hold *Public Meetings* on any great occasion, when they conceive they can promote the interests of working men; but on no occasion for party purposes, or private considerations for individuals.

They shall have a *Discussion* on some important subject once a week.

The other evenings of the week they shall take into account the best means of promoting or carrying into effect their general objects.

DONATIONS—Persons desirous of contributing money, books, maps, models, or anything likely to promote the objects of the Association, are respectfully requested to forward the same to the Secretary.

LIBRARY—The books in the library shall be circulated among the Members, subject to the regulations thereof; for which see the catalogue.

88a. [Add. Ms. 27822, f. 95. *Printed.*]

'An Address from the Working Men's Association in London, to their fellow-labourers,' appeared lately in the *London Dispatch, Weekly True Sun, Weekly Chronicle, The Dispatch,* and other Papers.

This address, written by a working man, is a paper of no ordinary character. It is indeed a most important production, and when taken as a whole, could not, probably, have been written by any man, unless he either was, or had himself been a working man. It inculcates sound moral principles. It recommends and enforces the necessity of acquiring knowledge, and it most ably points out the advantages which cannot fail to follow the putting its recommendations into practice.

Why it may be asked—why has it happened that the working people, who compose an immense majority of the nation, have never yet done any thing on a large scale, to advance any of their many interests? Why have they never adopted any plan to advance their own respectability? The answer is, want of union. If it be asked, why have they not been united? the answer is, the want of knowledge of their condition in relation to society. This ignorance has all along been their bane, it is still their bane. It is this which has ever made them look to others, and from time to time to rely upon those who neither understood, nor cared to understand their condition, and the consequence has all along been and ever must be disappointment, tending, as it should seem, to sour their dispositions, but not to instruct them in the great truth, that it is themselves, and themselves only, who have the means to better their condition, to increase their own respectability. It left them open to the delusion of every one who had a scheme to propose, of projectors, who having misled themselves, could only mislead others. It induced but too many of them to believe in the practicability of 'Mr. Owen's new state of society', or the proposals of others for a perpetual division of property, until none should remain to be divided. It induced them to cherish many projects, all equally impracticable in the present, and probably in any future state of society. Thus have they been led away from the consideration of every just view, of every practicable means of serving themselves, or even attending to any practicable suggestion whatever. It induced them to cherish hatred towards others, and neglect of their own most important interests; it led them to divisions among themselves, and tended to destroy whatever desire there might be in any who were able to assist, and who, but for these absurd notions and divisions, might to some extent have done them services.

The address now published, wisely avoids every subject which has a tendency to cause disputes. It points out the way by which every working man who thinks at all on the condition of the class to which he belongs, may advance his own and their interests, and it leaves the more remote question, 'What is the best state of society?' to be discussed and determined, when the working classes as a *body* shall be sufficiently instructed to ascertain it, and come to a just decision.

Let it be granted that some one of the many systems of the best possible government has been chosen. Call this a principle, if you will, and then, what follows? This, that the end aimed at must be obtained by practical means. No end ever was obtained in any other way, and this admirable 'Address of the Working Men's Association', shows plainly and clearly what are the first steps to be taken. To me it seems that this end can never be obtained, unless the steps, or some such steps as those recommended in the address are taken. It becomes, then, the duty, the solemn, sacred duty, of all working men, to read and thoroughly understand the matter contained in the address, and shame be upon them if they neglect to obtain the valuable information presented to them by a society of themselves, the members of which are acting as friends and brothers.

It may be asked, how are we to obtain the address? How are we to spread it among our fellows? Here is the answer. The address, together with the rules of the 'Working Men's Association,' have been reprinted by Mr. John Cleave, and sold by him at the price of One Penny. Any working man, or any one disposed to distribute the tract among working men, may have any number of copies, not less than twenty-five at a time, at the trade price. There are thousands of working men, who could sell from twenty-five to a hundred copies in a week, hundreds who could sell a larger number in half that time, and they who are desirous to do their duty in this respect, and cannot afford to purchase twenty-five copies, may club their money, become purchasers, sell as many as will repay them the pence they have advanced, and leave them some copies which they may give away. Every association of working men every trade-club throughout the nation, should purchase a large number, and induce its members to take an active part in disposing of them. If every such man did his duty in this way, the number sold would be immense, and the good done be great indeed. Here then is a test of the desire working men have to serve themselves and one another. Here is a test which will mark their feelings for their own class. It will at once show the disposition they have to advance their own interests, and if it should be demonstrated that the disposition generally exists, it will advance them in their own estimation, and tend greatly to increase their respectability in the opinion of every one else; and this alone, even if there were no further result to arise from their efforts, should be sufficient to induce them to use the most vigorous and unrelaxed efforts, to circulate this excellent tract as extensively as possible.

FRANCIS PLACE.

89. [Add. Ms. 27819, ff. 43–5. London Working Men's Association.]

On the 18 October the committee reported when after considerable discussion the following resolutions were adopted.

1st That the members of this association have no confidence in either Whig or Tory government believing both parties to be alike, the enemies of just legislation, and obstacles in the way of the establishment of peace and happiness in the country.

2nd That therefore one of the especial objects of our union shall be to instruct and caution our brethren against helping directly or indirectly to put down one of these parties and set up the other, as by so doing they will be instrumental in perpetuating their own social and political degradation.

3 That without seeking any particular form or theory of Government we nevertheless, desire to have, and we call upon our brethren to demand as a first and an essential measure, an equal voice in determinging [sic] what laws shall be enacted or plans adopted for justly governing the country.

4 That to these ends Universal Suffrage and the protection of the Ballot —Annual Parliaments—Equal Representation and no Property Qualification are all essential.

5 That with these grand objects in view we caution our fellow-men not to be diverted, nor led away by paltry questions of either policy or expediency; nor to place any confidence in men who under the guise of reformers; i Refused to repeal the rate paying clause by which the suffrage is much limited. ii Resisted the plan of voting by ballot. iii To shorten the duration of parliaments. iv Who voted for the slavery of Factory Children and spurned the application of 80,000 Hand Loom Weavers. v Who repealed the Malt tax on one night, and rescinded their own resolution the next night. vi Who hypocritically enquired into agricultural distress yet refused assistance and even to make a report thereon. vii And who, to complete the catalogue of their iniquities, passed the infamous Poor Law Bill.

6 That we are therefore ardently desirous that all minor questions shall give place to the major, *equal political rights*, and we now call upon our brethren to arouse from their apathy and to become active in the prosecution of this great good.

7 That we respectfully call upon the Farmers of England whose interests are identified with our own, and who like us under the present withering system are daily sacrificed to wealth and title to make common cause with us recover their just rights, and to have their state burthens reduced to their means of bearing them.

8 That we call upon the Agricultural Labourers of the United Kingdom who are being reduced to beggary and wretchedness to unite with us to have their grievances redressed.

9 That we also call upon all those benevolent and ardent friends in Town and Country whose interests may be opposed to ours in the present conflicting state of things but who are nevertheless zealously contending for equal rights and laws and justice for man, to come forward and cordially to unite boldly to demand a parliament in which all interests shall be represented.

10 That we feel assured that such a combination, all obnoxious and factious rivally [sic] would soon sink into oblivion, and give place to men who having no sinister interests apart from those of the people will labour diligently and wisely, to make all the sources of this favoured country tend to promote the happiness of the whole of its people.

90. [Add. Ms. 27835, ff. 131–2]

In the Autumn of 1836 Colonel Thompson read some lectures on free trade to the Working Mens Association. These lectures set several of the members thinking on the subject but no one became satisfied, every one still doubted. Some of them spoke to me on the subject and this induced me to propose a plan for free conversations on such matters of Political Economy as most immediately related to the working people, and in the month of december I laid the following plan before the association.

1 That a meeting should be held in the room of the association every sunday morning.

2 That a chairman for the day should be appointed exactly at half past 10 o clock, by the clock over the head of the chairman when the debate should commence and be closed exactly at one o clock.

3 That to prevent displays of oratory and efforts to obtain victory no one should rise from his seat to address the chair but should speak sitting.

4 That no one should speak twice on any subject until every one who wished had spoken once, and no one should speak three times until every one who wished had spoken twice, and so on for any number of times.

5 That the discussion on any question should be adjourned from time to time as the members present might by a majority decide, and the debate be continued until the subject was either exhausted or the company were unwilling to have it continued.

6 That there should be no division taken on any subject of debate.

7 That there should always be a subject for discussion, which should be hung up in the room for at least one week before it was discussed.

The plan was adopted and the discussion commenced on the first sunday in January 1836 [sic] and was continued until the month of June when it was adjourned, and was not renewed.

The questions discussed were Free Trade generally, and particularly profit and wages. The Principle of Population. Wages and Population etc. These discussions, carried on as they were compelled the members, who were desirous to speak, to enquire to read and to think, while the mode of speaking seated, prevent[ed] absurd displays of oratory and was the means of preserving order and decorum, as neither applause nor censure were expressed, and these arrangements had their use in inculcating forbearance and consequently good manners.

It was very gratifying to me, as it must have been to most of the members to observe the development of intellect which the enquiries necessary to enable the speakers to address the chair and the discussions elicited. The principle of Population, and its practical applications were continued to be discussed through three sittings. They were expounded by four of the members with a precision, clearness and conclusiveness which could scarcely have been surpassed in any assembly. A gentleman well qualified to judge of the proceedings in every respect who attended one of the sittings, sent me across the table a slip of paper on which he had written. 'I never heard more sense and less nonsense spoken among so many persons in the same time, on any subject.'

Nearly all the men who attended these discussions had been Owenites, but had abandoned it in consequence of their being unable to foresee any practical result. Much good must have resulted, in some instances I know that it has. It must have induced many to enquire to an extent they never before contemplated, and to pursue studies they never before paid any attention to, and it is very probable that some of the several small associations now existing (1841) each composed of select persons, for the purpose of discussing subjects of Political Economy, have emanated from the sunday morning meetings of the Working Mens Association.

91. [Add. Ms. 27819, ff. 264–9. Place's notes headed 'Hasty Sketch etc.' for the first of the Sunday meetings mentioned in **90**.]

Chairman   First meeting Jan. 1 1837

Before we proceed to the discussion of the question. It will I think be advisable that we should come to an understanding among ourselves of the purpose we propose and the mode of proceeding.

We are not met to dispute for victory but to search for truth. In searching for truth we should be open to conviction, and not at all afraid of any conclusion which the discussion may lead to however opposite that conclusion may be to the present opinion of any one of us. Unless we are thus prepared we shall only be wasting our time, in idle talk. Here however at least some among us are not in this state. Few men reason even with themselves as impartially as they ought. To do so is laborious and to most men highly disagreeable. The consequence is, that they either receive opinions upon trust or form them without taking into their considerations *the whole* of the circumstances, on which they are grounded. This was by far too much my own case when I was a young man, and the consequence is, that most of the opinions I then entertained have been abandoned, and others adopted: some are directly the reverse of those which I then believed were unquestionable truths. I do not think I ought to blame myself for the mistaken conclusion I then came too [*sic*]. I had little learning little experience and though I had read a good deal I like every thinking man at that time was placed in circumstances which were quite new. The French revolution had opened up new scenes and caused new modes of reasoning. It was not enough that a man should be a politician, it became necessary that he should be also somewhat of a philosopher and to become so it was necessary that he should make himself acquainted with many things which were not until then thought to be at all necessary to a politician. I was poor had little leisure, and consequently wanted the means of obtaining the necessary aids for information and even if I could have procured them I could not then have obtained the time necessary to make a right use of them. My views were therefore narrow and I consequently committed many errors. As my means increased both as to money & time and the oposition [*sic*] of clever men, I was enabled to study particular subjects attentively—to ascertain what belonged to them to bring them together and view them as a whole—: To consider certain matters called general principles and to correct my erroneous judgments. This was not only hard but at times very disagreeable labour, but I had learned to labour, and was too fearful of entertaining erroneous notions not to labour hard to procure information, and this I did cheerfully, and I hope I shall continue to do so as long as I live. I tell you this for the purpose of bespeaking you patience and indulgence, if at times I shall be found to entertain opinions directly the reverse of those entertained by some whom I am addressing. I wish you to believe that I would not utter one word which I did not believe was true, and being true calculated to promote the well being of the working men. I think it necessary to address you thus, because, unless you do sincerely believe that I seek the good of the working classes as much as any one among you I shall be talking in vain. I know well enough by experience that my position often prevents working men giving me the credit I ought to have among them. This want of confidence arises from two causes—1 suspicion of the intentions of every man who is not himself a working man—and at this I am not surprised because I know as well as any one can know the advantages that have been sought and taken of the working people. It would however be

172

much better for working men if this suspicion could be laid aside, and that they should reason thus. We are very well able to understand the matter addressed to us, and of that we will judge without caring at all for the intention of those who may address us—we will have to do only with the arguments. If this were the determination of the working men it would be out of the power of any one to deceive them, and all injurious suspicion would cease. 2 The notion working men entertain, and constantly act upon that however much a man like myself for instance may please them, in a great number of instances, if there be one in which he displeases them they may with reason directly condemn him as their enemy and treat him as an enemy—This is a grat bow [a great blow?] not only to improvement but to that social intercourse which might tend rapidly to the advancement of knowledge. I have experienced this sort of conduct many times and shall again experience it. Working men will often believe that I am their enemy; when if I were, I must be the meanest and basest of mankind, for I must seek to do them evil for the sole gratification of enjoying the mischief, and that only, since personally I can have nothing of what is usually termed 'interest' either in doing them good or evil.

May I hope then that among you who are some of the most enlightened of the working people my arguments, alone and not my intentions may be the subject for your consideration. It has long been my practice to act thus; I care nothing at all what a mans intentions are, I examine his arguments and if I am convinced they are good I admire them; if they are bad, I reject them; in this way I have learned, if not as much from enemies as from friends, I have yet certainly gained much useful information.

In this spirit I hope we shall proceed not to extort confessions from one another but to furnish matter for private serious thinking without prejudice; and come to such conclusions as the quantity and quality of the evidence may induce each of us sincerely to believe is just.

92. [Add. Ms. 27819, ff. 229–33]

The following statement will appear to many, to be, superfluous. In such cases as this it is not so, but on the contrary is necessary to make men who have never learned to reason correctly, or to push any matter presented to them to a conclusion as well as those who have not attended to the subject to understand its bearing. Great impediments are placed in the way of giving useful information, because they who should be the teachers of the people will not adapt themselves to the condition and capacity of the men they mean to teach.

In a few and only a few instances have I been able to convince some of the Trades delegates who have consulted me of the absurdity of the notion that every thing produced or manufactured, belongs solely to the people who made it, and this too without reference to the many hands it has gone through the manufacturing hands being alone contemplated by them.

I have proceeded thus. I will shew you that upon your system there never could be any property or even any thing deserving the name of a habitation, and consequently neither—conveniences—nor comforts—no books no knowledge, and that we should in no very long time be reduced to the condition in which the inhabitants of this Island were, a state which induced an eminent historian to call them, 'hairy naked savages'.

As one of the most perfect examples let us take a piece of Cotton-cloth.

In the Vale of the Mississippi in North America, many families of Farmers do all the work required by their own families, some of these families grow cotton. Let us then suppose that some of these families have a quantity of cotton wool to dispose of, for the purpose of procuring several things which their farms do not produce. It is plain that the cotton wool is theirs, they sell it, and in payment receive either, money—or produce or commodities or all three, but the money the produce, and the commodities are all of them produced by competition, and profit making, and but for which the purchaser of the cotton wool would have no means of paying for it, no capital, and as there would be no purchaser, so there would be no growers and consequently no cotton would be grown there, as was actually the case 100 years ago.

The cotton wool has thus changed hands it is no longer the property, or part of the capital of the growers, but it has become the property, the capital, of the man who made the purchase. This man employs people to pack and convey the cotton wool to the sea port, New Orleans, and to put it on board a ship. Does the cotton belong to these persons? No. They are intitled to the sum, no matter whether it be money or some of the cotton, according to the agreement they made to be paid for their labour. The cotton then remains the property of the man who purchased it from the growers. The ship brings him and his cotton to Liverpool. Is the cotton the property of the crew of the Ship? No—they are paid according to their agreement for the part they have performed. The owner of the cotton, lands it and puts it into a warehouse, paying those employed for this purpose, and engaging to pay the owner of the warehouse for ware room. The cotton still remaining his.

After some time the cotton wool is brought from the man whose property it was, it is now the property of the manufacturer who has paid for it, and he has it conveyed from Liverpool to Manchester. It is obvious that neither the warehouseman, nor the carrier, could have any right to the cotton wool beyond the quantity which would pay them for the labour and accomodation [sic] they had supplied and furnished, but as the manufacturer wishes to keep the cotton and the persons employed prefer having money to wool—the manufacturer pays them in money, and all the cotton remains his. He now employs people Men, Women, Children, to prepare and spin and weave, and the cotton wool becomes cloth. Will you now say that because these people have been employed to convert the cotton wool into cloth that the cloth is theirs? Is it not evident that only as much of the cloth is theirs as will pay them according to their contracts or agreements, wages, but as before money being more convenient for their purposes than cloth they are paid in money and the cloth remains with the manufacturer. The value of this cloth must be such as will pay all the costs and charges of growing—bringing to market and manufacturing, and also the reasonable profit of the grower; the purchaser who brings it to Liverpool and the Manufacturer. Their profits are not regulated by the will of the owner of the wool or of the manufacturer but by the supply and the demand. If there be much competi-

174

tion the profit will be small, but if there be little competition the profit will be large. But large profits produce competition and they are soon reduced to the average rate of profit of other manufacturers. It is the same with wages. If there be many hands, there will be much competition for employment and wages will be low, if there be few hands there will be little competition for employment and wages will be high; But high wages produce competition and they are soon reduced to the average rate for similarly skilled or unskilled labour, and if the number of hands be very great, the least skilled labour is paid for at the lowest rate at which hands will consent to labour. It is no more at the will of the labourer what wages he will have, than it is at the will of the manufacturer what profit he will have, labour like commodities will be cheap or dear as the demand is great or little, and the consequent competition among the labourers is also great or little.

If instead of the American farmers and his [sic] family being the cultivators of the cotton, he hired other persons to cultivate the land for him the case would not be altered, neither would the cost of production be increased, for so long as families in considerable number cultivated cotton, the value of the labour expended in producing it would be equal to the value of the labour which must be hired by him who employed labourers, since he must sell at the same price as he who did not hire labourers, or he must sell at less profit, for he could not raise his price, competition would keep the price where it was, and, as cultivation was improved and was extended, and the quantity of cotton produced was also increased competition would bring down the price to the lowest sum at which it could be sold so as to pay the growers and give them the average or common profit.

It follows then that without acumulation [sic]—that is—increase of wealth—or what is called capital; there could be no purchases, no exchanges, and that cotton wool would not be grown in America, and that there would be none made into cloth in Great Britain, as was the case at the commencement of the last century, when there was not so many as half the number of people there now is, and when the generality of the people's condition was worse than as may be ascertained by reference to the writers of the time, and by the conclusive fact that one with another the value of life has since that period increased [] years, that is one with another the people live [] years longer now than they did then.

The same sort of ownership is applicable to every other case. As for instance an oak tree. It must belong to somebody, when cut down, they who cut it down must share in its value and be paid accordingly. It would be the same did the tree become the property of those who cut it down and prepared it for the saw pit, and so it would be with the parts of it when it was sawed up—some might be used for Ship building—House building—Furniture—Fences etc. but the wood itself could not belong to those who merely bestowed labour upon it in converting it to its several uses, all that could belong to them could not exceed the increased value it would have when converted. If the converters purchased the wood, they would have the gross profit arising therefrom and the value of the wood, that is they would have, the money the wood cost them, the usual wages paid for the kind of conversion, and the usual profit on such articles. If some one of them bought the wood and employed the others to convert it, the wood would be his and

175

if we suppose, as has sometimes happened he was too poor to pay the men he had employed until the table they made was sold, the money for which it was sold would be divided thus. Payment for the wood, wages to the men employed, and profit to the man who employed them. Thus it is the produce of every article manufactured is divided, but in most cases the operation is not quite so simple. As for instance in the case of the price of calico. The sum it *must* sell for, if the business is to continue must be sufficient to pay for the cotton wool in the first instance and all the expenses thereon, to the time it is sold to the manufacturer, and also the usual profit to the man who bought it in America and brought it to Liverpool, all the expenses of the manufacturer—such as rent, for his factory cost of machinery— in wear and tear, replacement of the money the wool cost wages of work people and the usual profit of trade. No one article can continue to be manufactured unless it does all this. Profit for the purpose of acumulation as the means of distinction, comfort, enjoyment and increase of knowledge is the great stimulus to exertion, beyond the mere means of animal existence and without it, it would be impossible for the people of any country, but of this in particular, to be otherwise than as the historian said we were, few in number and that very small number—'hairy naked savages'.

93. [Add. Ms. 27819, ff. 47–8]

1837

The [London Working Men's] Association was every week increasing the number of its members, of its books—a considerable number having been presented, and also some newspapers and other periodical publications. It had become known extensively, its influence was spreading rapidly and similar associations were formed and being formed in a great many places.

The success of the association precipitated it into proceedings which exhausted its means too rapidly, and prevented it accomplishing many purposes which were of much more present and would have been thereafter of much more permanent importance than those they embarked in though they were of much importance as demonstrations of the actual influence of a body of self conducted working men. In proceeding thus, however they did no more than other political associations had done before them, and that too from the same cause their eagerness to come before and to be continually before the public. Scarcly [*sic*] has any one such society acted otherwise, all have to some, most to a considerable extent mistaken the noise they made, and the portion of public notice they obtained as evidences of power, and yet these demonstrations have never had but one tendency, namely to prevent them obtaining any portion of the consideration and consequently of the power a more deliberate and wisely conducted course might have enabled them to possess. This will be exemplified to a great extent in respect to the conduct of the working mens association and of all similar associations. The members of such associations have yet to learn to practice what they preach, to apply their homely proverb—'that you must first creep and then go' to themselves as aggregated bodies. That is only by long continued steady, patient, liberal conduct, accepting and using every kind of assistance which may at any time and in any way be available. Making no absurd pretension to any thing and especially not to superior wisdom and honesty, but acting with becoming modesty but with indomitable perseverance. Wheneve[r] they shall in considerable numbers, attain to this moral condition, they will be much more respected than feared, and will then be in the right way to obtain whatever of power it may be useful for them to exercise, and that too as it can be beneficially made use of. This is however a kind of wisdom which comes to any class of men but slowly, and can only be acquired by working men though their errors.

They determined to hold a public meeting in the great room at the Crown and Anchor Tavern in the Strand on the evening of tuesday the 28th of february, for the purpose of proposing a reform of the house of commons, the whole of the business to be conducted by working men. The reforms proposed were

1 Equal representation	2 Universal Suffrage
3 Annual Parliaments	4 No Property Qualification
5 Vote by Ballot	6 Sittings and payment of members

On the evening of the meeting the Great Room of the Tavern was densely filled. The Chair was taken by Robert Hartwell a journeyman printer, and the speakers were the following named working men.

Rob't Hartwell the Chairman	William Lovett Cabinet Maker
Henry Vincent Printer	White
William Hoare Shoemaker	John Cleave Pamphlet seller
Goldspink Carpenter	Cameron
Henry Hetherington Printer	John Rogers Tailor
Torney	

Besides these there were two speakers who were not of the working class —namely Feargus O Connor and John Bell both of whom were considered intruders.

The proceedings of this meeting were published in several newspapers as were also the petition[1] and resolutions passed at the meeting.

The members of the association were greatly elated with their success though it left them in debt. It assisted by making the association more generally known and what were called its principles more generally understood and to some extent facilitated the formation of other similar associations.

94. [Add. Ms. 35151, ff. 21–2]
Fellow Citizen   18 October 1837
            William Lovett
    I send you a copy of the third report of the Poor Law Commissioners and I beg you to read it carefully. I mean the Report which occupies 73 pages.

    I know how difficult it is, in a vast number of persons how impossible it is to remove preconceived opinions however erroneous they may be. Unfortunately a vast majority of our people, like indeed all other people, have

[1] For text of petition see *Life and struggles of William Lovett* (1967), 311–14.

not the capacity to receive new ideas, after they are—say 25 years of age—and this is the great impediment to general improvement, the reason why improvement in really useful knowledge goes on so slowly as it does. With this immense majority unless any new opinion that presents itself coincides with some old opinion, which they have they know not how obtained and for which they can give no accurate reasons,—they become incapable of examining the ground on which it has been formed and if therefore it be an erroneous opinion in error they must remain as long as they live.

Now I want you who can reason—to read this report—to attend to the facts—to put this question to yourself, and to answer, as free from prejudice as you may be able. Will the New Poor Law as it is, and as it is likely to be administered—elevate the character,

1st of that class of persons who have hitherto been the most depraved and debased. The Farm servants? Or will it not?

2nd Will it do the same by all, who are not really and truly vagabonds in the worst sense of the word? Or will it not?

If you decide that it will, you will approve of it, if you decide that it will not you will disapprove of it.

If you decide that it will you will have decided on several material points

1st The certainty, as it appears to me, of getting rid of the utterly degrading and demoralising system of *making* paupers which has been in existence upwards of 100 years.

2nd That men who became paupers and continued paupers for any considerable time were very seldom, scarcely ever again made useful to their fellow men in any way.

3 That any attempt made to induce such men to join other men in any attempt at improvement morally or politically must fail.

4 That whenever two thirds of England and Wales, a full half probably a much larger number of labourers were put into this condition, the effect was gradually to bring down, all sorts of labourers to an approximation to their own condition, in means of living and in understanding.

5th That at any amount of suffering to a comparatively small number of persons, it would [be] advisable to get rid of a system which so long as it continued could not fail to degrade the whole body of working people.

6th That children bred up as paupers could not make respectable men and women.

7th That children brought up in the Work-houses on the old system were unlike other children, were in fact qualified for evil courses, their condition being utterly inimical to any good purpose. That under the new system those unfortunate children will be extricated from the baneful effects of the old system and be placed in circumstances very superior to any in which it was ever possible to place them under the old system.

8 That if these be facts then the new poor law, will on a large scale, be one of the best possible means of preparing the common labourers and many others gradually to respect themselves and others, and thus prepare them to concert with the intelligent bodies of working men now being established to move systematically towards obtaining that knowledge which can alone enable them permanently to improve the condition of them all.

Observe that I make no reference to what is best or what is worst in government, my only purpose being to induce you to inquire seriously and to decide honestly, this question. Will or will not the present Poor Law aid in improving the large mass of common labourers throughout the country and be a step on the road towards that state which is so much desired by you and me and our fellow labourers in the good cause.

Yours truly,
Francis Place

95. [Add. Ms. 27844, f. 271. Written after Lord John Russell's 'Finality Jack' speech.]

229 Strand Nov. 24/37

My Dear Sir,

A new state of things in the March of Reform having now commenced I think there will be but little difference of opinion as to the course which Radical Reformers should pursue. The Westminster Reform Society met on Wednesday evening last, to determine if a Dinner should take place and instead of eating & drinking being uppermost in their minds a public meeting was resolved upon (see the Chronicle & Advertiser of this Morning) which I think may be held about next Monday week.

Now I want you to do some work for us—I want your Master Mind to be put into a state of activity as in olden times to produce the requisite Resolutions & possibly a petition to the House of Commons also to get us what funds you can. I have become in the first instance answerable for the expense.

We contemplate a Meeting at the Crown & Anchor the time is not suitable for Covent Garden. I sincerely hope that you are well—I could not attend the meeting of the Radical Club last night in consequence of residing out of town & the illness of my wife but I think that each member should now be called upon to convene meetings in the locality in which he resides for if there be inactivity *now* Radical Reform will be thrown overboard for many years.

I am
My Dear Sir
Yours truly

To Fras Place Esq. Thos Prout

96. [Add. Ms. 27844, ff. 272–5]

Mr Prout on the part of some persons who were about to call a public meeting of the Electors of Westminster wrote to me and requested I would propose resolutions and a petition—This I did—and accompanied them with the following observations.

Francis Place

Here are resolutions and a petition such as I am sure ought and I hope will satisfy your committee.

The first 4 resolutions are simple truths. I have put them in the present

179

words, and form and order, as a continuation of the old mode of proceeding in Westminster. Westminster took the lead for many years as well in the declaration of opinions, as in the good teaching sort of way in which they were put and they produced good results.

It is fit that Westminster should now again take to its old respectable station and lead the people on as far as possible on the road to liberty.

There is nothing new in any of these resolutions, nor need there be. In 1780 at a great public meeting of the Electors a committee was appointed to make a report on the state of the Representation of the people and to propose a plan of reform. They reported at length and proposed—Annual Parliaments—Universal Suffrage—Voting by Ballot—No money Qualification for members—The Country to be divided into equal Polling Districts —The election to be taken at the same time on a day certain.

Thomas Brand Hollis and Charles James Fox were the chairmen of the committees and they signed the Report & Declaration.

In 1819—Westminster went for Annual Parliaments, Universal Suffrage and Voting by Ballot. It must I think take its old position again in an open manly way or some of the large towns will take the lead and Westminster instead of being the good teacher will be looked upon as a worn out old driveller.

Don't on any account use the words *extension of the suffrage*—if you do there will be plenty of men present to ask what the words mean, the chairman will be embarrassed and an amendment will be proposed which will be carried that the words Universal Suffrage be substituted and the meeting will be made contemptible.

F P.

Resolutions

1 That the Electors of Westminster never did by any act of theirs admit that the acts to reform the representation of the people in the house of commons, were, or could be final measures.

2 That during very many [years] preceding the passing of the reform Acts in 1832 the electors of Westminster never ceased to require from the Legislature such acts as would secure to the whole people, 'full, free and equal right to elect representatives to serve in parliament'.

3 That upon every occasion when the electors of Westminster petitioned the house of commons for an extension of the right of suffrage they always coupled that request with another, namely that such acts might be passed as would restore to the people, the short parliaments which for centuries were enjoyed by their ancestors.

4 That on many such occasions the Electors of Westminster prayed the house of commons to protect the electors from all undue influence and intimidation, and from bribery and corruption by passing a bill which should direct the votes of the whole people to be taken by Ballot.

5 That the declaration made by Lord John Russell in the house of commons on the 20th of November last 'That voting by Ballot—Extending the Suffrage, and Triennial Parliaments were nothing else than a repeal of the Reform Act, to all of which he was opposed, and the tacit consent of the whole of her majesty's ministers to this declaration evinces a determination

in them to withold from the people all further reform and is nearly a repetition of the declaration of the Duke of Wellington which caused his expulsion from office.

6 That the declaration of Lord John Russell that it was always intended. That the Reform Acts should give a *preponderance* to the Landed Interest in the Election of Members of parliament is a *declaration* that it was intended to give to the aristocracy the power to appoint a *majority* in the house of commons.

That by the direct enactments of the Reform Acts,—by the direct and indirect influence—by the bribery, corruption and intimidation of the Aristocracy this intention has been accomplished.

That the power of the aristocracy thus to place a majority of members in the house of commons will wholly prevent any measure whatever being carried in parliament, unless it accords with the wishes and conforms to the interests of the aristocracy, to the utter exclusion of all influence of the people in what should be their own house.

That the pretence that the Reform Acts were intended to restore to the people their share in the legislature, and their wholesome controul [*sic*] over the aristocracy, was intended to be, and is a gross fraud upon the people.

That it is therefore necessary that the reforms proposed in the preceeding resolutions of this meeting, should be demanded and insisted on by the people until they have been obtained and a due share of the government of the country has been thus secured to them.

7 That a petition to the house of commons embodying these resolutions as follows be presented to the House of Commons—

The etc etc etc petition

Sheweth—

    That—(here take in the 1, 2, 3, & 4 resolutions and then as follows)

That your petitioners have been disappointed at finding that the house of commons during the five years which have passed since the first step towards a reformation of the representation of the people in your honourable house, —has made no advance in carrying the intentions of the reform acts into effect.

That your petitioners have been further disappointed and sorely aggrieved by various reports which they believe are true of a determination of her majesty's ministers to resist all attempts to procure for the people any of the above named necessary amendments without the whole of which there never can be even an approximation to a full fair free and equal representation of the people in your honourable house.

Your petitioners therefore pray that your honourable house will forthwith take into your serious consideration the allegations contained in this petition and grant

First—That the votes of the whole populace shall be taken by ballot.

Second—That the duration of parliament shall be restored to the shortest period consistent with the duties of your honourable house.

Third—That the right of suffrage be extended to every man of twenty one years of age who is capable of exercising that right.

97. [Add. Ms. 27844, ff. 277–9]

229 Strand Dec. 1 1837

My Dear Sir

The Committee met last night & feel very thankful to you for your kindness in framing Resolutions & Petition & for your offers & [?] in every way to assist us—but they think that it would be improper at this time to advocate Universal Suffrage, they suppose that the Constituencies are not *yet* sufficiently offended with the Ministry to adopt so decided a course. The Committee imagine that we should meet the Ministry upon their own ground & claim—that which they deny & in the first instance compel them *to entertain the question* & when that is accomplished *then* will be the time to name the *kind* of Reform desirable to have. Whether this be the wise course to pursue will admit of a difference in opinion but it was the general opinion of the Committee & the other course could not be carried.

Many thanks for your present of the pamphlet on Bribery & Intimidation etc.

I have no doubt of our meeting being well attended. We have written to above 50 including the Minority you mention but a request from you will have weight with many.

Again thanking you individually

I am

My Dear Sir

Yours truly

Thos Prout

To F. Place Esq.

P.S. I enclose the Resolutions agreed to.

1st That to secure to the People of the United Kingdom the right of choosing their Representatives in Parliament, to guarantee to them, the free & conscientious enjoyment of that right, against intimidation & corruption—& to provide for the responsibility of their Representatives, were the paramount objects of Parliamentary Reform at the passing of the Reform Bill, & will continue to be so until the House of Commons faithfully represents the Nation at large. That altho' from the rottenness of the system into which changes were introduced by the Reform Bill, such changes were necessarily amongst the first improvements demanded in the representation, yet for the absolute & lasting security of the great ends of Parliamentary Reform, further alterations of an equally important character were, & still are, required in the Electoral System, & to which those effected by the Reform Bill, were introductory & preparatory only. That this meeting deplores the fact that five years have been permitted to elapse by the party who introduced the Reform Bill & who (with the exception of a short interval) have enjoyed political supremacy in the Councils of the Empire during the whole of that time, without any attempts being made by them to place the Electoral System upon the solid basis of an extended suffrage, freedom of choice & frequent appeals to the Constituencies. That the consequences of such remissness to secure Parliamentary Reform in its full extent, to the Nation, by apt prompt & vigorous measures have been most disastrous to the cause of Freedom & Good Government in this country. That in as much as the Reform Bill increased the number of Electors, the opportunities for the exercise of Coercion & corruption have become multiplied, and as no measures have been introduced to protect the Constituencies against the perpetration of those flagrant offences, they are committed to an extent and in a manner more relentless & determined than was ever witnessed in this country at any former period. That whilst the independence & morality of the Electoral body is rapidly declining before these growing, & at present, irresistible evils, & the responsibility of the House of Commons to the Constituencies of the Empire is daily becoming less, the progress of useful & practical Amendments in every department of the State is arrested, & the benefits of the first steps already made towards improvement by the Reform Bill, entirely lost to the People.

It is therefore with sentiments of the deepest concern & regret that this Meeting looks upon the declaration made by one of Her Majesty's Ministers & tacitly assented to by his Colleagues in Office, that the Reform Bill is a final measure which the Electors of Westminster never considered it to be; & of the avowal made by the same Minister of his permanent hostility to the only measures by which a full fair & free choice can be made of National Representatives, & by which such Representatives can be made responsible to the People.

2nd That to secure one of the great objects of Parliamentary Reform, viz a faithful representation of the People in the House of Commons: a further extension of the Suffrage is required.

3rd That to protect Electors in the Conscientious exercise of the Suffrage, from the influence of intimidation & corruption, another of the great objects of Parliamentary Reform, it is necessary that the voting for Members of Parliament be by way of Ballot.

4th That in order to render the Representatives of the People responsible for the due discharge of the Trust reposed in them, another of the great objects of Parliamentary Reform, it is necessary to shorten the duration of Parliaments.

5th That the system of Registration created by the Reform Act and the present mode of Appeal to a Committee of the House of Commons do from their complication & uncertainty afford innumerable opportunities for causing vexation, annoyance, & expense as well to the Constituencies as the Representatives & require immediate Alteration.

6th That a Petition embodying these Resolutions be presented to the House of Commons, & that it be presented by our Representatives Colonel D. L. Evans & J. T. Leader Esq. who are hereby requested to support the prayer thereof.

98. [Place Collection, set 56, vol. 1. 1836–May 1838, ff. 8–9. Place's introductory comments on various documents and newspaper cuttings in this volume.]

May 8th Page 202 'The Peoples Charter, being the outline of an act of Parliament to provide for the just Representation of the People of Great Britain in the Commons House of Parliament embracing the Principles of Universal Suffrage, No property qualification, Annual Parliaments, Equal representation, Payment of Members and Vote by Ballot. Prepared by a committee of twelve persons, Six Members of Parliament and Six Members of the Working Mens Association and addressed to the people of the United Kingdom.'

The paper called the Charter was not however prepared by any committee.

The members of Parliament who were members of the committee never assembled never gave themselves any trouble about the matter. Mr Roebuck promised to draw a bill but his parliamentary duties and his long continued deplorable state of health totally prevented his keeping his promise—and the members of the Working Mens Association who were members of the committee found it too complicated and difficult in several respects for them. In this state Mr Lovett the Secretary earnestly intreated me to draw the bill. To this I consented provided the working mens Association would discontinue to countenance those who at various meetings *abused* the middle classes, calling them harsh names, imputing all manner of evil intentions to them and thus unnecessarily making enemies where they needed friends, and provided that he Mr Lovett would bring me a paper stating in exact words what were the points—and how his coadjustors thought they might be put into language the least offensive to any body since if any among them thought that any offensive expression was necessary I would not draw the bill. Mr Lovett was for himself satisfied and in a few days afterwards brought me the paper I had requested. I then drew the bill, and sent the draft to him with a letter requesting him to shew, the draft and the letter to Mr Roebuck. In the letter I requested Mr Roebuck to revise the draft, and assured both the Working mens association and Mr Roebuck that whenever the time should come when it would be necessary, that if he should be unable or disinclined, or no one more competent than myself should be found to convert the draft in as perfect a bill as it could be made, and give the reasons for every enactment, that I would do it myself.

Mr Roebuck thought the draft sufficient and was also at the time too ill and too much occupied to attend to the business and the draft was printed under the somewhat equivocal appellation of a *Charter* a name the Working Mens Association would not give up.

The Working mens association had been very diligent in circulating its very clever addresses, several of its members had been out as volunteer missionaries and the number of similar associations which had been formed by them was very great, and the circulation of the *charter* with the request in page 10 of the address which preceeds it—'that other Working Mens associations, would examine it and suggest improvements until it is so perfected as to meet as far as possible with general approbation' etc. caused it to be well understood by many thousands of persons. It was reprinted in some newspapers and long extracts were also published in a large number of country newspapers.

It was this circulation, and the great increase of Working mens associations which induced the Political Union at Birmingham to take up the matter. The addresses of *the* Working mens Association—the countenance they met with in a great many newspapers, the concurrence with the associa-

184

tion of a considerable number of members of the house of commons, the circulation and sale of the Charter, and the numerous addresses from other similar associations gave to the association a credit and an amount of popular consideration which had never before been given to any body of working men on the question of Reform.

99. [Add. Ms. 27820, ff. 184–5]

A copy of 'the peoples Charter', having been presented to the Radical Club with a letter recommending it to the notice of the members—Copies were ordered to be purchased and one to be sent to each of the members and a special meeting was called for the purpose of considering its contents. At this meeting it was resolved.

1st That the principles of Universal Suffrage. No property qualification. Annual Parliaments. Equal representation. Payment of Members and Vote by Ballot as contained in the proposed 'outline of an act to provide for the just Representation of the People in Parliament' and called 'the Peoples Charter' be recognised and approved of by this Club.

2nd That the secretary be directed to acquaint the Working-Mens Association that this club approves,

i of the principles of the Peoples Charter.

ii That they offer the accompanying suggestions for the approval of the Association.

As it was expected that these resolutions would lead to a conference a committee of the following persons was appointed viz. Francis Place, William James Fox, James Roberts Black, William Henry Ashurst, Thomas Prout, Henry S. Chapman, Thomas Falconer. A conference having been appointed Colonel T. Perronet Thompson and Mr Joseph Hume M.P. were invited and attended, when several alterations in the details were made.

100. [Place Collection, set 56, vol. 2. July–Dec. 1838]

6 Upper North Place
Grays Inn Road
Dear Sir,   Aug. 30th 1838

I am requested by the Working Men's Association to inform you that last meeting night the following list of persons was selected, by ballot, to be proposed at the Great Meeting, which is to be held in Palace Yard on the 17th September, as proper persons to represent London in the general committee that is now being formed. I doubt not of your being aware—that at all these large meetings Delegates are to be chosen to the amount of 49 in all, whose duty it shall be to take charge of the Peoples Charter and the National Petition and to otherwise promote the cause of Radical Reform. Several have already been elected for Birmingham and other towns, and we hope you will see the necessity at this critical period for uniting your talents and energies to promote the cause of the people as well as to prevent any folly or mischief that may arise if men like yourself stand apart or refuse to act in concert together.

I remain on behalf of the Association

J. A. Roebuck
F. Place
J. B. O'Brien
H. Hetherington
W. Lovett
J. Cleave
H. Vincent
R. Hartwell

Yours respectfully
W. Lovett Sec'y
F. Place Esq.
21 Brompton Square

P.S. An early answer in compliance will oblige etc.

101. [Add. Ms. 35151, ff. 86–7]

To Mr Wm Lovett   10 Sep. 1838
   Fellow Citizen

You will not I fear find the business on the 17th in Palace Yard all plain sailing. I see by the Posting Bill that the High Bailiff has called 'a meeting of the Inhabitants of Westminster', but has not used the word 'others', as I told you I thought he would not. Every one I have seen since you were here is in favour of a repeal of the Corn Laws. Each one agrees that this is just the time to commence vigorous proceedings the crops being short and bread dear—as the English Merchants have bought up all the corn which can be spared in the Baltic and at Odessa; all that has been saved from former seasons and left little which is not the produce of the present season, and as our next harvest must be a scanty one we not having produced enough for our consumption for many years, so the price of bread must be very high this time next year, and proper exertions may under such circumstances compel the repeal of the Corn Laws. They argue too that the Peoples Charter is not a measure that can be accomplished for some years to come, and that exertions may be made for a repeal of the Corn Laws now that the time is favourable, at the same time too that exertions are made to convince the people that the Charter is a great and most important measure, and also—if that be possible to convince the Legislature that it will be expedient for them to repeal the laws so justly complained of by the people. To me this reasoning appears sound and conclusive, and I therefore concur with them in thinking it is wise to make the most of present and probable events.

Mr Crawfurd is writing a series of letters in the Glasgow Argus. Colonel Thompson has undertaken to collect fallacies on the Corn Laws from the Newspapers, and from late Speeches in Parliament, to answer them seriatim, and the Sun is to insert these papers every Monday and Wednesday. He and others have written to the Editors of many newspapers and requested them to copy from the Sun which many will do. These proceedings must then go on, they cannot be stayed and if they could they ought not to be stayed. I think that with a little judicious management you may turn them to account for the Charter. Should you so determine great care must be taken to keep the two questions distinct. In no case where it can be avoided should they be confounded. The Charter must be continually held forth as the general and all comprehensive measure, the Corn Laws as a very momentous measure though only one of detail. He who is desirous to have the corn laws repealed should have impressed on him the necessity of promoting the adoption of the Charter as the means of causing the repeal of all laws which embarrass Trade and Commerce and are in any way inimical to the welfare of the people and preventing any such laws being again enacted.

From what you told me I apprehend an attempt will be made at the meeting to set aside all proceedings respecting the Charter, and if it does not succeed, then to endeavour to vote an adjournment of all proceedings to some distant day and to substitute a petition against the Corn Laws in its stead. This will be a very dishonest proceeding. The meeting is called for a specific purpose, and for any body of men without due and *proper* notice of their intention to propose that the proceedings of which due and *proper* notice has been give shall be set aside, or in any way embarrassed with widely different propositions which the people have not been called together to discuss is as dishonourable and dishonest as any public proceeding can be; yet this was not very long ago the deliberate course agreed to be pursued by the 'Associations of the Working Men'. To their disgrace be it spoken—though only as a bye gone act never to be repeated. You will recollect that when a public meeting was about to be called, for the one measure which would have told at that time—*The Ballot*—that the intention to hold the meeting was abandoned, simply and only because the working people declared their intention to come to the meeting in great numbers and there propose and carry *Universal Suffrage* for which the meeting was not called. Depend upon it, and that too especially, in public proceedings 'Honesty is the best Policy'.

To quarrel is to do mischief, extensive mischief, therefore whoever may chuse to quarrel with you, heed them not, do you quarrel with none; but as you cannot have your own way, take no part in any ill natured proceedings, and on no account because others may behave improperly, and act impassionately, do you follow their bad example. If your proposition should be opposed defend it, recollecting however that opposition may justly be made by those who may think the proposition unlikely to be useful, according to their notion of what may be useful—do you in such a case let it be put to the vote, and adopted or rejected as the people chuse. Whichever way they may decide you will have no cause of complaint.

No one can on any ground be justified in proposing a petition against the Corn Laws at the meeting, as the Inhabitants have not been called together to consider that question. Should any one propose to set aside the Charter for the purpose of proposing the Repeal of the Corn Laws, I advise you and your friends to take matters as coolly as possible and avoid most carefully all passion and invective and imputation, and to argue the matter on its own merits solely. Its merits are great and should not be lost sight of on any account, however offensive and unjust the conduct of others towards you may be, and pray remember that I am giving you the advice I have frequently under similar circumstances followed myself. The case is simply this. You have put forward in plain concise clear language a most important object. You have called a public meeting in the most correct and orderly way, to discuss the subject in the hope and expectation that the meeting will adopt the propositions. The meeting has been called and the expenses have been paid by those who thinking it most important have determined to go through with the business and never under any circumstances to abandon it, and for any number of persons to come and attempt to set aside the very purpose for which the meeting is called and the expenses incurred, not by negativeing [sic] the propositions, but by proposing other resolutions relating to something for which the meeting is not called, and for which no notice having been given nobody can be prepared to expect is a proceeding so very disorderly, dishonourable and disgraceful that I hope no such course will be persisted in, but if it is that it will be treated by the assembled people as it deserves to be. There is but one honest way of proceeding, and that is, to determine the matter for which the meeting is called and that done, they who think that any other subject should be discussed at such a meeting, may sign a requisition to the High Bailiff to call another meeting for the purpose. This mode of proceeding will I have no doubt put you right at once, if it should not, it is plain that the people are not friendly to your propositions, but that they should be so, it is impossible to imagine. If you proceed thus you will put yourselves before the Nation as a body of plain, honest, sensible, discreet men and compel even your enemies to respect your proceedings and this under present circumstances you can effect in no other way.

Pray think of these things dispassionately, think also of collateral matters, and then you will be better qualified to cope with the enemy should he attempt to interrupt or set aside your proceedings.

Your opponents will be very generally honestly disposed men though there will be some among them who are sad rogues, it will be your duty as far as it may be in your power by conciliatory conduct to prevent the honest men being misled by the rogues.

Yours truly
Francis Place

102. [Add. Ms. 27820, ff. 199–201]

On the same day a large Bill was posted. As follows

METROPOLITAN DEMONSTRATION

in favour of the

PEOPLES CHARTER and the NATIONAL PETITION

In pursuance of a Requisition to me addressed for the purpose of convening a public meeting of the *Inhabitants of the City and Liberty of Westminster* to take into consideration the propriety of petitioning parliament to pass into a law the *outlines* of a proposed act of Parliament intitled the *Peoples Charter* the object of which is to extend the Right of Suffrage and to enact such other Reforms as will effectually secure good and cheap government.

I do appoint such meeting to be held in Palace Yard on Monday the 17 September at twelve o clock.

Francis Smedley

August 29 1838   High Bailiff of Westminster

The High Bailiff called *a meeting of the Inhabitants of Westminster* which all the duty of his office entitled him to do, but the Working mens Association took upon themselves to supersede the authority of the High Bailiff and in a large Placard to announce a Metropolitan meeting in Palace Yard, the High Bailiff in the Chair, a liberty which none had ever before taken and was altogether improper.

At a meeting of the committee of the Working Mens Association five resolutions were adopted, and ordered to be proposed at the public meeting, a sixth was afterwards added, they were as follows [Printed].

1 That this Meeting are of opinion that the true cause of all the corruptions and anomalies in legislation, as well as the distress and difficulties of the commercial, manufacturing, trading, and working classes, is, that our REPRESENTATIVE SYSTEM is based upon *exclusive* and *unjust privileges*; and, therefore, believe that the time has arrived for establishing that system on a foundation more in accordance with principles of justice, brotherly love, and with the increased knowledge of the people.

2 That the principles of representation, as defined by the 'PEOPLE'S CHARTER', are just and reasonable, embracing, as it does, Universal Suffrage, No Property Qualification, Annual Parliaments, Equal Representation, Payment of Members, and Vote by Ballot; which, in their practical operation, would, in the opinion of this Meeting, be the means of returning just Representatives to the Commons House of Parliament—persons who, being responsible to, and being paid by the people, would be more likely to promote the just interests of the nation than those who now constitute that assembly. This Meeting, therefore, solemnly adopt the 'PEOPLE'S CHARTER' as a measure of justice they are resolved by all legal means to endeavour to obtain.

3 That the NATIONAL PETITION now read, as agreed to at Birmingham, Glasgow, and other towns, embodying the same principles as the CHARTER, be adopted and signed by the persons composing this assembly, and be presented to the House of Commons preparatory to the 'PEOPLE'S CHARTER' being introduced.

4 That this Meeting recommend the people of the United Kingdom to hold Meetings and to appoint Deputations to request their Representatives to support and vote for the 'PEOPLE'S CHARTER', and to support the prayer of the NATIONAL PETITION.

5 That the following eight persons be appointed by this Meeting to unite with the Delegates that may be selected by other Meetings in different parts of the Kingdom to watch over the CHARTER and PETITION when they are presented to Parliament.

6 That this Meeting warmly congratulate the French people on the practical efforts they are now making to obtain their elective rights; and earnestly hope that the National Guards of France will defeat the schemes of despots by emancipating their country.

The committee also appointed persons to move and second the resolutions thus

1 Lovett and Hetherington   2 Simpson and Cleave   3 Vincent and Hartwell   4 Moore and Whipple   5 Welford and Rogers.

It was customary at Westminster to permit any one who wished to speak, to do so, but none unless they were householders to move or second a resolution. The Working Mens Association put aside not only the inhabitant householders but even residents one[1] only of the movers or seconders appointed by them being resident in Westminster. . . .

This was an extraordinary proceeding in all its parts. The committee of the Working Mens Association went the length of excluding even the electors from the hustings, they admitted no one to the hustings but by a card, and no one knew where to apply for a card. Their own friends were more than the platform could accommodate.

103. [Add. Ms. 27820, ff. 202–19]

The Meeting in Palace Yard Westminster on the 17 September.

The people began to assemble early and at the time when the chair was taken the number assembled was estimated at 15,000.

The platform which is intended for the accomodation [sic] of those who manage the business those who intend to address the audience, the reporters for the newspapers and persons of distingtion [sic], is a very strong piece of carpenters work. It is put together by iron straps, long screws and nuts and can be put up in less than two hours, and will hold 100 persons conveniently. When set up in Palace yard the floor on which the people stand is level with the projecting window of the Kings Arms Tavern and the only access to it is through the Tavern.

The Ground in front of the platform descends gradually to the Great Door of Westminster Hall.

Mr Smedley the High Bailiff took the Chair at 1 o clock.

Close by him were John Temple Leader Esq. M.P. for the City and Liberty—Mr Dillon Browne M.P. Colonel Thompson The Reverend W. J. Fox. These were the only conspicuous persons and one of them and but one was a resident in Westminster.

From various parts of the country were the following persons.

Ebenezer Elliott from	Sheffield	Arch'd Downie	Stirling etc.
John Fraser	Edinburgh	G. F. Dennis	Colchester
Abraham Duncan	do	Jonathan Beaumont	do
R. K. Douglas	Birmingham	Reeves, Allen &	Brighton
P. H. Muntz	do	Fletcher	
R. J. Richardson	Manchester	Garrod & Birch	Ipswich
R. Lowrey	Newcastle	R. Hewett	Ipswich etc.
F. O Connor	Dewsbury	G. Taylor	do
	and 28 other	G. Layton	Brentford
	places	J. Leary	do
Hugh Williams	Carmarthen	J. Muagglethwhite [sic]	Worcester
J. Jones	Northampton	T. Smith	do

On taking the Chair the High Bailiff said. I have convened this meeting

[1] Hetherington. See Add. Ms. 27835, f. 128.

in consequence of a requisition addressed to me numerously signed by the Inhabitants of Westminster. The object of the meeting, as stated to me, is to take into consideration the propriety of petitioning parliament to pass a law with such amendments and modifycations [*sic*] as may be deemed necessary founded on the Peoples Charter.

Mr Lovett opened the business. He said that from the commencement of the present agitation, different portions of the press as each represented different parties, had attributed to the Working-mens Association different intentions. This they had also done by different associations and meetings. Singular enough said he, they will have it that we mean quite differently to what we say we mean. In order therefore that there may be no mistake as regards the object of this meeting, I have been requested on the part of the Working-mens Association to say that whatever speculative opinions we may entertain they form no part of our present agitation. We mean what we say when we declare, that the 'Peoples Charter' contains a full measure of political justice, which would give to the people the means of redressing all wrongs, and that with Gods help we meant to obtain it.

The National Petition embraces all the objects and the same principles of just representation as the Charter, and having already been hallowed by the approbation of hundreds of thousands of signatures will I trust be respected by this assembly.

We have embodyed [*sic*] these principles of Radicalism in the form of our Charter in order that we may not be agitating for one thing and at the eleventh hour be cheated with another.

We shall be told of the unreasonableness of our demand, of the necessity of taking our rights just as our lords and masters please to give them by instalments. We have been listening to them these six years and the instalments given to us have been, a coercion law for Ireland, several oppresive [*sic*] measures for Great Britain. Revolution and Distruction [*sic*] for Canada. We want no more such instalments.

We say if political power belongs to the people at all, it belongs to them in its plenitude, it belongs to them to the full extent of enabling them to restrain evil doers and to elect those who will do good.

He made a long speech, on these topics and moved the first resolution. . . .

John Temple Leader said the sight before him was glorious. It was a vast assemblage of working men met to consider what were their rights and to determine by every legal means to gain the moral influence in the country which would enable them to assert and to maintain them.

In former times when many thousands of people were called together the meetings were convened by a few leading men not of the working classes, who spoke to the masses for the purpose of inducing them to aid any purpose of their own and what was the consequence? This, the passions of the people were appealed to and the leaders having thus gained the notoriety they sought they deserted the people whom they had deluded. The people must trust to themselves. Every man amongst them had cause and reason to judge for himself and ought not let his judgment by [be] blinded by others.

This meeting was called by working men, it had been addressed by working men, they did not speak to the passions of their hearers, they gave reasons and used arguments, quite as well as was done in the house over the way, yet we are told the people ought not to have the franchise, they are by far too ignorant and don't know how to use it. For my part I never heard better arguments nor the English language better spoken than today. Such being the case, I recommend the working people to look to themselves and to themselves alone. I look upon this meeting and the agitation out of which it has sprung as a great step in a grand moral struggle. They must go on in this way, it was agreed that it was a grand moral struggle in which they would succeed.

He spoke of the state of Ireland and of the proceedings in Canada for the purpose of demonstrating the mismanagement of the Government.

It had been asserted by many prudent well meaning men that all the agitation and all the organization going on amongst the working men all over the country would lead to nothing but waste of time and loss of money. I deny it. I assert that you will get every thing you want if you agitate prudently and organize discreetly, but suppose you do not get all you want, will it not be better, more honourable and more worthy of englishmen to struggle against difficulties and all the obstacles which are or may be opposed to them? To persevere though defeated again and again would be more honourable than to sit down quietly and submit to their opponents. (Loud cheers)

He contrasted the proceedings of former times with those present and said the proceedings of other times were no longer adapted to our circumstances and must be discontinued. Magna Charter [*sic*] was a good thing in past ages. The Reform Bill was another Charter but it had not been carried out and was a failure. There said he is the Peoples Charter, holding up the publication, and round it I call on you the working people of London to rally. (cheers) This is your Charter, this is what you must support until you obtain it. (loud cheers)

He contended that it was in itself an answer to all objectors and concluded by saying. May you go on and prosper. . . .

Mr R. J. Richardson of Manchester said I stand here before you as the representative of the starving hand loom weavers of Lancashire. I am here this day to support the National petition and the Peoples Charter, and I will tell you why. I see a great and mighty nation possessed of all the requisites for good, a nation which has been called the admiration of the world and I now see it degraded both at home and abroad.

The people of Lancashire have long been struggling for the National Petition. In 1819 they met on the blood stained field of Peterloo for the very same petition and they will not shrink from it.

There the people have begun to arm themselves. I have in many places seen the arms over the fire places. They had determined not again to petition, but the National Petition has come most opportunely, yet still they would not have signed it, had it only prayed, they signed it because it demanded.

If the people again fail, if they have no redress of their grievances I cannot say what will be the consequence. The rifles will be loaded. That will be the next step, and I defy the power of any government, or any armed numbers any armed Bourbon force to put them down. It is of no use to disguise the matter, secrecy is the ruin of all things. Every thing will be done openly by the people of Manchester of Lancashire and it will be done constitutionally—legally.

Now for the peoples Charter, they demand it because it contains Universal Suffrage, because it gives them a vote in the choice of representatives. (loud cheering) They are justified in demanding it. Is it too much for those who produce all the food, all the clothing, all the luxuries of life, who fight all the battles of the country, to ask for a voice in the choice of representatives. Is not the whole system of the country from the Parish officer up to the Queen elective. Does not the Archbishop when he crowns the queen, ask the people whether they will have her for their Queen, and as matter of course do not the people in the abbey say 'yes'. She swears to maintain inviolable all the rights and liberties of the people, which our forefathers established, but which a corrupt government and a base parliament have perverted and are now hurrying the queen to danger. I will tell you what the people of Lancashire are going to do. They intend to hold a great meeting in Manchester on monday next. An aggregate meeting when they expect 300,000 men to be present of these two thirds will be fit to bear arms. I am sure the people will rally round the standard of real reform, that they will demand in a voice of thunder, Universal Suffrage, Annual Parliaments, Vote by Ballot, etc. If these things are not granted woe to them that interfere between the people and their God. The spirit of freedom is manifesting itself, in every town village and hamlet, whether commercial manufacturing or agricultural. All breath[e] the same essence of liberty, and the democratic storm now blowing throughout the empire will blast and overwhelm every petty consideration. The people will sweep away the scum of the aristocracy and all who oppose them; and they will ultimately have a republic, which is far from their intention at present. . . .

Mr Hethering[ton] would wind up the business of the day by moving a vote of thanks to the High Bailiff, for his courtesy in calling the meeting and the propriety and urbanity with which he had presided over it. It was carried by acclamation.

The High Bailiff returned thanks. He said that he should always be ready on proper requisitions, to call meetings as long as he considered the purpose for which they were called was constitutional.

It was said that at the least 30,000 persons attended during the proceedings many coming and going away again in consequence of their not being able to hear what was said.

It seems to me to be necessary to observe that

1st This was a very remarkable meeting, in which for the first time the electors took no part and the inhabitants of any sort so little as not to make themselves known as such at the meeting.

2nd as shewing the ardent state of feeling of the working people to an extent never before witnessed in Westminster. Few indeed of the middle class took part in these meetings any where Birmingham alone excepted.

The expense to the working people in sending delegates to London must have been very considerable, the distances from which many of them came were very great, and the purpose, to attend once at a meeting, had never before been sufficient to induce them to contribute their money for such a purpose.

3rd The speeches were almost wholly those of working men, yet they were as Mr Leader truly observed as much to the purpose and as well delivered as those in the house of commons usually were. It may be as truly said that [they] would bear comparison with those made at public meetings by their *betters*.

4th In respect to the concoction and conducting of the meeting. The Working Mens association which was composed almost wholly of working men and those of them who were not men working for wages were very small tradesmen only one remove from the others. They were altogether strangers to the Inhabitants who let them do just as they pleased, they themselves taking no part whatever in the proceedings. The High Bailiff permitting proceedings directly at variance with the custom of Westminster.

Of the twenty two persons who made speeches only two were inhabitants of Westminster, and of those who either moved or seconded resolutions one only was an inhabitant.

No known inhabitant in any of the long accounts given of the meeting was noticed as being on the Platform.

The expenses of meetings of the Inhabitants are always borne by those who promote them and by the donations they receive. These expenses consist of notices, advertisements—Placards—Bills, men to carry bills on poles, the expenses of the Tavern and the charge for putting up and taking away the platform. These have varied from £40 to £100 and can seldom be held for a less expence [*sic*] than £60. In this case they were all, or nearly all paid by the Working Mens Association.

Of the men chosen as delegates one only was a resident within the City and Liberty and he Hetherington was a newsvendor and pamphlet seller in a small way.

The delegates chosen for the General Convention and said to represent the Metropolis were

1 John Cleave Newsvendor and pamphlet seller Shoe Lane Fleet Street
2 Henry Hetherington do do Strand
3 William Lovett Journeyman Cabinet maker Grays Inn Lane
4 Henry Vincent do Printer St Pancras
5 Robert Hartwell do do Lambeth
6 James Bronterre O Brien writer for radical publications—nowhere
7 Richard Moore Carever [*sic*], chamber master Hinde Street Bloomsbury
8 George Rogers Tobacconist High Street St Giles's.

No public meeting for the same purpose was held in any other of the Metropolitan Boroughs.

The speech of Colonel Thompson was as he said in reference only to a particular subject, namely the impropriety of any attempt to introduce any subject for which the meeting was not called.

This was occasioned by the Sun, and Morning Chronicle newspapers recommending the Inhabitants to attend and move a resolution for the repeal of the corn Laws and thus altogether supersede the purpose for which the meeting had been called.

On a previous occasion the working men who usually took part in public meetings threatened, a number of middle class men, who were about to hold a public meeting at the Crown and Anchor Tavern for the purpose of supporting Mr Grote who was about to make a motion in the House of commons, for Vote by Ballot, that they would muster their force and move as an amendment, Universal Suffrage, and it was thought advisable not to hold the meeting. The leaders in this disgraceful matter were Hetherington Cleave and Lovett. These three men, and their followers alarmed at the recommendations of the Sun and the Chronicle, now applied to the persons whom they had prevented holding the meeting for ballot. It was remarked to them that they by their conduct had brought the difficulty upon themselves, but in as much as all such proceedings were wholly dishonourable and dishonest they would interfere to prevent the Corn Laws being brought before the meeting to be held in Palace Yard. Observing that the rule ought to be that whenever a meeting was called for one purpose people came prepared to speak to and to hear and attend to that subject and no other. That forcing another on their attention for which they were not prepared and when the persons who took an interest in that subject not being called upon to be present were absent was a proceeding which any man ought to be ashamed even to contemplate. In this the three concurred. Efforts were made and the two newspapers not only withdrew their recommendations but apologised for having made it and recommended that no such matter should be brought before the meeting.

At the meeting in Palace Yard Mr Duncan said that the Radicals at Edinburgh were resolved to attend all meetings in Scotland and move Universal suffrage as an amendment, for whatever purpose the meetings might be called. For this he was applauded by the multitude and neither Hetherington, Cleave nor Lovett said one word in reprobation of his or their conduct. It will be seen that as the number of foolish and of evil disposed persons became associated as Chartists they adopted the course recommended by Mr Duncan, and being a very numerous body many amongst them as there were good reasons for concluding were paid to intrude into all sorts of public meetings and by their motions as amendments, and by their riotous conduct broke up the meetings, and these were called in the news papers devoted to the Chartists 'Glorious triumphs' these foul proceedings were assisted by Hetherington and Cleave and countenanced by Lovett. When O Connor became the Great Leader of the Chartists, associations were formed under his direction and the direction of his people they made intrusion and rioting one of the articles of their confederation.

104. [Add. Ms. 27820, ff. 354–8]

A meeting was held at the large room in Theobalds Road, called *by some of the members* of the Working mens association, to consider the present state of affairs respecting the National Petition and the Peoples Charter. Mr Hetherington in the Chair.

Mr Hartwell said the meeting was called by himself and some others for the purpose of telling the people of the Metropolis the state of feeling in the country on the great objects of the Association. To hear from O Connor Vincent and others what was the excited state of the country, and to shew them that the apathetic state of the Metropolis was a disgrace to the working people congregated therein. The time was come when the men of London should either give in their adhesion to the principles of the peoples charter and the National Petition or to avow their dissent. It was necessary to say that they who were not with us were against us. It would not be enough for the men of London to say that they agreed to the principles, they must firmly and steadily support them, and *be prepared to do all that the Convention should say was for their benefit. Any man who flinched from that* was not a friend to the working people.

He described his tour in the West of England, the state of the people their dependence and destitution the tyranny of their employers and their *superiors* of the Magistrates and Parish authorities, and the reduction of their wages to 7/- a week and the charge they made to them of 9/6 a bushel for flour.

He announced a great meeting about to be held in Suffolk and requested some of those who were present to go to the meeting. He had applications from numerous places in the West of England requesting the association to send down deputations. He thought that the working men of London agitated as they would be in the ensuing month would join their efforts for the Charter and the National Petition. If the Convention were not supported in the Metropolis, the place of their meeting he knew not what responsibility might be cast upon them.

He moved a resolution. 'That those persons who approved of the Charter should pledge themselves to support the Convention'.

Mr O Connor addressed the meeting. He called upon the men of London to imitate the men of the north. He abused all persons and classes of persons, and in his usual manner he spoke to the worst feelings of the most ignorant of his audience. He said the Ballot and the repeal of the Corn Laws might be offered to them, but they must refuse both until they had the suffrage.

Mr Vincent also made a rambling speech, and the resolution was passed.

At this time there was much ill blood between O Connor and the Working-mens Association. It had gone on increasing from the first formation of the Association. The differences between the parties had been increased by the conduct of O Connor who looked at their proceedings with an evil eye, and had omitted no opportunity to bring the association into disrepute, and had, a short time before calumniated several of its leading members. Vincent and Hartwell both members of the association were desirous of a convulsion of any sort in the hope that it might lead to a revolution. Vincent had a family taint of insanity which at times made him uncontroulably [*sic*] desirous of mischief. At other times, he was mild considerate and good natured and was generally liked by those who knew him. Hartwell was a cunning ill disposed man, an intriguing, undermining reckless fellow who at length became disliked and shunned by his fellows. Hetherington was an honest man, with too little brains to guide him. One who always intended to do good but seldom understood the way to accomplish his own wishes, an odd character, true to his word, firm and unmoveable when set on for any purpose, yet easily led on other occasions, confiding and misled, abused and cheated by almost any one who would take a little pain with him.

The two first were dupes and partizans of O Connor. Hetherington disliked him and spoke of him without reserve as he thought he deserved to be spoken off [sic]. These three were the only members of the Workingmens Association who took part in the proceedings, and Hartwell acknowledged that the meeting had been called by himself and a few other persons.

O Connor had made progress in Foley Street Marylebone. In Theobalds Road near Holborn, and he and his new confederates therefore called another meeting in a very large room in the City Road near the northern part of Finsbury Square, an account of which was published in the Northern Star and in two or three other newspapers.

It was thus announced in the Northern Star.

'The National Convention. The Working-Mens Association. On thursday night the 20 Dec. there was a numerous meeting of the members of this association at the Hall of Science Commercial Place City Road for the purpose of taking into consideration the present state of the Country, and to determine upon the most efficient means of organizing the men of London in support of the National Convention.'

Mr O Connor was unanimously called to the Chair.

He commenced by abusing the Morning Advertiser, for having endeavoured to keep the people away from the meeting. He said, Whig like, O Connell like, it denounces me and cautions the people to beware of Feargus O Connor, and yet this very paper justifies the use of physical force, if it be necessary (great applause). He then abused the Morning Chronicle which had, he said, also denounced him. He challenged the whole Whig Press of London to come before him and face him, and in this way he went on to an extent, the report of which occupies a whole column in the Northern Star.

He denied having ever recommended or in any way encouraged the use of arms or what was called Physical Force. He had always taught the men of the North to depend on moral force alone. But by moral force he did not mean the moral power of the Scotch Philosophers (cheering) nor their chippings of the Excise and their attacks upon the Tea-pot. (great laughter)

He then came back to the Morning Advertiser, dwelt on it and the whig press for some time and then said the whole of that press were doing their best to set the moral force, and the physical force men together by the ears.

He then travelled to Ireland, still abusing the Morning Advertiser & the Chronicle and proceeded, in his way to state, his doings in that country. He then turned upon O Connell and abused him for some time. He then went to Edinburgh where he had been denounced but he would be in Edinburgh early in January and would then see if the men of Edinburgh would not be put to shame for what they had done. He called upon the whole people to meet in tens of thousands on the day the National Petition should be presented to the house of commons. He advised them to be resolute and to send in to the speaker and inform him that they would wait for an answer to the prayer of the petition.

197

He again returned to the Morning Advertiser and said, if ever I gave any one a good pickling I have given one to the Editor of the Advertiser.

He was going to Ireland to form an Union, and he would accomplish his purpose spite of O Connell and all his combinations.

This was Mr O Connors way of carrying forward the purposes for which the meeting was called, by taking no notice whatever of them.

Mr Whittle the Physical force delegate from Liverpool, said the people were entitled to Universal Suffrage and he pledged the meeting to obtain it. He scolded the Morning Advertiser and Chronicle.

He praised Mr Stephens, and declared that he was as good a man as ever lived. He praised O Connor. He declared that the National Petition had been signed by *two millions* and a half of people, (It had not been signed by one third of that number) and would soon be signed by more than three millions. He had much pleasure in moving

'That all the manifold evils of which the people complain are attributable to class legislation and can only be put an end to by Universal Suffrage.'

Mr Ireland seconded the resolution.

Still no allusion to the business for which the meeting was called.

Mr R. Moore a member of the Working-mens Association said 'Mr O Connor has made attacks upon friends of mine which I cannot permit to pass without notice.' He was well acquainted with Mr Duncan and Mr Frazer, he knew that they were as conscientious, well meaning, honest and determined friends to the cause as it was possible men could be; and he was sure their conduct could not be justly impugned for any thing they had done, much less because they had reprobated language which they thought likely to injure the good cause. He protested against the attack Mr O Connor had made upon these good men.

Mr Lovett: They had been called upon by Mr O Connor to put down any one who came there to produce dissension,—they might think that he had come there for that purpose; he assured them that he had not; but he was one who believed that the sentiments sent forth through the columns of the *Northern Star* and the *Champion* had been very prejudicial to the interests of those who were earnest in their wish for Universal Suffrage—(cries of 'No, no'). He expressed merely his own opinion, and wished to force it upon no person, but he trusted, though he differed from them, they would hear what he had to say. Mr Stephens might be a very good man, and might be a very humane man, but he had used language to the injury of their cause, and therefore they deprecated him. The language of Mr Stephens had kept away many from joining their ranks—(disorder). He had an experience of ten years in Radicalism, and he could say *it was because of the language,—the violent language,—used in 1830 and 1831 that prevented the working classes from then obtaining many of their objects*—(uproar). *He could assure them it was true, and he could mention names.* One he would give them. Benbow, at the Rotunda, said it would make his heart glad to hear of the burning of Bristol. Such expressions were extended by means of the Press, and a meeting which was to have been presided over by Mr Wakley was obliged to be given up in consequence. It would not have been allowed for fear of consequences, when such language was allowed to be spoken, and even applauded. The language of Mr Stephens has operated in the same manner. Many who would have joined us have kept back, because they saw language used calling upon the people to use the torch and the dagger, to bite with their teeth, and to tear with their nails— (uproar, applause and hissing). If it was doubted, he would read the very passages from the *Northern Star* and the *Champion*. As Feargus O Connor found fault with the friends of the cause in Edinburgh, he at once denounced them as enemies, and that merely because they deprecated language such as he had read—(hissing). He (Mr L.) thought they were deeply injuring their cause by using or approving such language; indeed he thought they ought to deprecate it. They were doing much harm to the cause by condemning all classes. There was not a class in which they had not thousands of friends; then why try to alienate them by denouncing them wholesale—(hissing and applause). It could only do harm by driving away many of their friends, then only those would be left who by using violent language will hurry them into some premature outbreak, and the moment they had done so they would leave them and become their bitterest enemies —(disorder). He did not think their cause would be promoted by abusing in coarse language the New Poor Law, or any other partial grievance— (hissing). . . . He would like to see the people educated—(hissing)—he would like to see noble powers and resplendent talent engaged in calling up the moral and mental energies of the people—(cheers). Instead of spending a pound to buy a useless musket, he would like to see it spent in sending out delegates among the people—(loud cheering and hissing). He was anxious to be understood clearly. If the people were to be called upon to arm—if they were to go on using violent expressions which must lead to mischief, he would have nothing to do with them—(uproar)—but if they were disposed to go on agitating as they had done for two years, he would do all in his power to forward the cause—(laughter and cries of 'No waiting.') If they were willing to push onward in a reasonable endeavour to arouse the moral and mental energies of the people, he would be one of them; he was one of them in heart; but if there was to be any arming, any fighting, he was not one of them—(cheers and hisses).

Mr O Connor was received with tremendous cheering. 'Words are but wind, actions speak the mind.' When he arrived that evening, four resolutions were put into his hand, one of them strongly reprobating the Edinburgh Delegates, but he at once said, 'No; don't move it, for it can do no good, and can only cause dissension;' and on his advice it had been withdrawn—(cheers). Not a word had fallen from his lips to cause dissension among the Radicals. Mr Lovett had asked who had done most for the cause. He (Mr O Connor) could only say that he had spent seven thousand pounds in it—(cheers). He had never travelled a mile, or eat [*sic*] a meal, but at his own expense—(loud cheers). He had formed upwards of 200 Associations and had created a feeling in the country that no man on earth could allay. He did not agree in every word that fell from Mr Stephens, but he was the friend of every man who had humanity at his heart, and that man was Mr Stephens. He for one would not be content to wait for two years— (cheers)—it might do very well for those who made a profit of it; but he thought they were now ready, and ought to proceed at once—(cheers).

They might fight their open enemies, but oh save us from our pretended friends. . . .

105. [Add. Ms. 27821, ff. 22–4]

On Sunday the 27 Jan'y [1839] was published the first number of the peoples paper 'The Charter'.[1] It was a large paper containing 16 pages each page 12 inches wide and 18 inches long, and was sold for sixpence.

The Title was 'The Charter. Established by the Working Classes.'

The Editor[2] of this paper was a particularly ill qualified man for his office, he had been a journeyman tradesman, then a sectarian preacher, was then employed upon a newspaper, and succesively [*sic*], on several others, every one of which he assisted to destroy. It was he who first suggested the Charter newspaper and being a very cuning [*sic*] fellow succeeded in persuading the Working mens Association to assist in its establishment. It was to be conducted by a committee of working men from different trades as set forth in the prospectus. The committee were led to suppose that Mr Carpenter would be able to employ the best talent in the country for each of the departments which he represented as necessary for carrying on the paper in a manner very superior to any other weekly paper. This was to be wholly under his direction, for which and his own able editorship he was to receive £30 a week. He never employed any able man, but got the paper up any how he could and pocketed the money.

The Paper having been announced as the political organ of the working men of London and also as the Official paper of the General Convention of which the Editor and several of the committee were elected members, it was sure to command a considerable sale amongst the middle classes, many of whom were very desirous to learn from time to time as much as they could of their proceedings. This had been calculated upon, and of the second number more than 5,000 were sold. It was not expected that many advertisements would be sent to it and it was therefore calculated that 7,000 must be sold to cover its expenses, but the projectors were sanguine and entertained no doubt that the sale would exceed 10,000. The first number was a poor thing and disappointed the expectations of many.

On Sunday the 2nd of feb'y was published No. 1 of a rival paper called The Chartist. It was not quite half the size of the Charter, was printed on bad paper and very much worn type. Its price was only $2\frac{1}{2}$d.

It commenced thus. 'To our Readers,—For the real wealth of England— for those who produce, for the mighty many this paper is started.'

It then says that 'the conductors well know the wants and privations of their labouring fellow men, and have perseveringly enquired, and reflected most anxiously how to supply their wants and how to remove their privations.' This is followed by a dissertation on the value of sixpence to a working man, and it asks how it is possible for most amongst them who are desirous to have an useful newspaper can pay sixpence a week for one. Every man should have a newspaper of his own to read when he has the time—at his leisure moments, and thus whilst he receives information and instruction save him from being driven to the Beer Shop where alone he can see a newspaper. To save him from this to promote his comfort and to

---

[1] See below, Appendix, pp. 249–54. [2] William Carpenter.

give him wholesome mental food in abundance for 2½d a week is the purpose of the paper.

This is followed by an exhordium [*sic*] well adapted to its readers, and intended to induce them to purchase the newspaper. It promises itself that in a fortnight, it will be found at every working mans fire side. It proceeded in a lively saucy stile [*sic*] but excepting the editorial articles it contained but little that the working people cared much about.

No. 2 of the Charter dated the 3rd of february contained accounts of proceedings at several public meetings, and an ill written attempt to persuade one and all to oppose the repeal of the Corn Laws. This advice was grounded on what O'Connor and others had carefully inculcated, namely that though the law was iniquitous the present attempt to procure its repeal was a contrivance of the middle class to increase their own profits and to lower the wages of the labourer, and the certainty that the corn and all other oppressive laws would be repealed when the Charter should, as it soon would, be the law of the land.

106. [*Place Collection, set 56, vol. 6. Sept.–Nov. 1839, ff. 257–8. Printed.*]

CHARTER OFFICE, 16, Catherine Street, Strand
November 14, 1839

Sir,—The Managing Committee of THE CHARTER NEWSPAPER respectfully solicit your attention to the following brief statement of the present position and future prospects of the Paper, and request your assistance towards extricating the Paper from its present difficulty, and placing it on a permanent footing.

THE CHARTER was established by a number of Working Men, in January, 1839, to be managed by a Committee chosen from amongst the Subscribers, and any profits that might accrue from its publication, to be appropriated to some public purpose connected with the moral, social, or political improvement of the Working Classes.

The Paper, from various causes, but chiefly from the want of the necessary fund to expend in placarding advertising, and otherwise pushing a New Paper, has never yet cleared its expenses; and the loss, upon an average, about £5 per week, exclusive of Editor's Salary, has fallen chiefly upon the Committee of the Paper, who are all Working Men, and unable longer to bear this expense. They would regret the necessity of giving up the Paper, feeling convinced that with the assistance of those Friends favourable to the object, they would now, in the course of a few weeks, be enabled to command a sale which would clear the expenses.

The Weekly Sale is now between 2,300 and 2,500; but in consequence of the large size of the Paper, and the quantity of matter contained in it, it will take an extra 1,000 to clear itself. This might be obtained if the Committee had at their disposal about Four or Five Hundred Pounds. The liabilities of the Paper are now about One Hundred Pounds. In the hope that you will feel disposed to render them some assistance, to prevent the necessity of relinquishing the Publication of the Paper, a deputation from the Committee will wait upon you, and who will answer any questions, or afford you any information on the subject.

We remain, Sir
Yours Respectfully,
THE MANAGING COMMITTEE
ROBERT HARTWELL, PUBLISHER

201

Dear Sir

I have received your printed paper and think the mode you have adopted is the only chance you have of putting the paper on its legs—and that even a very poor one.

I saw 5 men yesterday all of whom had taken the paper and had dropped it. I talked with them about the paper and said that if they and others were disposed to support it, any two of them for the others could investigate the state of the concern. They however declined and one of them said that he had dropped it, as had also the committee of the 'Reform Club' because it abused and held out the middle classes as little better than monsters, in this the others concurred, and said, if the working people were determined to stand alone, and to make war on the rest of the community they must themselves provide the means of maintaining their paper and their other means of offence. I thought myself bound to tell you this, for I believe that if the scolding etc. complained of could be refrained from and the paper continued on 'till the men, who are out of town returned, money might be raised to carry it on, if upon enquiry it should appear probable that it would be continued.

I send you a list of the members of the Radical club. They are all supporters of Universal Suffrage, but I very much fear that you will meet with the objection from them which I have mentioned. Yet they are promoting a subscription for Lovett, and have passed a resolution very properly condemning the conduct of Govt towards Lovett and Collins.

You will see by the paper inclosed that they did not order it to be inserted in the Charter. I was not at the meeting.

Yours truly
Francis Place

107. [Place Collection, set 66 f. 9] ⎰

85 Cornwall Road
Lambeth March 2 [1840]
Monday Evening

Sir

The money you were kind enough to advance for the use of the Charter Committee not having yet been paid I deem it necessary to write you a few lines accounting for the delay. It was only last week that the Committee were enabled to dispose of the paper, which they have done to Messrs Welford and Gaskell of the Statesman late Weekly True Sun. The Committee have decided that all borrowed money (which amounts to about £37) shall be paid before any other claims on the paper; they are to receive weekly instalments from the Statesman for six weeks (in proportion to the sale, as per agreement) and I can assure you that your loan, with that of Messrs Harrison and Travers will be amongst the first discharged; I hope either the close of the present or the beginning of next week. I thought it right to communicate the above to you, fearing that you might think we had forgotten you.

I am Sir
Yours Respectfully
Robert Hartwell

P.S. If you have occasion to write to me you will please address as above, my residence, as I have left the Charter Office and am working as journeyman on the Statesman Newspaper. I am sorry to say it will be some time before I recover the loss I have sustained by the failure of the Paper.

108. [Place collection, set 56, vol. 12, Jan.–Apr. 1841, f. 14]

6 August 1840

Mr Gotobed,

You were one of the persons who obtained £5 of me upon a serious understanding that it was to be repaid from the sale of the paper, it was to enable you to bring out, and it was lent for no other purpose. You obtained through me, £5 from Mr Harrison and £5 from Mr Travers. Mr Harrison now writes to me on the subject for himself and Mr Travers, and desires me to tell him why the money was not returned as it came to hand from the sale of the paper as was conditioned, and why he has heard nothing about the matter for months past. Shall I tell him that you are Swindlers, or what shall I tell him, or will you tell him any thing yourself. It would be needless for me to write to Hartwell to receive notes in reply which are disgraceful dishonest shuffles.

In almost every case where money has been concerned I have been ill treated and cheated by working men and it vexes me much as it does Mr Harrison to find, that in this respect, at least, they differ from all other men in being utterly dishonest.

Your obedient Servant,
Francis Place

109. [Add. Ms. 27821, ff. 42–6]

The Convention met on Monday 4th March [1839]. Mr Whittle in the Chair.

The secretary read a letter inclosing resolutions—passed at a public meeting called by the London Democratic Association, which had been transmitted to him, requesting him to bring the resolutions before the Convention at the earliest opportunity, which he now did, it was as follows.

'To the members of the General Convention

'At a public meeting held in the Hall of Science City Road the following resolutions were unanimously agreed to. G. J. Harney in the Chair.

'1st Moved by Mr Combe, seconded by Mr Fisher. That this meeting is of opinion that the Peoples Charter would be established by law within one month from the present time provided the people and their leaders do their duty—and—This meeting is of opinion, that it is essentially just and indispensably necessary to meet all acts of oppression with immediate resistance.

2nd Moved by Mr Rider seconded by Mr Marsden. This meeting

convey to the General Convention their opinion that for the due discharge of the duties of the Convention, it is essentially necessary to be prompt in the presentation of the National Petition; and we hold it to be the duty of the Convention to impress upon the people the necessity of an immediate preparation for ulterior measures.

'We the undersigned, appointed as a deputation, at the aforesaid meeting to communicate the foregoing resolutions to the General Convention, respectfully requesting that they will consider them at their first meeting.

Cornelius Bentley
Thomas Broome.'

Mr Richardson would confine himself to the motion moved and seconded by Mr Rider and Mr Marsden, over them they had control as members of the Convention. Their conduct was highly culpable and deserved censure, they as members of the Convention had acquiesed [*sic*] in an unanimous vote to suspend the presentation of the petition for two months, and then at a public meeting condemned the proceeding and proposed ulterior measures, which the good sense of the Convention had refused to entertain. The letter was an insult to the Convention and a libel on their constituents. The same attempt had been made at Manchester by the same parties who were prominent in this matter, and their perseverance in proposing matters at once criminal and dangerous, and not less absurd shewed a most criminal intention and looked like a conspiracy to destroy the Convention.

The chairman rose to order, he thought the language too strong, and the imputation of motives improper.

Mr Richardson thought he had drawn a fair inference.

Dr Taylor objected to Mr. Richardsons language.

Mr Marsden said that himself and Mr Rider had acted only with the view of conveying the sentiments of a public meeting to the Convention.

Mr Collins was astonished at the conduct of the two members, their duty was to have protested against and not to have moved and seconded such a resolution.

Dr Wade concurred with Mr Collins—such conduct was calculated to ruin their friends and encourage their enemies.

Many members spoke, some on one and some on the 'other side of the *house*' as Mr Neesom said, most of the speakers were physical force men and they seemed disposed to justify the members, Harney, Rider and Marsden, but they voted for Mr Richardsons motion.

Mr Carpenter towards the close of the debate said. He hoped an opportunity would occur when the question might be fully entertained. Incalculable mischief had been done by the repeated indiscretions of members of the Convention.

Mr Harney. Had put his name to the resolutions as Chairman of the meeting and because he highly approved of them. The resolutions were not a command but an opinion which the parties to them had a right to offer. As a member of the Democratic Union he would say what he pleased and do what he pleased. He called upon Mr Richardson to make good his charges and he would meet them, not by an appeal to the Convention, but by an appeal to his constituents.

Mr Richardson would meet Mr Harney at the Democratic Association and make good his charges there.

'The House' then divided for Mr Richardsons motion   22⎫
                       Against   6⎬M.16

17 were absent, some of them having left the meeting, but most of them being missionaries out of London.   Adjourned till Wednesday

A meeting of the Democratic Association was held at the assembly room in Theobalds road in the evening.

The account of the meeting was headed 'Recommendation to Arm'.

'The attendance was not large, this was said amongst other impediments to have been caused, by the proprietor of their usual place of meeting being alarmed at the violent language used. It was hinted that the refusal was caused by the intrigues of some of the members of the Convention, this elicited loud expressions of disapprobation against the treachery of that body to the cause of the people.

Mr Marsden one of the three delegates who had been censured by the Convention was voted to the Chair.

Williams moved that the National Petition should be presented at the latest early in April. He recommended that every shopkeeper should be called upon to contribute to the funds of the Convention, and that the people should deal with those only who should stick a receipt for the money given on one of his shop windows. Much as the employment of faggots and daggers had been condemned he thought it better for the people to redress their grievances by those means than to pine in hopeless misery. (loud cheering)

G. J. Harney condemned the proceedings of the Convention against him and his colleagues. He recommended the people to arm themselves and to resist to the death the continuance of the poor law. If any mercenary of the scoundrel government attempted to take his arms he should have them only with his life. He regretted the division in the Convention, but the truth was that, that body was no longer worthy of the peoples confidence. Mr Williams's motion was carried as was also another expressing confidence in the delegates who had fallen under the displeasure of the Convention.

                                 The meeting was dissolved.

110. [Add. Ms. 35151, ff. 146–8]

Friend and fellow Citizen   13 March 1839
       William Lovett

Many thanks for the papers, be so good as to let me have copies of every paper of which you have a duplicate.

I do not like the address, at all. It has neither the words nor the style which a paper issuing from a body of deputies appointed by the people should have. It is a common vulgar address, very much below any one issued by the Working Mens Association. It will do no good as a seperate [sic] transaction, it is offensive to all men, but a *portion* of the working people and to that portion it is misleading. It is the worst thing the deputies have done and it ought to have been the best.

The rules are good, and well constructed. I have attended to your proceedings with considerable anxiety because I take great interest in them.

Some of the speeches, and especially some of those made soon after the deputies assembled were in parts very absurd and calculated to lessen the importance of the assembly. This I regretted. Carpenter has taken much pains to put the best face upon every part of the proceedings, and he has done it cleverly without either committing himself or the deputies, but I who have had many years experience in committees and associations can see much which he does not expose to the general reader.

Upon the whole the proceedings have been better than I expected. I know well enough how inexperienced men must act, and I have observed nothing, except now and then in language, which I have not seen over and over again in each of our houses of parliament. At first the deputies, as you know I expected, they would, talked as if the whole power of the people was lodged in their hands and could be used by them at will. This mistake they were sure to discover and to act accordingly. This,—to some extent—they have done. They are learning a practical lesson of wisdom, and will return home wiser and better men than they came, but they will not generally have pleased those who sent them. They will have seen some part of the great difficulty of moving a whole people, and will each of them have learned patience and forbearance. I hope they will learn perseverance. They who sent them will not have had the same advantages and will have learned nothing, will be disappointed, impatient and will shew their displeasure. It will then become each of the deputies in his particular district, to bear with the people and not to give up the cause either from chagrin or despair.

Before the time comes for the deputies to disperse they will be thoroughly convinced that with a few exceptions, the people instead of being excited will become torpid. They—the deputies—will also be convinced how greatly they miscalculated their own power and influence and it will behove them, each one as far as his circumstances will permit him, to cheer up the people and encourage them steadily to pursue their object.

Upon the whole much good will be done, good far overbalancing all the trouble and expense which will be occasioned. They would were they to be reappointed on some future occasion, do a vast deal more good, they would then be experienced men, and would not commit the same errors twice.

Were they to know what I have here written, they would *all* probably,— some more, some less, be offended with me, this would however be wrong, since men called into public action for the first time, on a large scale, as they have been, and in the particular way in which they have been called could not avoid committing errors, and each should remember, that in most things, and most of all in public matters, men acquire much knowledge through their errors, which they never could obtain by any other means.

Yours truly
Francis Place

111. [Add. Ms. 27821, ff. 87–8]

A meeting was held on Monday the 15th of April headed in the Charter thus. 'Disgraceful conduct of members of the London Democratic Association'.

It seems that in consequence of advertisements in the Charter, and

Operative newspapers inviting two members to attend at the large room in the Old Bailey on Monday evening for the purpose of forming a general Metropolitan Radical Association on the plan set forth by the so called general association projected by O Connor Beaumont Harney and others but never carried out; a numerous meeting took place. Two members deputed from almost every Radical association in the Metropolis being present. Mr Neesom was called to the Chair and Mr Hartwell consented to act as secretary, but before the business for which they had been called together could be laid before them upwar[ds] of 50 members of the Democratic association headed by G. J. Harney and others burst into the room, and a miscreant who had been convicted of stabbing a man, whose name is Wall commenced an attack upon the Convention the Charter and all the political associations in London. Mr Rogers attempted to explain the business when as many of the Democratic Association as the Tables and unoccupied benches could hold jumped upon them and endeavoured to out vie one another in noise and abuse. Harney and Coombe declared that there should be no Union. The democratic association had raised the standard and they who refused to join the association were cowards and traitors. Utter confusion ensued and was continued during two hours, during which time many of the delegates went away. This was the thing the intruders wished and finding they had a majority, proposed a resolution the purpose of which was to throw the whole organisation of London into the hands of the leaders of the Democratic Association.

112. [Place collection, set 56, vol. 6, Sept.–Nov. 1839, f. 213. *Printed.*]

RADICAL CLUB

At a Meeting of this Club, held at Radley's Hotel, on Thursday, the 31st day of October, 1839, it was unanimously Resolved—

That this Club is desirous of marking the strong feeling of abhorrence and disgust with which it regards the cruelties practised by the Magistrates of Warwickshire, and sanctioned by the late Home Secretary, Lord John Russell, towards Mr Lovett and Mr Collins, sentenced to imprisonment for an *alleged* political offence. And that this Club determines to promote a subscription for the subsistence of the family of Mr Lovett, a member of the Club, during the time of his imprisonment.

That these resolutions be advertised in the Morning Chronicle, the Sun, Weekly True Sun, and the Birmingham Journal.

That Mr Harrison, Treasurer of the Club, be appointed to receive the Subscriptions, at Radley's Hotel, Bridge street, Blackfriars, or No. 4, Cumberland place, Grove lane, Camberwell.

R. G. Welford, Chairman

113. [Add. Ms. 35151, ff. 231–2]

Manchester 27 July 1840

My dear Sir

I think every possible effort should be made to get your proceedings into the London papers. The country is now just ripe to take the cue from the metropolis. Every movement upon the corn law will vibrate through the length & breadth of the land. A good stirring appeal—*short* & pithy— from the Metropolitan Association, calling upon the nation to unite & cooperate against the bread-tax, would be responded to & such an address is necessary to put the Association on its proper footing with the Country, & to give it claims upon the community for support. The address ought to appear immediately in the London papers, & it should recommend petitions to be forwarded immediately for the abolition of all taxes on the first necessaries of life. The Sun & Chronicle are the two most important papers for the country—The Advertiser is not much seen out of London. The object to be kept in view by your Association in my humble opinion ought to be to influence the country at large more than the metropolis. London is generally well represented so far as the Corn question is concerned. But we must change the parliamentary representation of a great many other boroughs before we can carry our point with the House of Commons. I hope you will bear in mind always the great power you have at command over the country through the London press. We in Manchester are looked upon with some jealousy by the agriculturists (I mean the populations of rural towns, as well as farmers & labourers) but they will follow the metropolis as their natural leader.

I throw this hasty suggestion before you & I remain
My dear Sir
Yours very truly

F. Place Esq.   R. Cobden

114. [Add. Ms. 35151, ff. 230 and 233]

Brompton 4 March 1840

To Richard Cobden, Esq.,

My Dear Sir,

I duly received your letter of the 27 February, but until now have had no time to reply to it. I do not say so as an excuse for neglect but as a fact for I have not lost an hour since its receipt. I have worked from 7 a.m. till midnight. Mr. Smith has told you how we have been going on, and he being one of the most sanguine and impetuous of men has no doubt told you from time to time that we were doing nothing. His eagerness to 'go a lecturing' would prevent him believing that we were not losing our time. He however will have enough to do in his time to satisfy him. He will have to lecture 6 nights a week, and sometimes in the day time also. Mr. Paulton will have as much to do as he can undertake without injury to his health. We shall need more lecturers not only for London but for many places within some twenty miles of it.

The people here differ very widely from you at Manchester. You some of *you* at Manchester resolve that something shall be done and then *you* some of you set to work and see it done—give your money and your time and need none but mere servants to carry out the details. Our men of property and influence never act in this way—they themselves must be operated upon and that too with care and circumspection to induce them even to give us

208

their *mites* and to permit us to put their names on the list of our General Committee. Of the committee of eleven appointed at the meeting which you attended and half a dozen who we put on the next day we have met no more in committee than three four or five until yesterday when we met to discuss our Constitution when seven attended. Our subscription does not amount to quite £100. I do not tell you this as a matter of complaint but simply as facts. The few who have met in committee, and the 3 or 4 who come constantly day by day were well experienced men and men of business—among them Peter A. Taylor, whom I believe you know, and with whose aid if no other person had attended the business would have been done just as it has been.

We have done an immense amount of business, but it is all preparatory —all absolutely necessary.

1. We have sent out some 600 notes to as many persons requesting permission to put their names on the General Committee list. About 250 are to M.P's. we shall have from 100 to 150 consents.

2. We have issued in like manner a much larger number to persons requesting them to become members of the association.

3. Time has, unavoidably, been consumed in discussing rules and regulations.

4. The same in preparing an address to the people.

5. In procuring places in which to read lectures and discussions.

6. In obtaining the consent of bankers to receive subscriptions.

7. In endeavouring to persuade a considerable number of persons of the right sort to consent to work for us in various ways.

We could not put forth an address without producing certain ruin until a considerable number of names were obtained for the general committee, Bankers to receive subscriptions and it would have been impossible either to have obtained subscriptions or men to join us until we published an address with names of committee, bankers etc. The necessity of delaying to come before the public without these formalities was seriously discussed when it was decided that it was not losing time by delaying until we had these things at our command. We could not hope to obtain any considerable accession of members until we had our rules and regulations to put into their hands. Two or three days more must yet pass away before we shall be able to make a public display. The moment we are in a condition to come before the public as we ought to do an extensive vigorous and I believe well planned scheme of business consisting of many particulars every one of which has been settled and preparations made to carry them fully into operation.

London differs very widely from Manchester, and indeed, from every other place on the face of the earth. It has no local or particular interest as a town not even as to politics. Its several boroughs in this respect are like so many very populous places at a distance from one another, and the inhabitants of any of them know nothing, or next to nothing, of the proceedings in any other, and not much indeed of those of their own. London in my time and that is half a century has never moved. A few of the people in different parts have moved, and those whenever they come together make a considerable number, still a very small number indeed when compared with the whole number, and when those are judiciously managed i.e. when they are brought to act together not only make a great noise which is heard far and wide, but which has also considerable influence in many places. But isolated as men are here, living as they do at considerable distances, many seven miles apart and but seldom meeting together except in small groups, to talk either absolute nonsense or miserable party politics, or to transact business exclusive of every thing else will tell you they have no time to give to the association, to help to repeal the Corn Laws, while the simple fact is that (that excepting the men of business and even they lose much time) 4/5th of the whole do nothing but lose their time.

With a very remarkable working population also, each trade divided from every other, and some of the most numerous even from themselves, and who, notwithstanding an occasional display of very small comparative numbers, are a quiescent, inactive race as far as public matters are concerned. The leaders, those among them who do pay attention to public matters, are one and all at enmity with every other class of society. True it is as they allege they have been cajoled and then abandoned by the middle class as often as they have acted with them, but their opinions are pushed to extremes and are mischievous prejudices. They call the middle class—'shopocrats'—usurers, (all profit being usury)—money-mongers—tyrants and oppressors of the working people and they link the middle class with the aristocracy under the dignified appellation of 'Murderers of Society'— 'Murderers of the People'. With such a population so circumstanced, the well informed honest zealous men, few in number, there is no way of making those who give a tone to any such project as ours, but by such preparatory measures as I have described, and by unweariedly working them out.

You who have seem much of the world, and written well, respecting some considerable countries will at once see how necessary it is for us to proceed as we have done, and that we had no other chance for success.

All we want is money, we shall come forth in a few days not as I hope a miserable puling brat but a young hercules and if we are well fed with money shall rapidly become a most powerful (as we shall then be called not) Hercules but Minister.

Yours truly,
Francis Place.

115. [Add. Ms. 27822, ff. 152–63]

A Brief Memorandum of circumstances connected with the first operations of the Anti-Corn Law League, and the Formation of the Metropolitan Anti-Corn Law Association.

It may be recollected that in the years 1828–9–30 there was great agricultural distress, and that in the rural districts incendiary fires spread over England. The Tories had not forgiven Wellington and Peel for Catholic emancipation—the country gentlemen were discontented with government finding difficulty in receiving their rents, patronage began to be more impartially distributed, and the ministry were turned out by the landed interest. These things happening at the same time with revolutions in France and Belgium, Parliamentary Reform began to be loudly demanded. This struggle was carried on for several years, and the Whigs were fortunate enough to enjoy the advantage of the fine harvests of 1831–2–3–4–5–6 and part of 1837. The struggle for reform and collateral measures of a Reforming kind, distracted the nation from all attention to mere fiscal and social legislation, and the manufacturers of Lancashire and Yorkshire particularly enjoyed great prosperity, and made large sums of money. New mills were everywhere erected, and large immigrations took place of agricultural families and paupers, to find employment in the manufacturing Districts, where Mr R. H. Greg, Ashworth and others complained of a want of hands.

In the end of 1837 a bad harvest gave a great check to the manufacturers —a worse year in 1838 made them very discontented, and stimulated many to look to the causes. At the end of 1838 the price of food rose high, every manufacturer was losing money, many were ruined. Then arose the vigorous movement in the Manchester Chamber of Commerce for the Repeal of the Corn Laws, which ended in a Town's meeting and a Subscription of £7,000.

On 30th December 1838 Mr Cobden, who had taken an active part in the proceedings, wrote to Mr William Tait his Edinburgh publisher 'We are now organising a society on a very large scale for following up the agitation. Money will be liberally raised, but we are badly off for talent, and are on the look out for a Secretary to whom we would give £200 or £300 a year, if we could find a man of energetic character, good education, and ability, and one whose heart is in the cause. Such a man would find himself placed in a career of permanent usefulness to himself and others here, for we shall always have work for him. Do you know of any young man of talent and *good conduct* (without the latter all else is valueless) in Edinburgh or the north.' Mr Tait recommended me.

I went to Manchester in January 1839. Mr Villiers brought on his motion, and delegates from Manchester London etc. watched its progress in Palace Yard. On its defeat Joseph Sturge moved the adjournment of the delegation to Manchester. There Mr W. Coates, Mr G. A. Young (Marylebone) Mr P. A. Taylor, and I *think* T. F. Gibson attended, to represent London. At the Corn Exchange I heard and saw Mr P. A. Taylor for the first time. His speech was a noble one, and made a great impression on all. I was deeply struck with it.

In March 1839 I lectured at Huddersfield, Doncaster, Louth, Boston, Peterborough, Huntingdon, Cambridge etc.

Mr Paulton & Mr J. B. Smith laboured to raise the metropolitan community, but without any success so far as permanent effect was concerned.

I was instructed by the League to go to London and to establish an Association. I got letters to Mr Henry Warburton M.P. I also saw Mr Joseph Parkes. He referred me to Mr Francis Place for advice and assistance, as the person most competent to put me on the best way of organising a society, or a Branch of the League. I waited on Mr Place, and received from him the heartiest assurances of sympathy, and a consent to make use of his name in any way I considered useful. I also received much advice and information suited to the peculiar character and circumstances of the London community. I consulted him as to calling on various gentlemen in a list I had received at Manchester. Mr Place pointed particularly to Mr Taylor's name. I waited on Mr Taylor and he gave me great encouragement of which

I had had much need, considering the gloomy views entertained by many on whom I waited, as to the uselessness of attempting any thing in London. Mr Taylor gave me a letter to Mr John Travers Swithins Lane.

I waited on Mr Travers, who was very zealous in the cause, and received me with all his hearty kindness. He sent for Mr G. A. Heppell. They looked at each other as I developed my scheme of rousing London, and laughed at my sanguine tone, considering it very hopeless to attempt anything. They however said they were very anxious for the great cause, they liked my hopefulness and resolution, and plan, and they gave me a list of leading liberals, the liberty to make use of their names to others, and a hearty pledge to help with money.

I showed the list to Mr Place, and got one of West End people from him. With the liberty to use the names of Messrs Place, Taylor, and Travers, as approving of the formation of an Association, I canvassed others, and got more approvers.

I then issued a Circular to all whose names were on the lists with which I had been furnished, stating the importance of forming a London Association, and that when I had received their answers stating whether they consented to become members I would call a meeting. I got to 400 circulars only ten or twelve answers. After reporting progress to Manchester, I resolved to proceed as if an Association was already resolved on and established.

I took our first rooms in the Strand, put up a great Board with 'Metropolitan Anti-Corn Law Association' painted on it, and called a meeting of all to whom circulars had been sent, for the purpose of constituting the Association. The meeting was so numerously attended that the place of meeting could not contain above half of those who came. Mr Place came and brought Mr Warburton with him. Mr Travers came, and exerted all his influence to get men of mark to support Resolutions and subscribe. A good deal of money was subscribed on the spot—Mr Warburton as chairman heading the list with £100. Mr Lloyd Jones, who has since been so conspicuous as a member of the City Improvement Committee, took an active part in the business part of the new society. Mr Place remained with some others whom he detained after the public meeting, to put the Society at once into a business shape. For the first month the Committee met every day. Mr Place drew out a code of rules—the principle of which was that the society had one sole object, and could not by its constitution ever entertain any other 'the Total and Immediate Repeal of the Corn and Provision Laws'. A strict adherence to this rule kept the Society out of many scrapes, and sometimes was the means of saving its very existence. Mr P. A. Taylor and Mr Place, who had given me the most valuable assistance, advice, and, what was of far more consequence than either at that time, hope and encouragement that we would succeed in rousing London, were present at every meeting—once a day at first, and afterwards once at least every week for seven years of toil, excitement, contention, struggle, sometimes hopelessness and alternate encouragement. For a long time also Mr William Arthur Wilkinson and the Right Honourable Thomas Milner Gibson the present vice President of the Board of Trade were very punctual and actively useful attenders at the Committee meetings, as also Messrs

Thomas Field Gibson, R. Ricardo, R. B. Whitesides, and a little later Samuel Harrison and James Wilson Editor of the Economist.

Mr H. S. Chapman the present Chief Justice of New Zealand was appointed Secretary, and the Society immediately commenced operations in the way of agitating London. I lectured at a great many places opened and paid for by the Society, as did also Mr G. Greig of Leeds. In all [] public meetings were held under the society in the course of the first year.

The Lecturers being called away by the League to the country, and the League itself languishing for want of funds caused by the high price of food, and consequent manufacturing depression, the Metropolitan Association fell back. To get up the lecturing again Mr Place wrote me a letter from the Committee, asking me to become Secretary, and although their funds were at zero they offered me a most liberal salary. I referred them to Mr Cobden as having from the first placed myself at his disposal. A deputation was sent to Manchester to negotiate my engagement with the League, and in January 1840 I entered on my labours as Secretary of the Metropolitan Anti-Corn Law Association.

The society collected	and spent
In 1840 £	£
1841	
1842	
1843	
1844	
1845	
1846	

It held [] Public meetings and lectures. It published and distributed [] number of Tracts and Reports. It organised [] branches in the Metropolis.

It held lectures and meetings in all the principle towns of Middlesex, Surrey, Essex, Northamptonshire, Sussex, Wiltshire, Hampshire, Berkshire, Kent, Buckinghamshire, and it was, by its branches, the chief instrument in the return of Mr Pattison for the City of London, prepared the way for the establishment of the League in the Metropolis, by enlightening the public mind, and organising societies; and it was by its Branches that the first Great London Meetings were so crowded and made to go off with a spirit which afterwards established their success, and overawed the Chartists, who had formerly routed public meetings.

By the Metropolitan Anti-Corn Law Association the voice of London was effectively heard in Parliament by [] Petitions signed by [] and by [] Memorials presented to the Queen for the repeal of the Corn Laws.

I was seven years the Secretary of the Association, and look back to my intercourse with its members with the greatest pleasure. I had no sooner become officially connected with its business Committee, than I found myself among a society emphatically of *Gentlemen*. Mr Place's great experience, and the thorough business habits of all, reduced the whole management of the Association to the greatest order, regularity, and method. I found myself treated with great friendliness, perfect courtesy,

213

and respect. I found that the Committee were determined to do their own business with care and punctuality, making me strictly responsible for what it was my official duty to do, but taking a labouring [role?] themselves, and consulting with and assisting me with the most valuable advice and experience, without over-ruling me, or taking my own proper functions out of my hands. I can most safely say that we never could have achieved the great success we accomplished but by the methodical punctuality and business experience of the Committee, and that I never could have worked with heart, zeal, and pleasure, but for the kind and judicious way in which the Committee discriminated betwixt what was their own department and duty, and what was mine. Their meeting every week, and having reports from me every week in every department, compelled order and diligence, and acted as a stimulus on every member of the Association. I ought also to observe that, as a lecturer and public speaker, entire freedom of speech was always completely conceded to me, and I was never asked to do other than to make a fair and unqualified declaration of my own honest convictions.

Notwithstanding the comparative magnitude of our operations, the Association was never a shilling in debt—and in its political action before the public which was constant and extensive, it is enabled to say that neither in print nor in speech did its members or its officers ever commit an act of indiscretion calling for the animadversion of any kind, or from any quarter. Mr P. A. Taylor one of its most active and efficient members of Committee, was uniformly chosen President of the aggregate meetings of League Delegates, and did great service to the cause by agitating it in the Common Council, and in getting City meetings in Common Hall to petition for free Trade. I refer with confidence to our minute Books reports, and other Documents, for the evidence of the valuable services of Mr Place the Chairman of the Business Committee. Such proceedings, so recorded and arranged, could never have been so conducted without the superintendance [sic] of a vigilant and effective chairman. These Books also are the best testimony of the public spirit, and silent and unostentatious usefulness of such men as Mr Samuel Harrison, T. F. Gibson, R. Ricardo, W. A. Wilkinson and others, who without placing themselves before the public, or in any way of procuring distinction, were always to be found at their post, doing that real business without which nothing effective could have been accomplished.

Such is a naked and meagre memorandum of bare facts in relation to the history of the Metropolitan Anti-Corn Law Association.

Sidney Smith   13 March 1847
London 4, Charlotte Row.

116. [Add. Ms. 35151, ff. 261–3]

To Peter A. Taylor Esq.   July 14 1840
Dear Taylor

Thanks for your letter. The matter is true and well put. Mitchell is a sample of the out and out active leaders of the radical working men of London. There are others much more vehement, inconsiderate and reckless than he is, and many who are less so. Some of the worst among them, unfortunately have the most time to spare and are most active in getting up the dinner in honour of Lovett & Collins.

There was an association, in London, of working men, a small one, which called itself the 'democratic association'. At the head of this was, George Julian Harney, who had been shop boy and cheap publication hawker to Hetherington, it was composed of half crazy not over honest fellows, who abused and quarelled [*sic*] with every body who did not concur with them in every move they made or proposed to make. Some of these men still continue to meet, and they are pushing on the dinner. They are hawking the tickets about for sale and others are helping them. There will be a great assemblage of people and much harm will be done by the countenance they will afford to one another, and the encouragement they will give to the talking of mischievous nonsense.

Great apprehension has been entertained by the Chartists all over Great Britain lest there should be a combination of working people and middle class people, and special pains have been taken in the newspapers which advocate the Charter to keep the breach between these classes as wide as possible and this is still done. There is not however now one paper in London which advocates the Charter, every one has driven itself out of existence, by its perpetual abuse of all who are not working men, and consequently confining the sale to those only among working men who are chartists, and there are not enough of these who are able and willing to support a weekly newspaper. A short time before the dissolution of the Convention Hetherington with some assistance composed a conciliatory address to the public in which he shewed that the working people could not of themselves, in their present state obtain the Charter, and he shewed the necessity for combining as much as possible with the middle class, the Convention adopted the address and published it. This alarmed some of the members, a muster was made and in about a week another address was published, in it pains were taken to offend the middle class who among other imputations were called 'Murderers of the people', 'murderers of society'.

It may perhaps seem strange to you that men who are otherwise sensible and discreet men should fall into and continue in such gross errors, but so it is. The dinner is intended to put the whole affair in its very worst position and it will accomplish the intended purpose. Ill will and malice will be spread further and wider than ever. The middle class have committed a deadly sin, never to be either forgiven or forgotten, and this is the feeling of even the best and wisest among the chartists. The very narrow view they take shuts out all hope of present amendment. It was they say the duty of the middle class to come forward and support the Convention—why say they—why did not the middle class do their duty? Why did not they come forward and join the convention? if they had done so the Charter would now be the law of the land. They still think that the middle class has nothing to complain of, in being held out in newspapers, in addresses, in speeches at public meetings, as 'base, cruel tyrants'—'bloodsuckers—usurers—robbers—murderers' etc. nothing to fear from the perpetual denunciations against their holding property which belonged to the hands which created

215

it, and were about to resume it, but were bound in justice & reason to join the Convention, and for not having done so they are to be punished. The very best among the members of the Convention hold the language of complaint on this account against the middle class people and do not wish that any of them should join them. Argument to shew how impossible it was for the middle class to join the working class is useless. The reply is. 'Well we shall do without them', and to do without them; and against them is the desire of the present leaders. I doubt that there is one man who was a member of the Convention who does not entertain a more rancorous feeling towards the middle class than he did a year ago. For this there is no present remedy and much mischief will be done.

The two great, conspicuous and constantly pervading faults of the working people are Impatience and Intolerance. You saw both in Mitchell. At our April dinner when I was in the Chair I humoured Mitchell and Huggett. They wished the [Radical] Club to present a petition to the House of Commons in favour of Vincent, and they wished the petition to be such an one as they would have caused to be drawn which none of the members would have signed. Now these men like other working men have been too ill educated and have seen too little of the ways of men in associations for business to become either patient or tolerant. The proposal for a petition was to them the whole universe, and excluded every thing else, they could not imagine that any other mans notion could deserve attention. Their notion was to them all important, and hence the petulance, impatience and intolerance manifested by both. Mitchell spoke 13 times, Huggett 9 times. I was offended at the abrupt departure of Galloway and Lawrance, both had been working men, neither of them have acquired any considerable scope of intellect, nor any thing in their demeanour, which could make their contumely pass of[f] easily, it was awkward, out of place and offensive. Men like Mitchell and Huggett want the knowledge of the ways of men which induce them to pay respect to the opinions of one another, and there was an appearance of difficulty which I could only get rid of by allowing them to exhaust themselves, and then to permit me to draw the petition. They were impatient intolerant, and vehemently suspicious of our sincerity and the time was consumed in allowing them to talk down their own misconceptions & absurd apprehensions. It was not time lost, the petition effected more than was expected, and they poor fellows were intitled to the indulgence. I was well pleased to see you indulge them in a similar way at our last meeting though the result was different. Mitchell understood the men he was acting with, and fully concurred with them, he had no disposition to join with us in any proposition, and dared not to have done so even had he wished. Depend upon it he had so completely cajoled himself as not in the least to understand us, and will be surprised when I on some occasion shall tell him of his bad conduct in writing the paragraph for the Northern Star.

Apply what I have said to any matter in which you may be engaged with such men, attend to what they say as indicating what they think but mean to conceal; observe what they applaud and what they condemn and you will discover that Impatience and Intolerance are the especial vices which govern them. In the present case the whole proceeding is bad. Besides my intercourse personally with some of the committee I have applied to the committee by letters, and have represented the danger to Lovetts health, and the probable injury to the reputation he has acquired which should be turned to account to enable him to maintain his family, the danger the language which some will use at the dinner to a subscription which I am raising for him, and the still greater danger of mischief from the Commissioners of Stamps. Lovett was one of the securities to the Stamp Office for advertisement duty for the Charter Newspaper. He being in prison that paper was allowed to run into debt, or was rather pushed into debt in every possible way with every possible person and terminated in a disgraceful swindle. Sometime since I caused enquiry to be made at the Stamp Office and found that Lovett was liable for a debt of £61 and some costs in a Law suit against Hartwell. I am negotiating for his release from this claim and I represented to the committee that nothing should be done until I was able to get the matter adjusted, not the least attention has been paid to the request, though Mitchell, Moore and others who are members of the dinner committee were also members of the newspaper committee and knew how this affair stood, before I wrote to them. The notice was given to them before our Club dinner, of course before the vituperative paragraph for the Northern Star was written.

Mischief is brewing. About 6 months since, fearing there would be a mischievous reaction, Dr Black and I set to work, quietly to revive the London Working mens Association, in the hope that as we should be able to assist them with some money and put them at the head of such associations into a similar but more respectable condition than they were in when the Brumagem men pushed in and caused the mischief, which now presses heavily in several respects. The men think our proposal will not do, it will move too slowly for them. There must be more activity, more bustle, to stand in the place of making progress, and our project has failed. There are however no less than 6 projects to obtain the Charter at once, from four of them I have been addressed, each has a plan, utterly illegal in all its parts. I have written to each shewn them the law and the '*transportation*' they will risk if they go on, and I have shewn them that they must, or rather should begin again with the working mens associations, spread them upon one plan every where, make them schools of instruction and teach the multitude, and thus from time to time have cognisance of their actual state, and let one another know what they are about. Not one of them has replied, nor do I expect that any one will, unless they get into danger or difficulty. Nothing of any importance will be done, disappointment will result from every one of the many silly schemes now in embryo, and there will be a pause presently, a death it will be called, but it will be no death, and no consequent resurrection but there will be '*a revival*'. Four of the Scheming sets have invited Lovett to become their secretary, and 6 or 7 places have invited him and Collins to a jollification. Lovett has not learned much if any thing by his imprisonment, he has been worried and like a worried animal, when he is recruited, he will be operated upon by increased excitement of his enemies and the shewey noisy nonsense of his friends.

Yes, we are all infirm of purpose and this it is which gives the enemy the power he has over us.

The Statistical committee and Hume have made a sad mess of their business. I am ashamed of them, but I have long been used to such things, so I let that pass.

The Manchester men are noodles after all, but that too must be let go by, and we must make the most of whatever means we may have.

Wilson says, we shall have a crop above the average, he ought to know best, but I cannot reconcile myself to his prediction, or to the possibility from what I read and hear of their being an average crop however good the season may be.

Come to the rooms on friday, I have ordered the committee to be summoned,

Yours truly

Francis Place

I have cleared myself from every political connection for any particular purpose, Corn Laws alone excepted, and I will embark in no new matter. however large or small, or important or insignificant it may be, unless there should be some really national matter started.

117. [Place Collection, set 56, vol. 12. Jan.–Apr. 1841, f. 321]

London, 183, Tottenham Court Road

Dear Sir, March 1841

The following Address[1] is intended to be submitted to all the leading Chartists throughout the kingdom that we can have access to, in order to obtain their signatures, when it will be printed and published as their joint address; *previous to which it will be considered a breach of honour for any individual to cause its publication.* It is also intended that the persons signing it shall form a provisional board of management for six or twelve months, (as may be deemed advisable,) to aid in forming the association by the sale of cards, or otherwise, after which the board of management is to be elected by the members according to the rules and regulations. By returning this to Mr Lovett, 183, Tottenham Court Road, signed or otherwise, by return of post, you will oblige yours respectfully,

WILLIAM LOVETT
JOHN COLLINS
HENRY HETHERINGTON
JOHN CLEAVE
GEORGE ROGERS
HENRY MITCHELL

118. [Add. Ms. 27821, ff. 328–9]

183, Tottenham Court Road

Sir, 1842

The want of a cheap & commodious place in which the Working & Middle Classes might hold their Public Meetings has long been experienced

---

[1] For text see *Life and struggles of William Lovett*, 202–7.

by all friends to the improvement of the people. The extravagant sums required for the use of our large public rooms prevent meetings from being held in them unless on occasions of great and urgent importance, & then only by those who can command the necessary funds, the consequence is, that the Working Classes, being too poor to hire such places are frequently compelled to hold their meetings in public houses. The members of the National Association have for some time past been endeavouring to provide a remedy for this evil, & have eventually succeeded in obtaining the lease of a large building in a central situation capable of containing upwards of two thousand persons. This place they intend to fit up as a Public Hall, to be used for Public Meetings, Lectures, Discussions, Musical Entertainments, & all objects promotive of the political and social improvement of the people. As this place will require considerable repairs entailing expenses beyond the present means of the Association, they have appointed a deputation to wait upon all those friends who may be disposed to render pecuniary assistance in furtherance of so desirable an object. The persons appointed have therefore requested me to write to you to ascertain your earliest convenience when you can favor [*sic*] them with an interview.

I am, respectfully, your Obed. Serv't,
Wm Lovett

P.S. I have been requested to subjoin the following objects of the National Association, & also to inform you that they have established a weekly periodical, price three halfpence, entitled the 'National Association Gazette'. It advocates the political, social & moral improvement of the people— it is opposed to all monopolies & contends for universal popular education, unconnected with any sect or party

Objects of the National Association

1 To unite in one general body, persons of all creeds, classes and opinions, who are desirous to promote the political and social improvement of the people.

2 To create & extend an enlightened public opinion in favor of the People's Charter.

3 To erect or obtain Public Halls, or Schools for the people, such halls to be used as Schools for the children during the day, & of an evening by adults for lectures, discussions, readings, musical entertainments etc.

4 To establish Normal or Teachers Schools, in such Towns or districts as may be necessary.

5 To establish Agricultural & Industrial Schools for the education & support of the orphan children of the Association.

6 To establish Circulating Libraries, to be sent in rotation from one town or village to another.

7 To print & circulate Tracts & Pamphlets promotive of the objects, as also a national periodical.

8 To offer premiums for School books, & such works as may promote the welfare of the people.

9 To send out Missionaries to explain the views & objects of the Association.

119. [Add. Ms. 27810, f. 1. Rough Minute Book of the Metropolitan Parliamentary Reform Association.]

At a meeting of the Radical Club held at Radley's Hotel, Bridge St., Blackfriars, on Monday the 31st of January 1842, it was resolved;

1st That the club do agitate for the People's Charter.

2nd That the following persons be a committee to consider the best mode of agitating for the Charter.

Francis Place, Peter A. Taylor, Sam'l Harrison, Wm H. Ashurst, John Epps M. D., J. Roberts Black, Col. Thompson, Geo Huggett, Hy Mitchell.

At a special meeting of the Radical Club held on the 7th March 1842, at Radley's Hotel, the committee reported that in their opinion the intention of the Club would be best carried out by concurring with a plan for a Reform of the House of Commons which had been sometime before agreed to by the following persons

Francis Place, J. A. Roebuck, John Travers, E. Frazer, J. Roberts Black, Jos. Philps, Sam'l Harrison, Thos Prout, Joseph Hume, Hy Ellis, Wm Molesworth, Geo. Bubb, John Temple Leader, Wm Geesin, J. C. Hector, Jos. Smith, Stephen Erratt, Dr. John Epps, Joseph Watts, Edward Rainford, E. W. Field.

120. [Add. Ms. 27810, ff. 91–4]

Dear Harrison   Tuesday 15 Feb. 1842

I dare not come to the Radical Club. I regret it very much—and as I can communicate in no other way I claim your serious attention to what follows, in answer to the request contained in your note just now received at 4 p.m.

You liked Sturge's meeting, so did I—because it not only shewed the progress of opinion, but it was conducted much more rationally than might have been expected—the fault however of nearly every active political reformer is, that he mistakes indication for conclusions, acts upon them, is disappointed, vexed, does foolish things and thus plays the game of the *enemy of us all*—the *Aristocracy*.

This has been the case ever since 1776 when Major Cartwright first put reform of Parliament into a form in which it could be entertained to any useful purpose. It never was a matter of any concern to the working classes and of but very few indeed of those who were not either persons of property or what are called public men.

In Nov. 1792 was commenced the London Corresponding Society, whose story I begin to fear will never be told—there now remains no one but myself that can tell it. I have all the documents and publications of the society and much collateral matter of various kinds in pamphlets, books, newspapers, MSS and parliamentary proceedings—but I am called off and occupied with other matters of which none have cognizance, but those I serve and each of these either as an individual or as one of a small body gives himself no concern as to me, in respect to any thing else, and it would be absurd to expect it could be otherwise, whenever therefore any one of the matters I wish to occupy myself with is mentioned each one either wonders why I do not set about it, or why I have not accomplished it, his own affair, or the affair in which he is conversant with me, occupying only a portion of my time and according to his wishes, all the rest is applicable to the special purpose. This I fear must be my case to the end—one only way remains by which it can be put aside and that is now out of my power —namely removing some 3 miles or so farther from town.

The London Corresponding Society was a well organized well conducted business society. Its business consisted in good teaching. It was the first and last of the kind. It was seen by the men in power to be utterly inimical to the domination of the Aristocracy and they resolved to put it down, but even in the time of Pitt, Grenville and Dundas in the days of terror it required seven years to effect the determined purpose of the bitter un-relenting, never for a moment ceasing enmity of the aristocracy to put it out. In 1793–4 they put it down in Scotland by transporting for 14 years three brave Scotsmen and two englishmen who were deputies from the London Society—and by establishing a system which assured every man, that if he dared to shew his thoughts either by speaking or writing in favor of good government or of any approximation thereto—'*Botany Bay*' would be his future residence. This atrocious triumph of tyranny, led the King, Lords and Commons—the Aristocratic conspiracy against the people, to conclude that the people of England were as debased and vile as were the law officers of Scotland. They were not without reason for the conclusion— the numbers of the 'Society against Republicans and Levellers'—the City life and fortune men, whom, if I recollect aright, to the number of 3,000 had signed a declaration not merely to support the conspiracy in any thing informal, but in spirit to put down in any way—the Regicides, the bloody Jacobins, as any man who did not basely submit to their dictum was called —to do which they pledged their lives and fortunes—they had the assistance of Church and King Mobs in many ways but in none so decidedly as in the plundering and burning the house of Dr Priestly at Birmingham, and in a multitude of acts, scarcely less atrocious but smaller in extent. They there-fore seized 11 and indicted 12 men of good character and high intellectual powers, for high Treason or as Earl Stanhope in the House of Lords truly said '*of a Suspicion of a suspicion of high Treason*'. They never doubted that they could make out a case of *constructive* Treason, to which a Jury would say guilty and by the force of their verdict change the government to a despotism—they made a prescription list to commence with, in which among a very large number of others, was it is understood, I believe on sufficient evidence, the name of the present *Earl Grey* and eighty others— they failed—they caused a jury to be occupied during nine successive days in the trial of the worthy, exemplary man Thomas Hardy—the whole force in every way of the Government was employed for a conviction—Law officers conducted proceedings as infamous as any at the worst periods of our history,—the late Lord Eldon as Atty General led the bar—infamous as are many so called legal proceedings to be found in our history and in the State trials, there is not one, which, when the whole circumstances of the case are considered, including the different states of society can be equalled in infamy with the proceedings of 1794—the good man, the quiet harmless inoffensive man, who may be said never to have made an enemy and who certainly never contemplated the doing a wrong to any one was, after a trial which lasted nine days, acquitted. But the men whose thirst of domination could not be assuaged—went on, they brought John Horne Tooke to the bar, his trial lasted six days, but he also was acquitted—still the evil spirit could not be calmed, it brought John Thelwall also to the bar, his trial lasted four days, but he too was acquitted—the remaining nine were arraigned and discharged.

Tyranny was thus foiled and this Society continued its steady honest businesslike cause and after some time increased rapidly—the foul conspiracy then went to work in another way, and the Treason and Sedition Bills of Pitt and Grenville after much opposition both within and without the Houses of Parliament were passed into laws on the 18 Dec. 1795—by these the liberty of the helpless people was greatly circumscribed, and new fangled treasons were enacted—(I was at this time one of the General Committee when in our great committee room the delegates and sub delegates amounted to 120 persons).

Infamous as these laws were, they were popular measures—the people—aye, the mass of the shopkeepers and working people, may be said to have approved them, without understanding them—such was their terror of the French Regicides and democrats—such the fear that 'the *Throne* and the *Altar*' would be destroyed and that we should be 'deprived of our holy religion'—that had the knowledge of the Grand Conspiracy been equal to their desires, they might have converted the government into any thing they wished for the advantage of themselves.

All unauthorised societies were limited in number to fifty persons and this it was concluded would destroy the London Corresponding Society—but not so—the good and true and sensible men who at that time had been appointed to conduct it were neither to be dismayed nor in the least to be put from their purpose, they reorganised the Society anew and it went on —the necessary changes were made, as the Bills became law and tyranny was again defeated, there was no abandonment of purpose, no shrinking in any way—no lowering of tone—no dissention—no one who reads their publications, will say there was the least difference in tone—in no instance could the Atty General the diabolus regis, fix his crooked talons in them— and in those days of persecution, no ex officio was filed, no bills preferred against them for libel—this could not be borne and therefore in 1798 about one hundred men were seized, as smaller numbers were before them, the Habeas Corpus act was suspended as it had before been, the men were committed by the King's Cabinet Ministers to various Gaols and most of them subjected to penitentiary discipline—no legal charge was ever made against any one of them—green bags were presented to both houses of Parliament, containing reports so false, calumnious and altogether infamous as cannot now be believed by any one not intimately acquainted with the circumstances—a new act of parliament was passed to put down all political societies and among these the London Corresponding Society was put down by name and by special enactments.

Why was all this uneasiness? Why did the grand conspiracy fear its existence?—solely because the character of the society was not publicly demonstrative—it did hold public open air meetings, but these excepting two, were only when the conspiracy was legislating against them—they

222

held occasional meetings, (not many) in Taverns, and each of these was called for by some special proceedings of the conspiracy—the character of the Society was good teaching—'Universal Suffrage and Annual Parliaments' were what is usually called its principles—but its especial and never for one moment suspended purpose, was to form a 'Political Public' and continually to increase its number—this made it useful—this made it feared, and its business character made its existence continuous—hence it became unbearable to the grand Conspiracy and hence its extinction.

There had been many Political Clubs and Societies—and many meetings of delegates prior to the existence of the London Corresponding Society. The Six points of the Charter (now so called) were all decided upon as things necessary to good government in April 1780—publicly by the sub committee of Westminster—the six volumes of political papers published by the Rev. C. Wyvill—the 'proceedings of the Society for Constitutional Information'—the writings of Major Cartwright and others, all shew, the desire there was among well informed men from 1780 to 1792 for a 'full and fair representation of the people in Parliament' the proceedings of the many societies that existed in common with the London Corresponding Society, from 1792 to 1798 shew the same desire—the many which have existed since, do the same. In 1836 the Working mans [sic] Association was commenced—this was the first association which can fairly be said to have consisted solely of working men, that proceeded on system—it went on well, it spread its influence in all directions and numerous societies were formed under the names of Working men's Associations—Radical Associations and Universal Suffrage Associations, but it and all of them partook too much of a mere club—this was unavoidable, it and they wanted means, i.e. money in sufficient quantities to become business associations—for its means, it did wonders—when, in 1838 the currency men of Birmingham, disappointed and vexed by their scheme being rejected by government, commenced an agitation for Universal Suffrage, which gradually spread out, so as to include the ballot and short parliaments—and then to the six points of the Charter the currency plan being at the bottom of all—amongst them were men of wealth and influence, they laid down a large plan, acted with great vigour and little judgment—the result was—the farrago of nonsense as a whole, called the '*National Petition*'—the nonsensical and mischievous abortion, called the 'General Convention' and the 'National Rent'—their influence and their vigour, carried the whole body of the working men who were politically associated along with them and amalgamated them into one mass of most deplorable folly, every rational expectation was pushed aside, the Birmingham men were as certain as absurdity could make them, that their scheme of currency would be adopted by government—the working people became quite as certain that the Charter would be the law of the land in a few months, and folly and rashness unequalled was exhibited. All these persons thought as most of the politically associated working men still do, that—noise and clamour, threats, menaces and denunciations will operate upon the government, so as to produce fear in sufficient quantity to insure the adoption of the Charter—they have yet to learn that these notions and proceedings contain no one element of power—that the Government as mere matter of course

223

will, as every Government must, hold people very cheap who mistake such matters, as have been mentioned, for power—in fact, in their political capacity, they have no power whatever, and can of themselves carry no useful political change into effect. They have proved not only as a body but as individuals without one solitary exception that they have not a glimpse of their own, much less of the actual condition or relation of the several portions of society, who must concur, before any great organic change can be even put in progress—proof so demonstrable and so demonstrated to those capable of seeing the whole case, never before was given—it lies in the general refusal to assist in procuring the repeal of the food laws, and especially in the manner in which they have shewn their determination to do wrong from want of knowing how to do right. In their abuse of the Corn Law repealers—in the scandalous epithets they have showered upon them and the middle class as a body and as individuals, which is still but too prevalent—their infamous conduct at many public meetings, all founded on the absurd notion that the Charter could be and can be obtained by themselves alone, and that when obtained they may do as they will. This is no exaggeration, in the least—there is not one speaker, one writer among them, who untill [*sic*] very lately has not labored [*sic*] to make the division between the working people and the middle class people, (and more especially they who advocate the repeal of the Corn Laws) as wide as possible—I speak from facts—I have copies of every publication put forth by or for them, and I can shew, that—each and all, has and have been active in the (to themselves and every body else) bad work—they act from feeling, not from reason, lamentable it is, that it should be so, but so it is— they do not see, they cannot see, that the repeal of the food laws *must* precede the enactment of the Charter—they believe to a man that the Reform bill was a matter of no importance—they do not perceive that the passing of that Bill was a most useful demonstration of popular opinion, they suppose too, that it was carried by the clamour of the working people —few indeed, in any rank, seem to understand the matter—the agitation among the working people was necessary—the exertions of all were necessary, but even these exertions would not alone have prevented the return to power of the Duke of Wellington on the 18th April 1832—it was the quiet operation of the tradesmen and others of London with other places on their bankers, and the fear that the same process would as it was about to be put into practice on the saving banks which caused the return of Earl Grey and his colleagues—this then was an operation of the people upon the aristocracy—upon the grand conspiracy against the people—it was the first of the kind—it was No. 1 and No. 2 must be the repeal of the Corn laws—the aristocracy lost no power over the House of Commons by the Reform bill, it was only changed—the change operated against them for a time, but it was not difficult to foresee how it would act in their favour, when the means of using the power it gave them should be understood— this was foreseen and clearly explained.

The aristocracy feel however that though their power over the House of Commons remains to them, they have suffered greatly in what is to them and to us, matter of great moment—they have lost consequence—and they know well that it is consequence, in a popular sense, which *alone* supports them as a class and that if it was wholly gone they would cease to exist.

This they know well and they will therefore make a stand—a brave one against No. 2—the loss when it must come, will not be like No. 1, but a loss in geometrical progression whose ratio is a high one—they know well too that whatever they lose in this respect can never be recovered—they have another cause too for resistance of smaller moment but yet a powerful one —loss of income—all the agitation—noise etc.—that can be made, will weigh but little with the grand conspiracy, they know that these alone, however general they may be, can effect nothing that they need care for, but the most shrewd and least proud, conceited or ignorant among them are apprehensive that the efforts making for a repeal of the Corn Laws, may lead to an operation like that of 1832—and to this, it should be our purpose to bring it—to this it will probably be brought and when the time has come, that it *can* be put in practise [*sic*] ten days will suffice—to compel an assurance of the total repeal of the food laws.

Look at the whole matter, look at it in all its bearings, and see, as you may, that this may be accomplished, without the Chartists, while they alone, can never have the least chance of carrying the Charter, neither numbers nor any thing which they can do, could in any conceivable case, carry the Charter.

Had the Chartists only kept aloof, and abstained from foolishly alarming the Middle Class, it is probable, that the progress of the repeal of the Corn laws, would be nearer than it is—but it is now well upon its legs, has learned to walk and is beginning to run.

The repeal of the Corn laws must precede the enactment of the Charter. It is now most extensively acknowledged by men of all castes, religious, moral and political, that to tax the people's food, to waste a large portion of the tax raised that the remaining portion may be pocketed by a comparatively small number of men, of whom, almost all are convinced are of no real use to society, is, not only grievous injustice, but practical and extensive robbery of all—more than this too has become known and the knowledge is spreading daily, that the food laws prevent the expansion of trade, commerce, and manufactures—throw out, and keep out of employment, thousands upon thousands of honest well disposed people, at the same time, that it reduces their wages—all this has been urged ever since 1814 when the first attempt at the atrocious laws was mooted to the present moment, but it has only been within the last two years that public attention could be drawn to the facts, but happily as they came to be understood, every one, not actually interested in the evil, who dare do so, will raise his voice against them—this has been brought about by the increase of the evil to an extent which has made it conspicuous to the blindest eyes—the dullest understand the moment it is pointed out or exhibited.

Now then ask yourself, lay this paper before any man, not resolved that he will resist evidence however plainly and condensely stated, and ask him —can these things be said, truly said of the Charter? It stands out, a bold truth, some day to be acknowledged generally, but that is all that it can be for a long time to come—men must be much more rational—much wiser than they are, before they will be able to see what good government consists of, before they will go for the Charter, on the only grounds on which it can ever be obtained—namely—*a sound act of justice*. It never can be carried on the ground on which it was gravely put at a large meeting at Birmingham and has been mooted ever since—namely '*a Bread & Cheese Question*'.

This brings me to our present question. 'What should be done in agitating for the Charter?' The case seems clear, the road one, and one only—and a good, solid, level, broad road it is.

I have shewn that all the parliamentary reform associations, one only excepted were mere clubs, meeting, now and then, to talk, to print an address, to promote a petition and to die away.

The steps to be taken should be the establishment of one association in London, which should have an office conducted by an able, active, energetic but discreet man—who should have as many clerks, as he might find necessary.

He to be responsible to a business committee of the association—the office being open daily would be a central place, where might be efficiently transacted all the requisite business—one material part of which would be an active carefully conducted correspondence with *thousands* of individuals, and the consequent establishment of hundreds of similar associations—the proceedings of every one of which should be made known, weekly, through a common medium, which can as easily as legally be accomplished—if there be a desire for such associations—in other words, if there really be a desire for such an extensive reform in the commons House of Parliament.

To these societies every body generally—nobody particularly should be requested to become a member.

The purpose of all should be, by every means which could be used, to convince every one, that good government consists in all having the right of voting, secured, as its exercise must be, by certain other particulars.

I am satisfied that no other plan can be efficient.

This would be move No. 3—a move of infinitely more importance than all other moves put together.

Move No. 2 will be a sacrifice of dignity, of revenue to some extent, to the aristocracy—Move No. 3 is annihilation to them, it will be a long time before the people necessary to make the change will concur in it—the aristocracy will make an ultimate stand against it & fight it out.

Much has been written and said of our admirable government of checks—yet we never had a government of checks—our government can never be a government of checks—No man can shew that in any one case since the revolution of 1688 it has been a government of checks—It has all along been a grand conspiracy against the people and whenever the house of Commons has made a stand, it has always been in consequence of a dispute between the members of the Aristocracy—and the question has always been which of the disputing parties shall for a time, be dominant.

Lord Grey said he would stand by his order. Lord John Russell said he would oppose whatever measure should be proposed which had a tendency to bring the house of Commons into collision with the House of Lords—He might as truly have said 'You are the tools of the Aristocracy—the

226

would be refractory members must and shall submit'. There is and there will be a majority in this house, who do and will make common cause with the aristocracy and with them compose a grand conspiracy against the nation. Is not this so? has it not always been so—will it not continue to be so, untill the people do really chuse the members of the House of Commons? and when they do, will the house be talked to in this way? will they act as they have and do still act? will they not be in collision with the House of Lords? One only answer can be given—they will, and then what? aye that is the question—who is to give way?—the Commons backed by the people? not they—the Lords? not they—see the beautiful system of checks—things are then brought to a stand still? not they—will the Commons—will the people be stultified? not they—what then? why, the Commons will vote the Lords useless, the people will support them—the army will abandon or shoot them—and there goes the beautiful system of checks. Let no man deceive himself, there can be no checking of a representative body by a body which represents nobody but appears personally to do its own business against the representative body—no all the power must be with the Aristocracy or none—their is no medium, there can be none—Yet our silly chartists have persuaded themselves to believe most firmly, that the mere apprehension, excited by their *talk* and nothing else, will induce these Aristocrats to give them the Charter—oh no—the *training* which must lead to this, has not yet commenced.

And this leads to the next question—has the time come when the training can be commenced? I reply, I do not know, but I am willing to try what can be done, upon the plan, before stated.

I will waste no time in merely meeting to be useless. The first thing to be agreed to, is, what do we mean by Reform of Parliament? I reply—the six points of the Charter—but I object to the use of the word 'Charter'—1st as an inappropriate expression for Acts of Parliament—but 2nd and mainly—as a word brought into disrepute and calculated to impede, if not, to prevent all progress.

Next I object to 'Universal Suffrage' for the 2nd reason—and I would not push aside the means of propagating sound knowledge likely to lead to important results by insisting upon '*Annual* Parliaments'. Here then is what I mean and what was agreed to by those, who signed the book which contains the project, only expressed in a more concise manner.

Metropolitan Parliamentary Reform Association
Objects

1 To obtain for every man of the age of 21 years the right of voting for a representative in the House of Commons.
2 To equalize the number of voters for each such representative.
3 To shorten the duration of Parliament.

Means

Each man shall be registered in some one polling district and no more. To secure to each man this important right it is necessary
1 That each man whether he be the occupier of a whole house or of only some part of a house as a lodger or is a servant or an inmate in any house,

227

who has been rated to some parochial or corporation rate or tax for 6 months, shall be put upon the district voting register in which he resides and upon payment of the voting rate shall receive his polling card.

2 That each man whether he be the occupier of a whole house or of only some part of a house as a lodger or a servant or inmate in any house if he be not rated as before mentioned, may cause himself to be rated to the voting rate and when he has been rated for 6 months and has paid his rate he shall receive his voting card.

N.B. No fee shall be taken, nor no more money shall be levied than is sufficient for the payment of the election expences [sic] in each district.

3 That the country be divided into as many polling districts as there may be representatives in the House of Commons.

4 That the duration of parliament may be shorter but shall not be longer than 3 years.

5 The day of election and of dissolution of parliament to be certain and unalterable by the will of any person or persons.

6 That every man who is eligible to vote, shall be eligible as a representative.

7 That the right of voting be exercised secretly by way of ballot.

8 That each representative be paid for his attendance in the House of Commons.

F.P.

121. [Add. Ms. 27810, ff. 97–8]

Dear Harrison   Monday 21 Feb. 1842
            I sent you a note written yesterday—this may be considered a continuation.

It seems to me that the Committee should make a written report to the Club, to be entered upon their minutes.

It also seems to me that it should be somewhat after the following form.

Your Committee appointed on the (30 Jan.) for the purpose of etc. etc. Report

That having taken the whole matter into their consideration are of opinion that the intention of the Club will be best carried into effect by adopting a plan sometime since proposed and signed by a number of well judging persons. In this plan all the points of the Charter so called are preserved, excepting only that the duration of Parliament is not limited to one year, but cannot exceed three years.

In the plan recommended for adoption by the Club, certain words which have become obnoxious to great numbers of persons are carefully and judiciously avoided—as—

'*Universal Suffrage*' a term very vague in itself, but well understood to mean the right of voting for members of Parliament by every man in the Nation.

'*Charter*' a word which in its usual acceptation has no application for the purpose for which it is used.

'*Household Suffrage*' words which have been used in a very vague manner, and of which the meaning has never been clearly defined.

The words '*Universal Suffrage*' and '*Charter*' and the appellation to those who support the '*Charter*' of '*Chartists*' have been used by nearly all, if not every Chartist Association and at every public meeting of those, denominating themselves Chartists, not only in a vague obnoxious manner, but as words of fearful import, which have as they were intended they should driven away vast numbers of the best informed and most useful members of the community.

Under the name of Chartist well meaning inconsiderate men and other misled men have in very many cases, all over the country from the extreme west to the extreme east and from Brighton in the south to nearly the extreme north of Scotland, denounced every man who is not a working man, applied to him, the grossest epithets and most atrocious intentions and conduct, have threatened them with vengeance and in some places, have proposed plans for the seizure and division of their property—numbers of misled men and others of bad character, under the self denomination of Chartists have gone from place to place and in the most violent manner disturbed and dispersed meetings of various kinds.

That these and other unwarrantable acts—and the countenance and support given to such conduct from time to time by every periodical publication favorable to Chartism—and by every Chartist Association—have as they could not fail to do—and as in most cases they were intended to do, caused the most fearful apprehensions of mischief among the middle classes—whom it would therefore be utterly unreasonable to expect would concur in any plan of reform which retained either of the words Universal Suffrage or Charter.

Every observing, every reasoning man, understands the association of ideas, which certain words give rise to, and no one who has any considerable knowledge of mankind would expect to succeed in any project headed with words, which by their association excited apprehension of evil, and it has in the opinion of your Committee become necessary that in proposing a scheme of suffrage as extensive as are the men of the United Kingdom, the words objected to should be omitted, the more especially as it will be seen that neither of them are at all necessary for the promotion of the most extensive representation of the people in parliament.

Your Committee object to the words Household Suffrage since under any honest definition of the words—they would exclude a large majority of the men of these kingdoms—and because they have become reasonably obnoxious to the political portion of the working people and defraud them of what they justly believe would of all things most contribute to their well being—namely, the power to vote for representatives in parliament.

Your Committee are of opinion that they cannot honestly perform the duty with which they have been charged, by suppressing or in any way paltering with matters of such serious importance to many millions of people—they are confident that these opinions will be countenanced by the Club, and they fully expect concurrence in the opinion they entertain that the reformers of this country have made sufficient progress in correct thinking to hear the truth and to act upon it, however its announcement may be obnoxious to many—they are not in a condition to carry out any extensive plan of reform or to support (if they possessed it) any system of government which should deserve the appellation of 'good government'.

Your Committee have had laid before them a plan of a permanent association for promoting and maintaining the most extensive reform in the Commons House of Parliament.

For the plan, see the close of Report.

Your Committee recommend the adoption of the plan and that as many of your members as chuse shall sign it, and assist to carry it into practise [*sic*].

Your Committee have been informed, that it was, and is the intention of the persons whose names are attached to the plan, that one general association should be formed in London.

That rooms as offices for business, should be taken, a comprehensive yet precise system of business be adopted and a well qualified man of punctual business habits be placed at the head of it, with power to engage from day to day, such assistance as may be found necessary to carry on the concerns of the association with precision & dispatch.

That correspondence should be carried on with *individuals* (not with associations) all over the kingdom, that similar associations should be formed in as many places as possible without delay and increased from time to time.

That the terms on which members may be admitted into associations and the amount of their contributions shall be settled by each association for itself in accordance with the circumstances of each particular case.

That in as much as the matter is of national importance it shall be conducted with the consideration so serious a matter deserves and requires.

That it will not therefore enter into any dispute with any other body whatever, nor with any other individuals, neither will it indulge in imputation or fault finding with any body of men, who may in any manner intend to promote the well being of their fellow men however much they may think the parties mistaken or whatever may be their conduct towards this association or any of its members—but believing their cause to be just, will leave to time and the good understanding of their fellow men to decide upon the conduct of the association—confident that if they act honestly, discreetly and free from all sinister intention, they will progress continually and ultimately succeed in the attainment of their object.

N.B. Means can be adopted to have a weekly communication of what passes in all the associations—by means of a stamped paper which shall not come under the claws of the Lawyers.

P.S. It strikes me (Harrison) that if any thing is published by the Radical Club that it should appear at once as proceeding from the Club without reference to any individual and if therefore the Committee on tuesday determine so, and then call a meeting of the Club—that any paper laid before them should be considered as laid upon the table by an indifferent person.

I am sure it will produce more effect in this way than in any other.

I hope to have some remarks in writing from all who may read the rough drafts.

Hume was here today during two hours—he is most anxious to be doing and he will be at the Club meeting.

Black was here and Hume was told some truths, which he did not like to hear, but he promised to conform. He however without understanding the scope of any argument will be for making alteration in parts, but this he shall not do in any paper of mine—if he will put his propositions on paper, I will give them all the consideration of which I am capable, as I will those of any one else—you, at least will give me credit for not being very fastidious about words nor inapt to receive suggestions and to work them out.

If you determine to print, I suppose the proceeding will be thus

The Committee will decide on some course and agree to recommend it to a meeting to be called of the Club—the Club will decide as to what it will do & if it agrees to print, then the papers will be sent to me for revision and the Committee be ordered to see them printed—probably in octavo and not exceeding one sheet of 16 pages.

(Thanks for your note) Yrs truly   Francis Place

122. [Add. Ms. 27810, f. 100]

Dear Place   Croydon 21 Feb'y 1842

Dr Black gave me yr paper no. 4 today which I have read carefully & entirely approve. I suppose there is a no. 2 & 3 which I have not yet seen. I will send no. 4 to Mr Harrison & tomorrow the Committee meet at my counting house when the matter is [to] be fully discussed.

I think the present time most peculiarly favourable to carry out such a plan as you propose—it will meet the views of all honest Chartists & neutralise the influence & power of such men as Feargus O'Connor who must either join in or make himself comparatively a cypher—it will also induce them to join us in our agitation for the repeal of the Bread Tax & convince them of the sincerity of our intentions.

If a number of our Radical Club will sign such a document I think we should advertise it & the names in the newspapers (communicating it to Sturge & S. Crawford & obtain their co-operation with us) & if funds can be raised (& without that we can do nothing) we should forthwith go to work—either Lovett or the Editor of the Nonconformist would make capital managers, the latter especially who is a capital & effective writer, much more so than Lovett. I have most fears upon the subject of funds— what hopes have you upon that point.

I was, as you were, very much pleased with the unity & enthusiasm of the Conference they were the most glorious public meetings I ever witnessed & I feel a proud satisfaction in the honour conferred upon me of presiding in such an assembly.

You do not say how you are. I hope better & wish you were able to be at our Committee—but you must run no risks—we can at this juncture especially ill afford to lose you & such as you.

Yours dear Place
ever most sincerely
P. A. Taylor

231

123. [Add. Ms. 27810, f. 106]

Dear Place

I have seen Taylor who tells me he has written you chiefly on the subject of Black and his qualifications as Sec'y—he says he shall be guided entirely by your opinion (which he knows will be an honest one) as to his being the most fit—the only other party of whom he has thought was Milne the editor of the Nonconformist. Taylor has some recollections of Blacks neglects etc. more especially in the Craven St Corn law Soc'y, and speaking of this it occurs to me that Col. Thompson on Monday at the Strand read a letter which he had rec'd from Wood a printer for work done in 1836–7 for that defunct soc'y but that the Col. having been Chairman at some one meeting he calls upon him to get the amount for him £9. Of course the Committee all disclaim it—but I told the Col. that I thought he had better speak to you about it—& to let us subscribe rather than let the papers charge us with such arrears—I said I would pay £1—but if so I shall not subscribe this year to our society & I shall give this as the reason—now if Dr Black had to do with this affair at first & never brought it forward as also the former business of the Newspaper Stamp arrear which some of us were called upon last year to pay. I confess it augurs ill for future management but you are the best judge & you will observe that I do not connect Black with these matters having only some faint recollection of his having to do with them.

I have written to Mr Hume briefly explaining what we have done. Taylor thinks he should take the Chair—get the report rec'd & adopted & prepare a resolution recommending an association etc. which may be printed & that names be obtained forthwith. I wish it could be fine enough on Monday for you to be with us.

Yrs etc.
S. Harrison

N.B. Roebuck is in the country & sends an excuse.   3 March 1842

124. [Add. Ms. 27810, ff. 104–5]

Dear Taylor   Brompton March 3 1842

Black is not the man which if I could command the manufacturer of men I would have made for me, but under circumstances I think he is by far the best man we are at all likely to procure. He has more means for the purpose than any one else can have—and he has a very ardent desire to prove that he has the precise habits necessary for the office.

When the Anti Corn Law association was formed it was impossible to lay down precise rules for conducting the business—and when the time came it was impossible to carry them into practice and the association has done less in every department than it would have done had we started with a good organization and with money.

If we start at all in the Reform association we shall have both—since unless we have both, neither you nor Harrison—nor I—will go on with it.

And 1st as to money—an effort must be made to raise £500.

2nd In the mean time an organisation for business can be perfected. It will be our fault if it be allowed to be either deviated from or neglected in any particular.

3 By the time money has been obtained if it can be obtained we shall be ready to call the subscribers together to appoint
    i. a business committee for a year
    ii. The Business committee to adopt the plan of business.
    iii. To appoint a secretary.

If we can proceed thus far we shall be firmly on our legs—I concur with you in thinking that town after town will come in rapidly. If it be not so, then we shall have learned what cannot be otherwise known—that the time has not yet arrived when men are either wise enough to understand their own position or to anticipate the probability of the impending evils—and we must wait let whatever may happen.

If they are wise enough to comprehend their position then we shall get a float and go right ahead.

Yours truly
Francis Place

125. [Add. Ms. 27810, ff. 108–9]

Dear Harrison   Saturday evening 5 Mar. 1842

             I return the so called report you left with me; here are my remarks upon it.

I object to it in toto, as one of these conventional, compromising proceedings, which drivvles [*sic*] down good purposes to nothing.

How stands the matter? Thus.

1 I drew a draft of a report—and gave the reasons why I thought it should be somewhat of the kind I had made it.

2 This draft was objected to as containing references not needed, and because it reasoned on circumstances which could well be omitted.

3 It was therefore cut down in committee, and written instructions were sent to me for another, omitting the objectionable matter.

4 I drew another strictly conforming to the instructions of the committee

5 This has been laid aside altogether, and another written which has all the vices and objections of the first draft, put into the worst possible form.

This is I believe a correct account of the proceedings.

The Report I drew was for the purpose of having upon our Minute Book, an entry which, under any circumstances, all could refer to as a text of our plain honest proceedings.

When it was objected to by the committee, I gave it up at once. This I should not have done, had it been written by any one but myself, and I immediately conformed to the directions of the committee and drew another.

This second draft you informed me was approved of by Taylor.

Without any cause assigned this has been put aside, the directions of the committee evaded, and all the objections made to the first report reinstated, and in the worst possible form.

In paragraph 1 it says, the intention of the Club will be best carried into effect by the formation of a distinct association etc. This is equivocal—does

233

it mean by the Club—or by someby [*sic*] else? If it is intended that the new society should be formed by others, then it should have said so.

Then comes a list of 6 objects. It seems to me to be absurd to put them as they are here put. As I put them, they are in the words of a former agreement which, if any thing is done, MUST be retained. The wording in Black's book was the work of three months consultation and discussion and were the only words to which those who signed them, would consent to put their names. They agreed that they should not be again changed, lest we should have to go through all the disputing again. In Black's book as consenting thereto are the names of Hume, Harrison, Travers, Black, Place, Roebuck, Molesworth, Leader, Philps, Prout, Epps, Rainford, Field, all members of the Club, and thus more members of the Club have signed the plan than will probably attend on Monday at the dinner.

Paragraph 2 avoids the only reason why the words which have become obnoxious notwithstanding the written obstructions of the committee to me, are retained. They are essential, and should not be omitted.

Paragraph 3 It is as absurd as unbecoming to say—'that we respect those who entertain a prepossesion [*sic*] in favour of the Charter'. Not one of us does so. What does any one of us know of any of the body of Chartists, excepting as individuals and these but few—but as we know them by their public acts. And not one of us who is acquainted with their public acts, can respect those whose conduct has been so reprehensible as theirs has been in almost all cases, not to say as might of many—very many of them be said—that they are *atrocious*.

Were this paragraph to become public the noisy, violent, unprincipled O'Connorites would treat it and us as we should deserve. They would call us, in the plainest terms—'*lying imposters*', and caution their followers to have nothing to do with the '*ten more humbugs*'.

The words which compose the latter part of the paragraph are devoid of sense—they have no meaning or I am too stupid to find any.

Paragraph 4 I for one can say I have no fear, because I shall not be frightened nor even surprised at any thing that may happen. But this I can also say, without much or any chance of making a mistake, that if the riotous Chartists, and these are all, or nearly all who have for many months past shewn themselves in public meetings, will—if ever they have the opportunity, make *fearful* work enough. (Vide Cooper & Markham at Leicester)

Paragraph 5 is inconsequent.

'If the Chartists have been violent.' 'The Commons have been negligent.'

Whence we are left to conclude that 'two blacks make a white'—Should we write thus?

Paragraph 6 The reference to the Corn Law League is out of place, is see sawing. The inference that they have effected *no* beneficial change is in bad taste—and equivocal. They have effected *some*, I should say a considerable change—and a very beneficial one, they have made a difficult subject plain, and caused many thousands of people to whom it was obnoxious to entertain it and act upon their convictions. This is the whole, that they could do, and the forerunner of great good. The paragraph is useless, unless it be to shew cause to the Chartists why the League should be repudiated.

Paragraph 10 I—'doubt'—very much—the very best that we can do, by the most perfect organization will be an experiment, to ascertain how far the sort of people who must take the lead before any thing can be accomplished, are disposed to concur, and act together—if they in considerable numbers will act on one simple plan, for some time steadily—all who are worth having of the honest working people will fall in.

Of any argument to work well our committee is a very bad specimen.

I believe—after much serious thinking & conversing with all sorts of people, especially Chartists—and reading at great cost of time, almost every thing that has been published on the movements of *the* people during the last five years—that even the doing as much may remove—'doubt', can be done in no way but that which is contained in Black's book.

The latter part of this paragraph has no meaning.

Paragraph 11 is liable to the charge of ambiguity, and as being an attempt at deception. If the members of the Club—who have not already signed Black's book are prepared to sign that book—why not say the project agreed to by many members and other persons who are willing to assist in carrying the said plan into effect.

The whole report seems to me to be a sad falling away from any thing like a steady purpose, and utterly incapable of being made useful.

F.P.

126. [Add. Ms. 27810, f. 25]

Metropolitan Parliamentary Reform Association,
Office, No 9 John Street, Adelphi, London,

Sir,   1842

We take the liberty to enclose a prospectus and an address by which you will perceive the utility of our proceedings.

The Association was projected more than a year ago, but its establishment was delayed as it was thought the time was not come when it could be proposed with the success which circumstances now promise.

Amongst its most active supporters are Henry Warburton, Esq., Joseph Hume Esq.M.P., John Temple Leader Esq.M.P., William Williams Esq. M.P., Howard Elphinstone Esq.M.P., John Bowring Esq.M.P., John Marshall Esq., Swynfen Jervis Esq., Thomas Potter, Jun. Esq., Messrs. John Travers, Peter Alfred Taylor, Thomas Prout, William Ellis, Francis Place, William Henry Ashurst, Dr John Epps, Samuel Harrison, Richard Taylor.

The plan of the Association while it includes every reformer who desires 'Complete Suffrage' for the people, carefully avoids all the usual causes of ill will and contention amongst reformers.

It will neither take offence at the proceedings of others, not enter into disputes with any, however much its organization or proceedings may be impugned.

The Association to be as eminently useful as it is hoped it will be must make its proceedings as generally known as possible, and inasmuch as what concerns all should have the countenance and support of all. We respectfully apply to you to aid in the good work, by promoting as far as you can, the establishment of similar associations, and by inducing other persons to assist in the same way.

We invite correspondence with individuals, and shall be much obliged by your supplying us with the names of as many persons as possible who may seem to you likely to attend to applications like this now made to you.

All enquiries respecting the establishment of similar associations and the laws relating thereto will be prompty answered.

By order of the Committee

P. A. Taylor	Chairman
J. Robts Black	Secretary

127. [Add. Ms. 27810, ff. 5–8. *Printed.*]

ADDRESS. THE METROPOLITAN PARLIAMENTARY REFORM ASSOCIATION

THIS ASSOCIATION proposes nothing new, nor any thing which has not received the sanction of, and been supported by, many of the best and wisest men of the last century.

This address is made to the men of the present day, in the hope that the plan of Reform proposed by the Association, will be adopted and carried on steadily, until, in due time, its objects shall be peaceably, but fully accomplished.

The first attempt, free from all party bias, to induce the people to concur in efforts to obtain a radical reform of the Commons House of Parliament, was made by the late Major John Cartwright in the year 1776, in a pamphlet entitled 'Take your Choice', which he greatly enlarged and re-published in 1777, heading the title page—'Legislative Rights'.

Speaking of the composition of the then House of Commons, the major says:—

'Whether, indeed, the House of Commons be in a great measure filled with idle school-boys, insignificant coxcombs, led-captains, and toad-eaters, profligates, gamblers, bankrupts, beggars, contractors, commissaries, public plunderers, ministerial dependants, hirelings, and wretches that would sell their country, or deny their God for a guinea, let every one judge for himself. And whether the kind of business very often brought before the House, and the usual manner of conducting it, do not bespeak this to be the case? I likewise leave every man to form his own opinion.'

Speaking of the Election of Members, he says:—'All men will grant that the lower House of Parliament is *elected only by a handful of the commons instead of the whole*, and this chiefly by means of bribery and undue influence. Men who will employ such means are villains; an assembly of such men is founded on iniquity; and, consequently, the fountain of such legislation is poisoned.'

Speaking of the corrupt proceedings of the House, he says:—'This has been, more or less, the condition of our Government ever since we have had long Parliaments We see the same corrupt, or impolitic, proceedings going on in the administration of a Harley, a Walpole, a Pelham, a Bute, a

236

Grafton, and a North; and we see every Parliament implicitly obeying the orders of ministers. Some ministers we see more, some less, criminal; some parliaments more, some less, slavish; but we see all ministers, and all parliaments, guilty; inexcusably guilty, in suffering the continual and increasing prevalency of corruption from ministry to ministry.'

Whether or not the words of the honest patriot be applicable to the House of Commons in 1842, we also leave every man to form his own opinion.

The efforts made by the Major at that time were not lost; his opinions were adopted and acted upon; several noblemen, and many gentlemen, headed by the Reverend Christopher Wyvill, held meetings in various English counties, and appointed delegates, who met in convention, from time to time, at the Thatched House Tavern, and at the St Alban's Coffee House, in St James's.

At the commencement of the year 1780, just sixty-two years ago, a great public Meeting of the Inhabitants of the City and Liberty of Westminster was held, for the purpose of promoting a Reform in the House of Commons, and at this meeting a general committee, consisting of a large number of persons, was elected; this committee met, and appointed a sub-committee, which, in the month of April, made a report to the general committee, in which they recommended:—

1 Annual Parliaments 2 Universal Suffrage 3 Voting by Ballot 4 Equal Polling Districts 5 No Money Qualification of Members 6 Payment of Members for their Attendance.

For each of these six propositions the committee gave satisfactory reasons.

The report was adopted, was printed in very large numbers, and copies sent to every political body in the kingdom, and to very many private individuals.

In the same month, the 'SOCIETY FOR CONSTITUTIONAL INFORMATION' was established in London; at the head of *this society* was

The Duke of Richmond, President

Supported by

The Earl of Derby,	The Earl of Selkirk,
The Earl of Effingham,	Viscount Mountmorres,
The Earl of Surrey,	and Lord Kinnaird;

by eleven members of the House of Commons, all of whom were well known and popular; by a considerable number of gentlemen, many of whom were eminent in various professions; and by many who afterwards became conspicuous for their great talents and eminent services. The number of members was 166.

This society adopted the 'report of the sub-committee of Westminster', reprinted it in great numbers, and distributed it to the utmost extent in their power.

The report, in some cases, with an extension of the duration of Parliaments, was also adopted by several associated bodies of Reformers, and by them distributed.

237

At this time there was no political public, and the active friends of parliamentary Reform consisted of noblemen, gentlemen, and a few trades-men.

Neither these societies nor the other political bodies at that period had any continuous existence; they met occasionally, talked over the concerns of the moment, ordered a tract to be printed or an advertisement to be inserted in the newspapers. Their proceedings were neither adapted for, nor were they addressed to, the working people, who, at that time, would not have attended to them.

Efforts to procure a reform in the House of Commons were made in many places. The number of public meetings and of petitions to the House of Commons increased continually, when the coalition of Lord North and Charles James Fox, in the spring of 1783, caused an opinion to be generally entertained that no faith could be reposed in public men, and suspended all active proceedings in favour of parliamentary Reform; which lingered on, and were, at length, nearly extinguished.

In this state of things, in November 1792, the London Corresponding Society was founded. This was the first attempt ever made to induce the working people to interfere in political matters, which it has ever been contended, they were incompetent to understand. Hitherto, they had never, of their own will, interfered in any political concern, but as supporters of some party or person; and then only as mobs, or as tools, when they were ill-used, or sacrificed to party interest.

The London Corresponding Society was established on a plan for doing business; it soon extended, and was formed into small portions, called divisions; every division met once a week at a time certain, and as much oftener as it pleased. Each division had a secretary, and other officers, to form a general committee, which met once a week. This committee was the legislative body. The divisions also elected five members, who formed the executive committee, which made a weekly report of its proceedings to the general committee. Each division elected a secretary, an assistant secretary, and a treasurer.

The secretaries and treasurer were bound to attend the general com-mittee.*

In its arrangements for business and in some other particulars, the society differed from all others which preceded it, as it did from all which succeeded it, excepting some few of the political unions during the time the Reform Bills were before parliament in 1831–2. . . .

The men who originated and those who conducted the London Corres-ponding Society, did not expect to carry any reform for a number of years; their first business was to form a political public of the middling and smaller tradesmen, and others whose circumstances were similar, and of the working people. This could only be done by giving them such political information as should induce them to detach themselves from the control of political adventurers, and enable them to see their own welfare and the prosperity of their country in a House of Commons, as independent of the aristocracy as it

* The matter has been stated at some length, as it was against this organization that the Acts of 1795, 1798, and 1817, were especially directed.

238

could be made. They, therefore, confined their agitation to the two points only which, under their circumstances, were the most easily understood, and the most likely to be adopted, namely:—

1 Universal Suffrage; and,
2 Annual Parliaments.

In 1793, the Society sent two of its members as delegates to a convention about to be held at Edinburgh, where one had previously met; several of the delegates, including the two from the Society, were seized, tried on charges of sedition, and transported for fourteen years.

That atrocious stretch of power terminating so favourably to the government, induced them to expect that London juries would follow the example set by the Scotch courts; and, making too sure of their victims, they, on the 12th May, 1794, seized *eleven* men, nearly all of whom were members of the London Corresponding Society, and caused these men, of unexceptionable conduct in life, to be indicted for high treason. Three of them were tried at the Old Bailey, and acquitted; and the remainder were discharged from the close confinement to which they had been subjected during seven months.

This was a great mortification to ministers, and compelled them to abandon their list of proscriptions, of the existence of which no doubt has been entertained, and, with it, their project for further abridging the freedom of the people.

Disappointed and vexed beyond endurance, the bad Government, at the head of which were Pitt, Grenville, and Dundas, the session in the Autumn of 1795 was commenced by the introduction of two bills, one in the Lords by Lord Grenville, enacting 'new-fangled treasons'—the other in the Commons, by Mr Pitt, enacting new seditions, and both for the purpose of coercing the people to the greatest possible extent. Pitt's Bill limited the number of persons who should be permitted to meet for any political purpose to fifty, and thus extinguish the London Corresponding Society; but ministers were again to be disappointed; the Society altered its arrangements, and conformed to the law; rapidly increased its numbers and its importance, and was gradually forming a political public. This could not be borne, and, therefore, in 1798, ministers again 'exerted a vigour beyond the law'; they caused a very large number of persons to be seized, and confined them in various prisons; they suspended the *Habeas Corpus* act, and these persons, against whom no offence could be alleged, were detained in prison nearly three years; they were then discharged, without trial or public inquiry.

A Bill was laid before Parliament, and, with the same indecent haste with which that to suspend the *Habeas Corpus* act had been passed, the two Houses of Parliament passed the bill to put down political societies, naming the London Corresponding Society as the society especially to be extinguished.

All the stringent enactments of that bad law were re-enacted and made more stringent by Lord Castlereagh's Act of 1817.

These acts do not, however, forbid the existence of associations for procuring a reform of the House of Commons; and this Society will conform to the Pitt and Castlereagh laws, bad as they are, and disgraceful to the nation as is their continuance in the Statute Book.

From the commencement of the London Corresponding Society to the present time, there has been a steady increase of political knowledge among all ranks of people.

The lessons so carefully and wisely taught by the London Corresponding Society, have been well learned by vast numbers of people; and, notwithstanding the late irregularities of bodies of men whose information is still imperfect, the strong conviction that the future prosperity of the people must depend upon their having a House of Commons, fairly elected by the whole body of the people, has continually increased, and is increasing.

It was expected that the Reform Bill, brought into Parliament in 1831, would put an end to the corruptions of the House of Commons; but in the progress of the bill through the House, clauses were inserted in it which, together with the small number of electors in very many of the boroughs, made the elections of members mere matters of *influence* and *money*; and the House of Commons is now as corrupt as it was when in the power of the boroughmongers before the Reform Bill was passed in 1832.

The unjust laws which the corrupt House of Commons have suffered to remain, have prevented the improvement of agriculture, limited trade, commerce, and manufactures, and, consequently, reduced the employment of the people and the real amount of their wages; they have destroyed the small comforts of millions, deprived hundreds of thousands of a portion of their food, the forerunner of disease and death, and compelled them to believe that no remedy for any of these evils can be found but in a House of Commons elected by the whole people.

The extent of information amongst the people appears to warrant the conclusion that the time has come when Associations, to procure a thorough Reform of the House of Commons, may be formed, without reference to classes or parties, and free from any particular denomination, excepting that of parliamentary Reformers. That such associations may be expected to be very numerous, and be composed of every rational man, who wishes for good government, to promote and sustain the well being of the people.

A plan, which, while it can give no offence to any person who really believes that a House of Commons truly representing the people is necessary to their welfare, has been adopted by several public men, and others; an Association will be commenced immediately, and the good work carefully, honestly, and vigorously carried on.

The plan of the Society is as follows:—

METROPOLITAN PARLIAMENTARY REFORM ASSOCIATION

Objects:—

1 To obtain for each man of twenty-one years of age the right of voting for *a* representative to serve in the Commons House of Parliament.

To secure to each man this important right, it is necessary—

That every man, whether he be the *occupier* of a whole house, or a *lodger* in some part of a house, who has been rated to any parliamentary, county, municipal or parish rate for six months, shall be rated to an election rate, and be put upon the voting register, for the polling district in which he resides; and every such person, so qualified, shall receive his voting card, entitling him to vote at all elections within that district.

That every man, whether he be the occupier of a whole house, or a lodger in some part of a house, or a servant or inmate, not being rated as above directed, shall have the right to cause himself to be rated to the election rate; and when he has been rated for six months, he shall be put upon the voting register for the polling district in which he resides, and every such person so qualified, shall receive his voting card, entitling him to vote at all elections within that district.*

2 That the country be divided into as many polling districts, as there may be representatives in the House of Commons.

3 That the duration of Parliaments may be shorter, but shall not be longer than three years.

4 That every elector shall be eligible to be elected.

5 That the right of voting for a representative shall be exercised secretly by ballot.

6 That each representative of the people shall be paid for his services.

For the purpose of carrying this plan into effect generally, it is necessary that a sufficient amount of money be raised, to enable the Association to take rooms in an eligible situation for offices.

To employ a well-qualified man to act as Secretary.

To employ as many assistants as may be necessary to carry on the business with precision, punctuality, and energy.

To correspond with as many *individuals* in every part of the country for the purposes of the society, and for the promotion of other similar societies in as many places as possible.

To devise and carry into effect a plan, by which a weekly account of the proceedings of every such society may be published, and thus to make the proceedings of all known to all, without in any way breaking the obnoxious laws which limit the intercourse of reformers in different parts of the country.

It is believed that the time has arrived when this comprehensive plan of Parliamentary Reform will be acceptable to very large numbers of persons in every part of the country, and that it will be eminently successful.

One great advantage of the plan, is its easy adaptation to every man's means, inasmuch as the rate of subscription of each particular society, to support its necessary expenses, may be made to conform to the particular circumstances of the Members and of the locality. No expense can be incurred in any society, unless it originates within the particular Association, and at the will of the Members thereof.

By order of the Committee,

Office, 9 John Street, Adelphi   P. A. Taylor, Chairman
1842   J. Roberts Black, Secretary

---

* 'No more money to be raised by the election rate than may be found necessary to defray the legal charges of returning a representative to parliament for the particular election district.'

128. [Add. Ms. 27810, ff. 203–4. *Printed.*]

THE METROPOLITAN PARLIAMENTARY REFORM ASSOCIATION TO
THE PEOPLE OF GREAT BRITAIN
FELLOW COUNTRYMEN,

The Reform Bill has been tried for ten years.
Four General Elections, and a number of intermediate contests have
fairly and fully brought it to the test of experience. And what has it done
for you? Are you represented? Have you obtained the long desired blessings of good and cheap government? The very questions seem like a
mockery.

In the worst days of the unreformed Parliament, the great mass of the
people never were further from the possession of their rights, and the
enjoyment of legislative security for their interests, than they are at the
present moment. Never was the country more entirely under the domination
of a class. The landed proprietary overrides both the political parties in
Parliament; untaxing itself, and taxing all others, at its own sovereign
pleasure. We are enthralled in a sordid slavery, of which the worst feature
is, that it can be enforced under the forms of a reformed representation.
Nay, it is through the agency of those forms that the landed oligarchy has
attained its absolute and unprecedented ascendancy.

Such is the reward of the magnanimous efforts by which you neces-
sitated a change in the old system of corruption and nomination. That
a change took place, was your work. In May 1832, the Whig Ministry
shewed its weakness, and the Court its treachery. But the political unions
mustered in their strength; the people every where evinced their determination, and their energy; the momentary triumph of corruption was baffled;
and the Bill was carried,—which has disappointed all your just expectations.

What have you got by the Reform Bill? In the first Parliament elected
under it, an overwhelming majority for the Whig Ministry was returned.
And what did that majority do for you? It passed the infamous Irish
Coercion Bill; a measure worthy of the worst days of Pitt and Castlereagh.
It left untouched the atrocious laws against popular meetings and associations. It voted the continuance of flogging in the army, and of impressment
in the navy. It peremptorily refused the Ballot, and proclaimed the anti-
reform and absurd doctrine of finality. These were the first-fruits of the
Reform Bill, while the popular enthusiasm that procured its enactment was
yet unabated, while Toryism was yet stunned and prostrate; and while the
authors of the Bill had ample power to carry through Parliament whatever
it pleased them to propose.

What did you get by the Reform Bill when the crisis came of a Tory invasion of the Government in 1835? The demon which politicians dreamed had
been laid for ever, arose and stared you in the face. What power confronted
this prompt and insolent attempt? The new system gave a majority of just
ten votes against the old oppressors. That paltry majority sufficed to
restore the Whigs to office, and it also sufficed to show that you had gained
no security against misgovernment. The feebleness of the ministry became a

constant apology for disgraceful concessions to Toryism; it never acted as a motive for the extension of popular rights. Even in what was called the Repeal of the Taxes on Knowledge, there was a spirit analogous to that of Sir Robert Peel in his proposed revision of the Corn Laws; the working people were deprived, by severe restrictions, of such publications as had circulated amongst them; and the daily press was preserved, an untouched and inpenetrable monopoly.

Another election came, in consequence of the demise of the king. The Whigs had now the advantage of court favour. But the result was, the same little majority; the same vacillating and imbecile conduct. What did you, the People, gain by the last Parliament, the third under the Reform Act? What one great measure in your favour did it entertain? Its course ended by rejecting even a Government proposition, for partially, and only partially, untaxing your daily bread.

And now, the last election has delivered you up, bound hand and foot, into the power of those who seem disposed to turn the screw so long as a drop of blood is to be squeezed out of your veins. Tory faction and landed oligarchy are triumphant and uncontrolled. So much for the working of the Reform Bill of 1832. Is it not time we had another, and a better?

The causes of this miserable failure may be easily traced. The Reform Act never realized even the limited extent of the Elective Franchise it professed to establish. Two large classes of dependent or corrupt voters were added to the original scheme,—the corrupt freemen of corporate towns, and the agricultural tenants-at-will. Protected by the Ballot, both might have voted honestly, and been practically taught political integrity. Without such protection, they have unavoidably become the tools of the profligate wealthy. Over other classes of voters, all the corrupt influences have been preserved in their full force. To these have been added the expense and annoyances of a complicated and vexatious system of registration. Some have been disfranchised, and others enfranchised, no one could tell why or wherefore. The rights and duties of citizenship are surrounded by a hedge of thorns; the money power, which is the power of corruption, guarding the only access. Venal boroughs, with small numbers of electors, have sprung up to supply the place of nomination boroughs; and have been defended by the authors of the Reform Bill, on the same grounds and with the same arguments. There has been no representation of the people; nor can there be under the present system. In its practical working, it has given various results; a large majority for Whigs; an even balance of parties; and a large majority for Tories; but it has never given a real House of Representatives, guarding and extending the rights of the people, and promoting their interests.

The time, then, is come to demand a new Reform Bill. In the statement of the objects of the *Metropolitan Parliamentary Reform Association*, we have described the provisions which, in our opinions, would secure a true and full representation. It is inconceivable to us that the existence of a slave class should be necessary to national freedom. We aim at obtaining a vote for every man, free voting, proportionate representation, and responsible Parliaments: that the nation may be well-governed. It cannot be worse governed than it has been by factions. Even the authors of the

243

Reform Bill compromise, must now feel that it is a failure. After progressively changing the relative position of parties in favour of Toryism, its last result has been to give a commanding majority, for the express purpose of upholding a bread tax. Do you require further demonstration? The present Government and Parliament bid fair to furnish it.

People of Great Britain, are you content with this state of things? If you are, we can only make our own solitary and unavailing protest against a policy which threatens with speedy destruction our commercial and manufacturing interests, starving the workman, and ruining the capitalist; against a class ascendancy, which sacrifices the many to the few, and permanently impoverishes the nation for the sake of temporarily enriching the landowners; against a legislation in which every great public object is made subordinate to the tactics, and the ambition of political parties; and against a nominal representation, the root of all these evils, which distinguishes the privileged from the enslaved, by no plausible or consistent test whatever, but trampling upon principle, makes a mockery of the forms of freedom, and debases humanity in the name of all that should secure its elevation and its progress.

For you, People of Great Britain, we demand a real Representation. It is for you to decide whether we do it effectually, or only so as to clear ourselves by denouncing a servility, degradation, and ruin, the tide of which we cannot stay. It is obviously vain any longer to put your trust in political parties; or to seek relief from the guidance of party leaders. The folly of compromising measures is amply demonstrated by experience. There is no hope but in the simple, broad, first principles of representation. They are our watch-word; whoever shrinks from it, or whoever abuses it. They are our standard, and we nail it to the mast. For real representation we associate; for nothing else, and nothing less. The nation has no other hope. Without it, the millions of this great people, so long esteemed an heroic race, have no chance or prospect but that of being plundered, cheated, insulted, spurned, despised, and ruined. Will you associate with us to work out our deliverance? We will shew you how to do so legally. If you come forward like men, we cannot but do so triumphantly.

Union is strength. Let us fairly try its force. We need no arms, no illegal combination, no secret confederation. Our objects and plans, our numbers, proceedings and determination, will all be bared to heaven and earth. It is for those who are ashamed, or fearful, or intent on sinister purposes, to shun the light. With us, the end and the means are alike honourable. We seek the freedom of a citizen for each, and the prosperity of a community for all. Join with us; arouse yourselves, People of Great Britain! in a spirit worthy of your national character; associate, with the resolve never to relax or compromise, until you have a complete, free, and equal Representation; and the day of triumph over the sordidness of faction, the servility of forms, and the insolence of aristocracy, will not be far distant.

By order of the Committee,
Office, 9, John Street, Adelphi,   P. A. TAYLOR, *Chairman*
15th April, 1842   J. ROBERTS BLACK, SECRETARY

129. [Add. Ms. 27810, f. 28]

9 John Street, Adelphi
May 7th 1842

Sir,

The subjoined list, in which your name is included, is proposed for the General Committee of the Metropolitan Parliamentary Reform Association for the current year.

Should you have any objection to your name standing as one of that Committee, will you have the goodness to inform me of it by Tuesday Evening next.

I am Sir,
Your obedient Servant,
J. Roberts Black

Ashurst W. H.	Harrison Samuel	Rogers L.M.
Brown, F.C. M.P.	Huggett Geo.	Saul W.D.
Bowring Dr M.P.	Hewett Thos	Smith James
Boothby B.	Hodgskin Thos	Scholefield J. M.P.
Courtauld Sam'l	Jervis Swynfen	Tayler P.A.
Charlwood Geo.	Leader J. Temple M.P.	Travers John
Cumming Wm	Marshall John	Tayler Rich'd
Ellis Wynn M.P.	Mottram E.	Trott Wm
Ellis William	Miall E.	Theobald Wm
Elphinstone Howard M.P.	Prout Thomas	Tayler P.A. junior
Epps Dr	Place Francis	Warburton Henry
Field E.W.	Phelps Joseph	Williams Wm M.P.
Gibson, T.M. M.P.	Radnor Lord	Webber Thos
Hume Jos. M.P.	Roebuck J. Arthur	Westerton Charles
Heppel G.H.	Revell Henry	Crawford W. Sharman M.P.
Hetherington H.	Mitchell Henry	

130. [Add. Ms. 27810, f. 29. Meeting of the Committee of the Metropolitan Parliamentary Reform Association, 19 May 1842.]

Secretary reported that he had sent out 47 circulars to persons nominated on the General Committee, 41 of whom had consented to serve.

That he had sent out 923 general circulars enclosing No. 1 and 2 printed papers, and read an abstract of the answers already received, which are very favourable.

That he had called, according to a list handed in by him, upon a number of persons for donations without much success.

131. [Add. Ms. 27810, ff. 39–42. Metropolitan Parliamentary Reform Association.]

At a meeting of the Business Committee held at the office of the Association on Friday June 3rd 1842, there were present:—Francis Place (in the chair), P. A. Taylor, S. Harrison, H. Hetherington, J. R. Black

245

The business sheet being laid before the chairman, and the minutes read and confirmed.

1 The Secretary laid before the Committee the address of the Association to the inhabitants of Nottingham, which was read, and ordered to be sent immediately with a number of the printed papers no. 1.2.3.

2 The Secretary read the titles of the newspapers as far as has yet been ascertained who had noticed the proceedings of the Association,

Favourably. Weekly Dispatch, Morning Advertiser, Spectator, Examiner, Morning Sun, Evening Sun, British Statesman, Bell's Life in London, National Association Gazette, Morning Chronicle, Globe, Cambrian, North Staffordshire Mercury, Stockport Chronicle, Gateshead Observer, Doncaster Gazette, Hull Rockingham, Suffolk Chronicle, Leceistershire (*sic*) Mercury, Welshman, Sheffield Iris, Aylesbury News, Kent Herald, Hampshire Independent, Gloucester Journal.

Unfavourably. Morning Post, Yorkshire Gazette,

3 A list of letters received was read as follows:—

From Geo. Burton, Stamford sending a list of names of active men in that place.

From Sir John Morris, Skilly Park, agreeing on the necessity of a union of all classes for a Reform of the House of Commons, but being as yet unwilling to extend the Suffrage as far as the Association proposes.

From Mr Beadon, Taunton sending a list of names, and stating that he & others are busy in establishing an Association.

From Thomas Gibson, Morpeth sending names, and engages to go to work to persuade the chartists there to join him in cooperation with us.

From E. Clarke, Snaresbrook, sending names, & expressing his great interest in the movement.

From P. R. Arrowsmith, Bolton, sending names, and will endeavour to establish an Association there.

From J. Noble, Boston, sending names of active reformers there.

From Geo. Lea Pringrose [?], Cambridge, expressing strongly his approbation of our plans & promising to aid in Cambridge.

From Thomas Thompson, Bishop Wearmouth, sending names, saying chartists are very strong there.

From Provost Little, Annan, saying that they are about to form an Association there, a provisional committee being appointed composed of half electors & half non-electors.

From J. Lotherington, Sunderland, sending names of active reformers, & saying the prejudices against chartists operate for the moment against the formation of an Association there.

From J. Holebrooke, Slateford, sending names of active reformers, and will assist.

From S. Donkin, Bywell, Northumberland, sending names of active reformers & will try to form an Association & do any thing in his power for that county.

From Wm Thomason, a delegate of late Chartist Convention, now on a Chartist tour, favourable to our Association.

From C. Phillips, Bridgenorth, who will endeavour to form an Association there.

From J. D. Bassett, Ilfracombe, offering a donation of £20 & promising active aid in Devonshire.

From Sir F. McKenzie, Chateau Talhoiret, France, respecting the system of French Electoral Colleges.

4 The Secretary reported that he had held a second meeting of the Lecture Class on Thursday evening, when three more members had been added to the class, making now 11.

Also, that Mr Prout was to make arrangements for a Lecture at Wandsworth; that P. A. Taylor jun'r had agreed to lecture for the Association, and that Jonathan Duncan, had likewise agreed to do so, and would go to Deptford to arrange with Mr Wade, for delivering a lecture there, and that it was probable Mr Roebuck would agree to deliver a lecture at the Crown & Anchor.

And that, some doubts having been raised as to the legality of lecturers going forth by authority of the Association, he had written to Mr Roebuck & since waited upon him, as counsel of the Association, for his opinion.

5 Mr Hume's letter to the Secretary, Mr Hume's letter to Mr Prout, and Mr Prout's letter to Mr Hume, were read, and ordered to [be] placed together in the letter book (see letter book p5) The secretary was directed to write to Mr Prout requesting him to press Mr Hume for an answer to his letter.

6 The Secretary reported that he had made applications to nearly all those gentlemen who had not yet paid their donations.

7 Mr Huggett's report was read. Friday visited 17 persons, with no result. Saturday visited 26 persons, with no result. Monday visited 32 persons, with no result except 2 declining. Tuesday visited 17 persons, with no result, except one declining. Wednesday visited 22 persons, of whom one will be a member, 4 decline, & 17 as yet no result. Friday visited 21 persons, of whom 9 will be members, 1 declines & 11 as yet no result.

8 Accounts were examined & passed, the expenses for the week being £12–13–1.

Adjourned.   [signed]   Francis Place.

132. [Add. Ms. 27810, ff. 55–6. Metropolitan Parliamentary Reform Association.]

At a meeting of the Business Committee on Monday March 6th 1843. there were present:—Francis Place (in the chair) P. A. Taylor, S. Harrison, J. Robts Black.

The business sheet being laid before the chairman and the minutes confirmed.

1 The secretary read the annexed report. [Missing]

2 The accounts were examined & approved.

3 Cheque No. 33 was drawn for Forty seven Pounds, 17/11 signed by F. Place, P.A. Taylor & J. R. Black.

4 Cheque No. 34 was drawn for Fourteen Pounds 14/- & signed by F. Place, P. A. Taylor & J. R. Black.

5 The following outstanding accounts were ordered to be paid.

Mitchell	for printing	£4 . 3 . 0
Crozier	do	3 7 0
Sabberton	do	5 6
Stratford	do	8 0
Austin	do	3 6
Silvester	do	1 4 6
Waterlow	do	10 0
Westerton	do & stationery	1 8 0
Mudie	newspapers	17 6
Purdon	do	18 0
Stiles	hire of seats	15 0
Bowket	hire of room	5 0
Ball	posting bills	9 0

6 The secretary was directed to write to the auditors requesting their attendance at the office of the association on Thursday next at one o clock to audit the accounts of the association.

7 Mr Place undertook to audit them previously, that he might be able to answer for their correctness should the auditors fail to attend on next Thursday.

8 The secretary was directed to summon all the members of the association who had paid their subscriptions, to a General Meeting, on Friday next, at 12 o'k precisely, to consider the propriety of dissolving the association.

9 The secretary was directed to prepare an address in anticipation of the dissolution of the association.

10 The ballance [*sic*] of cash on hand after paying outstanding accounts, and rent becoming due, with the proceeds of the furniture if the association be dissolved, to be paid to the secretary as all he is to receive for the settlement of his unpaid salary.

133. [Add. Ms. 27810, ff. 56–8. Metropolitan Parliamentary Reform Association.]

At an adjourned special general meeting of the association, held at the offices, on Friday Mar. 17th 1843, to consider the propriety of dissolving the association there were present:—H. Warburton Esq. in the chair, F. Place, P. A. Taylor, Samuel Harrison, Thos Prout, Geo. Beacon, J. Lyon, C. Elf, J. Dawes, J. Duncan, Dr Wade, A. Morton, C. Westerton, B. Wills, W. D. Saul, Dr Bowkett, Dr Latzky, Muntz, J. B. Brown, J. R. Black.

1 The accounts up to Mar. 4th as audited by W. Williams Esq. M.P. were examined. Mr Place requested that any member not satisfied would ask whatever question he liked relating to the accounts in order that the most satisfactory explanations might be given. After some questions and explanations, and the Secretary had read the 10th entry of the last mtg of Bus. Com., the accounts appearing satisfactory to the meeting they were passed.

2 The Secretary was directed to read the Report of the Business Committee, narrating the proceedings of the association, & recommending its discontinuance till circumstances arise more favourable to the prosecution of its objects.

3 Mr P. A. Taylor moved 'That this Association be dissolved'. Mr F. Place, seconded the motion.

4 Mr Prout opposed to the dissolution & would move an amendment, which Mr Wills seconded. 'That a committee be appointed to procure an Honorary Secretary, & to make arrangements for the occasional meeting of the association, at some room not incurring any considerable expenses.'

After much discussion the amendment was substituted for the resolution of Mr Taylor.

5 When Mr Warburton proposed that the resolution should be shaped differently, to which the meeting assented. And it was resolved 'That the meetings and expenses of this Association be for the present discontinued.'

'That a committee be appointed for the purpose of finally auditing and paying the outstanding accounts.'

'That the present Business Committee, with Messrs Wade & Beacon be the committee.'

6 Mr Prout then moved and Mr Duncan seconded 'That a committee be appointed to procure an honorary secretary and to consider further proceedings, with a view to occasional meetings in order to be in readiness for action when necessary', which was carried; the following gentlemen being appointed the committee: Thos Prout, Dr Wade, Dr Latzky, Mr Mentz [sic], Mr Morton, Jon. Duncan, Dr Bowkett.

APPENDIX

(See document 105)

[Add. Ms. 27820, ff. 382–3. *Printed.*]

AN ADDRESS FROM THE PROVISIONAL COMMITTEE FOR THE ESTABLISHMENT OF A WEEKLY NEWSPAPER, ENTITLED THE CHARTER, DEVOTED TO THE INTERESTS OF THE WORKING CLASSES, THE PROFITS OF WHICH ARE TO BE PLACED AT THEIR DISPOSAL.

Of all the various instruments for promoting the great interests of society, and carrying forward the work of civilization and social happiness, there is none at once so potent and so generally available as the Newspaper Press. It dispenses knowledge at the same time that it supplies motive for action; it appeals alike to the judgment and the feelings; and by commanding a wide sphere for its operations—by introducing itself into the privacies of domestic life, and inciting and rewarding the thirst for novelty common to all men, it unobtrusively and imperceptibly changes the aspect of social life, and implants new elements in society.

But it is not only as an instrument of good that the Newspaper Press may be employed, it has a like potency for evil; and in the hands of bad men it may become the means of diminishing, instead of augmenting, the sum of human happiness.

When the Newspaper Press is employed for party purposes—for advancing the objects of particular classes—for securing political or civil immunities for any one section of society, at the expense of the rest—for creating or maintaining monopolies, commercial or political—for giving an undue preponderance to capital over labour, by artificially increasing the power of the one, and unjustly curtailing the rights of the other—for promoting and protecting combinations *against* the people, and assailing, maligning, and deprecating union *amongst* them;—in a word, whenever the Newspaper Press is employed to separate the interests of society as a whole, and to secure for one class immunities and enjoyments not equally distributed amongst all, it then becomes an instrument of surpassing evil, disorganizing the community, and creating and calling into active operation all those malificent influences, social and political, which have in bye-gone times involved states and empires in intestine wars and ultimate ruin.

It would not comport with the necessary brevity of such an Address as the present, to inquire in how far the present state of society, and of the working population in particular, is attributable to the misdirection of the Public Press. Suffice it to say, that every class, *save the labouring class*, has its representative in the Newspaper Press. Commercial capitalists, the monetary classes, the shipping interest, the legal and medical professions, and jobbers and speculators of every description, find in this the ready and powerful instrument for advancing their own immediate objects, and for modifying the proceedings of the legislature and the government in their favour.

Why are the Working Classes alone destitute of this mighty auxiliary? Their numbers, their intelligence, their thirst for knowledge, and, above all, their multifarious grievances, and the necessity for well sustained self-exertion, in order to effect their removal, render the possession of such an instrument of self-advancement and social and political emancipation, of all objects the most desirable.

The Newspaper Press, daily and weekly, is the property of capitalists, who have embarked in the enterprise upon purely commercial principles, and with the purpose of making it contributive to their own personal and pecuniary interests. It is the course that is *profitable*, therefore, and not the course that is *just*, which necessarily secures their preference. So long as it is deemed compatible with the main object of newspaper capitalists to advocate the claims and interests of the labouring classes, will that advocacy be afforded; when it ceases to be so considered, it will be at once abandoned. It may and does happen, therefore, that many a time when the working population stands most in need of a free organ of communication, a broad shield of defence, or an active weapon of attack, that one upon which their reliance is placed will wholly fail them; and not unfrequently has it, in the day of their utmost extremity, been handed over to their antagonists.

But, let it be supposed that no such unfavourable contingency attached itself to the existing Newspaper Press; it is, nevertheless, obvious to ask, why so large and really powerful a section of society, as that constituted by the labouring classes, should consent to remain in a position which compels them to receive as a favour what they might secure as a right? Why should they not—like the other and more favoured classes in society—have their own Press, instead of being reduced to a passive and humiliating reliance on the Press of those who can have but little sympathy with their wants or wishes, and who only render them service so long as such service can be made subservient to their own individual gain? And why, furthermore, should they not themselves enjoy the *pecuniary profits*, as well as the public services, to be derived from the publication of a well-conducted Newspaper? No reason can be given why this should not be the case; the only matter for surprise is, that no well considered plan has hitherto been devised for the purpose of realizing so desirable an object.

The time has now fully arrived when some vigorous, extensive, and well-combined effort should be made to achieve this two-fold object.

First.—To secure for the Working Classes a WEEKLY NEWSPAPER, of the size and price of the *Weekly Dispatch*, and in no way inferior to that Paper in any of its literary qualities or mechanical features: a Weekly Newspaper which shall advocate unflinchingly and uncompromisingly the right of all men to full and equal representation in the legislature, and all those other essentials of just government embodied in the 'People's Charter,' also a national and liberal system of education, as well as those social and commercial reforms identified with the permanent interests of the people at large; and which shall, in its miscellaneous department, include all those matters of novelty and interest necessary to constitute a popular Weekly Journal.

Secondly.—To constitute out of the profits, derivable from the sale and advertisements of such a Paper, a *fund* available for any object which shall be deemed promotive of the individual or collective comforts and interests of that class for whose special benefit the paper is proposed to be established; and to place such fund, moreover, at the sole and entire disposal of its delegated representatives.

To expatiate upon the importance of such a project, or upon the great objects that may be realized by carrying it into effect, is wholly unnecessary. It is enough to advert to the fact, that profits amounting to from £20,000 to £30,000 a year, are derived from more than one Weekly Newspaper, now supported almost wholly by the labouring classes, to indicate what might be effected for themselves, by such a union and co-operation as is now proposed. With a fund of such an amount as that just referred to, what might not the industrious population of this country do for themselves, and what advances might they not make towards improving the character of society at large! They would in such a fund have resources adequate to meet at once the demands of distress and destitution, the aggressive movements of commercial capitalists, and the unjust proceedings of the legislature or the government. They would be relieved from the degrading necessity of soliciting the eleemosynary aid of others to educate their children, or to relieve their own distresses, when the stagnation of trade or the embarrassments of commerce temporarily deprived them of the ordinary means of subsistence. In the pursuit of social and political reforms, it need not be said that such a fund would be found of the highest value and importance, enabling them steadily and perseveringly to press after objects, which their present limited and uncertain means compel them now to pursue with many intermissions and much lack of energy. To realize all this, nothing is necessary beyond the co-operation and support of the Working Classes themselves. They will not be asked to contribute to the fund to be created, otherwise than by diverting into it the moneys they now put into the private purses of newspaper proprietors. It is proposed to publish a Weekly Paper, of large size, which shall be conducted by men of first-rate talent and long tried patriotism and service, on behalf of the class to whose interests such Paper is to be devoted. All that is required to insure its success, and render it a source of considerable profit, is, that it should be purchased by those amongst whom it is proposed to distribute the profits. A wide circulation for the Paper, and a proportionate demand for its advertising columns, are the two things necessary to achieve the object proposed; and the former will inevitably secure the latter.

Having thus adverted to the object and advantages proposed to be achieved by THE PEOPLE'S PAPER, it remains to show in what manner it is intended to place the profits to be derived from the undertaking at the disposal of those by whom they are to be contributed.

1. It is proposed that any Trade's Union, Benefit Society, Political or Social Association, or other organized body of persons coming under the denomination of working men, which shall obtain fifty subscribers to the Paper, shall participate in the management of the fund, by electing, annually, one of their own body to serve upon the committee hereafter provided for; and an additional delegate for every fifty subscribers.

2. It is proposed that the funds derived from the profits of the Paper shall be placed under the management of a committee, constituted of the delegates appointed by the several societies or bodies of men, in conformity with the provision of the preceding paragraph. All questions in committee to be decided by a majority of votes.

3. It is proposed that the funds shall be vested in four Trustees, to be chosen at a general meeting of the committee of management.

4. It is proposed that the editorship and literary management of the Paper shall be confided to the person with whom the project for its establishment originated; who has been for many years connected with the Newspaper Press of the metropolis; who has given ample evidence of his unceasing devotion to the interests of the Working Classes; and who is ready to enter into the most satisfactory sureties for sustaining the political, literary, and other necessary characteristics of a popular Newspaper. The financial management of the property will be vested in the committee provided for in clause 2.

The establishment of such a Paper, and the consequent realization of the advantages above adverted to, cannot of course be effected without an earnest and well-directed effort being made by the class of persons for whose benefit they are intended. Nor can we think that they will refuse to make such an effort on their own behalf, now they are called upon to do so. They are not required to incur any risk, or the contingency of any pecuniary loss; they are offered a Weekly Newspaper, at least equal in size and general interest to any one now extant; devoted, moreover, to the advancement of their own interests, and placing at their disposal all the profits to be derived from its circulation. They are called upon merely to co-operate with the provisional committee in their attempt to achieve this desirable object, by

252

first resolving to purchase the Paper themselves, and next, by inducing as many other persons as they can to purchase it also. This Appeal is made in the full confidence that it will not be in vain. The opportunity now offered to the Working Classes of possessing themselves of at once a powerful instrument of social and political advancement, and of large profits, will not, it is believed, be suffered to pass by unimproved. 'A long pull, a strong pull, and a pull altogether,' and the thing is done. The extent and importance of the result no man can adequately estimate.

It is earnestly requested that this Address may be read in every Trades' Society, Benefit Society, Political Union, Social Association, and in all other bodies of the Working Classes; and that the respective secretaries of such Societies, severally, do communicate to the secretary of the provisional committee, *as early as possible*, the number of subscribers to the Paper, whose names can be handed over to the committee, so that the necessary instructions may be forthwith given for the election of a member from each society comprising fifty subscribers, to serve upon the committee for managing the funds to be derived from the Paper.

Any fifty persons of the Working Classes, not now members of any society, may form themselves into a body for supporting the Paper, and elect a member to serve upon the committee.

Any two or more societies, not having a sufficient number of members each to furnish fifty subscribers, may unite to elect a member to serve upon the committee; and societies at too great a distance from town to send a delegate to the committee, may empower the representative of any other society to act and vote for them.

PROVISIONAL COMMITTEE

J. KILLINGBACK, Pressman.
W. CRAIG, Compositor.
T. TATE, Carver and Gilder.
S. HASSELL, Mason.
J. KENDRICK, Carver and Gilder.
J. HEPPEL, Engineer.
T. J. DUNNING, Bookbinder.
J. JAFFRAY, ditto.
B. TEASDALE, ditto.
W. SLY, Ladies' Shoemaker.
J. WRIGHT, Morocco Leather Finisher.
T. BARRATT, Cork Cutter.
T. MATHEWS, Smith.
T. HURLY, Bricklayer's Labourer.
T. DALLAWAY, Basket Maker.

J. CARBERY, Hatter.
J. W. TICKLE, Hatter.
J. ANSTIS, Carpenter.
W. H. COTTERELL, ditto.
J. KAY, Engineer.
M. GOTOBED, Carpenter.
E. BLEWITT, ditto.
R. HARTWELL, Compositor.
T. ALLDIS, Musical Instrument Maker.
G. TOMEY, Smith.
J. C. LOCKET, Bricklayer.
J. STODDART, ditto.
W. ISAACS, Typefounder.
J. JONES, Smith.
J. H. FORSYTH, Carpenter.

W. LOVETT, Cabinet Maker, Hon. Sec.

All Secretaries and Officers of Societies, as well as all persons desirous of obtaining Subscribers to this Paper, are requested to forward the names and addresses of such Subscribers to the Secretary (*post paid*), 6, Upper North Place, Gray's Inn Road, of whom copies of this Address may be obtained; also of Mr. HARTWELL, 85, Cornwall Road; of any Member of the Committee; and of Mr. DOOLEY, Bell Inn, Old Bailey, where the Committee will meet for the present. Friends in the Country willing to assist in this project, are solicited to form themselves into a Provisional Committee, for the purpose of obtaining Subscribers, and to communicate with the Committee in London.

*** The outline of the propositions contained in the above Address, was submitted to a numerous Meeting of Members of Trade Societies at the Bell Inn, Old Bailey, on Friday, September 7th, 1838, by a gentleman, long connected with the Public Press as an editor and a reporter. A Committee was formed from that Meeting to investigate into the practicability of the undertaking, who, after a patient inquiry, reported in favour of the proposition at a subsequent Meeting; also stating that they had made an estimate of the expenses on a liberal scale, with the number of copies necessary to be sold to clear them; and that as soon as a sufficient number of Subscribers should be obtained, the projectors of the Paper would bring out the first number. It was thereupon resolved that the above Address should be published; and that those persons whose names are attached, should form a Provisional Committee, with power to add to their number, to carry the object into effect.

HARTWELL, Printer, 85, Cornwall Road, Lambeth.

INDEX

Adams, W., 15
Adelphi, 14, 235, 241, 244, 245
Agassiz, —, 23
Ainsworth, H., 155
Albany, 17
Albany Road, 128
Albany Street, 71, 77, 120
Aldersgate Street, 68, 71, 116
Aldgate, 23
Alldis, T., 253
Allen, —, 190
Allen, T., 68, 69
Althorp, Viscount, *see* Spencer, J. C.
America, 139, 140, 159, 174–6
Andrews, W. E., 2
Anglesey, Marquess of, *see* Paget, H. W.
Annan, Dumfriess., 246
Anstis, J., 253
Anti-Corn Law League, xii
Archer Street, 68
Argyle Arms, public house, 140
Argyle Street, 68, 71, 140
Arnot, S., 70, 113
Arrowsmith, P. R., 246
Ashurst, W. H., 120, 185, 220, 235, 245
Ashworth, —, 211
Association of Working Men to Procure
  a Cheap and Honest Press, 153–6
Athenaeum, 70
Atkinson, H. T., 69, 71
Attwood, T., 10, 45, 149
Augero, F. A., 2, 69, 70, 72
Austin, A., 120
Austin Friars, 120
Aylesbury News, 246

Baber, G., 69
Bagnigge Wells, Middx., 127
Bainbridge, Dr. J. N., 116
Baker, —, 113, 128
Baker, E. H., 155, 161
Baker Street, Upper, 68
Ballot, 52, 55, 141
Bank of England, 10, 89, 91, 124
Bankside, 120
Barbican, 71, 116, 120
Barker, T. B., 116
Barnes, W., 116
Barratt, G., 68
Barratt, T., 253
Barrett, D., 2

Barrett, T., 2
Bartholomew Lane, 120
Bartholomew Place, 68
Basinghall Street, 116, 120
Bassett, J. D., 247
Bateman's Buildings, 68
Baxter, —, 36
Bayley, —, 125
Baylis, A., 120
Baylis, S., 120
Beacon, G., 248, 249
Beadon, —, 246
Beak Street, 15, 70, 116
Beauclerk, Major A., 21, 45, 48, 49, 59,
  61, 66, 68, 70, 97
Beauclerk, C., 21
Beaumont, A. H., 159, 161, 207
Beaumont, B., 66
Beaumont, J., 190
Beck, —, 145
Beckett, W. a', 15
Beckford, W., xiv
Bedford Row, 120
Bedford Square, 69, 70, 77
Bedford Street, 15
Belgium, 10, 143, 210
Belgrave Square, 70, 116, 120
Bell, J., 177
Bell Inn, 253, 254
Bell's Life in London, 246
Belvedere Road, 156
Benbow, W., 38, 49, 53, 54, 64, 77, 85,
  97, 105, 141, 144, 145, 198
Bennett, J., 68, 69, 116
Bentham, J., ix, 21
Bentley, C., 204
Berkeley, G. S., 69, 113, 116
Berkshire, 213
Bermondsey, 143
Berners Street, 116
Bethnal Green, 42, 69, 120, 142
Bethnal Green Road, 155
Birch, —, 190
Birkbeck, G., x
Birmingham, 10, 88, 145, 184, 190, 193,
  221, 223
Birmingham Journal, 207
Birmingham Political Union, xx, 45, 66,
  184, 185, 217
Bishopsgate, 75
Bishop Wearmouth, Co. Durham, 246

Black, Dr. J. R., xxiv, 120, 151–3, 156, 158, 185, 217, 220, 231, 234–6, 241, 244, 245, 247, 248
Blackfriars, 120, 207, 220
Blackfriars Bridge, 10, 37, 38, 137
Blackfriars Road, 49, 142
Blackman Street, 23
Blacksmith's Arms, public house, 156
Blake, G., 116
Blake, R., 116
Blewitt, E., 253
Blind Beggar, public house, 142
Bloomsbury, 29, 40, 68, 69, 116, 120, 155, 194
Bloomsbury Householders' Union, 87
Bocking, Essex, 120
Bohm, W. H., 116
Bolton, Lancs., 246
Boothby, B., 245
Borough, see Southwark
Boston, Lincs., 211, 246
Bow, 155
Bowkett, Dr., 248, 249
Bowling Square Chapel, 122
Bowring, Dr. J., 235 245
Bowyer, T., xxiv, 39, 40, 61, 68, 69
Brackenborough, E., 69
Breeches-Makers' Benefit Society, viii
Brentford, Middx., 190
Brewer Street, 68
Bridge House Place, 116
Bridge Road, 65
Bridge Street, 207, 220
Bridgnorth, Salop, 246
Briggs, A., xviii n.
Brighton, Sussex, 190, 229
Bristol, 51, 78, 144, 145, 198
Bristol, 2nd Marquess of, see Hervey, F. W.
British Association for Promoting Co-operative Knowledge, 138–41
British Statesman, 246
Broad Street, 68, 71
Brompton Square, xii, 120, 156, 186, 208, 232
Brookes, J., 116
Brooke Street, Lambeth, 155
Brooks, —, policeman, 128–30
Brooksbank, T., 120
Brook Street, Holborn, 68
Brook Street, Ratcliffe, 156
Broome, T., 204
Brown, —, 122
Brown, F. C., 245
Brown, J. B., 248
Browne, D., 190
Brownlow Street, 69
Brunswick Square, 76
Bryanstone Square, 120
Brydges Street, 15

Bubb, G., 220
Buckinghamshire, 120, 213
Buckle, J., 68
Bucklersbury, 120
Buller, A., 21
Buller, C., 21, 70
Bulls Head Court, 125
Bulwer, E. L., 21, 105
Bunhill Row, 155
Burdett, Sir F., vii, ix, x, xiv, xix, 13, 14, 21, 48, 49, 56–8, 63, 64
Burnard, J. P., 70, 116
Burton, G., 246
Burton Crescent, 68, 71, 116, 120
Butler, J., 13th Baron Dunboyne, 132
Byng, —, 43, 44
Bywell, Northumb., 246

Calthorpe Arms, public house, 133
Calthorpe Street, 129
Camberwell, 120, 207
Camberwell New Road, 120
Cambrian, 246
Cambridge, 211, 246
Camden Town, 69, 155
Cameron, —, 177
Canada, 191, 192
Carbery, J., 253
Carmarthen, 190
Carnaby Market, 68
Carpenter, W., 2, 69, 70, 78, 84, 96, 116, 132, 133, 200, 205, 206
Carpenter's Buildings, 69
Carpenters' Hall, 69, 120
Carpenter's Magazine, 141
Carpue, —, 48
Carrick, J., 68, 69, 71
Cartwright, Major J., xiv, 220, 223, 236
Castlereagh, Viscount, see Stewart, R.
Castle Street, Finsbury, 68, 70, 116
Castle Street, Holborn, 120
Castle Street, Oxford Market, 141, 142
Catherine Street, Strand, 201
Catherine Street, Vauxhall, 68
Cavanagh, P., 2
Cave, O., 2
Chadd, Miss E., vii
Chad's Place, 116
Champion, 198, 199
Chancery Lane, 75
Chapel (Chapple) Street, 68, 70, 116
Chapman, H. S., 120, 185, 213
Charing Cross, vii, xi, xii, 15, 68, 71, 116
Charles Place, 116
Charles Street, 68
Charlwood, G., 120, 245
Charter, 200–3, 206, 217, 249–54
Charter, xiv, xxi, 183–93, 207, 217, 220, 223–9, 234, 251

Chartism, xii, xvi–xviii, xxiii, xxiv, xxvii, 213, 215
Chartist, 200
Chatham, Kent, 40
Cheapside, 12, 68, 117, 120
Cheeseman, R., 68–70, 116
Cheltenham, Glos., 120
Chenies Street, 71
Chester Street, 68, 70, 116, 120
Chitty, —, 106
Chrestomathic Schools, x
Christian Corrector, 120
Christopher Street, 68, 71, 117
Chubb, —, 10
Churchill, H. B., 68–71, 78, 83, 97, 116, 120
Church Street, Hackney, 70, 116
Circus Street, 161
City Road, 1, 70, 75, 161, 197, 203
Clairville, Old Brompton, 68
Clapton, Upper, 68, 71, 116
Clare, Eire, 146
Claremont Square, 42
Claremont Terrace, 70, 116
Clarke, E., 246
Cleave, J., 2, 37, 50, 51, 58, 61, 64, 70, 72, 85, 121, 122, 125, 139, 141, 152, 161, 169, 177, 186, 189, 194, 195, 218
Clerkenwell, 42, 69, 87, 117, 139
Clerkenwell Green, 42, 145
Cleveland, Duke of, *see* Vane, W. H.
Coates, W., 211
Cobbett, W., 116
Cobden, R., 208, 211, 213
Coddington, Ches., 122
Colchester, Essex, 190
Cold Bath Fields (Calthorpe Estate), xxiv, 122, 125, 132, 133, 146
Cole, C., 155
College Hill, 68
College Street, 155
Collins, J., 202, 204, 207, 215, 217, 218
Collinson, J., 68
Combe, —, 203, 207
Commercial Coffee House, 52, 64
Commercial Place, City Road, 197
Commercial Place, Hampstead Road, 68, 71
Commercial Road, Hampstead Road, 116, 155
Commercial Road, Whitechapel, 143
Common Hall, 87, 214
Complete Suffrage Movement, xii, xxiv
Compton Street, 116
Coode, G., 68, 116, 120
Cook, J., 2
Cooke, W., 70, 113, 116, 120
Cooper, T., 234
Copenhagen House, 143
Copley, J. S., Baron Lyndhurst, 81
Cornhill, 75

Cornwall Road, 202, 253, 254
Cottage Green, Camberwell, 120
Cotterell, W. H., 253
Courtauld, S., 120, 245
Courtenay, —, 133
Court of Common Council, 87
Covent Garden, 117, 120, 155, 161, 179
Cowell, J., 15
Craig, W., 253
Cramphorne, R., 68
Craven Street, 232
Crawford, W. S., 231, 245
Crawford Street, 36, 58, 71
Crawfurd, J., 21, 120, 186
Cray, J., 155
Cray, R., 155
Crescent Place, 116
Crescent Street, 155
Cripplegate, 87, 120
Cross Street, 68
Crown & Anchor Tavern, 23, 36, 45, 54, 57, 59, 60, 64, 81, 83, 118, 132, 177, 179, 195
Crown Tavern, 29
Croydon, Surrey, 231
Culley, J., 128
Culley, R., xxiv, 130, 131, 133
Cumberland Place, 207
Cumberland Street, 117
Cumming, R. D., 116
Cumming, W., 68, 69, 116, 120, 245
Curwood, J., 116

Dallaway, T., 253
Davis, —, 113
Dawes, J., 248
Dawson, A., 2
Dean, J., 15
Dean Street, 70
Dennis, G. F., 190
Deptford, 87
Derby, 11th Earl of, *see* Stanley, E. Smith
Despard, Colonel, viii
Detrosier, R., 61, 69–72, 79, 83, 105, 151
De Vear, Thomas, 15, 21, 23
Dewsbury, Yorks., 190
Dispatch, 167, 251
Doctors' Commons, 120
Doncaster, Yorks., 211
Doncaster Gazette, 246
Donkin, S., 246
Dooley, —, 253
Doris Street, 71
Doughty Street, 120
Douglas, D., 4th Earl of Selkirk, 237
Douglas, R. K., 190
Douglass, S. M., 69
Douglass, W., 69, 116
Downie, A., 190
Downing Street, xxvi, 92

Drake, J., 46, 48, 68, 70
Draycott, F., 68, 69, 116
Drewett, J., 116
Drummond Street, 70
Drury Lane, 69
Duce, J., 120, 155
Duffey, —, 105, 115, 145
Duke of York, public house, 142
Duke Street, 68, 69, 116
Dunboyne, 13th Baron, see Butler, J.
Duncan, A., 190, 195, 198
Duncan, J., 247–9
Dundas, H., 221, 239
Dunning, T. J., 253
Durham Street, 70

Eagle Street, 155
Eagle Tavern, 1
Eaton Place, 68, 70, 120
Edgeware Road, 68, 70
Edinburgh, 190, 195, 197, 199, 211
Edwards, —, 36
Effingham, 3rd Earl of, see Howard, T.
Eldon, Earl of, see Scott, J.
Elf, C., 248
Eliot, G., 15
Elizabeth Street, 68, 117, 120
Elliott, E., 190
Ellis, H., 220
Ellis, R., 2
Ellis, William, 61, 235, 245
Ellis, Wynn, 245
Elphinstone, H., 68, 70, 120, 235, 245
Ensor, —, 143
Epps, Dr. J., 116, 120, 220, 234, 235, 245
Erratt, S., 220
Essex, 120, 213
Essex Street, 69
Euston Place, 120
Euston Square, 68, 70, 120, 155
Evans, D. L., 15, 106, 132, 133, 183
Evans, E., 15
Evans, T., 15, 70, 116
Evans, W. B., 21
Evening Sun, 246
Examiner, 246

Falconer, T., 120, 185
Fall, G., 71, 72
Farn, E., 120
Farrell, J., 155
Farringdon Street, 75
Fetter Lane, 69, 116
Field, E. W., 120, 220, 234, 245
Fielden, J., 116, 149
Finsbury, 34, 68, 70, 71, 74, 75, 116, 117
Finsbury Square, 68, 74, 75, 120, 142, 197
Fisher, —, 203
Fleet Street, 7, 54, 64, 75, 120, 194

Fletcher, —, 190
Fleur-de-lis Court, 155
Flood, —, 36
Foley Street, 197
Forsyth, J. H., 253
Foskett, G., 139–41
Fountain Court, 68
Fowler, —, 122
Fox, C. J., ix, xiv, 180, 238
Fox, C. J., bookseller, 120
Fox, H. R., 3rd Baron Holland, 9
Fox, J., 155
Fox, Rev. W. J., 59, 61, 68, 71, 116, 120, 185, 190
France, 143, 210, 247
Franks, R. H., 61, 68, 71, 93, 113, 116, 120
Fraser, J., 190, 198
Frazer, E., 220
Frederick Place, 69, 116
French, D., 2
Fulham, 71
Fursey, George, 128–30

Gains, —, 113
Galloway, A., 68, 71, 116, 120, 216
Garden Court, 120
Garnault Place, 117
Garrod, —, 190
Gaskell, W. P., 120, 202
Gast, J., 38, 151, 155
Gateshead Observer, 246
Geesin, W., 220
George IV, x
George Street, Hampstead Road, 68, 69, 116
George Street, New Road, 120
George Street, Tower Hill, 155
Gibson, T., 246
Gibson, T. F., 120, 211, 213, 214
Gibson, T. M., 212, 245
Glasgow, 120
Glasgow Argus, 186
Glashan, G., 155, 161
Glazier, G., 120
Globe, 246
Globe Lane, 69
Globe Tavern, 7
Gloucester Journal, 246
Gloucester Street, 76
Godwin, W., ix, 143, 157
Golden Square, 15
Goldspink, —, 177
Goodwin, S., 116
Goswell Road, 155
Gotobed, M., 203, 253
Gouger, R., 20, 21, 25
Gowan, Captain, 68
Gower Street, 71
Grady, J., 2, 69, 72

Graham, G. J., 120
Granbourn's Buildings, 116
Gravesend, Kent, 40
Gray, A., 139
Gray, J., 155
Gray's Inn, 68, 71, 117
Gray's Inn Lane, 75, 194
Gray's Inn Road, 133, 164, 185, 253
Gray's Inn Square, 120
Great Dover Street, 68, 69, 116
Great Ormond Street, 68, 71, 76, 116, 120
Great Russell Street, 120
Great Union Street, 70, 116
Greek Street, 15
Greenford, 71
Green Street, 70
Greenwich, 87
Greg, R. H., 211
Greig, G., 213
Grenville, W. W., Baron Grenville, 221, 222, 239
Greville Street, 68, 69, 116, 138, 139, 151, 152, 155, 161
Grey, C., 2nd Earl Grey, xii, 9, 35, 36, 41, 47, 48, 81, 82, 86, 87, 90–3, 95, 98, 101, 221, 224, 226
Griffin, C., 2
Grosvenor Place, 68, 120
Grote, G., 91, 195
Grote, Prescott & Co., 22
Grove Lane, 207
Guildford Street, 75
Guildhall, 8, 93, 101
Guthrie, —, 145

Hackney, 70, 116
Hackney Road, 68–70, 116, 117, 120
Halifax Arms, public house, 143
Hall, C., 68
Hall, T., 68
Hammersmith, 143
Hampshire, 213
Hampshire Independent, 246
Hampstead, 116, 143
Hampstead Heath, xx, 88
Hampstead Road, 68, 69, 71, 116, 155
Hand, C. J., 2
Hanger's Lane, 120
Hankin, H. B., 68, 69, 113, 116
Hanover Crescent, 155
Hanover Street, 15
Hanover Terrace, 120
Harding, J., 15
Hardy, T., viii
Harley Street, Upper, 120
Harney, G. J., 203–5, 207, 215
Harper, G., 15
Harper Street, 116
Harrison, B., xvii *n.*

Harrison, S., 68, 71, 112, 113, 116, 119, 120, 202, 203, 207, 213, 214, 220, 228, 230–5, 245, 247, 248
Harrison, S. B., xii *n.*, 61, 68, 71
Hart Street, 116
Hartwell, R., 152, 155, 161, 177, 186, 189, 194–7, 201–3, 207, 217, 253, 254
Hassell, S., 253
Hatton Garden, 68, 69, 116, 127, 138, 139, 151, 155, 161
Heath Street, 155
Hector, C. J., 120, 220
Heenan, B., 69
Hendley, G., 155
Henley, J., 2
Heppel, G. H., 120, 212, 245
Heppel, J., 253
Hercules Buildings, 69
Hervey, F. W., 2nd Marquess of Bristol, 44
Hetherington, H., xx, 2, 75, 125, 138–43, 152, 161, 164, 177, 186, 189, 190 *n.*, 193–7, 215, 218, 245
Heward, R., 63
Hewett, R., 190
Hewett, T., 245
Hewitt, D., 69
Hibbert, J., 141
Hickson, W. E., 61, 68, 71, 120
High Holborn, 120
High Street, Bloomsbury, 68, 70, 71, 116, 117, 194
High Street, Bow, 155
High Street, Southwark, 70
Hinde Street, 194
Hoare, W., 161, 177
Hobhouse, Sir J. C., vii, ix, x, xx, xxvi, 8, 13, 14, 91, 92, 106, 121
Hobhouse, T., 21
Hobsbawm, E. J., xxv
Hodgskin, T., x, xv, xxiii, 58, 245
Hoile, J., 71
Holborn, 68–70, 75, 116, 117, 119, 120, 197
Holebrooke, J., 246
Holland, 3rd Baron, *see* Fox, H. R.
Holland Place, 69
Hollis, T. B., xiv, 180
Holloway, 70, 116
Holmes, T., 68
Holywell Street, 10
Horns Tavern, 65
Horse Bazaar, 34, 35
Hovell, M., xvii *n.*, xviii
Howard, C., 16th Duke of Norfolk, Earl of Surrey, 237
Howard, T., 3rd Earl of Effingham, 237
Howell, H., 68, 71, 72
Howland Street, 76
Hoxton, 68, 120
Huddersfield, Yorks., 211

Huggett, G., 216, 220, 245, 247
Hull Rockingham, 246
Hume, J., vii, ix–xi, xiv, 2, 10, 16, 17, 20, 21, 24, 35, 36, 43, 44, 106, 116, 120, 133, 185, 218, 220, 231, 232, 234, 235, 245, 247
Hunt, H., xv, 1, 2, 10, 143, 145
Hunt, J., 69, 71, 72
Hunter Street, 76
Huntingdon, 211
Hurly, T., 253
Hyde Park, 35, 74
Hyde Street, 155

Ilfracombe, Devon, 247
Ipswich, Suffolk, 190
Ireland, —, 198
Ireland, 73, 121, 122, 143, 191, 192, 197, 198
Irvine, J. G., 69
Isaacs, J., 253
Isabella Street, 68

Jaffray, J., 253
James's Place, 69, 70, 116
Jermyn Street, 15
Jerusalem Passage, 139
Jervis, S., 235, 245
John Street, 235, 241, 244, 245
Jones, J., of Northampton, 190
Jones, J., smith, of London, 253
Jones, L., 212
Jones, Colonel L. G., 21, 56
Jones, Sir W., 98
Jones, W. H., 2

Kay, J., 253
Kemp, R., 15, 71
Kendrick, J., 253
Kennington, 65, 69
Kensington, 69
Kent, 213
Kent Herald, 246
Kent Road, 117, 128
Kent Terrace, 120
Kentucky, 153
Keppel Street, 68
Kilkenny, 121
Killingback, J., 253
King, J. B., 69, 116, 120
King, T., 15
Kings Arms Tavern, 190
Kings Cross, 69
Kings Mews, 74
Kings Road, 75
King Street, 68–71
Kinnaird, G., 7th Baron Kinnaird, 237
Kirby Street, 69
Kitran, W., 155
Knapp, G., 68
Knight, G., 69

Lafayette, Marquis de, 143
Laing, —, 127
Lamb, G., ix, 132
Lamb, W., 2nd Viscount Melbourne, x, 40, 83, 126, 127, 145
Lambeth, 65, 68, 69, 71, 87, 155, 156, 194, 202, 254
Lambeth Marsh Gate, 68
Lambeth Reform Union, 65
Lamb's Conduit Street, 75
Lancashire, xii, xv, 192, 193, 211
Lancastrian Schools' Society, ix, x
Lancet, 55
Lane, C., 2
Lane, W., 68
Langley, —, 113, 114
Lansdowne, 3rd Marquess of, *see* Petty-Fitzmaurice, Sir H.
Lant Street, 116
Latzky, Dr., 248, 249
Lawless, —, 145
Lawrence, W., 68, 120, 216
Layton, G., 190
Leadenhall Street, 68
Leader, J. T., 120, 183, 190, 191, 194, 220, 234, 235, 245
Leary, J., 190
Lee, J., 121, 125, 127, 145, 146
Lee, J. G., 116
Leeds, Yorks., 21, 213
Leicester, 234
Leicestershire Mercury, 246
Leicester Square, 23, 70, 79, 93, 104, 110, 113, 152
Leicester Street, 15
Lennox, C., 3rd Duke of Richmond, 237
Leonard, H. P., 69, 88, 97
Lillie, Sir J. S., 71
Lillingstone, D., 68
Lime Street, 120
Lincoln's Inn Fields, 57, 58
Lisle Street, 15, 23, 100
Lisson Grove, 142
Little, Provost, 246
Little Britain, 120
Little Charlotte Street, 68, 70, 116
Little Russell Street, 69
Liverpool, 174, 176, 198
Livery of London, 93, 101
Locket, J. C., 253
Lockett, E., 68
London Co-operative Trading Association, 139
London Corresponding Society, vii, viii, xiv, xviii, 156, 220–3, 238–40
London Democratic Association, 203–7, 215
Londonderry, 3rd Marquess of, *see* Stewart, C. W.

260

London Dispatch, 167
London Mechanics Institute, x
London Tavern, 93
London Wall, 68, 69, 116, 120
London Working Men's Association, xii, xxi, xxiv, 146, 151, 158, 161–73, 176, 184, 185, 189–98, 205, 217, 223
Long Acre, 15, 68, 69, 71
Longford, —, 61
Longmate, J., 68, 69, 113, 116, 120
Lotherington, J., 246
Louth, Lincs., 211
Lovett, W., xxiv, 2, 37, 58, 59, 61, 64, 68, 69, 72, 75, 77, 125, 136–9, 141–5, 151, 152, 155, 161, 164, 177, 184, 186, 189, 191, 194, 195, 198, 199, 202, 205, 207, 215–19, 231, 253
Lowrey, R., 190
Lucas Street, 155
Ludgate Hill, 10
Lynch, —, 145
Lynden, G. W., 15
Lyndhurst, Baron, *see* Copley, J. S.
Lyon, J., 248

Maberley, —, 35, 36
Macdiarmid, W., 68, 69, 117
M'Donnell, D., 155
Machin, G., 68
McKenzie, Sir F., 247
Mackinnon, Dr., 21
Maclesfield Street, 15
Magna Charta, 3, 192
Malthus, T. R., x
Manchester, 53, 78, 140, 159, 174, 190, 192, 193, 204, 207–9, 211–13, 218
Manor Place, 116
Mansion House Street, 120
Manwaring, W., 68
Markham, J., 234
Mark Lane, 120
Marsden, R., 203–5
Marsh, J., 69, 71
Marshall, J., 21, 235, 245
Marsham Street, 68–70, 116
Martin, J., 155
Martin, Call & Co., 22
Marylebone, xiv, xxii, 34–7, 43, 45, 46, 58, 68, 70, 87, 117, 120, 144, 161, 197, 211
Mason, —, 113
Mathews, T., 253
Matland, J., 2
Mawbey, C. E., 2
Mayne, R., 127
Mazzini, G., 120
Medway, T., 155
Mee, J., 2, 85, 121, 122, 124, 125, 127–9, 145, 146
Melbourne, 2nd Viscount, *see* Lamb, W.

Melville, J., 120
Menteath, C. G. S., 68, 70, 71
Mercer, R., 2
Merchant, —, policeman, 128
Merle, —, 46–8
Metropolitan Anti-Corn Law Association, xii, 207–14
Metropolitan Parliamentary Reform Association, xii, xiii, xviii, xxiv, 220, 227, 235–49
Metropolitan Political Union, xv, xxii, 1–7, 45
Metropolitan Radical Association, 207
Metropolitan Trades Union, 33, 140
Miall, E., 245
Michie, W. A., 71
Middlesex, x, xiv, xv, xxii, 71, 213
Middlesex Hospital, 70, 116
Middleton Street, 69
Midwinter, W., 69
Milbank Street, 71
Mile End, 143
Mill, J., ix, x
Mill, J. S., x
Millard, W., 68, 69, 88, 112, 116, 139
Milne, —, 232
Milner, J., 120
Milner, T., 69, 116
Milton Street, 155
Mitcalf, —, 36
Mitchell, H., 214, 216–18, 220, 245
Molesworth, Sir W., 120, 220, 234
Mongredien, A., 68, 69, 80, 113, 116, 120
Moore, J., 65
Moore, R., 116, 155, 161, 189, 194, 198, 217
Moore, W., 69
Mordan, S., 68, 71, 116
Morgan, —, 139
Morning Advertiser, 179, 197, 198, 208, 246
Morning Chronicle, 13, 35, 64, 74, 78, 86, 87, 97, 107, 179, 194, 195, 197, 207, 208, 246
Morning Post, 246
Morning Sun, 246
Morpeth, Northum., 246
Morres, H. R., 2nd Viscount Mountmorres, 237
Morris, Sir J., 246
Morton, A., 155, 156, 161, 248, 249
Mottram, E., 120, 245
Mountmorres, 2nd Viscount, *see* Morres, H. R.
Muagglethwhite, J., 190
Muntz, —, 248, 249
Muntz, P. H., 149, 190
Murphy, T., 56, 57, 59, 61, 68–71, 81, 84, 113, 116
Murray, J., 120

261

Museum Street, 29, 68, 69
Myddleton Street, 68

Nash, E., 71
National Association, 218, 219
National Association Gazette, 219, 246
National Petition, 185, 188, 191, 192, 196–8, 204, 205, 223
National Political Union, xii, xvi, xviii–xx, xxiii, xxiv, 15, 16, 40, 48, 53–64, 66–72, 77–84, 91, 92, 96–8, 102, 109–19, 134
National Reform Association, 27–9
National Union of the Working Classes, xv, xix–xxiv, 29–34, 37–9, 49–53, 64, 66, 73–7, 84–7, 96–8, 105, 115, 116, 120–32, 134–46
Neale, R. S., xvii *n*.
Neesom, C. H., 204, 207
Nelms, R., 36
New Basinghall Street, 120
Newberry, W., 71
Newcastle Street, 155
Newcastle upon Tyne, xv, 190
New Cut, 68
Newgate Prison, 130
Newgate Street, 75
Newington, 68, 116
Newington Green, 68, 71, 116
New Kent Road, 68, 70, 116
New Road, Marylebone, 161
New Road, St. Pancras, 76, 120
New Street, Holborn, 116
New Street Square, Covent Garden, 68, 69, 117
Newton Street, Holborn, 116
Noble, J., 246
Noble Street, 155
Noel, R. R., 71, 78, 116
Nonconformist, 231, 232
Norman, J., 70, 116
Norminton, E., 69
Northampton, 190
Northamptonshire, 213
North Crescent, Bedford Square, 69, 77
North End, Fulham, 71
Northern Star, 197–9, 216, 217
North Staffordshire Mercury, 246
Northumberland, 246
Norton Folgate, 155
Norwich, Norfolk, 36
Nottingham, 145, 246
Notting Hill, 71, 116
Nyse, —, 113

O'Brien, J. B., 186, 194
O'Connell, D., 1, 2, 21, 116, 120, 121, 133, 145, 146, 197, 198
O'Connor, F., xiii, 159, 161, 177, 190, 195–9, 201, 207, 231, 234

O'Connor, R., 159
Ogilvey, —, 36
Old Bailey, 129, 207, 253, 254
Old Broad Street, 22, 71, 117
Old Brompton, 68, 71
Old Change, 68
Old Jewry, 151
Old Street, 42
Operative, 207
Osborne, J., 51, 52, 74, 120, 141
Ossett, —, policeman, 128
Owen, Robert (d. 1858), ix, xv, xxiii, 96, 135, 136, 139, 140, 143, 147
Owen, Robert, of James's Place, Hackney Road, 70, 116
Owen, Robert Dale, 116, 120
Oxford Arms Passage, 70
Oxford Market, 141
Oxford Street, 36, 71, 116

Paddington, 43, 46, 87
Paget, H. W., Marquess of Anglesey, 121
Paget, J., 15
Pain, J., 68, 70
Paine, T., xiv, 143
Palace Yard, 74, 75, 185, 186, 189, 190, 195, 211
Pall Mall, 12, 22, 44, 120
Palmer, R., 68, 70
Paper Buildings, 68
Paris, 120
Parkes, J., vii, 89, 211
Parkins, —, 85, 120
Park Lane, 120
Parliamentary Candidate Society, xiii, xxii, 15–26, 103
Partington, Mrs., 44
Paternoster Row, 120
Pattison, —, 213
Paulton, A. W., 208, 211
Pearce, —, 113
Pearson, C., 2
Peel, Sir R., 8, 98, 210, 243
Penton Place, 68, 69
Pentonville, 42, 68–70, 116
Pepper Street, 116
Perceval, S., 73
Percy, H., Baron Percy, ix
Percy Street, 71, 117
Perry, T. E., 15–17, 19–21, 45, 47–9, 59–61, 68–71, 78, 116, 120
Peterborough, Northants., 211
Peterloo, xv, 11, 126, 192
Petrie, G., 64, 122, 124, 125, 141, 146
Petty-Fitzmaurice, Sir H., 3rd Marquess of Lansdowne, 9
Phelps, J., 120, 220, 234, 245
Philadelphia Chapel, 34, 75
Phillips, —, 130
Phillips, C., 246

Phillips, R., 2
Philps, J., *see* Phelps
Piccadilly, 15, 23, 120
Pigou, W., 15
Pimlico, 70
Pitfield Street, 68, 120
Pitt, —, 14
Pitt, J., 15
Pitt, W., 67, 150, 221, 222, 239, 240, 242
Place, S., vii
Place, T., 61
Pleydell-Bouverie, W., 3rd Earl of Radnor, 245
Plummer, —, 121, 122, 125
Plummer Street, 70
Poland, 143
Poor Law, x, 177–9, 199
Poor Man's Guardian, xix, 49, 51, 73, 74, 85, 115, 141–6
Popay, —, xix, 130, 146
Portland Place, 42, 43
Portman Market, 142, 161
Portugal Street, 57
Potter, T., 36, 46, 48, 71
Potter, T., jun., 235
Potts, R., 155
Powell, J. H., xxiv, 39–45, 68–70, 116
Powell, M., 68
Powell, T., 139
Pratt Street, 69
Prendergast, M., 120
Preston, —, 122, 125, 145
Preston, Lancs., 143
Priestley, Dr. J., 221
Prince's Road, 69
Princess Street, 155
Prince's Street, 120, 161
Pringrose, G. L., 246
Pritchard, W., 120
Prockter's Hotel, 65
Prout, T., 120, 179, 182, 185, 220, 234, 235, 245, 247–9
Putney Street, 155

Queen Square, 117, 120
Queen Street, 76

Radical, 152, 159–61
Radical Club, 119, 120, 179, 185, 202, 207, 216, 220, 228–31, 233–5
Radley's Hotel, 207, 220
Radnage, Bucks., 120
Radnor, 3rd Earl of, *see* Pleydell-Bouverie, W.
Rahere Street, 155
Rainford, E., 68, 70, 71, 112, 113, 116, 118–20, 220, 234
Ralay, J., 70
Ransom & Co., 22
Ratcliff, 156

Raven, R., 155
Raymond Buildings, 120
Red Cross Street, 68, 71, 116, 120
Red Lion Court, 7, 120
Red Lion Passage, 68, 71, 116
Red Lion Square, 120, 139, 155
Red Lion Street, 71, 116
Redman, D. W., 68–70, 113, 116
Redman, E. H., 68
Redwood, —, policeman, 128–30
Reeves, —, 190
Reform Club, 120, 202
Regent's Park, 35, 36, 71, 120
Regent Street, 15, 43, 70, 116
Regnault, E., 120
Rennie, —, 61
Revans, S., 120
Revell, Major H., 43, 68, 70, 71, 97, 116, 120, 245
Reynolds, C., 70
Reynolds, W., 68
Ricardo, R., 213, 214
Rice, Rev. Dr., 42
Richardson, R. J., 190, 192, 204, 205
Riches Court, 120
Richmond, 3rd Duke of, *see* Lennox, C.
Rider, —, 203, 204
Rigge, J., 68
Riley, C. M., 7
Roberts, James, 155
Roberts, John, 116
Robert Street, 155
Robinson, J., 155
Rockingham Place, 117
Roebuck, J. A., vii, xxiv, 21, 59, 61, 70, 71, 78, 80, 133, 184, 186, 220, 232, 234, 245, 247
Rogers, G., 47, 61, 68–72, 78, 84, 116, 118, 194, 207, 218
Rogers, J., 155, 161, 177, 189
Rogers, L. M., 245
Rosser, C., 61, 116
Rotherhithe, 155
Rotunda, 34, 37, 38, 42, 49, 54, 55, 59–61, 64, 72, 97, 120, 122, 137, 138, 142, 144, 145, 198
Rowan, Colonel, 127
Rowe, D. J., xviii *n.*, xxiii *n.*
Royal Exchange, 120
Royal Street, 68
Rudé, G., xxv, xxvi
Russell, J., 122, 125, 137, 141, 146, 159, 161
Russell, Lord J., xiii, xxi, 12, 13, 46, 48, 179–81, 207, 226
Rutt, J. T., 68, 71, 116
Rye, Sussex, 106

St. Ann Soho, parish, 107
St. Bride Fleet Street, parish, 87

263

St. Clement Danes, parish, 87, 107
St. George Westminster, parish, 107
St. George's Fields, 120
St. Giles Holborn, parish, 47, 71, 116, 194
St. James's Square, 43
St. James's Street, 44
St. James Westminster, parish, 43, 68, 107
St. John Westminster, parish, 106, 107
St. Luke Old Street, parish, 42, 68, 87
St. Margaret Westminster, parish, 107
St. Martin in the Fields, parish, 107
St. Martin's Lane, 116, 156
St. Mary Axe, 70, 116, 120
St. Mary Islington, parish, 42
St. Mary le Strand, parish, 107
St. Mary Newington, parish, 43
St. Pancras, parish, 43, 87, 194
St. Swithin's Lane, 120, 212
Santos, E. D., 2, 70–2
Saull, W. D., 68, 69, 71, 113, 114, 116, 120, 142, 245, 248
Saunders, H., 65
Savage, James, 120, 141
Savage, John, xx, 36, 37, 58, 71, 88, 113, 114, 161
Saville House, 79, 81, 87, 104, 110, 112, 113
Savoy, 107
Saxton, N., 120
Say, J. B., x
Scales, Alderman, 21, 22
Scarfe, —, 113
Scholefield, J., 245
Scott, J., Earl of Eldon, 221
Scott Street, 155
Seamore Place, 155
Selkirk, 4th Earl of, *see* Douglas, D.
Selles, J. T., 120
Sellis, J., 70, 116
Senior, N., x
Serle Street, 57
Serpentine, River, 35
Sewell, J., 117
Seymour Place, 68
Sheffield, Yorks., xv, 190
Sheffield Iris, 246
Sheppard, F. H. W., xvi *n.*
Sheridan, C. B., 21
Shirley, J., 68, 70
Shoe Lane, 70, 161, 194
Simpson, —, 129, 189
Simpson, H., 117
Skene, G., 139
Skene, P., 139
Skinner, J., 116
Skinner Street, 75, 116
Slateford, 246
Sly, W., 253
Smedley, F., 189, 190
Smith, —, 113, 118

Smith, C. F., 23, 59, 61, 68–71, 78, 113, 116, 120
Smith, J., 220, 245
Smith, J. B., 211
Smith, S., 208, 214
Smith, T., 190
Smith, W., 36
Smithfield, 68, 71, 116, 120
Snaresbrook, Essex, 246
Snow Hill, 70
Society for Constitutional Information, 237
Soho, 68, 70, 116
Somers Town, 68
South Crescent, Bedford Square, 70
Southwark, 'Borough', 23, 69, 70, 71, 87, 116, 117
Sparks, A., 155
Spectator, 246
Spencer, J. C., Viscount Althorp, 46, 47
Spitalfields, 74, 139, 155
Stamford, Lincs., 246
Stamford Street, 120
Stanhope, C., 3rd Earl of Stanhope, 221
Stanhope Road, 69
Stanley, E. Smith, 11th Earl of Derby, 237
Statesman, 202, 203
Stephens, J. R., 198, 199
Stephen's Court, 116
Stephenson, H. L., 15
Stevenson, G., 68
Stewart, C. W., 3rd Marquess of Londonderry, 44
Stewart, R., Viscount Castlereagh, 67, 126, 239, 240, 242
Stiles, J., 68
Stirling, 190
Stockport Chronicle, 246
Stockwell, 120
Stoddart, J., 253
Stokenchurch, Bucks., 120
Stone's End, 68, 71, 116
Strand, 23, 36, 45, 68, 69, 120, 134, 155, 161, 164, 177, 179, 194, 201, 212
Stratton Street, 120
Sturge, J., xxiv, 211, 220, 231
Sturges, J., 156, 161
Styles, J. D., 70, 80, 113, 116, 118, 120, 151, 155
Suffolk, 196
Suffolk Chronicle, 246
Suffolk Street, 120
Sun, 40, 186, 194, 195, 207, 208
Sunderland, 246
Sun Street, 75
Surrey, 10, 38, 120, 137, 213
Surrey, Earl of, *see* Howard, C., 16th Duke of Norfolk
Surrey Road, 34, 55

Sussex, 213
Sutherland, L. S., xiv *n.*
Sydney Arms, public house, 143
Symons, J. C., 120

Tait, W., 211
Tate, T., 253
Taunton, Som., 246
Tavistock Place, 71
Tavistock Street, 152, 155, 161
Taylor, G., 190
Taylor, J., 68, 71, 88, 117, 120
Taylor, Dr. J., 204
Taylor, P. A., 120, 209, 211, 212, 214, 220, 231–3, 235, 236, 241, 244, 245, 247–9
Taylor, P. A., jun., 245, 247
Taylor, R., 120, 235, 245
Teasdale, B., 253
Temple, 68, 70, 71, 116
Temple Bar, 52, 54, 75, 141
Templeman, J., 71, 117
Thames, River, xvi, 10
Thelwall, J., 43
Theobald, W., 245
Theobald's Road, 68, 69, 116, 143, 195, 197, 205
Thomas, —, inspector of police, 11
Thomas, E. C., 68, 70, 71, 117
Thomas, W., 70
Thomas, W. E. S., vii *n.*, xii
Thomason, W., 246
Thompson, E. P., xiv *n.*, xv *n.*, xxv
Thompson, T., 246
Thompson, Colonel T. P., 21, 68, 120, 170, 185, 186, 190, 194, 220, 232
Thompson, W., 139
Thomson, J., 156
Threadneedle Street, 22
Three Compasses, public house, 143
Thurston, G., xxiv
Tickle, J. W., 253
Tillotson Place, 120
Times, xi, 116, 127, 128
Titchfield Street, 120
Todd, J., 117
Tomalin, J. B., 120
Tomey, G., 253
Torney, —, 177
Tottenham, 120
Tottenham Court Road, 70, 71, 76, 117, 218
Tower Hamlets, 155
Tower Hill, 155
Tower of London, 12, 124
Tower Street, 155
Travers, J., 120, 202, 203, 212, 220, 234, 235, 245
Treason and Sedition Acts of 1795, vii, xv, 222

True Sun, 159, 160
Tucker, R., 117
Turner, J., 68
Tuson, W., 70

Union Place, 70
Union Row, 68
Union Street, 68, 70, 117
Universal Suffrage Club, 152, 159–61
Upper North Place, 164, 185, 253
Upper Street, 156
Upton, G., 117
Usiglio, Dr., 120

Vane, W. H., Duke of Cleveland, 44
Vauxhall, 68, 116
Vear, Thomas de, 15, 21, 23
Vesey, W., 68
Villiers, C. P., 211
Vincent, H., 177, 186, 189, 194, 196, 216
Vintry, 68

Wade, Dr., 145, 204, 247–9
Wade, J., 120
Wagg, M., 68
Wakefield, D., 21, 61, 68–71, 82, 83, 117
Wakefield, W., 61
Wakley, T., 15, 52, 55–61, 71, 78, 142, 144, 149, 198
Walker, J., 2
Wall, —, 207
Wallas, G., vii, x *n.*, xii *n.*, xiii, xviii
Wallis, G., 68
Wallis, W., 69, 70, 97, 117, 120
Walworth, 68, 116
Wandsworth, 247
Warburton, H., 16, 106, 211, 212, 235, 245, 248, 249
Ward, G. G., 2, 68, 70, 113, 117
Warden, B., 2, 36, 139–41
Warwick Lane, 70
Warwickshire, 207
Waterloo Bridge, 120
Waterloo Place, 74
Watkins, D., 64, 70
Watling Street, 120
Watson, J., 2, 37, 49, 52, 68, 74, 75, 77, 138, 139, 141, 144, 145, 161
Waylen, E., 2
Webb, —, 36
Webber, T., 245
Weekly Chronicle, 167
Weekly Dispatch, 246
Weekly True Sun, 167, 202, 207
Weir, W., 120
Welford, R. G., 120, 189, 202, 207
Wellard, S., 70
Wellesley, A., Duke of Wellington, xx, xxvi, 10, 12, 37, 44, 78, 82, 88–95, 114, 181, 210, 224
Wellington Street, 23

265

Welshman, 246
West, J., xviii
Westerton, C., 245, 248
Westminster, vii, ix, x, xii–xv, xviii, xix, xxii, 13–15, 26, 68–71, 81, 82, 84, 87, 99, 100, 107–9, 116, 180, 183, 186, 188–91, 193, 194, 237
Westminster Hall, 190
Westminster Reform Society, 179, 182
Westminster Review, 23, 104
West Street, Smithfield, 68, 71, 116, 120
Whipple, —, 189
White, —, 177
Whitechapel, 87
White Conduit Fields, 155
White Conduit House, 51–6, 59, 144, 145
Whitecross Street, 120
Whitehall, 8
Whitesides, R. B., 213
Whitford, J., 71
Whittle, J., 198, 203
Wigg, R., 139
Wilkes, J., xiv
Wilkinson, G., 69
Wilkinson, W. A., 212, 214
William IV, 12, 73, 90, 91, 93–5
Williams, H., 190
Williams, J., 205
Williams, W., 120, 235, 245, 248

Willington Square, 155
Wills, B., 248, 249
Wilmot Square, 155
Wilmot Street, 120, 155
Wilson, E., 120
Wilson, G., 218
Wilson, J., 213
Wilton Crescent, 120
Wiltshire, 213
Winchester Street, 68, 155
Windmill Street, 68, 75
Windmill Street Chapel, 142
Wire, D. W., 120
Wood, —, 232
Wood, J., 2
Wood, W. R., 117
Worcester, 190
Wright, C., 70, 113, 117
Wright, H., 70, 117
Wright, J., 253
Wyvill, Rev. C., xiv, 223, 237

Yearly, —, 121, 122, 125
Yorkshire, xiv, 211
Yorkshire Gazette, 246
Yorkshire Grey, public house, 143
York Terrace, 120
Young, —, 40
Young, G. A., 211

LONDON RECORD SOCIETY

The London Record Society was founded in December 1964 to publish transcripts, abstracts and lists of the primary sources for the history of London, and generally to stimulate interest in archives relating to London. Membership is open to any individual or institution; the annual subscription is £3 3s (£3·15), which entitles a member to receive one copy of each volume published during the year and to attend and vote at meetings of the Society. Prospective members should apply to the Hon. Secretary, Mr Brian Burch, c/o Leicester University Library, University Road, Leicester.

The following volumes have already been published:

1. *London possessory assizes: a calendar*, edited by Helena M. Chew. (1965)
2. *London inhabitants within the Walls, 1695*; with an introduction by D. V. Glass. (1966)
3. *London Consistory Court wills, 1492–1547*, edited by Ida Darlington. (1967)
4. *Scriveners' Company Common Paper, 1357–1628, with a continuation to 1678*, edited by Francis W. Steer. (1968)

Price to members £3 3s (£3·15) each, and to non-members £3 15s (£3·75) each.

The following Occasional Publication is also available:
London and Middlesex published records, compiled by J. M. Sims (1970). Price free to members, and to non-members £1.

A leaflet describing some of the volumes in preparation may be obtained from the Hon. Secretary.